Student Interactive

myView® LITERACY

Savvas Learning Company LLC, 15 East Midland Avenue, Paramus, NJ 07652

Cover: The Artchives/Alamy Stock Photo; JPL-Caltech/Institut d'Astrophysique Spatiale/NASA; Dan Lewis/Shutterstock; Dmitri Ma/Shutterstock; Jefunne/Shutterstock; Rtem/Shutterstock; Vangert/Shutterstock; Stefan Petru Andronache/Shutterstock; Imagefactory/Shutterstock; World History Archive/Alamy; Npeter/Shutterstock; James Steidl/Shutterstock; Kovalov Anatolii/Shutterstock; CWB/Shutterstock

Attributions of third party content appear on page 632, which constitutes an extension of this copyright page.

ISBN-13: 978-0-134-90887-8
ISBN-10: 0-134-90887-2
11 22

Julie Coiro, Ph.D.

Jim Cummins, Ph.D.

Pat Cunningham, Ph.D.

Elfrieda Hiebert, Ph.D.

Pamela Mason, Ed.D.

Ernest Morrell, Ph.D.

P. David Pearson, Ph.D.

Frank Serafini, Ph.D.

Alfred Tatum, Ph.D.

Sharon Vaughn, Ph.D.

Judy Wallis, Ed.D.

Lee Wright, Ed.D.

UNIT 3 CONTENTS

Reflections

UNIT 4

CONTENTS

Liberty

UNIT 5

CONTENTS

Systems

UNIT 3

Reflections

Essential Question

How do experiences of others reflect our own?

WATCH

"Reflecting on Our Lives"

TURN and TALK

What does the word *reflections* mean to you?

SAVVAS realize™

Go ONLINE for all lessons.

VIDEO

AUDIO

INTERACTIVITY

GAME

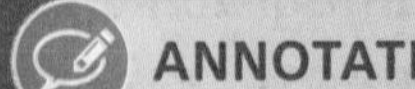
ANNOTATE

BOOK

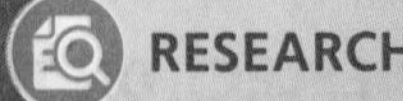
RESEARCH

Spotlight on Realistic Fiction

READING WORKSHOP

READING-WRITING BRIDGE

- Academic Vocabulary • Word Study
- **Read Like a Writer** • **Write for a Reader**
- Spelling • Language and Conventions

WRITING WORKSHOP

Opinion Essay

- Introduce and Immerse • Develop Elements
- Develop Structure • Writer's Craft
- Publish, Celebrate, and Assess

PROJECT-BASED INQUIRY

- Inquire • Research • Collaborate

Independent Reading

In this unit, you will read realistic fiction with your teacher. You will also read on your own. One of the best ways to become a stronger reader is to read genres that interest you.

Follow these steps to help you select a book you will enjoy reading for a sustained period of time on your own.

Step 1 Determine a purpose for your reading. Next, pick a genre that best matches your purpose.

I want to read a book in the
__________ genre because
__________________________.

Step 2 Select a book and read the first two pages. Use this strategy to determine if the book is right for you. If not, try a different title.

Is this book right for me?
After reading two pages, ask yourself:

	YES	NO
Does the topic interest me?	○	○
Do I understand most of the ideas?	○	○
Can I read the text smoothly?	○	○
Do I understand most of the words?	○	○

Independent Reading Log

Date	Book	Genre	Pages Read	Minutes Read	My Ratings
					☆☆☆☆☆

Unit Goals

Shade in the circle to rate how well you meet each goal now.

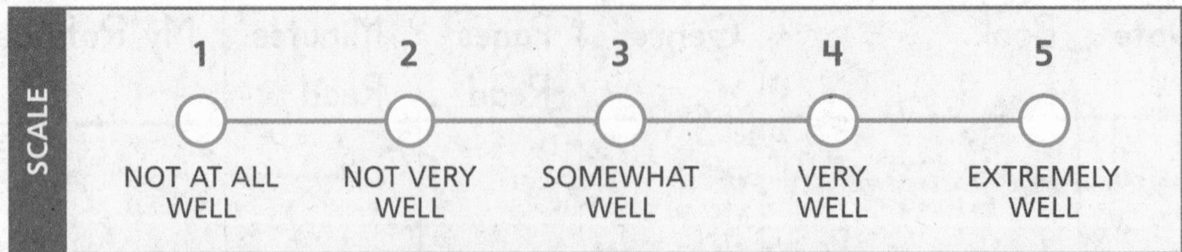

Reading Workshop	1	2	3	4	5
I know about different types of fiction and understand their elements.	○	○	○	○	○

Reading-Writing Bridge	1	2	3	4	5
I can use language to make connections between reading and writing.	○	○	○	○	○

Writing Workshop	1	2	3	4	5
I can use elements of opinion writing to write an essay.	○	○	○	○	○

Unit Theme	1	2	3	4	5
I can collaborate with others to explore how the experiences of others reflect our own.	○	○	○	○	○

Academic Vocabulary

Use these words to talk about this unit's theme, *Reflections: demonstrate*, *perspective*, *recall*, *appeal*, and *confide*.

TURN and TALK Read the words and definitions. Place an X inside the box in the chart that best shows your background knowledge of each word. Explain your chart to a partner.

demonstrate: to display something

perspective: how someone sees the world

recall: to remember

appeal: the quality of beauty or interest

confide: to trust someone with a secret

Academic Vocabulary	I know this word, and I can use it in a sentence.	I know this word, but I cannot use it in a sentence.	I have seen or heard this word.	I do not know this word.
demonstrate				
perspective				
recall				
appeal				
confide				

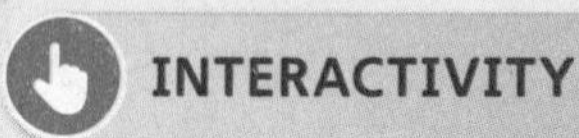

MORNING Serenade

My bus driver is seemingly powered by song.
Potholes and puddles make a splashy trip;
sha-thud sha-thud-thump the bus lurches along.
The rain on the roof taps, plinks, and drips.
The driver sings along like she thinks it's jazz.
I don't know how she's so cheerful; it's some secret she has.

She opens the doors and carols hello.
I stomp up the steps, sleepy and surly.
What makes you so merry, I demand to know,
I'm tired and grumpy, you're working, and it's early.
You're not really that happy, honestly, are ya?
She answers with something from opera: an aria?

You don't talk but trill. What makes you warble and sing?
Kid, some days it rains, and some days it pours,
but it won't get you down if you've just got that swing.
The day may start gloomy, but with music that soars,
my spirit is lifted. When you decide to live your life
with a tune,
the hard times pass quickly, my wise bus driver crooned.

Weekly Question

What can we learn from the experiences of older generations?

Quick Write How does the bus driver's attitude affect the speaker in the poem? What is a behavior or attitude that you admire in an adult you know? Briefly describe the trait and what you like about it.

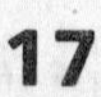

Learning Goal

I can learn more about realistic fiction by analyzing characters.

Spotlight on Genre

Realistic Fiction

Fiction tells made-up stories to entertain readers. **Realistic fiction** tells stories that are made up but could really happen. It includes

- **Characters** who are believable
- **Settings** that are or seem like places in the real world
- **Plots** based on realistic events and actions
- **Themes**, or messages, that relate to real life

Look for these characteristics of the genre as you read well-known literature during your independent reading.

TURN and TALK Think about some of your favorite stories and describe their characters. Use the anchor chart to talk with a partner about the elements of realistic fiction that are present in the stories. Take notes on your discussion.

My NOTES

Realistic Fiction Anchor Chart

Purpose:

- ✓ To entertain

Elements:

- ✓ Believable, fully developed characters
- ✓ A real or realistic setting
- ✓ A plot that could happen in real life
- ✓ An overall message, or theme

Text Structure:

- ✓ Chronological sequence of events

Meet the Authors

Alma Flor Ada grew up in Cuba in a family of storytellers, which notably included her grandmother. Ada often writes about "the joy of family" and the power of stories to connect people.

Gabriel M. Zubizarreta has coauthored two books with Alma Flor Ada. As a parent and novelist, he hopes his books encourage readers to become authors of their own stories.

from

Love, Amalia

Preview Vocabulary

As you read the excerpt from *Love, Amalia*, pay attention to these vocabulary words. Notice how the words relate to the characters and their relationships.

enthusiasm	**shattered**	
reassuring	**encompass**	**inseparable**

Read

Readers of **realistic fiction** follow these strategies when they read a text the first time. Before you begin, establish a purpose for reading.

First Read

Notice	**Generate Questions**
where the story is set and who the characters are.	about parts that confuse you.
Connect	**Respond**
characters' experiences to events from your own life.	by discussing parts you find effective or important.

Genre Realistic Fiction

from Love, Amalia

by Alma Flor Ada and Gabriel M. Zubizarreta

AUDIO

ANNOTATE

BACKGROUND

Twelve-year-old Amalia is heartbroken when she learns that her best friend is moving away. She turns to her grandmother for comfort. Abuelita shares with Amalia the stories of her relatives and how she uses cards and pictures to feel close to them across great distances. Amalia must decide whether she can overcome her pain and hold on to her friend.

CLOSE READ

Analyze Characters

Underline details that tell you about Amalia's relationship with her grandmother.

1 "What is it, Amalia? Is something bothering you?" Amalia's grandmother removed the boiling honey from the stovetop to let it cool. Then she wiped her forehead with a tissue and looked at her granddaughter. The light from the setting sun entered the small window over the sink with a soft glow. The geraniums on the windowsill added a subtle hint of pink. "You are too quiet, *hijita*. Tell me what's bothering you," her grandmother insisted. "It is obvious that something is wrong."

2 "It's okay, Abuelita, *de verdad*. I'm fine."

3 Amalia tried to sound convincing, but her grandmother continued, "Is it because Martha did not come with you today? Is she all right?"

4 Going to her grandmother's home on Friday afternoon was something Amalia had been doing since she was little. For the last two years, since they started fourth grade, her friend Martha accompanied her most Fridays. Every week Amalia looked forward to the time she spent at her grandmother's house. But today was different.

5 Amalia paused before answering, "She is not coming back anymore, Abuelita. *¡Nunca más!*" Despite Amalia's efforts to control her feelings, her voice cracked and her brown eyes watered.

6 "*¿Qué pasa, hijita?* What's going on?" Amalia's grandmother asked softly, gently hugging her and waiting for an explanation.

7 Amalia shook her head, as she frequently did when she was upset, and her long black hair swept her shoulders. "Martha is going away. Her family is moving west, to some weird place in California. So far away from Chicago! Today she had to go straight home to start packing. It's not fair."

8 “That must be difficult.” Her grandmother's voice was filled with understanding, and Amalia let out a great sigh.

9 For a while there was silence. The sunlight faded in the kitchen, and as the boiled honey cooled into a dark, thick mass, its sweet aroma filled the air.

10 “Shall we knead the *melcocha*, then?” Amalia's grandmother asked as she lifted the old brass pot onto the kitchen table and poured the sticky *melcocha* into a bowl. The thick white porcelain bowl, with a few chips that spoke of its long use, had a wide yellow rim. Once, the bowl had made Amalia think that it looked like a small sun on the kitchen table. Today she was too upset to see anything but the heavy bowl.

CLOSE READ

Make Connections

Think about someone who means a lot to you, such as a family member or friend. How would you feel if that person moved far away?

Highlight details on both pages that show how Amalia feels about Martha moving away.

CLOSE READ

Vocabulary in Context

Context clues are words and phrases around an unfamiliar word that help readers understand the word.

Use context clues in the sentence to determine the meaning of *slathered*. Underline the context clues that support your definition.

11 They washed their hands thoroughly in the sink and dried them. Her grandmother's kitchen towels each had a day of the week embroidered in a different color. Since today was Friday, the cross-stitched embroidery spelled VIERNES in *azul marino*, deep blue. Abuelita had taught Amalia the days of the week and the names of the colors in Spanish using these towels. Although her grandmother never seemed to be teaching, Amalia was frequently surprised when she realized how many things she had learned from Abuelita.

12 After drying their hands, they slathered them with soft butter, which prevented the taffy from sticking to their fingers or burning their skin. Then, with a large wooden spoon, Abuelita scooped some taffy from the bowl and poured it onto their hands.

13 As they pulled and kneaded, the taffy became softer and lighter. They placed little rolls of amber-colored taffy on pieces of waxed paper. Amalia had helped her grandmother pull the *melcocha* many times, but she never ceased to marvel at how the sweet taffy changed color just from being pulled, kneaded, and pulled again. It transformed from a deep dark brown into a light blond color, just like Martha's hair. Thinking about Martha made Amalia frown.

CLOSE READ

Analyze Characters

Underline details that tell you how Abuelita feels about loss.

14 Her grandmother might have seen her expression but made no comment about it. Rather, she said, "Wash your hands well, Amalita. Let's sit for a moment while the taffy cools down."

15 Before washing her hands, Amalia licked her fingers. Nothing tasted as good as "cleaning up" after cooking. The butter and taffy mixed together made a sweet caramel on her fingers, which was every bit as good as the raw cookie dough they "cleaned up" when she and Martha made cookies at Martha's house.

16 Once Amalia had washed and dried her hands, she followed her grandmother to the living room. They both sat on the floral sofa, which brightened the room as if a piece of the garden had been brought inside the house. Abuelita's fondness for the colors of nature could be seen in each room of her house.

17 "I know how hard it is when someone you love goes away. One moment you are angry, then you become sad, and then it seems so unbelievable you almost erase it. Then, when you realize it is true, the anger and the sadness come back all over again, sometimes even more painfully than before. I have gone through that many times."

Analyze Characters

Underline details that show how Amalia feels about loss.

18 Amalia listened closely, trying to guess who her grandmother was talking about. Was she thinking of her two sons who lived far away or her daughter who always promised to visit from Mexico City but never did? Or was she referring to her husband, Amalia's grandfather, who had died when Amalia was so young that she could not remember him?

19 "But one finds ways, Amalia, to keep them close," her grandmother added. And then, smiling as if having just gotten a new idea, she said, "*Ven*. Come with me." She then got up and motioned Amalia to follow her to the dining room.

20 Amalia just wanted to end the conversation. It was bad enough that Martha had told her that she had a surprise and it had turned out to be that Martha was moving to California very soon. Martha's leaving sounded so definite and permanent that she hated even the thought of it. Talking about it only made Amalia feel worse. She wished she did not need to wait for her father to pick her up and could just walk home. Maybe then she could call Martha and hear her say that it all had been a great mistake and they were not moving after all. And it would all disappear like bad dreams do in the morning.

21 Abuelita signaled Amalia to come sit at the massive dining room table. Before she sat down, Abuelita put on a CD quietly in the background. Amalia could not remember Abuelita's home ever without some soft music. On the lace tablecloth there was a stack of Christmas cards, several red and gold leaves, and a box made of beautiful olive wood that Amalia immediately recognized. Her grandmother used that box to save the special cards and letters sent by relatives and close friends. At the bottom there were old letters neatly kept in bundles tied with ribbons. Amalia loved the feel of the old polished wood, the gentle waves that had been stroked so many times before.

22 "Are you writing your Christmas cards already, Abuelita? It's not even Thanksgiving!" Amalia was relieved to change the subject. "What are the dry leaves for?"

23 "I like writing my cards slowly," her grandmother replied as she picked up an unfinished card. "That way I can really think about what I will write on each one. There are so many things I want to say."

CLOSE READ

Make Connections

Think about the details that make a place special to you. What do those details look like?

Highlight details about what makes Abuelita's home special to Amalia.

CLOSE READ

Make Connections

Highlight examples of advice Abuelita gives Amalia that is similar to advice someone has given you.

24 After a moment, almost as if talking to herself, Abuelita added, "I've made terrible mistakes in my life when I didn't think before speaking."

25 Amalia looked up, surprised. Abuelita always looked so calm and sure. It was almost impossible to imagine her acting foolishly.

26 Looking at the half-written card, Abuelita continued, "As I was telling you, one must find ways to keep loved ones close, even if they move away. This year I have decided to send a little bit of my backyard with each card. Every year at this time, my children and I had many good moments getting ready for the holidays. So I have gathered some of this autumn's leaves to remind them of those times. Look at this one!" and she held a maple leaf that had turned a deep crimson. "See how red it is? One of the things I have always loved about this house is seeing the trees change colors with the seasons.

27 "The same is true with the things we treasure: They happen, bloom for a time, and then fade away. Then sometimes they may reappear again, or something else will take their place."

28 Holding the leaves up one by one, she added, “There is a poem I like very much. The poet says that a dry leaf is not an elegy, a song of death, but rather a prelude, a promise of a distant spring.”

29 Abuelita almost seemed lost in her own thoughts, but then she returned to Amalia, saying, “Before writing each card, I like to read ones I received from the person to whom I am about to write. This reminds me that I am not the only one who wants to stay close. Do you want to look at some of last year’s cards with me?”

30 “Sure, Abuelita,” Amalia said, pushing back the lock of hair that kept falling in her face. She always enjoyed listening to her grandmother’s stories, especially stories about their family. The distant relatives, some of whom Amalia could not remember ever meeting, came alive when Abuelita spoke about them. Even things that happened a long time ago, like the story of how her grandfather’s parents had come from Mexico to Chicago, became so real when Abuelita told them that Amalia felt as if she had actually been there. Today she did not feel much like listening, but making an effort to show some enthusiasm for her grandmother’s offer, she added, “You can tell me all about the people who sent them.”

CLOSE READ

Analyze Characters

Underline details that help you understand the power of Abuelita’s storytelling on Amalia’s mood.

enthusiasm high interest, excitement

Analyze Characters

Underline phrases that tell you how Abuelita deals with her son Patricio living far away from her.

31 Abuelita began pulling cards out of the box one by one. With each card she had something to say, and although she had spoken about these faraway relatives many times before, it seemed to Amalia that today she was adding special details to every story.

32 Holding a card with a picture of a lush landscape, Abuelita spoke for a while about her oldest son. Amalia's *tío* Patricio had fallen in love with a Costa Rican girl he met at the University of Chicago. Soon after they graduated they got married, and because she did not want to live far away from her family, they moved to Costa Rica.

33 "He was very concerned about leaving me and moving away. However, I reminded him that we, too, had moved away, and sometimes that is necessary," Abuelita said. "It's true that I gained a beautiful daughter-in-law and grandchildren, but it has been hard having my eldest child live so far from me. Yet they love each other and have a happy family, and that, Amalita, is one of life's greatest gifts. See how happy they look in this picture they took as soon as they arrived in Costa Rica."

34 It wasn't easy to imagine Tío Patricio and Tía Graciela as two young people in love when Amalia thought of the pictures her mother had received from them recently. In those pictures Tío Patricio was a balding man and Tía Graciela a rather proper-looking lady, but in the old photo Abuelita held, they were a handsome young couple looking adoringly at each other under a palm tree, almost like a movie poster. Abuelita gently put away the card with a pleased look on her face.

35 "Someday you must go to Costa Rica, Amalia, and visit them. It is an amazing place."

36 The next card was in the shape of a large Christmas tree and said FELIZ NAVIDAD in bold letters. Abuelita opened it and read it in silence, very slowly, as if pausing on every word.

37 "Your tío Manuel is quite a person, Amalia. When my brother, your great-uncle Felipe, said it was becoming hard for him to manage the old rancho alone, Manuel went back to Mexico, to help his uncle. Who do you know that goes back to Mexico to work on a farm? Everyone says they would like to go back someday, while the truth is, most people just come here and stay. But no, not your uncle Manuel. He kept saying how important that land was for his family, and that he was not going to give it up. So even though he was born and raised here in Illinois, he went back and learned how to work the rancho. And he has done such a good job of it." Abuelita looked very pleased.

CLOSE READ

Analyze Characters

Underline details that tell you how Abuelita feels about her son Manuel.

Make Connections

Highlight details that show how Manuel changed over time.

38 "There was a time when I was not sure your uncle would turn out as he has. He did many dumb things when he was in high school, and ended up dropping out. Your grandfather was very hard on him, and it broke my heart at the time." She paused, and for an instant Amalia could see the pain those memories brought, but then Abuelita smiled. "Yet he has managed to save our rancho. When he first talked about organic farming, people laughed at his idea, but now he is doing just great. There are no tomatoes that can compare with the ones he produces."

shattered broken into many small pieces; damaged or destroyed

39 Amalia continued listening with interest. It was comforting to hear Abuelita retelling the familiar stories. Especially today, after Martha's announcement had shattered her, it was good to hear once again the words she had anticipated Abuelita would say, as she had on other occasions:

40 "Ay, *hijita*, how we loved that rancho. It was there where my brother Felipe and I were born—on the kitchen table! There was no doctor, of course . . . we were born with the help of our aunts. Who would ever have thought I would end up living so far away?

41 "When I married your grandfather, he knew how homesick I was for the ranch. We went back there as a couple once before we had children, and then when our children were very little we went several times during the summer. When they grew older it got harder to travel, but we all loved those visits!"

42 It seemed to Amalia that as her grandmother spoke of those distant memories, her eyes sparkled like the lake when the sun's rays hit it at midday.

43 Amalia wished Abuelita could just pick her up and hold her tightly as she used to do when Amalia was smaller, reassuring her grandchild that she belonged to something that would never change. But Amalia was bigger now, and Abuelita seemed to keep getting smaller, so Amalia just let herself feel surrounded by the warmth of her grandmother's voice.

CLOSE READ

Analyze Characters

Underline details on this page that help you contrast Amalia's mood with Abuelita's mood.

reassuring giving comfort; reminding someone not to worry

Make Connections

Consider the reasons people you know live in the places they do. Highlight details about why Amalia's aunt lives in Mexico City.

44 Holding a Christmas card with a huge poinsettia, her grandmother began to speak of Amalia's aunt, who lived in Mexico City and made costumes for movie and television actresses.

45 "Here is another one who went back. My daughter is just so in love with Mexico City. She's been fascinated by dresses ever since she was a little girl. She would draw them and color them and cut them out for her paper dolls. Each doll had quite a wardrobe. They had clothes for work and play, for traveling and for the theater, for going to dances and even for picnics. There was no end to their clothes!"

encompass surround or completely cover

46 Abuelita gestured with her hands as if to encompass the huge table, and Amalia could just see it covered with colorful paper doll clothes.

47 "And that is why she lives in Mexico City, in the capital, *en el D.F.* She says she could never have the same opportunity in Hollywood, but in Mexico she dresses all the most famous stars."

48 She paused for a moment, and when she spoke again, her voice had a joyful ring to it.

49 "You can't imagine, *mi amor*, how your mother and her sister would play together when they were little girls. Well, you do know that's why your mother called you Amalia, so that you'd have her sister's name. They were inseparable, those two. Whether they were jumping rope or playing jacks, they spent all their time together. What they liked best, though, besides those paper dolls, were the times they spent playing in the yard. They would climb trees, play tag, build pretend castles, and imagine being princesses. In the summer, your *abuelito* would set up a small plastic pool, and they loved swimming in that pool. It was very small, but they didn't care because they had each other."

50 Abuelita probably would have continued telling more stories, but she was interrupted by a light knock on the door. It was already dark, and Amalia's father had come to get her.

51 As Amalia was leaving, her grandmother hugged her and whispered in her ear, "You will find a way to stay close to Martha."

52 Riding in the car, Amalia pondered her grandmother's words. They had brought back the sorrow she had been able to forget while listening to the family stories.

53 *Who cares about staying close?* she thought. *I don't want to care about someone who won't be here.*

CLOSE READ

Analyze Characters

Underline details that show the differences between Amalia's and Abuelita's attitudes about loss.

inseparable never apart; unable to be split up

Develop Vocabulary

One way authors help readers understand characters is by choosing words that have precise shades of meaning. For example, the words *happy* and *enthusiastic* express similar emotions, but the second word has a stronger effect.

My TURN Place each word on the scale in order from negative to positive. Then write a new sentence for each word to describe Amalia or Abuelita.

Word Bank

enthusiasm **inseparable** **reassuring** **shattered**

more negative more positive

1. ______________________________

2. ______________________________

3. ______________________________

4. ______________________________

Check for Understanding

My TURN Look back at the text to answer the questions.

1. How do you know that *Love, Amalia* is realistic fiction? Give examples.

2. What is the authors' purpose? How do you know?

3. How does Amalia feel at the beginning of the story? Why? Make a prediction about what Amalia will do after the story ends, based on her characteristics and actions.

4. What does Abuelita teach Amalia about how to react to disappointment? What does Amalia learn about how to keep people close even when they live far away? Use text evidence to infer themes, or messages, in the story.

Analyze Characters

Readers can notice the interactions and conflicts between characters. Readers think about how the characters think, feel, and act to analyze the characters' relationships. Readers think about the characters' opinions and differences to analyze characters' conflicts.

1. **My TURN** Go to the Close Read notes in *Love, Amalia* and underline the parts that help you analyze the relationship between Amalia and Abuelita.

2. **Text Evidence** Use the parts you underlined to complete the chart.

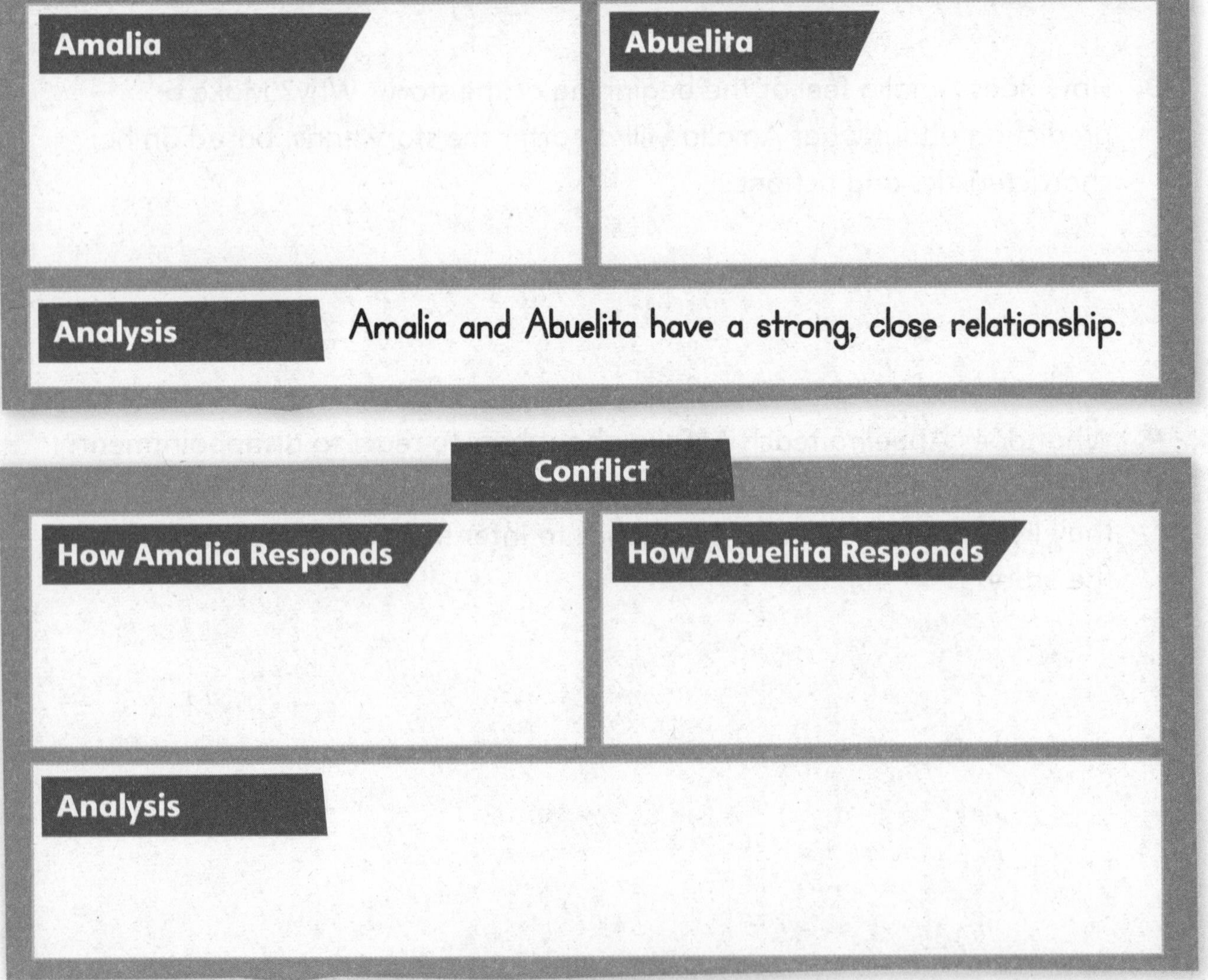

Make Connections

Relate what you read to ideas in other texts, your own experiences, or society. Making connections can help you better understand texts.

1. **MyTURN** Go back to the Close Read notes and highlight details that help you make connections.
2. **Text Evidence** Use your highlighted text and your own connections to complete the graphic organizer.

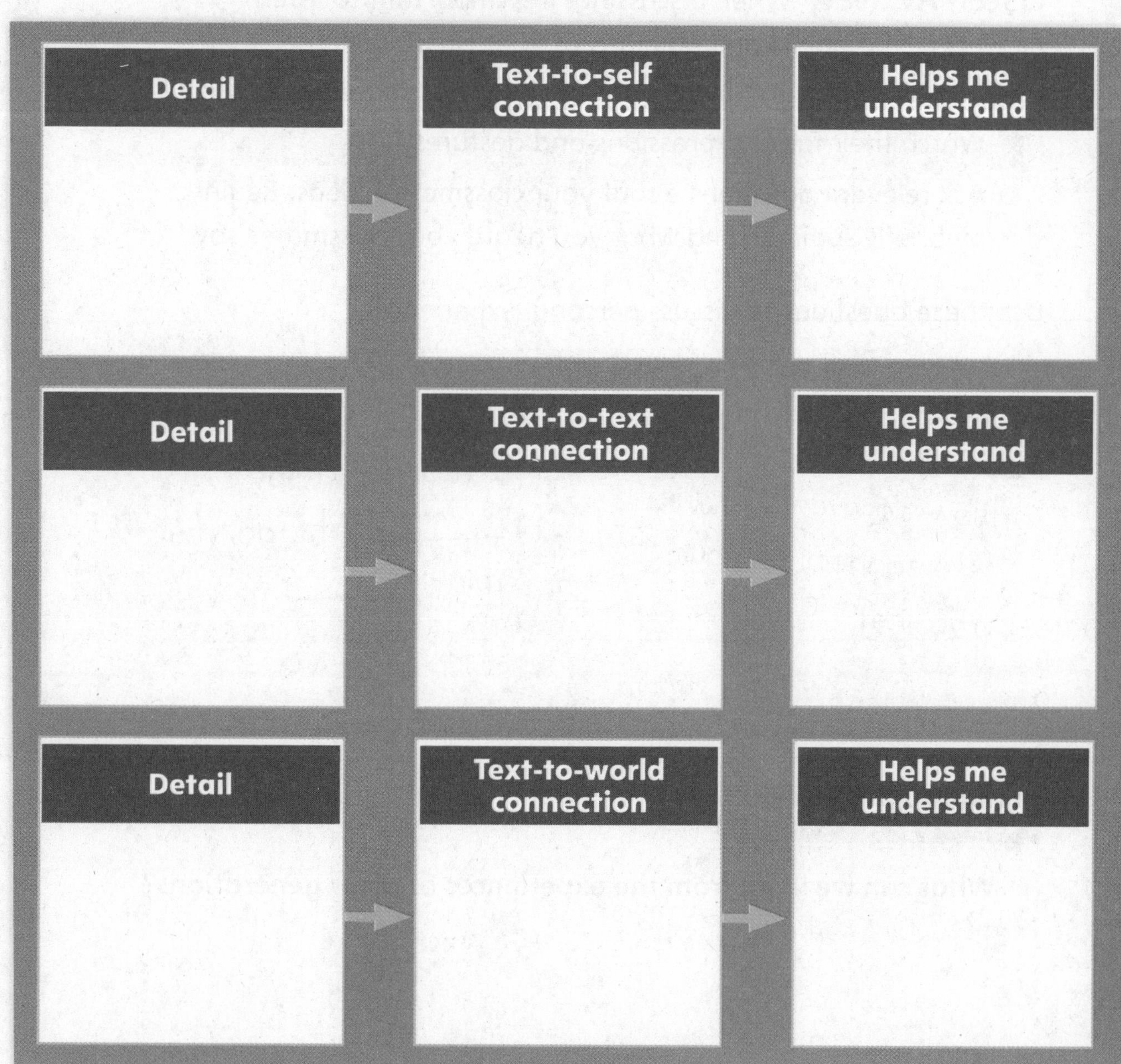

Reflect and Share

Talk About It In *Love, Amalia*, Amalia is upset because her best friend is moving away. Consider all the texts you have read this week. What other separations have you read about? Discuss how your experiences can help you understand a text.

Listen Actively When discussing, it is important to listen actively to the points and opinions of your classmates.

- Remain quiet, and focus on what your classmates are saying.
- Watch their facial expressions and gestures.
- Ask relevant questions about your classmates' ideas. Begin by briefly summarizing what you heard your classmates say.

Use these questions to discuss personal experiences:

How do events in the text connect to your own life?

I heard you say ______. Why do you think ______?

Weekly Question

What can we learn from the experiences of older generations?

Academic Vocabulary

Learning Goal

I can develop knowledge about language to make connections between reading and writing.

Adding different suffixes to a base word creates **related words** and often changes the word's part of speech. For instance, the suffix *-or* means "one who does something." Adding *-or* to the base word *demonstrate* creates the word *demonstrator*, and changes a verb to a noun. A demonstrator is "a person who demonstrates."

My TURN For each word,

1. **Identify** the suffix added to *demonstrate*.
2. **Use** a print or digital resource, such as a dictionary, as needed to define the suffixes.
3. **Write** the meaning of the word.

Word	Suffix and Meaning	Meaning of Word
demonstrator	-or: one who does something	a person who demonstrates
demonstration		
demonstrative		
demonstrable		

Words with Latin Roots

Latin roots are the basis for many words in English. Knowing the origin of words can help you define unfamiliar words.

For example, the Latin root *port* means "carry." Knowing this meaning can help you define words with this root, such as *transport*, which means "carry from one place to another."

Other Latin roots include *dict*, *ject*, and *terr*. Use a print or digital dictionary to confirm the origins of word parts you read.

My TURN Read the chart. Add two related words for each root. Then, on a separate sheet of paper, use two words with Latin roots in sentences.

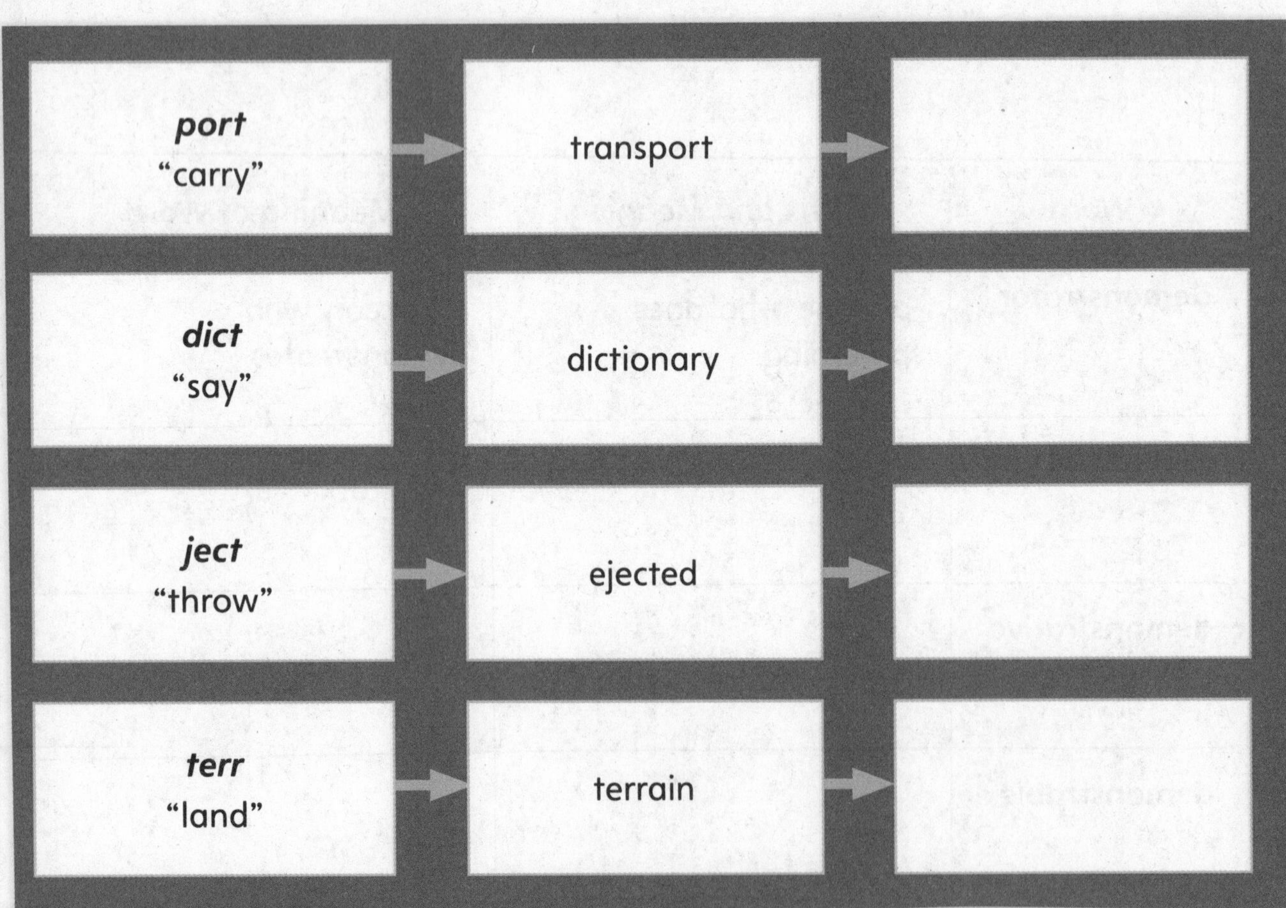

Read Like a Writer

Authors use images, or sensory language, to help a reader experience the way things look, feel, smell, sound, or taste.

Model Read the text from *Love, Amalia*.

> The light from the setting sun entered the small window over the sink with a soft glow. The geraniums on the windowsill added a subtle hint of pink.

imagery

1. **Identify** The authors use the sensory language "light from the setting sun," "a soft glow," and "a subtle hint of pink."
2. **Question** How does this imagery help me experience the text?
3. **Conclude** The imagery develops an emotion and helps me experience how the setting looks.

Reread paragraph 9 of *Love, Amalia*.

My TURN Describe how the authors' use of imagery creates a feeling or experience.

1. **Identify** The authors use the sensory language ______________________ ______________________.
2. **Question** How does the imagery help me experience the text?
3. **Conclude** The details appealing to the senses of ______________ help me experience ______________ and develop a feeling of ______________.

Write for a Reader

Authors use elements of craft, such as imagery, to show vivid descriptions and to help create a mood, or atmosphere.

My TURN Think about how the authors' use of imagery in *Love, Amalia* affects you as a reader. Now identify how you can use imagery to affect your own readers.

1. If you were trying to show a friendly and loving character, what kind of sensory language, or imagery, would you use?

2. If you were trying to show a harsh or threatening character, what kind of imagery would you use?

3. Write a passage about one of the characters you described. Use imagery to help readers clearly imagine your character.

Spell Words with Latin Roots

Many words in English are formed by adding word parts to **Latin roots** including the roots *port*, *dict*, *ject*, and *terr*. For example, adding the suffix *-age* to the root *port* creates *portage*, a word that means "the act of carrying or transporting."

My TURN Read the words. Spell and sort the words by their Latin roots.

SPELLING WORDS

subjective	transportation	portage	contradict
terrarium	terrace	reject	projectile
conjecture	reporter	dictator	indictment
dejected	contradiction	injection	subterranean
prediction	unpredictable	supportive	objective

port	dict	ject	terr

Prepositions and Prepositional Phrases

Prepositions are words that show location, time, direction, or other details. A **prepositional phrase** is made up of a preposition and a noun or pronoun called an **object**.

Type	Prepositions	Examples with Prepositional Phrases
location	*above, behind, between, from, near*	It has been hard having my eldest child live so far **from** me.
time	*after, at, before, during, on, until*	**Before** dinner, Amalia washed her hands.
direction	*across, down, from, over, to, toward, through, up*	Sunlight entered the small window **over** the sink.

These nouns and pronouns in prepositional phrases are never subjects of sentences. The verb in the sentence should agree with the subject of the sentence, not with the object of a prepositional phrase.

The books on the table were shelved by the librarian.

The plural verb *were* agrees with the plural subject *books*, not the singular object *table*.

My TURN Edit this draft by adding prepositional phrases as indicated. Check for subject-verb agreement.

Amalia could not believe her best friend was moving. (direction) They made taffy together. (time) Amalia and Abuelita walked together. (location) Abuelita opened the wooden box.

Organize an Opinion Essay

Learning Goal

I can use elements of opinion writing to write an essay.

An **opinion essay** is a type of argumentative text that gives the writer's point of view about a topic. A writer supports an opinion by providing reasons for his or her point of view. Those reasons are supported by facts, details, examples, and other information.

MyTURN Use an opinion essay you have read to complete the chart.

Title

Topic	
Reason	**Reason**
Examples	**Examples**
Writer's Opinion	

Analyze a Point of View

In opinion writing, a writer shows strong feeling for or against something. The writer carefully chooses words, facts, and examples to support that opinion.

While shows that the writer's opinion conflicts with a popular point of view.

The terms *cruel* and *helpless victims* show the writer's strong opinion about the subject.

While many believe testing beauty products on animals is acceptable, the cruel truth is that these animals are helpless victims.

The writer believes this practice is unacceptable.

The writer asserts that what he or she believes is the truth.

Analyzing the information a writer includes can help a reader better understand the writer's purpose.

My TURN Reread an opinion essay from your classroom library. Answer the questions to identify the writer's point of view.

What words show the writer's opinion?

What piece of information supports the writer's point of view?

What does the writer say about other points of view?

Analyze Reasons and Information

A writer carefully chooses the reasons and information he or she includes to support an opinion. The reasons may give information about what is important to the writer.

The transition *because* shows that the writer is about to list reasons for his or her opinion.

Running is a healthy pastime because it boosts a person's self-esteem. It also gives an outlet for anger and frustration. For example, most runners feel a rush of positive energy after a run, even when they are exhausted by the exercise.

The writer provides an example to support his or her reasons.

These reasons show the writer is interested in how running feels.

My TURN Work with a partner. Read an opinion essay from your classroom library. Complete the chart to analyze the writer's reasons and information.

Title		
Reason	**Reason**	**Reason**
Examples	**Examples**	**Examples**

How do the reasons and examples show the writer's opinion?

Brainstorm a Topic and Opinion

A writer begins planning an opinion essay by choosing a topic that he or she feels strongly about.

MyTURN Complete the boxes as you prepare to write your opinion essay. Highlight your best idea. Then, clearly state your opinion about the topic.

A topic related to school

A topic related to home

A topic related to a sport or activity

My Opinion

Plan Your Opinion Essay

Writers brainstorm to generate ideas for their opinion essays.

My TURN Follow the steps to brainstorm ideas for your opinion essay. Consider your topic, purpose, and audience.

1. In your writing notebook, build a chart that resembles this one.

State Opinion	
Reason #1	
Example	
Reason #2	
Example	
Restate Opinion	

2. Identify reasons for your opinion. List examples that support each reason.
3. Reread the reasons and examples you wrote.
4. Highlight the reasons that best support your opinion. Consider which reasons will have the greatest effect on your readers.
5. Use those details as you continue to outline and write your article.
6. Work with your Writing Club to discuss your plan.

INTERACTIVITY

How Many PETS?

Millions of people around the United States own millions of pets. House pets add a lot to our lives. Taking care of an animal helps us feel and express positive emotions. It also teaches us to be responsible for the needs of another living thing.

85.8 MILLION

Cats

9.5 MILLION

Saltwater Fish

Birds

14.3 MILLION

95.5 MILLION

Freshwater Fish

WEEK 2

Weekly Question

What are some different ways in which people can reach a goal?

Quick Write Briefly summarize the data about pet ownership. Then think about what a person can learn from a pet. What are the goals of owning a pet, and how do pet owners achieve those goals? Give an example from real life or from a book you have read.

Hamsters, Mice, and Rabbits

12.4 MILLION

Reptiles

9.3 MILLION

Dogs

77.8 MILLION

Source: American Pet Products Association's 2015–2016 National Pet Owners Survey

Learning Goal

I can learn more about realistic fiction by analyzing plot elements.

Spotlight on Genre

Realistic Fiction

Realistic fiction entertains readers with imaginary, but believable, characters and events. The **plot**, or main events of the story, has five main parts.

- The **introduction** presents the characters, setting, and conflict, or problem.
- The **rising action** develops the conflict through a series of events.
- The main conflict reaches its peak at the **climax,** or turning point, in the story.
- Events after the climax are the **falling action.**
- The **resolution** provides a solution to the conflict or concludes the story.

Establish Purpose The **purpose**, or reason, for reading realistic fiction is often for enjoyment. You could also read to determine how the author's words develop the story's characters and events.

To identify realistic fiction, consider whether the characters could exist in real life.

TURN and TALK With a partner, discuss different purposes for reading realistic fiction. For example, you may want to analyze the story's events and determine if they could happen in real life. Set a purpose for reading this text.

Plot Anchor Chart

3 Climax is the turning point of the conflict.

4 Falling action includes events after the climax.

2 Rising action develops the conflict.

5 Resolution solves the conflict and concludes the story.

1 Introduction introduces the characters, setting, and conflict.

Meet the Author

Barbara Robinson started writing poems and short stories as a child. She always had a talent for generating fresh ideas from her imagination. She is best known for her humorous children's books.

A Pet for Calvin

Preview Vocabulary

As you read "A Pet for Calvin," pay attention to these vocabulary words. Notice how they all describe worms, their environment, or characters' reactions to them.

loamy **tolerate**

wriggled **quarters** **tingled**

Read

Before you begin, establish a purpose for reading. Then follow these strategies as you read this **realistic fiction** text for the first time.

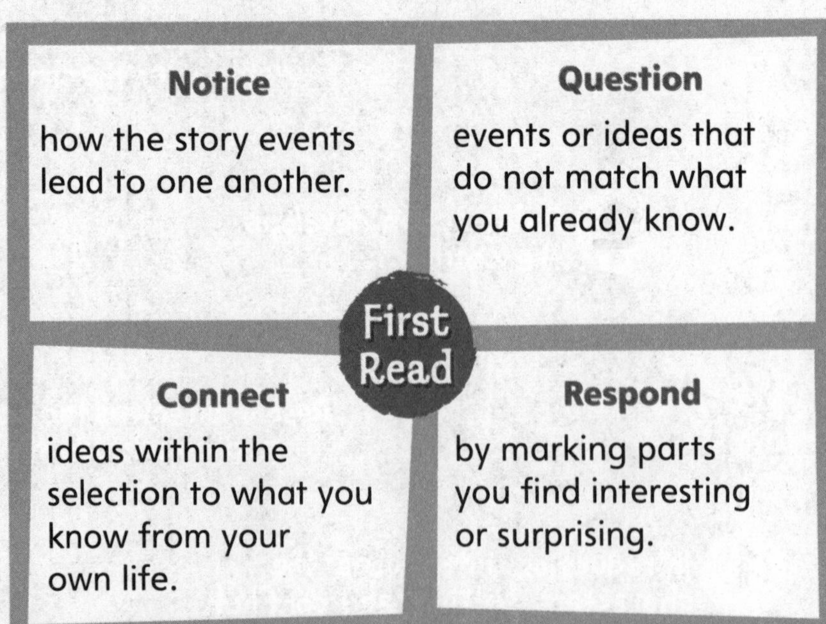

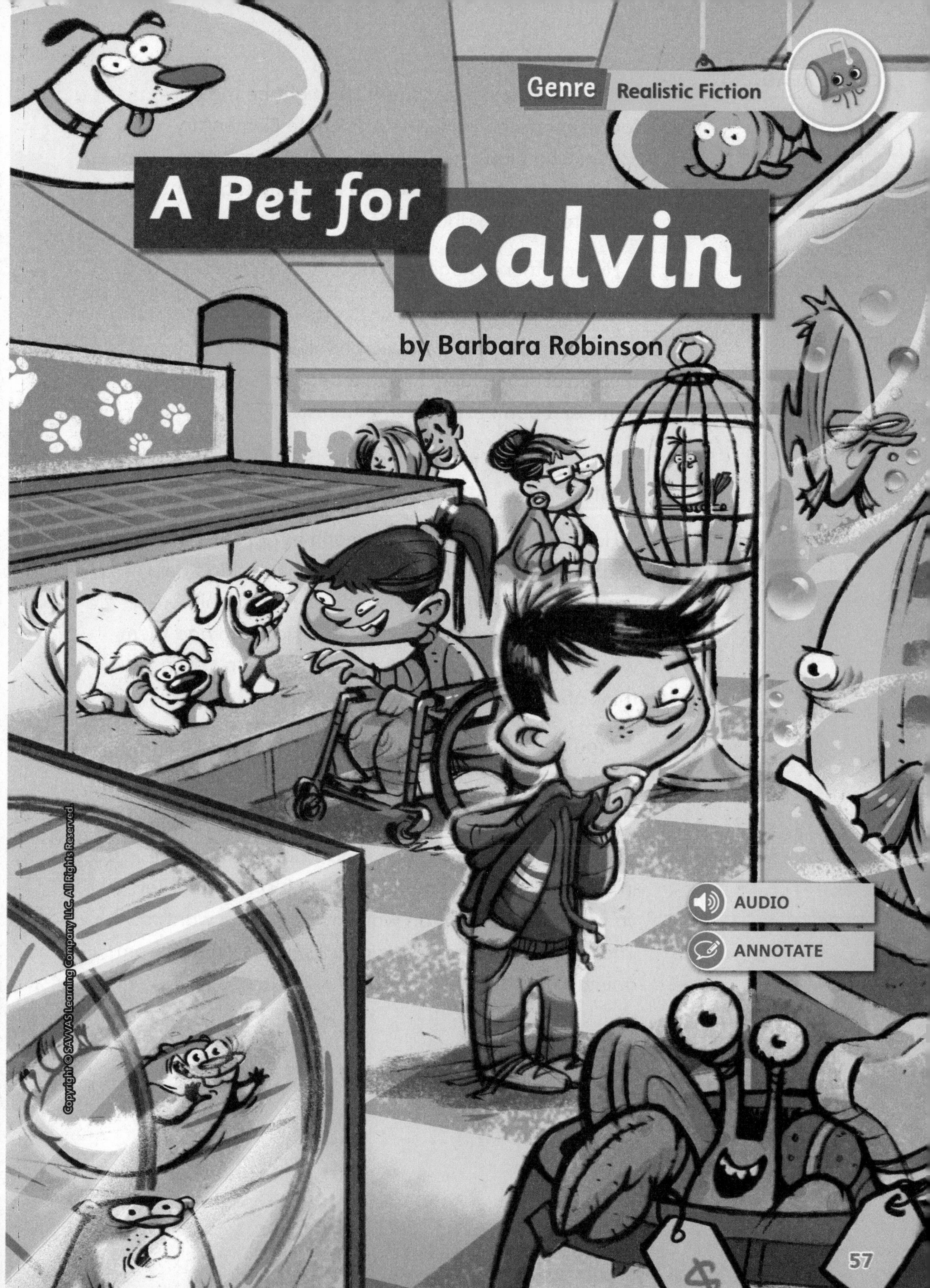

A Pet for Calvin

by Barbara Robinson

CLOSE READ

Analyze Plot Elements

Underline the sentence that tells the story's conflict, or problem.

1 Calvin McCandless thought he might be the only fourth-grade kid in Homer Applegate Elementary School who didn't have a pet. But he wasn't sure about that—some of those kids were girls, and they didn't talk to him about pets or anything else.

2 His best friend, Roger Stratton, had two pets—a dog and a hamster.

3 "I *don't* have two pets," Roger always said when this subject came up. "I have a dog. My sister has the hamster. I don't even *like* the hamster."

4 "But you have two pets in your house," Calvin insisted.

5 He knew that his friends sometimes got tired of hearing him complain this way, but he couldn't help it. Probably kids who had pets—dogs, cats, gerbils . . . a kid in the fifth grade had a ferret—kids who *had* them were so used to having them that they didn't even think about it.

6 "You don't even think about it," he told Joe Coolidge. "You've got your dog, he's always there . . . "

7 "I do too think about it," Joe said. "I *have* to think about it. I have to feed him, and walk him, because in our dumb neighborhood he can't just run free. Tell ya what, Calvin, you can walk my dog if you want to. That would be outside . . . do you still get wheezy from animals outside?"

8 Calvin sighed. “In or out,” he said, “it doesn’t matter.” He spoke from experience because his parents did once let him bring a dog home, but before they were even in the house, his eyes had closed up and he couldn’t breathe.

9 “Outstanding!” his grandmother said when she heard about this. “Were they trying to kill you? Death by dog?”

10 As always, his kooky grandmother made Calvin laugh and feel better . . . but, as always, she made his father sigh and roll his eyes.

CLOSE READ

Summarize

Highlight details that develop the conflict of the story.

Summarize

Highlight a detail about a past event.

tolerate allow; accept; put up with

11 "Mother," Mr. McCandless said, "don't say things like that. We thought, maybe, with the new medicine, Calvin could tolerate—"

12 "A short-haired dog," Calvin's mother put in. "It was a short-haired dog."

13 "Not short enough," his grandmother said . . . but then she hugged everybody, to show that she wasn't really mad at them, that she was just sad for Calvin.

14 There was a possibility that Calvin would outgrow his wheeziness, but that would be a long time to wait. Besides, would he still need a pet when he was grown up? His father didn't seem to need one, although maybe he would if it weren't for Calvin's allergy.

15 "Not at all," his father said, "I have you, and your baby sister, and your mother. I have my job and our home and things to do . . . like today, I have to go to Home Depot, and I have to watch the ball game, and I have to spade up the vegetable patch. Want to come along?"

16 Of course he did want to. This was what they did every Saturday: Home Depot, ball game, some house chore.

17 The Home Depot was always fun, and then the Red Sox won, and now he could dig up dirt and get chore points for it. It was great dirt, too—loose and loamy—and he liked to pick up a shovelful and run it through his fingers.

loamy having of a certain mixture of clay, sand, and organic material; having a texture good for growing plants

18 He made a small cone of the dirt, and with a stick he made a careful hole in the middle, like a model of Mount Vesuvius . . . and up through the hole came, not hot lava, but a worm.

19 It stood up—which Calvin had never seen a worm do, but of course this one was in a hole, which helped—and it looked at him.

20 He was so sure of this that after a second or two he said "Hello" . . . even though he knew the worm couldn't hear him. He knew, from science class, that worms didn't have ears.

CLOSE READ

Analyze Plot Elements

Underline the most important event in the rising action.

CLOSE READ

Summarize

Highlight details that show Calvin making both a decisive and unexpected action.

wriggled moved by twisting

Vocabulary in Context

Words and phrases that help readers understand an unfamiliar word are called **context clues.**

Underline context clues that help you understand what *sensory receptors* are.

21 Worms didn't have much of anything, really, except what the science teacher called "sensory receptors"—"Like gooseflesh," the teacher had said, "when you're chilly or scared." Or, Calvin thought, like the funny thrilly feeling in the soles of your feet when you step, barefoot, onto sand and gravel.

22 Worms, he assumed, must be all feeling, and he reached out to touch this worm. His fingers were inky, from keeping score in the ball game, and he left a black mark on the worm, which wriggled back into the hole.

23 "Calvin!" his mother called. "It's almost dinnertime. You need to come in and wash up."

24 To his amazement, the worm wriggled back out and . . . looked at him again.

25 He picked it all up—mound of dirt, worm, extra dirt, pieces of grass and leaves and twigs that were lying around—and carried it to where his father had been planting squash seeds, saved from last year in a plastic container.

26 The plastic container made a perfect worm house, he thought, and added some more grass and twigs and, later, a cover of plastic wrap, with airholes, of course.

27 Last of all, he wrote SPOT on a piece of tablet paper and taped it to the container. It was the perfect name for his worm, he thought, looking at his own inky finger.

28 He didn't mention the worm to anyone, but he didn't deliberately *not* mention the worm either. The subject didn't come up, and the only family member who would be interested was his baby sister, and she would just want to eat it.

29 That night he put the worm house on the shelf above his bed, with his important things—his baseball cards and signed program, his Morphagon transformer, his Coke bottle that fell from the third floor of the school and didn't break—and before he went to sleep, he took the plastic wrap off and very gently poked around in the dirt till he found the worm, curled up. He stirred the dirt a little more, and the worm curled up a little more, and went back to sleep.

30 He checked up on his worm, off and on, the next day, but there wasn't much he could do for it. It didn't need water or food . . . but it did need dirt. Tomorrow, after school, he would take care of his worm's dirt.

CLOSE READ

Analyze Plot Elements

Underline one or more actions on both pages that Calvin does to turn the worm into a pet.

CLOSE READ

Analyze Plot Elements

Underline details that help you compare and contrast Calvin's interactions with his pet to John's experiences.

Summarize

Highlight details on both pages that show how Calvin wants Spot to have a good home.

31 At first he thought he would just add dirt, but maybe this was like Kitty Litter that had to be changed, according to his friend John Hazeltine, who had two cats.

32 "Gotta change the Kitty Litter," John would say, and he would go change the Kitty Litter while Calvin and Roger or Joe would hang around and wait for him to come out and ride bikes.

33 Of course John could just throw out the old Kitty Litter, but Calvin had to empty the dirt into his mother's big mixing bowl, then transfer his worm into new dirt in the worm house.

34 *He probably likes it in the bowl,* Calvin thought, *because there's lots more room. Maybe he thinks it's vacation.*

35 He scooped up a handful of dirt, and worm, and put it all back in the plastic container on nice new dirt. He could tell—he *thought* he could tell—that his worm liked it because he wriggled right down in, and when Calvin looked in the side of the container, his worm looked back.

36 On Friday his mother cleaned his room, and she asked him about the container of dirt. "I guess you're growing something in there . . . seeds . . . lima beans . . . "

37 "No," he said, "it's my worm. He's in there."

38 "Oh, Calvin!" his mother said. "A worm! You'll just knock that thing down and spill dirt all over your bed."

39 "Pretty close quarters for a worm," his father said. "It's used to a little more territory."

40 Calvin suddenly remembered thinking almost that very same thing when he had changed the worm dirt. He had even thought it might seem like a vacation . . . but a big mixing bowl wasn't much of a vacation when you're used to the whole backyard.

CLOSE READ

Analyze Plot Elements

Underline details that show what Calvin's parents think about him having a worm as a pet.

quarters living space; a place to stay

Summarize

Highlight sentences that show the conflict between what Calvin wants to do and what he does.

41 "Of course," his mother said, "I know worms don't have any feelings. . . ."

42 *Wrong,* Calvin thought. *They're all feelings, with their sensory receptors. A worm could probably feel comfortable . . . or uncomfortable. Maybe even scared . . . or nervous . . .*

43 After supper, he took his mother's garden trowel and scratched out a big path of soft, sifty dirt in the backyard . . . and, sure enough, Spot wriggled right down into it.

44 *Comfortable*, Calvin thought. . . .

45 In another week or two, he would have changed the dirt six or seven times; he and his worm would have looked at each other through the side of the worm house; he might even have taken him for a very short walk; he would have taken him to school on Bring Your Pet Day . . .

46 Now none of those things would happen, and it didn't help to think about them.

47 The next day was Saturday, and there was Home Depot, but then his parents went to an all-day barbecue, and his grandmother came to stay with him.

48 "Calvin," she said after lunch, "tell me your life story since last week . . . all the good stuff."

49 So he told his grandmother about his worm.

50 "Outstanding!" she said. "A perfect pet! Your father was right, though. A worm needs a lot of room. We'll get that great big lasagna dish, the glass one . . . where's the worm?"

51 "Well, I dumped the dirt, Grandma, so . . . "

52 "Hmm. Worm, too, then. Back in the garden?" She didn't wait for him to answer. "Come on, let's see."

53 *Kooky, kooky,* he thought as his grandmother fished up a worm, said, "Oh, this is an old one," and dropped it back in the dirt.

54 "Was your worm very fat?" she asked. "Some worms are."

55 "I don't know, Grandma . . . just an average worm."

56 "Best kind," she said.

57 Right then Calvin decided to announce that any worm his grandmother produced was his worm. "That's it," he was going to say. "You found my worm!" because it would make her happy, and it wouldn't make any difference to him.

CLOSE READ

Analyze Plot Elements

Underline details that help you infer how Calvin feels about looking for his worm compared to how his grandmother feels.

CLOSE READ

Analyze Plot Elements

Underline the climax, or the turning point, of the story.

Then underline details of the falling action of the story.

tingled felt excitement; felt a prickling sensation

58 She discarded several worms—"too thin . . . too lazy"—and then she crowed. "Here we are! If this one could talk, it would say, 'I'm Calvin's worm' . . . Yes?" And she handed him . . . Spot.

59 All Calvin's sensory receptors shivered and tingled, "Yes," he said, his voice a little shaky. "I would know him anywhere," and of course he would, because of the black mark he, Calvin, had put there, on this very worm.

60 There must be hundreds of worms in this garden. His father had once said, "Too bad I'm not a fisherman, with all these worms." And out of all these worms, his grandmother had found his worm . . . or, maybe, his worm had found his grandmother, because he had heard her say, "That's some outstanding worm. Stood right up in the dirt."

61 Now Spot had curled up in the palm of his hand, so Calvin had to use his other hand to scoop dirt into the lasagna dish.

62 "This is just for now," he told Spot—because maybe his science teacher was right about worms and ears, but even so, it didn't seem right to have a pet and never talk to it. "But next Saturday, at Home Depot, we'll get a really big plastic box to be your house, and a lot of new dirt, and one of those toy ladders that you see in hamster cages . . . "

63 By next week, he would have changed the dirt at least twice. "Gotta change the worm dirt!" he would say; he and Spot would have looked at each other each morning and night through the side of the worm house; he would have taken Spot on a walk—just like now, on the palm of his hand.

64 And this year, on Bring Your Pet Day, he would be the only fourth-grade kid in Homer Applegate Elementary School—maybe the only kid anywhere!—who had a worm for a pet.

CLOSE READ

Analyze Plot Elements

Underline the sentence that states the resolution, or solution to the story's conflict.

Develop Vocabulary

In realistic fiction, descriptive words help the reader understand the characters, setting, and events. Precise language helps readers use their five senses to imagine what the details look, sound, smell, taste, and feel like.

My TURN Write the definition of each word. Then explain how the author's word choice in "A Pet for Calvin" affects readers' senses, thoughts, or feelings.

Word	Definition	Effect of Word on Reader
loamy	having a texture good for growing plants	helps readers imagine what the dirt feels and looks like
quarters		
tingled		
tolerate		
wriggled		

Check for Understanding

My TURN Look back at the text to answer the questions.

1. What examples help you determine that "A Pet for Calvin" is realistic fiction?

2. How and why does the author use humor?

3. How do different events of the plot show that Calvin thinks more and more about the worm's needs? Use text evidence to analyze plot elements.

4. How do Calvin's parents' reactions to his pet worm differ from that of his grandmother? Analyze this conflict between the characters.

Analyze Plot Elements

Plot elements include parts of a story's plot, or organization of a story's events. A plot includes the story's conflict, or problem; the events that rise to the climax, or turning point; the events that result from the climax; and, finally, the events that resolve the conflict.

1. **My TURN** Go to the Close Read notes in "A Pet for Calvin" and underline the parts that help you analyze the plot elements.
2. **Text Evidence** Use the parts you underlined to complete the graphic organizer.

Conflict: ______________________

Rising Action:

- ______________________
- ______________________
- ______________________
- ______________________

Climax: ______________________

____

Falling Action: ______________________

____

Resolution: ______________________

Analysis: How does the plot change Calvin?

Summarize

Summarizing means retelling the most important events of a story in the order they happened. A summary is always shorter than the story itself, and it should maintain the story's meaning.

1. My TURN Go back to the Close Read notes and highlight details that help you summarize one event while maintaining logical order.
2. **Text Evidence** Use your highlighted text to help you summarize an event to complete the graphic organizer.

First
Second
Third
Fourth
Last

Reflect and Share

Write to Sources In "A Pet for Calvin," Calvin overcomes many obstacles to keep his pet—even if it is a pet worm! How does determination help people reach their goals? Use the following process to write and support a response to the question.

Freewrite For many writers, characters and events can inspire ideas. For your response, consider the texts you have read this week. Choose texts about characters who face challenges or problems as they try to attain a goal. Identify evidence in each text that tells you how or if the characters met their goals.

Next, freewrite to explore what you think about these texts. In freewriting, you write ideas without editing them. To get started, ask yourself questions, such as *What problem or challenge does this character face?* or *How does the character try to reach a goal?*

Use your freewriting to compose a brief response about how determination helps people reach their goals.

Weekly Question

What are some different ways in which people can reach a goal?

Academic Vocabulary

Learning Goal

I can develop knowledge about language to make connections between reading and writing.

Words that have the same or similar meanings are **synonyms**. Words that have opposite meanings are **antonyms**. Finding synonyms and antonyms can deepen your understanding of vocabulary words.

My TURN For each word,

1. **Read** the definition.
2. **Write** two synonyms and two antonyms.
3. **Use** a print or digital resource, such as a thesaurus, as needed.

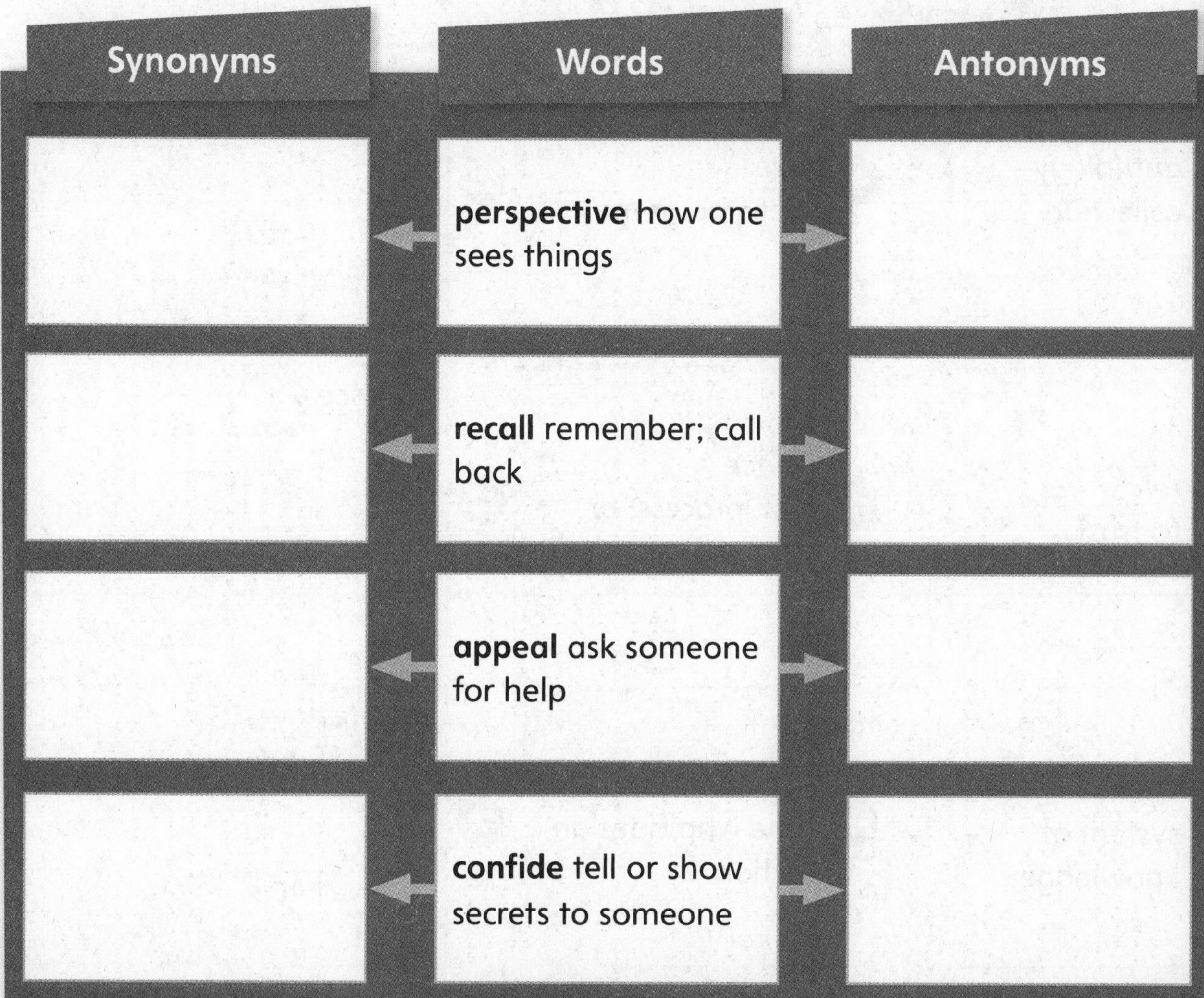

Synonyms	Words	Antonyms
	perspective how one sees things	
	recall remember; call back	
	appeal ask someone for help	
	confide tell or show secrets to someone	

Suffixes *-ize, -ance, -ence, -ist*

A **suffix** is a word part added to the end of a word or word part. Suffixes change the meaning or part of speech of a word.

The word *summary* means "a brief statement that includes only main ideas or events." If you know what *summary* means, you can figure out that *summarize* means "to give a brief statement including only main ideas or events."

My TURN Read each word and meaning. Then use the meaning of the suffix to write a definition for each new word. On a separate sheet of paper, use each new word in a sentence.

Word	+	Suffix	=	New Word
anthology collection	+	*-ize* become or make	=	*anthologize*
rely to trust	+	*-ance* act, process, or state of	=	*reliance*
science system of knowledge	+	*-ist* one who does an action	=	*scientist*

Read Like a Writer

One way authors entertain readers is through humor. **Hyperbole**, or exaggeration, is something overstated and made greater than it actually is. Another humor device is a **pun**. A pun is a play on the different meanings of a word or on two words with similar sounds but different meanings.

Read the text.

> After an allergic reaction, Sara's dad asked, "Killed by kitten? That would be a perfect death."

hyperbole

pun

1. **Identify** Sara's dad exaggerates and also uses the word *perfect*, which is similar to the *purring* sound cats make.
2. **Analyze** Why are the hyperbole and pun entertaining?
3. **Conclude** The text is humorous because of exaggerated and funny comments about a possibly serious problem.

Read the text.

> Gary thinks his grasshopper is the best pet ever! But he knows it bugs his mom.

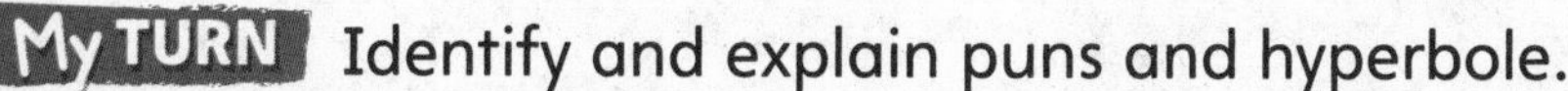

My TURN Identify and explain puns and hyperbole.

1. **Identify** Gary exaggerates that ______________________.
   The author uses the pun ______________________.
2. **Analyze** Why are the hyperbole and pun entertaining?
3. **Conclude** The text is humorous because ______________________
   ______________________.

Write for a Reader

Hyperbole and puns are types of figurative language used to create humor. Hyperbole is exaggeration, often for humorous effect. Puns create humor through a play on the different meanings of a word or on similar-sounding words.

My TURN Think about how Barbara Robinson's use of hyperbole in "A Pet for Calvin" affects you as a reader. Now identify how you can use hyperbole, as well as puns, to create humor to entertain your own readers.

1. If you were trying to show a funny response to a serious event, what hyperbole and puns would you use?

2. Write a passage that includes two or more lines of dialogue in which one character responds in a funny way to a serious event. Use hyperbole and puns to emphasize the humor.

Spell Words with *-ize, -ance, -ence, -ist*

Adding the word part *-ize*, *-ance*, *-ence*, or *-ist* to a word as a suffix may require spelling changes. For example, when adding *-ize* to *memory* to spell *memorize*, the *y* is replaced by the *i* in *-ize*.

My TURN Read the words. Spell and sort the words by their word parts.

SPELLING WORDS

appearance	disappearance	familiarize	sanitize
pessimist	optimist	brilliance	physicist
colonize	insurance	coherence	protagonist
influence	antagonist	memorize	italicize
existence	clearance	performance	preference

-ize

-ance

-ence

-ist

Pronouns and Antecedents

Pronouns are words that take the place of nouns or groups of nouns. **Antecedents** are the nouns to which the pronouns refer. Like nouns, pronouns have singular and plural forms. A singular pronoun refers to a singular noun, and a plural pronoun refers to a plural noun or multiple singular nouns.

Singular pronoun and **antecedent**

Calvin did not have a pet, but his friends did.

Plural pronoun and **antecedent**

Two **people** were looking, and they found the worm quickly.

Plural and singular pronouns and antecedents

Grandma and Calvin found a new home for **the worm.** They put it into a large container.

My TURN Edit this draft by replacing the repeated noun or pronoun with the correct pronoun for each antecedent.

Calvin has a problem, and Calvin is not sure how to solve the problem. Calvin's friends like to play with Calvin's friends' pets. Calvin's mom and dad give him medicine. The parents make sure Calvin finishes the medicine.

Develop an Opinion

Learning Goal

I can use elements of opinion writing to write an essay.

An opinion essay focuses on an idea that a writer has thought deeply about. The writer structures the essay by introducing a topic and clearly stating what he or she thinks about that topic. The writer carefully chooses words, facts, and details that show his or her point of view.

Swimming is the **best** summertime activity **because** it's good exercise, it's a great way to make friends, and it's a way to keep cool on hot days.

Swimming is the topic.

Best shows the writer's opinion about the topic.

Because shows that the writer is going to list reasons for his or her opinion.

The writer gives reasons that are important to him or her.

My TURN Read an opinion essay from your classroom library. Use the chart to record information about the text and the writer's opinion about the topic.

Title	
Topic	
Writer's Opinion	
Words That Show Opinion	

My TURN Plan your own opinion essay in your writing notebook. Develop an idea, and carefully choose facts and details that support your thoughts and opinions.

Develop Reasons

Develop reasons for an opinion by asking *What makes me think that?* Then review your reasons to make sure they are relevant. Use examples, facts, and other details to support each reason.

Topic: My Favorite Book

Opinion:	I like the main character because we are similar.
Reason:	We both work hard to achieve our goals.
Example:	She doesn't get a spot on the basketball team in fourth grade, but she makes the team in fifth grade. The same thing happened when I tried out for the dance team.

My TURN Use the outline to develop an opinion based on the topic provided. Reasons for your opinion must be supported by examples, facts, and details.

Topic: Your Favorite After-School Activity

Opinion: ______________________________

____

____

Reason: ______________________________

____

Example: ______________________________

____

Develop Facts and Details

Writers use facts and details to convince readers to agree with an opinion. **Facts** are pieces of information that can be proved to be true. **Details** are bits of information, including facts, that help explain or support a writer's ideas.

A claim that is supported by opinions may not convince readers who do not already agree with those opinions.

> The Sumatran elephant deserves to be on the endangered species list because elephants are beautiful and fascinating creatures that should be protected.

The revised claim is supported by a fact. This makes readers more likely to agree with the writer's opinion about protecting elephants.

> The Sumatran elephant deserves to be on the endangered species list because the elephant is a major part of an ecosystem that supports many other species.

My TURN Choose a fact that supports the following opinion.

The destruction of the Amazon rainforest is a loss for humanity.

_____ The Amazon is home to many animals.

_____ The rainforest houses about 10% of the known species of plants and animals on Earth.

_____ The Amazon is an amazing place that all people should visit.

My TURN As you develop your own opinion essay, support your reasons with facts and details.

Include Graphic Features

A writer can make an opinion essay more coherent by including facts and details in visual form. Tables, charts, graphs, and diagrams can help a reader quickly understand an issue discussed in a text.

Data included in a graphic feature must come from a reputable, or trustworthy, source. Scientific or government Web sites and books published by experts in the subject are good sources of information.

Cats make the best pets. If you don't believe me, just ask your doctor. Studies have shown that people who own cats have a slightly decreased risk for heart attack, stroke, and other diseases. Dog ownership has not shown these benefits. So if you are at risk, consider choosing Fluffy over Fido the next time you adopt a furry friend!

Study of Disease in Cat Owners and Non-Cat Owners

Current Cat Owners

17% suffered heart attacks, strokes, or other diseases

Never Owned Cats

20% suffered heart attacks, strokes, or other diseases

Source: National Institutes of Health, *Journal of Vascular and Interventional Neurology*, 2009

Clear opinion statement

Links writer's credibility to an expert's

Introduces research that supports opinion

Addresses other opinions or questions reader has

Data from expert research supports the opinion

My TURN Compose your opinion essay. Make it more coherent by including a graphic feature that visually displays facts or supporting details.

Use Technology to Produce Writing

Writers can produce their writing in several ways. Many writers use a computer to revise, edit, and print their work. Others may decide to write a blog post or an online letter to the editor of a newspaper.

My TURN Highlight the ideas you might want to try when you are finished writing your opinion essay. Write in your own idea for producing your work.

- Print your essay on paper.
- Format it for a class blog or Web site.
- Format your essay as an e-mail to the editor of your school newspaper.
- Turn your essay into a script, and then record it as a video with a partner.
- Use an online design program to create illustrations for your essay.
- ______________________________

My TURN Use technology to produce your opinion essay. The checklist can help you choose a method. Share your ideas with your Writing Club.

USING TECHNOLOGY TO PRODUCE YOUR WORK

The digital format you chose

- ☐ is appropriate for your topic.
- ☐ accomplishes your assigned task.
- ☐ appeals to your audience.
- ☐ does not distract from your work.

Use this checklist when you use technology to produce your writing!

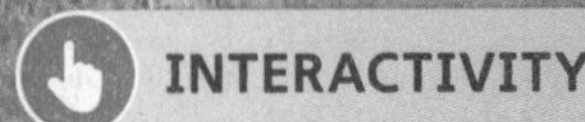

ART: Then and Now

PAINTING

Cave dwellers—the earliest painters—mixed powders with grease to paint on cave walls. Ancient Egyptians painted murals on the tombs of their rulers. The ancient Egyptians also developed watercolor paints. **Today,** tablet computers allow contemporary artists to create art in new ways and share it with the world.

ORIGAMI Origami—the ancient art of folding paper into decorative shapes and figures—originated in East Asia in A.D. 105. In ancient Japan, origami was built from simple designs and used in religious ceremonies. **Today**, people from all over the world enjoy and practice origami. Mathematicians and scientists even use origami to solve mathematical puzzles!

WEEK 3

Weekly Question

How are the experiences of people in ancient times similar to those of people in the modern world?

TURN and TALK With a partner, discuss how you express yourself creatively. You might dance, sing, or play a sport. How is your form of creative expression different from or similar to that of an adult you know? Take notes on your discussion.

CERAMICS

Early hunter-gatherers created ceramics, or pottery, to store items and to cook their meals. **Today**, artists still make vases, bowls, and cups. People visit museums to view pottery from ancient and contemporary artists.

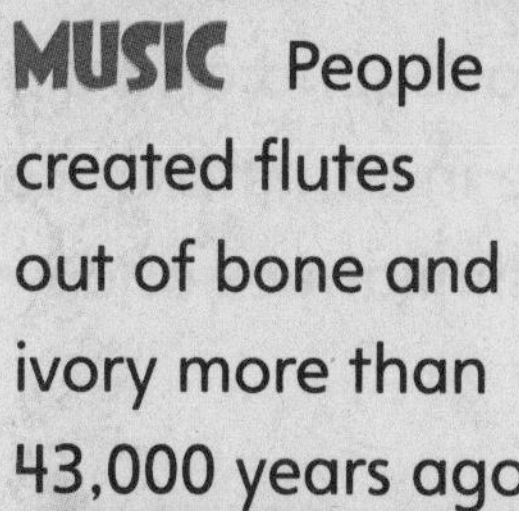

MUSIC People created flutes out of bone and ivory more than 43,000 years ago. Since then, new types of music have developed slowly as different groups have made new instruments and invented ways to play them. **Today**, different technologies offer new ways to access and create music.

Learning Goal

I can learn more about *Reflections* by comparing literary structures in a legend and a drama.

Legend and Drama

A **legend** is a type of folktale based on a real cultural hero but with made-up parts. It includes

- Some real people and events
- Exaggerated or made-up details
- Stories that are linked to a historical time and passed down from generation to generation

Look for these characteristics of the genre as you read well-known legends during your independent reading.

A **drama**, or play, is written to be performed and to entertain. A drama

- Tells the story through **character tags,** or the names of who is speaking, and **dialogue,** or the lines the characters speak
- Includes **stage directions,** or instructions telling characters how to act or move on stage
- Is structured in **acts** (major divisions) and **scenes** (minor divisions)

Dramas are meant to be performed for an audience.

TURN and TALK With a partner, use the anchor chart to compare and contrast a legend and a play. What do both genres have in common? How are they different? Explain the similarities and differences in structure.

Drama and Legend Anchor Chart

Meet *the* Author

Marie Yuen writes poems, short stories, plays, and musicals, and she sometimes writes for TV, too. She lives in Chicago, once lived in Hong Kong, and has vacationed in Kyoto, where this legend takes place. Back in preschool, she had a pet fish, although it was not a carp.

The Carp

Preview Vocabulary

As you read *The Carp*, notice the vocabulary words. Pay attention to how the words help develop the characters and their responses to events.

quell **tactics**

persevere **conscientious**

Read

Before you begin reading the first text, establish a purpose for reading. Keep in mind that you will read two texts. Active readers follow these strategies.

First Read

Notice	**Generate Questions**
how the words and pictures help you better understand the story.	about how the author presents characters and events.
Connect	**Respond**
this text to your personal experiences.	by discussing the challenges the characters experience.

The Carp

by Marie Yuen

AUDIO

ANNOTATE

CLOSE READ

Explain Literary Structure

Underline details on both pages that introduce the setting or situation.

1 Long ago in Japan, there lived a boy named Rosetsu who dreamed of becoming a painter. Not just any painter, but the greatest in all of Japan.

2 Rosetsu's mother and father scraped and saved every penny so Rosetsu could attend art school. When the time came, Rosetsu kissed his parents goodbye and headed down the road to Kyoto, home of the famous Maruyama School, where Rosetsu hoped to study with the master painter Maruyama Okyo. Under the guidance of this brilliant sensei, teacher, Rosetsu might learn to be a master painter himself.

3 Rosetsu had a long walk ahead of him, but his heart was filled with joy and excitement. "This is the way my future lies!" he said to himself as he walked along the dusty road. He paused to watch a sparrow flying overhead and whistled softly to the bird as it soared over the treetops and out of sight.

4 "Making ink, preparing paper and silk, and learning the proper way to hold a brush will be bliss, and what paintings I shall create when I have learned all I have to learn from my sensei!" Rosetsu said. By now it was midday, so Rosetsu found a shady spot to eat his lunch, beside the Katsura River. As he ate, he watched two turtles sunbathe on a nearby log.

5 Just as Rosetsu finished his lunch, an elderly man, gray-bearded and bent from years of toil, appeared before him. Without so much as a hello, the man shook his crooked walking stick at Rosetsu and demanded, "Who are you, and what do you want?"

6 "My name is Rosetsu, and I want to go to Kyoto so I can study at the feet of Sensei Maruyama Okyo and become a great painter," Rosetsu replied.

7 "What makes you think you can be a great painter?" asked the man.

8 "When I dream at night, that is what I am."

9 "Hmm, it's a mystery how you can become a painter when you don't even have a painting brush," replied the man, nodding and stroking his beard.

10 Rosetsu's eyes widened, and he asked, "How did you know that I have no brush?"

11 The man seemed not to have heard Rosetsu. "Let's see how you do without one. Paint a picture for me."

12 "Without a brush, or ink, or paper, or silk?"

13 "Long ago, painters worked without any of these," the man answered. "If you are meant to be a painter, prove it now, to quell the doubts inside you."

14 "But I have no doubts about—"

15 "Yes, you do."

CLOSE READ

Synthesize Information

Highlight text on both pages that shows how the author introduces the main character.

quell put an end to something

CLOSE READ

Synthesize Information

Highlight details that show how Rosetsu and the stranger interact.

16 Rosetsu looked around in a panic until his eyes landed on a nearby tree. He broke off a twig and picked off a few berries, mashing and mixing them to form a kind of ink, and then he peeled off a piece of pale bark to paint on. With a few strokes of the twig, Rosetsu painted a picture of a sparrow and two turtles, and then he handed it to the stranger.

17 The man stared at the painting in silence, as Rosetsu nervously drew circles in the dirt with his foot.

18 Suddenly, the stranger clapped Rosetsu on the back and announced, "You young man, are a painter—one destined to paint pictures more wondrous than the world has ever seen."

19 "Thank you!" Rosetsu said, a smile spreading the width of his face. Then he remembered where he was going, and that he had many miles to walk before he reached Kyoto, so he bowed and said, "Now, if you'll excuse me, I must be on my way."

20 "Not before I give you this," replied the man, and suddenly, as if from thin air, he produced a painting brush—old and worn and nothing to look at—and placed it in Rosetsu's hand.

21 Rosetsu didn't want to hurt the stranger's feelings, so he smiled and thanked him, and he put the brush in his pack. Then he said goodbye to the stranger and continued on his journey.

22 By the time Rosetsu arrived in Kyoto, it was nearly evening, and he worried the school would be closed. He was relieved to arrive at the gate and see the gatekeeper dozing there.

23 The boy coughed loudly and then announced, "I am Rosetsu, and I have come to see Sensei Okyo. It has long been my dream to learn from the sensei. One day I hope to become a great painter like him."

24 The gatekeeper yawned, rubbed his eyes, and then said, "That is a noble dream, my boy, but what if the sensei does not want to teach you?"

25 This idea had never crossed Rosetsu's mind. "Then I would plead with him to reconsider," he replied. "I know he is a generous man, and when he hears my dream he will surely take me on as his student."

26 "Hmm," said the gatekeeper, furrowing his brow. "How long have you been painting?"

CLOSE READ

Explain Literary Structure

Underline descriptive language that shows how the setting shapes the characters' actions.

CLOSE READ

Synthesize Information

Highlight an example of dialogue that develops the conflict and the plot.

27 Rosetsu's heart beat faster as he responded, "Not long, sir, but I am eager to learn. I also have a brush. . . ." As Rosetsu pulled the painting brush from his pack, the gatekeeper stared at it, his face reddening.

28 "Where did you get this brush?" he demanded. "Did you steal it?"

29 "No!" cried Rosetsu. "I met a stranger on my way to Kyoto. He told me to paint a picture, and then he gave me the brush!"

30 "Did he tell you his name?"

31 "No, I have no idea who he was."

32 The gatekeeper laughed and replied, "I now know you didn't steal this painting brush because you don't know its owner or its true worth. The brush once belonged to my own sensei, the great Ishida Yutei!"

33 "Ishida Yutei!" Rosetsu repeated, his eyes widening. "He taught Sensei Okyo!"

34 "Yes, I am Sensei Maruyama Okyo, and the stranger you met on your way here was Sensei Yutei. If my sensei gave you his brush, he must think highly of you indeed. Of course you will be admitted to Maruyama School. Here is your brush. Keep it safe so that one day—after proving yourself worthy—you will be ready to paint with it."

35 "Thank you, sensei!" cried Rosetsu.

36 Rosetsu began to work and study in Sensei Okyo's studio. He started by preparing ink, paper, and silks for painting, and learning to care for and repair brushes. Each morning he eagerly awoke in hopes that he'd be found worthy enough to paint with Sensei Yutei's brush, and every night he told himself, "Soon, soon."

37 Three years passed quickly. Rosetsu worked and studied, but he didn't make as much progress as he'd like. As his classmates finished school and went on to become great painters, Rosetsu was left behind. He often felt discouraged and full of self-doubt.

38 One day as when Rosetsu was grinding more ink for class, he heard two students speaking in the hall.

39 "Rosetsu has never completed a painting, not even once!" one student said, adding, "It must be because he is missing something—like talent, or taste."

40 "Sensei Okyo is very hard on Rosetsu—much harder than he is on the rest of us," the other student said. "I think he's disappointed that Rosetsu will never be great."

41 As the sound of their footsteps died away down the hall, Rosetsu was flooded with embarrassment and shame. He packed up his belongings and ran out of the school, relieved to escape into the cold winter night.

42 He trudged through the snow for hours with no thought to his destination. Finally, when he could walk no more, he collapsed into a snow bank beneath some pine trees, where he burrowed under the snow and fell asleep.

CLOSE READ

Explain Literary Structure

Underline a descriptive paragraph that marks a turning point in the story.

CLOSE READ

Synthesize Information

Highlight words on both pages that show that the story is organized chronologically, or in time order.

tactics planned actions for a specific purpose

persevere do something in spite of discouragement

43 The sun was overhead by the time Rosetsu awoke. As he shook the snow off, he heard a loud splashing nearby. Soon he found the source. A giant carp was jumping wildly in the middle of a half-frozen pond. Just out of reach, on the ice, lay a sembei—a sweet-salty Japanese cracker.

44 Rosetsu watched the carp as it twisted and turned and tried all sorts of tactics to reach the sembei. He marveled at the carp's determination. Each time the fish jumped, it broke a tiny bit of the ice and moved closer to its prize.

45 Morning passed, noon came and went, and the sun began to sink, yet the bruised and exhausted carp still did not give up. Finally, with one last leap, the fish broke through the remaining bit of ice between it and the sembei, grasped its hard-won treat in its mouth, and swam away.

46 Rosetsu laughed and clapped, cheered by the carp's spirit and determination. "If I am to succeed," Rosetsu said to himself, "I must be just like that carp: determined, persistent, and unwilling to give up. I'll ask Sensei Okyo how I can become worthy of Sensei Yutei's brush, and then I'll persevere until I gain my prize."

47 Rosetsu returned to the Maruyama School with a fire in his belly and a gleam in his eyes. The next day, he was granted permission to meet privately with Sensei Okyo.

48 "I must know why I have been kept behind these three years, when all of my classmates have surpassed me," Rosetsu said. "Have I been careless with my work?"

49 "No," the sensei replied, "you are a conscientious worker, but your own doubts have held you back. A great painter doesn't abandon his paintings halfway through for fear they won't be good enough! You must believe in your own talents if you want others to do so."

50 Rosetsu said, "So you don't think I am without talent?"

51 "Had you no talent, I wouldn't have accepted you in the first place. Did not Sensei Yutei give you his brush?"

52 "Yes!" Rosetsu said. He smiled and bowed. "Thank you, sensei. I shall do my best every day from now on, and soon, I hope, I will be ready to use my brush."

53 Rosetsu studied and worked harder than ever, and he completed many paintings, each one more dazzling than the last. After another year passed, his skills and knowledge were almost equal to those of Sensei Okyo.

54 Then came the glorious day he was allowed to paint with Sensei Yutei's brush. His choice of subject matter? It was a carp, of course, in honor of the one that inspired him to persist no matter what. And so it was that Rosetsu became not only one of Sensei Okyo's best pupils, but one of Japan's greatest painters of all time.

CLOSE READ

Explain Literary Structure

Underline details that show how the author resolves the conflict of the story.

conscientious diligent; thorough

Meet *the* Author

Dana Crum is an award-winning poet, novelist, and journalist. He loves animals (especially cats), music (especially hip-hop), and words (especially ones kids like reading).

The Hermit Thrush

Preview Vocabulary

As you read *The Hermit Thrush*, watch for the vocabulary word.

supportive

Read and Compare

Before you compare texts, establish a purpose for reading. Active readers follow these strategies when they read and compare texts.

First Read

Notice	**Generate Questions**
how the texts are similar and different.	about themes, or messages, *The Hermit Thrush* shares with *The Carp*.
Connect	**Respond**
what you read in the *The Carp* to what you read in *The Hermit Thrush*.	by discussing the most interesting parts of *The Carp* and *The Hermit Thrush* with a partner.

The Hermit Thrush

by Dana Crum

Explain Literary Structure

Underline details that show how the playwright introduces the situation of the drama.

Then underline details that tell you which character is speaking and how he or she should behave on stage.

1 **CHARACTERS**

HAYATE WATANABE, a 13-year-old boy

WAKANA, HAYATE's 15-year-old sister

MOM

DAD

BEN, HAYATE's best friend

2 **SETTING**

The Watanabe home in Los Angeles, California.

ACT 1

Scene 1

3 *It's Saturday, the day of the family's weekly concert.* MOM, DAD, *and* WAKANA *sit in the living room. An acoustic guitar leans against Dad's chair.* MOM *holds a pair of drumsticks in her lap.* WAKANA *thumbs through a book of sheet music.* HAYATE *is last to arrive, carrying his saxophone. He sits in the corner and stares down at his sneakers.*

4 DAD (*to* HAYATE). You made it!

(HAYATE *shrugs.*)

5 MOM. Let's get started. Who would like to go first this week?

6 WAKANA. HAYATE, didn't you say you wanted to go first?

7 HAYATE. (*He looks up. He stares at* WAKANA.) No, I didn't.

8 MOM. I'll start. I'm going to play the drum solo from a song I loved in college.

(MOM *plays her drum solo expertly. When she finishes, she stands.*)

9 WAKANA. That was awesome!

10 DAD. Yes, it was a little *too* good. Don't leave us and join a rock band, okay?

(MOM *smiles.*)

11 MOM. So who's next?

12 HAYATE (*sighing*). I'll go. I might as well get it over with.

13 DAD. What will you play this week, HAYATE?

14 HAYATE. Just a jazz piece my music teacher taught me.

(HAYATE *stands and raises his saxophone to his mouth. He takes a breath. Harsh sounds come from the saxophone. Beads of sweat appear on* HAYATE'S *forehead. He stops playing before finishing the song.*)

15 WAKANA. Yikes, your sax sounds like a sick moose.

16 MOM. Wakana!

17 DAD. Be more supportive of your brother.

18 WAKANA. Sorry, HAYATE. I was just joking!

(HAYATE *storms out of the living room.* MOM *follows him and stops him in the hallway.*)

19 MOM. Don't pay attention to WAKANA.

CLOSE READ

Synthesize Information

Highlight details that show how a drama develops characters differently than a story.

supportive
encouraging; helpful

Explain Literary Structure

Underline details on both pages that help you determine how Act 2 is different from Act 1.

20 HAYATE. She's right, though. I can't play well. I've been taking lessons for a long time now, and I practice every day. But I don't think I have what it takes.

21 MOM. I know you're frustrated, but just keep at it. Everyone struggles sometimes.

22 HAYATE. I don't see you, DAD, or WAKANA struggling. You all play your instruments perfectly, and it seems to come to you naturally. Why don't you have these Saturday concerts without me? I should do something else—something I'm actually good at.

23 MOM. Don't give up so easily. Why don't you come back to the concert? Your father and WAKANA haven't performed yet.

24 HAYATE. Can I just go to my room, please?

25 MOM. Okay, I suppose so.

(HAYATE *slumps as he walks down the hall to his room.*)

ACT 2

Scene 1

26 *It's Sunday, the next day.* HAYATE *is standing in his room, clutching his saxophone. His friend* BEN *is glancing at* HAYATE'S *sheet music.*

27 BEN *(looking up).* Let's go shoot some hoops.

28 HAYATE. Okay. I don't feel like practicing this song anymore, anyway. What's the point? I'll never be any good.

29 BEN. Not with that attitude you won't, young man!

(HAYATE *frowns at* BEN.)

30 **BEN.** Just kidding, dude. That's what my parents said all the time when I wanted to quit piano. Lessons and practicing scales and all that—I got really sick of it. It made me all stressed out, too. My parents kept insisting I should have a better attitude. I told them I'd have a better attitude if I could quit!

31 **HAYATE.** So they just let you?

32 **BEN.** Well, no. It was kind of strange, actually. They gave me an electronic keyboard for my birthday. And for some reason, when I started playing that, it was fun. I didn't feel anxious when I played it—I just loosened up. And that helped me relax when I played our big grand piano, too.

(**HAYATE** *starts quietly playing a tune he made up.*)

33 **BEN.** Whoa—that's good!

34 **HAYATE.** I'm just messing around. That's the only time I sound okay.

35 **BEN.** You know, maybe you need to loosen up, too. Spend more time playing what you want to play and less time trying to be perfect.

36 **HAYATE** *(his voice full of doubt).* Maybe . . .

CLOSE READ

Synthesize Information

Highlight details from the dialogue in Act 2: Scene 1 that develop the conflict.

Explain Literary Structure

Identify the setting of Scene 2. Underline your answer. Consider how Scene 2 builds on the events of Scene 1.

Scene 2

37 *It's Monday.* HAYATE *is practicing in his room, staring at his sheet music. His saxophone wails. He throws the music aside.*

38 HAYATE. I don't even like that song! I never want to play it again.

39 WAKANA *(peering around his open doorway)*. Sounds like a good idea to me!

40 HAYATE. Yeah, yeah, I know—I sounded like a sick moose.

41 WAKANA. No, it wasn't bad. You should only play music you love, though.

42 HAYATE. I'd ruin that too. Maybe I shouldn't play anything at all.

43 WAKANA. If you don't like the saxophone, why don't you tell MOM and DAD you want to quit?

44 HAYATE. I love the sax—I'm just not good. Anyway, they'd be so disappointed.

45 WAKANA. Well, you should only keep playing if you like to. Do you know this quote? "The bird doesn't sing to please others. It sings because it is happy."

46 HAYATE. What?

47 WAKANA. Just something I read once.

Scene 3

48 *It's Thursday. After practicing his sax,* HAYATE *has gone outside to the backyard to get some fresh air.*

49 HAYATE *(talking to himself)*. Why can't I learn to play better? Last week I left the concert early. This week I won't go at all.

(Suddenly, HAYATE *hears the beautiful sound of a hermit thrush singing in a nearby tree.* HAYATE *watches and listens.)*

50 HAYATE *(to the hermit thrush).* If only I could play as well as you sing, little bird.

(He listens as the bird finishes its song and then starts again.)

51 HAYATE *(to the hermit thrush).* You don't study music. You can't read notes. But you sing beautifully. (HAYATE *looks thoughtful.*) Maybe I should do what you do. I should play what's in my heart. I should feel the music and stop thinking so much. *(The hermit thrush continues to sing.)*

Scene 4

52 HAYATE *goes back to his house and returns to his room. He picks up his saxophone. He starts to play a melody with his eyes closed, swaying gently as he plays. The notes sound fuller and rich, not harsh as they usually do. The tune has some echoes of the hermit thrush's song.*

CLOSE READ

Synthesize Information

Identify how Scene 4 fits into the structure of the drama.

Highlight details in the scene that create the climax of the drama.

Synthesize Information

Highlight details that show how the setting of a play develops. Consider how this differs from how the setting of a story develops.

Vocabulary in Context

Context clues are words or phrases that surround an unfamiliar word and help you to understand its meaning.

Underline words that help you understand the meaning of *ode*.

ACT 3

Scene 1

53 *It's Saturday.* MOM, DAD, WAKANA, *and* HAYATE *sit in the living room.* DAD *is the first to perform. Hunched over his acoustic guitar, he strums and sings a beautiful tune.*

54 WAKANA. That was great, DAD.

55 MOM. Who'd like to go next?

56 HAYATE. I'll go. *(He stands.)* I'm going to perform a song I'm writing. It's not finished yet. *(He begins to play. His performance is heartfelt and animated, and he smiles and sways as he plays. He hits a few off notes, but mostly he plays well.)*

57 WAKANA. You sounded good, HAYATE—and you looked happy for a change!

58 MOM. I didn't know you were writing your own music!

59 HAYATE. Yeah, I just got inspired, I guess.

(HAYATE *grins as he sits down.* MOM *winks at him.* DAD *pats him on the back.)*

Scene 2

60 *It's Saturday, two months later. In the living room, the Watanabe family watches and listens while* HAYATE *plays his saxophone. He looks relaxed and happy he plays.*

61 DAD *(smiling).* That was great, HAYATE! What was that song?

62 HAYATE. It's the song I started writing a couple of months ago.

63 MOM. It's beautiful! It sounded almost like a birdsong.

64 HAYATE *(blushing).* Thanks. I call it "Ode to a Hermit Thrush."

Develop Vocabulary

Authors use precise words to describe and develop characters' emotions and relationships. These words make details vivid and help readers connect with the characters and story.

My TURN Complete the graphic organizer. For each vocabulary word, write three other words with related meanings. You may use words from *The Carp*, *The Hermit Thrush*, or a print or online thesaurus.

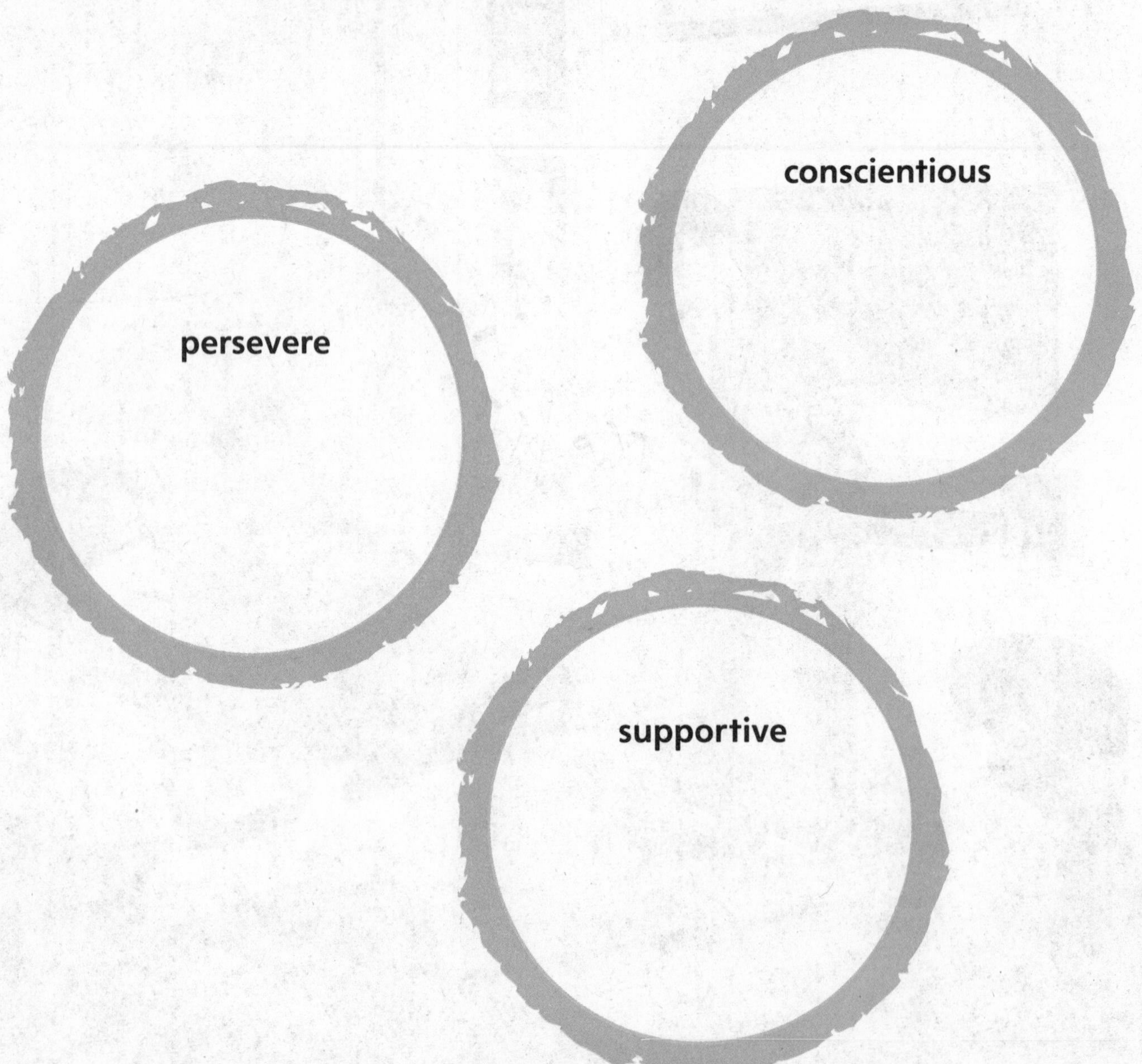

Check for Understanding

My TURN Look back at the texts to answer the questions.

1. How is the legend *The Carp* different from the play *The Hermit Thrush*? Use examples in your explanation.

2. What is the author's message in *The Carp*? How do you know?

3. Visual elements add to the meaning, beauty, and tone, or feeling, of a text. How do the illustrations in *The Carp* affect your understanding of the text?

4. Compare and contrast Rosetsu's experiences to those of a character in another legend you know.

Explain Literary Structure

Authors and playwrights use dialogue and description as well as a sequence of events to develop stories. A playwright can group major events into **acts**, which can be divided into **scenes. Character tags** tell which character is speaking, and **stage directions** explain what the actors are doing. These elements work together to provide structure and meaning in a story or drama.

1. **My TURN** Go to the Close Read notes in *The Carp* and *The Hermit Thrush*. Underline parts that show the structure of each text.

2. **Text Evidence** Identify the text or texts that use each element. Use the parts you underlined to explain how the elements work together.

Stage Directions

Dialogue

Acts and Scenes

Descriptive Paragraphs

Synthesize Information

When you read two texts that have a similar structure, characters, or theme, you can **synthesize information** about both texts. Combine details about what you know with what you read to create new understanding.

1. **My TURN** Go back to the Close Read notes and highlight details that help you synthesize information about the legend and the play.

2. **Text Evidence** Complete the graphic organizer by using your highlighted text to synthesize information from both texts.

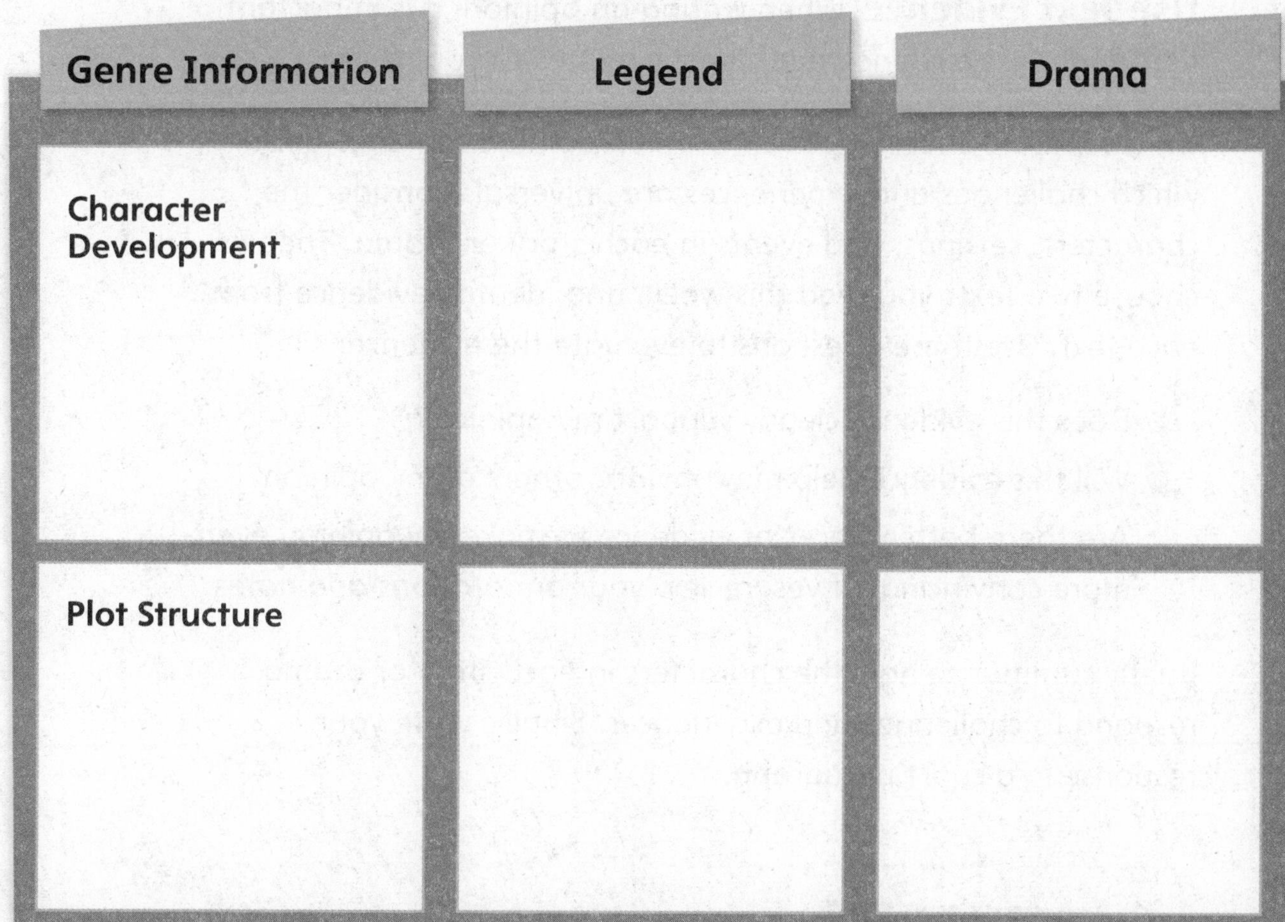

Genre Information	Legend	Drama
Character Development		
Plot Structure		

How does genre affect the structure of these literary texts?

Reflect and Share

Write to Sources In this unit, you have read about characters and their experiences. Compare and contrast the texts you have read this week. Do people from different times and cultures share challenges and experiences? Use this question to help you explain which experiences are universal.

Use Text Evidence When writing an opinion, it is important to include text evidence that directly relates to your claim.

On a separate sheet of paper, write an opinion sentence about which challenges and experiences are universal. Consider the characters, settings, and events in each story or drama. Then choose two texts you read this week, and identify evidence from each text. Use these questions to evaluate the evidence:

- Does this evidence clearly support my opinion?
- Will this evidence help me convince others of my opinion?
- Are there better pieces of evidence to make my opinion even more convincing? If yes, review your annotations and notes.

Briefly summarize how the characters in each story or drama respond to challenges and experiences. Finally, write your response in a short paragraph.

Weekly Question

How are the experiences of people in ancient times similar to those of people in the modern world?

Academic Vocabulary

Learning Goal

I can develop knowledge about language to make connections between reading and writing.

Context clues are the words and sentences around a word that can give clues to a word's meaning, such as a definition, example, synonym, or antonym. Use context clues to determine the meanings of unfamiliar or multiple-meaning words.

My TURN For each item,

1. **Underline** the context clues for each boldfaced word.
2. **Confirm** the meaning of the boldfaced word in a dictionary.
3. **Write** a new sentence using the word.

1. Our teacher had a different **perspective** on our quiz scores. From her point of view, we had not studied enough.

2. The general chose to **recall** the soldiers after the battle. Military intelligence supported the decision to withdraw.

3. The medical board had to **appeal**, or ask for assistance, for funding for a new research wing at the hospital.

4. Sofia wished she could **confide** in her sister. However, Sofia knew that if she did, everyone in town would know her business.

Unusual Spellings

Many English words sound different than how they are spelled. Some words have letters you do not hear, such as the *b* in *doubt*. Other words you hear may not give you clues about how they should be spelled, such as the word *anxious*.

To verify the spelling or pronunciation of a word you do not know, use a print or digital dictionary. When searching in print, keep in mind that the letters may be in an unexpected order.

My TURN Read each word. Think about how the word might be pronounced. Then check a print or digital dictionary to see if you were correct. Mark the result in the chart. If you had the wrong pronunciation, write a tip that can help you remember.

Word	Was I correct?	How I can remember
indict	No	rhymes with *right* and *kite*
liaison		
language		
colonel		

Read Like a Writer

A **stereotype** is a flat, or undeveloped, character with general traits of a group of people but no individual traits. Literary stereotypes are not the same as stereotypes of real people. An **anecdote** is a story that illustrates a point.

Model! Read the text.

The stranger wore tattered clothes and carried a cane. "In my youth, I was always in a hurry. I never took time to enjoy life," he croaked in a weak voice.

stereotype

anecdote

1. **Identify** The stranger seems old but wise. The anecdote shows he did not appreciate his youth when he was young.
2. **Analyze** What is the purpose of the stereotype and anecdote?
3. **Conclude** The stereotype helps me picture the wise, old character, and the anecdote emphasizes a theme.

Read the text.

Giang's sister ignored him, texting her friends instead of helping him with his homework. It was just like last summer, when Bian would not drive him to music class.

My TURN Explain the purpose of stereotyping and anecdote.

1. **Identify** Bian ______________________. The anecdote describes ______________________.
2. **Analyze** What is purpose of the stereotype and anecdote?
3. **Conclude** The stereotype helps me picture ______________________. The anecdote ______________________.

Write for a Reader

One purpose of literary stereotypes is to establish a certain kind of character quickly. Stereotypes often appear in traditional literature, but most contemporary authors choose to write well-developed, complex characters instead of stereotypes. Writers use anecdotes to make a point or highlight an important theme.

My TURN Think about how stereotypical characters and anecdotes affect you as a reader. Now identify how you can influence your readers by using anecdotes and avoiding flat characters in your own literary text.

1. If you were trying to show an interesting and well-rounded character in a legend or myth, what anecdotes would you use? What stereotypes would you avoid?

2. Introduce a well-rounded character for a scene or story. Be sure to avoid stereotypical traits. Use anecdotes to reveal the theme.

Spell Words with Unusual Spellings

Some sounds are not spelled in a regular way. Vowel sounds can be spelled several different ways.

My TURN Read the words. Spell and sort the words in alphabetical order.

SPELLING WORDS

league	embarrass	epitome	depot
sergeant	vague	intrigue	cordial
yacht	anxious	villain	disguise
fatigue	genealogy	cantaloupe	jeopardy
debt	queue	flood	liaison

Possessive Pronouns

Pronouns are words that can take the place of nouns or groups of nouns. Pronouns that show ownership are **possessive pronouns**. Unlike possessive nouns (*the dog's*, *Maria's*), possessive pronouns do not use an apostrophe.

	Singular	Plural	Before a Noun	By Itself
first person	*my* *mine*	*our* *ours*	This is **my** book. This is **our** book.	This book is **mine**. This book is **ours**.
second person	*your* *yours*	*your* *yours*	This is **your** book.	This book is **yours**.
third person	*his* *her* *hers* *its*	*their* *theirs*	This is **his** book. This is **her** book. This is **their** book. This is **its** book.	This book is **his**. This book is **hers**. This book is **theirs**.

My TURN Edit this draft by replacing each possessive noun with the correct possessive pronoun.

Rosetsu left Rosetsu's parents behind when he went to be a painter. "I am starting Rosetsu's great adventure," he thought, "and the future will be Rosetsu's!" A stranger offered Rosetsu the stranger's brush. The gatekeeper at the school accused Rosetsu of theft. "That brush is not Rosetsu's!" he exclaimed. Sensei Okyo's and Sensei Yutei's techniques were taught at the school.

Develop an Introduction and a Conclusion

Learning Goal

I can use elements of opinion writing to write an essay.

Argumentative writing, including opinion essays, needs structure to make sense. Begin with a strong introduction that clearly states your opinion. Sum up your point of view in a conclusion.

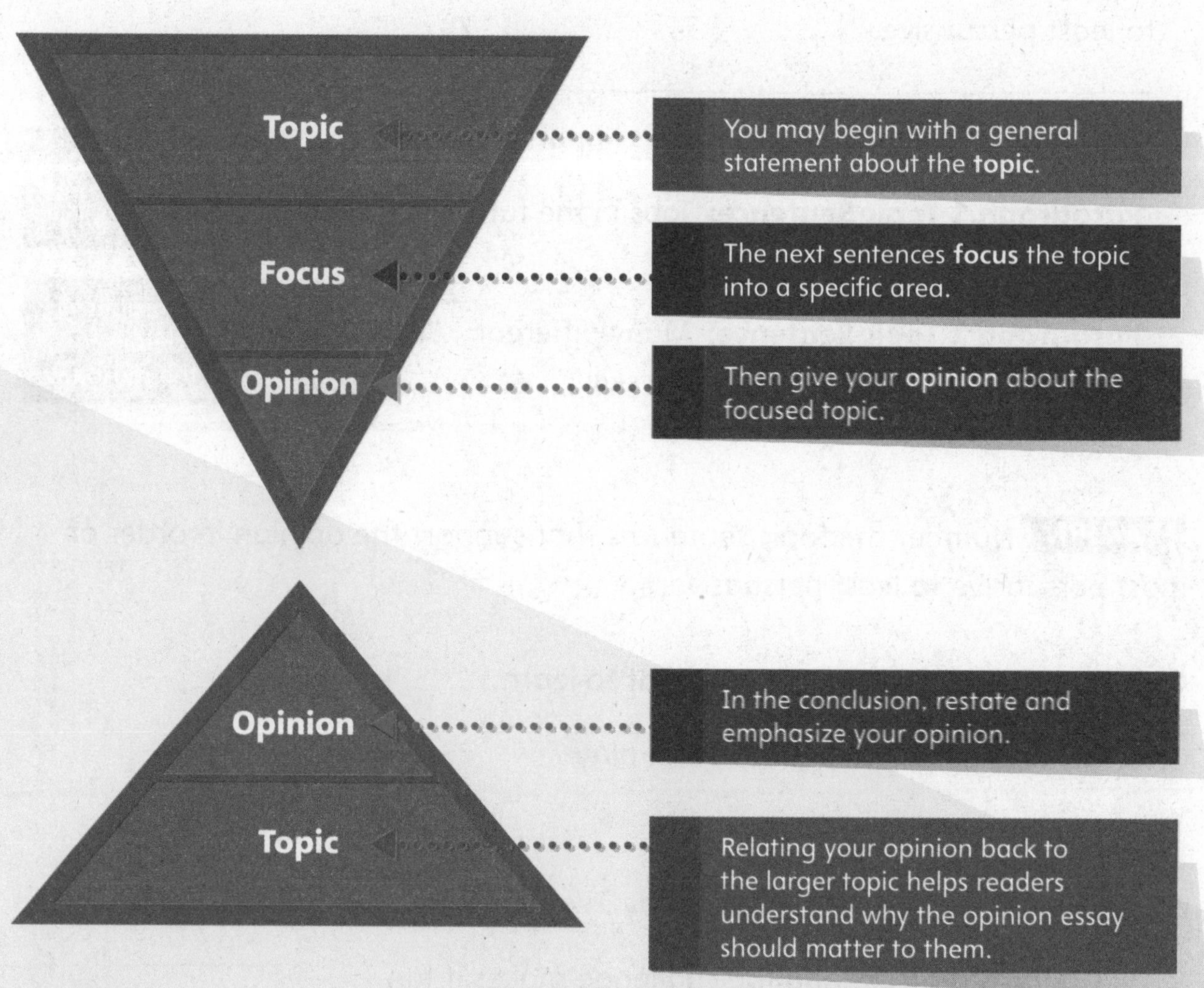

MY TURN In your writing notebook, develop a draft of the introduction and conclusion of your opinion essay. Use the organizer as a guide to making your writing clear and coherent.

Develop Reasons and Supporting Information

Writers organize opinion essays to make their reasons clear and persuasive. Paragraphs:

- show how examples, facts, and details support reasons.
- show how reasons relate to the larger opinion.
- may be organized from least to most persuasive or most to least persuasive.

Opinion: I think learning to code is important.

Paragraph 1 Topic Sentence: Jobs in the future will depend on technology.

The first paragraph may explain the most persuasive reason.

Paragraph 2 Topic Sentence: Many different industries now require coding as a skill.

Other paragraphs may give details to support the reason.

My TURN Number the topic sentences that support the opinion in order of most persuasive to least persuasive.

Opinion: Guitar is the best instrument to learn.

_____ My dad has an old guitar I can play.

_____ I enjoy listening to guitar music.

_____ Someday I might be able to play in a band.

_____ Guitar is difficult, and the challenge makes it fun.

My TURN In your writing notebook, develop a draft of your opinion essay. Use paragraphs to create a logical structure.

Compose with Transition Words, Phrases, and Clauses

Use transitions—or linking words, phrases, and clauses—to guide readers through your opinion essay. These words make your writing coherent by creating logical relationships between reasons and facts and details.

Some common transitions that writers use in opinion essays include *additionally, consequently, for, since, even though, in fact, next, then, clearly, specifically,* and *because*.

My TURN Add transitions to complete the opinion paragraph.

Soccer is my favorite sport to play. I think it's the best ________________ a soccer player gets great exercise. ________________, kids get to play on a team. ________________, they learn skills that help them succeed in life, ________________ how to get along with others and how to follow directions. ________________ practices can be long and tiring, soccer is worth the effort. ________________, others agree with me, because more than 3 million kids play soccer in the United States each year.

My TURN In your writing notebook, develop or revise a draft of your own opinion essay. Include transitions to make your essay clear and coherent.

Use Formatting

Formatting allows a writer to highlight important information. Headings, or titles for paragraphs and sections, are one kind of formatting. Headings guide a reader through a text by briefly summarizing each section.

My TURN Read each paragraph and write a heading for it.

Indoor Gardening

____

The first step to indoor gardening is understanding the kind of soil, sunlight, and watering your plants need. Air is drier in the winter, so plants may need more water. Sun-loving plants need a south-facing window so they can get enough light.

____

Because they are hearty and require little care, plants such as grape ivy, fiddleleaf fig, and snake plants are perfect for indoor gardens. If you avoid overwatering, these will live happily in any room that gets a little light.

____

Having a garden indoors can help people enjoy greenery during even the most brutal winters. But aside from looking pretty, houseplants actually remove pollutants from the air and help keep air from becoming too dry.

My TURN In your writing notebook, develop a draft of your opinion essay. Include headings to create a logical organization.

Use Technology to Interact and Collaborate

To **collaborate** is to work together to accomplish a goal. Writers often collaborate to brainstorm ideas and to revise or edit their work. Technology has made it easier for writers to work together and communicate with each other.

My TURN Work with a group to research an opinion essay on a topic that interests you. Highlight the ideas you want to try within your group. Add other ideas to this list based on resources available in your classroom.

- Use your classroom's social media to share opinions about the essay.
- Work together to type a response to the opinion essay.
- As a group, draft a post for your class blog about the opinion essay.
- Use the Internet to research facts and details that support your opinion.
- Participate in a video chat with another class to share ideas.
- Research how other writers have approached the same topic.
- Have a video chat with an author about his or her writing process.
- ______________________________
- ______________________________

My TURN Identify a topic, purpose, and audience. Then select any genre, and plan a draft by mapping your ideas.

Remember to be open to feedback and ideas for improving your work.

INTERACTIVITY

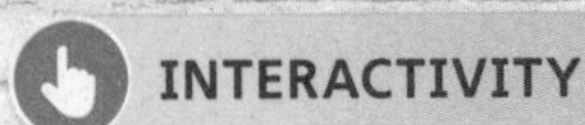

Riddle Me This!

When he married my sister, I promised this mister I'd name my first son after him. I am your mother, and he is your

____

When her brother, your dad, goes to see a movie with your mother, she takes care of your brother and you. She is your

____

We are first or second, once or twice removed, because either our parents or grandparents were siblings. We are

____

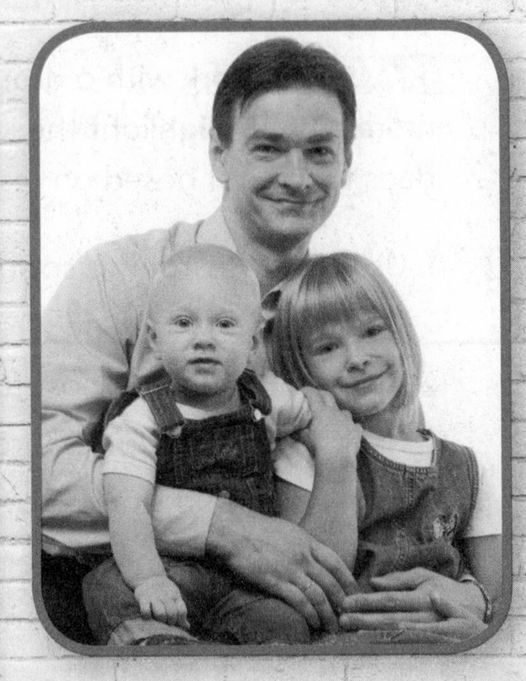

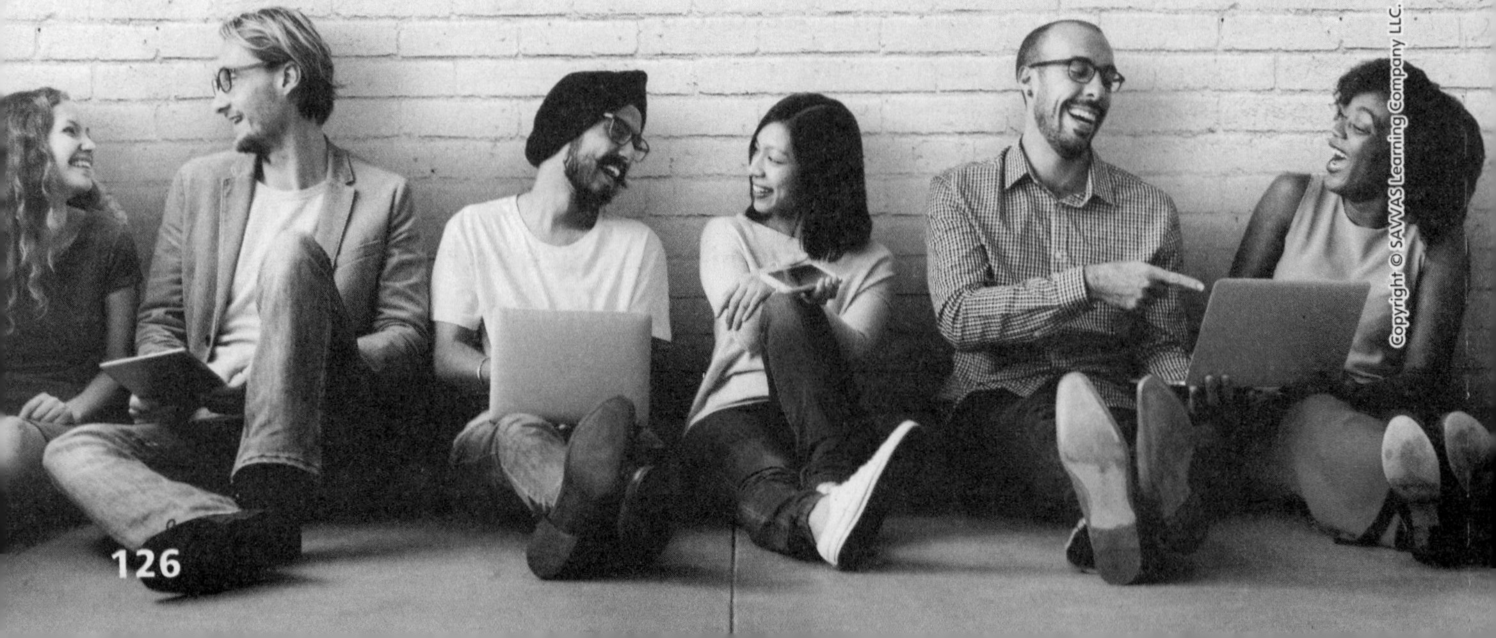

WEEK 4

Weekly Question

What can our families teach us about ourselves?

TURN and TALK Share a piece of advice given to you by someone in your family or a trusted adult. Talk about how this advice helps you and why you remember it.

They come to play with you when your parents, their children, have to travel for work. They are your

____

When your dad married my mom, we became

____

siblings.

Learning Goal

I can learn more about *Reflections* by reading poetry.

Poetry

Poetry, also called **verse**, is a form of literature that may feature sound devices. Poets use sound devices to create a mood or emphasize the message of a poem. Poetry often features

- Content focused on **imagination, ideas, images,** and **emotions**
- **Rhythm,** a regular or varied pattern of sounds
- **Rhyme,** two or more words with the same ending sound
- **Repetition,** use of sounds, words, thoughts, or sentences over and over again
- **Onomatopoeia**, words that sound like their meaning

Why is a poem fun to read? How is a poem the same as, or different from, a story?

TURN and TALK Contrast poetry and realistic fiction. Use the chart to compare and contrast the genres. Take notes on your discussion.

My NOTES

PURPOSE:

To please and entertain the reader and to express ideas or feelings using sound devices and mental images

ELEMENTS:

- Rhythm
- Rhyme
- Onomatopoeia
- Imagery (sensory details)
- Repetition

POETRY TEXT STRUCTURE:

Words are arranged in lines and groups of lines called stanzas.

Meet the Author

Malathi Michelle Iyengar learned to play the clarinet while growing up in North Carolina. She studied music and education in college and spent a year in Asia studying clarinet. Now Iyengar lives in California and teaches at a public elementary school.

Poetry Collection

Preview Vocabulary

As you read the poems, pay attention to these vocabulary words. Notice how the words add meaning and make images sharp and memorable.

vivid **retired**

trembles **crinkled** **melodic**

Read

Before reading, think of how you will approach **poetry** differently from other texts. Follow these strategies as you read the poems for the first time.

First Read

Notice
how different elements of poetry create different effects.

Generate Questions
about parts that confuse you.

Connect
the poems to each other and other texts. How are they similar and different?

Respond
by discussing your thoughts and feelings about the poems as you read.

Genre Poetry

Poetry Collection

Artist to Artist

by Davida Adedjouma

Sepia

by Malathi Michelle Iyengar

Spruce

by Malathi Michelle Iyengar

AUDIO

ANNOTATE

Explain Figurative Language

A **simile** is a kind of figurative language that compares unlike things using the words *like* or *as*.

Underline a simile.

Vocabulary in Context

Context clues can help you understand the phrase *oils & acrylics*.

Underline clues that support your definition.

Artist to Artist

by Davida Adedjouma

I write books, now, because my father wanted
to be an artist he grew up & he was good
at it, too. Drew people with meat on their bones
in flesh-colored tones from my 64-colors box
of crayons. But
every night—& sometimes even weekends & holidays—
he dressed in the blue uniform & black shoes
of many other fathers who also weren't doctors or lawyers,
teachers or preachers, & rode the 10:00 p.m. bus
to the downtown post office. Sorted mail by zip code—
60620, 60621, 60622. He sorted mail all night &
into the day because we had bills to pay. For 30 years
my father rode the bus feeling black and blue. He
never drew & his degrees in art & education sat
hardening on a shelf along with his oils
& acrylics. But
along with his gapped teeth, his bow legs & his first name
with an A at the end, he gave me the urge to create
characters with meat on their bones, in flesh-colored tones
written in words as vivid as a 64-colors box of crayons.
I write, he drew. Daddy, thank you!
& now that you're
retired . . .
. . . what do you want to be?

vivid clear, bright, and lifelike

retired no longer working

Sepia

by Malathi Michelle Iyengar

Brown.
  Sepia brown.
    Inky, crinkly sepia brown.

Aunty's brown hand
trembles with age
but her voice rings with laughter: *Look!*
A photo from when I was young.

Wistful, muted brown.
Soft, nostalgic brown.

Is that really you, Aunty?
I see a girl with my face!

Look closer.
Aunty holds the photo up
next to her crinkled cheek.

The eyes! I realize.
The girl has Aunty's eyes,
  soft and shining,
    sepia brown.

Explain Figurative Language

Imagery is language that appeals to the senses—sight, hearing, touch, taste, and smell.

Underline an example of imagery in the poem. Consider how the speaker's thoughts and point of view help reveal the theme of the poem.

Visualize

Highlight pairs of lines that help you see a scene.

trembles shakes slightly

crinkled wrinkled or creased, as a crushed piece of paper

Spruce

by Malathi Michelle Iyengar

Brown.
Spruce brown.
Rich, melodic spruce brown.

Violin, guitar and bass
built of spruce wood, burnished brown.
A honey-colored melody
drifts along our narrow street.

Humming, strumming brown.
Ringing, singing brown.

Abuelito's precise brown fingertips
move along the violin's strings.

Papá's guitar travels
through a maze of shifting chords.

Tío winks at me from behind the *contrabajo*
as my hands clap out a staccato pattern:
taka taka tak,
rapid spruce brown.

CLOSE READ

Explain Figurative Language

Underline words that sound like their meanings. These are examples of **onomatopoeia**.

Visualize

Highlight descriptive details that help you form a picture in your imagination.

melodic pleasing and harmonious to hear; sweet sounding

Develop Vocabulary

In poetry, writers use descriptive words to create sound devices and guide readers to form mental images.

My TURN Read the vocabulary words. Match each clue with the number in the puzzle and write the word.

WORD BANK

vivid **retired** **trembles** **crinkled** **melodic**

CLUES

1. Shakes in fear or excitement
2. Clear and bright
3. Synonym for *harmonious*
4. Rhymes with *wrinkled*
5. No longer working

1

2

3

4

5

Check for Understanding

My TURN Look back at the texts to answer the questions.

1. How do you know that "Artist to Artist," "Sepia," and "Spruce" are poems? Give three examples.

2. Which two sound devices are used most effectively in these three poems? Use text evidence to support your opinion.

3. Illustrations can provide details that words alone do not. How do the illustrations contribute to the meaning, tone, and beauty of the poems?

4. Choose a poem and identify the speaker. Then analyze how the speaker reflects upon a topic in the poem.

Explain Figurative Language

Poets reveal themes and deeper meanings of their poems by using figurative language. These words create dense, vivid images for readers. **Similes** compare unlike things using *like* or *as*. **Imagery** uses words that appeal to the senses to create strong descriptions. **Onomatopoeia** uses words that sound like their meanings, such as *bang* or *pop*. Sometimes readers experience events in a poem through a speaker's eyes. The speaker is not necessarily the poet.

1. **MyTURN** Go to the Close Read notes in the poetry collection and underline examples of figurative language.

2. **Text Evidence** Use your evidence to complete the chart.

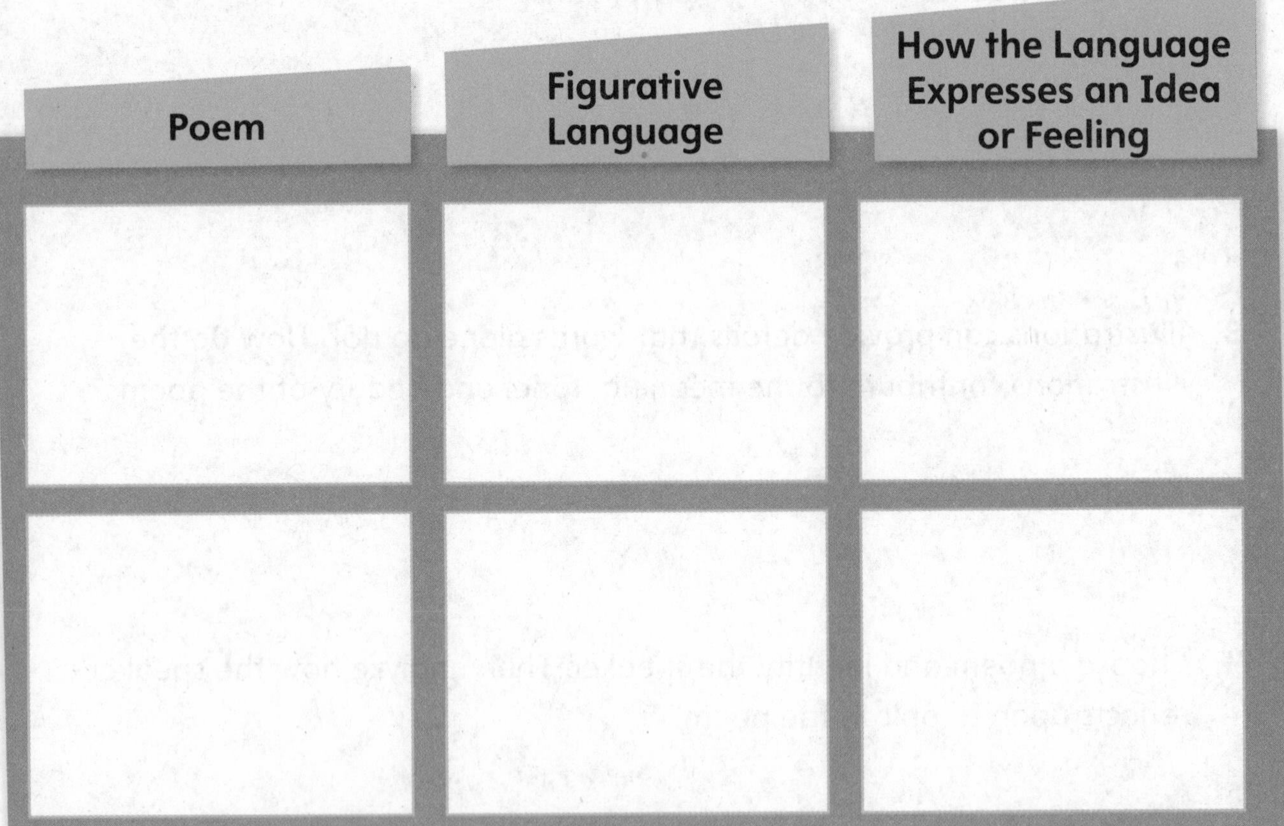

Poem	Figurative Language	How the Language Expresses an Idea or Feeling

Reread "Sepia." What is the speaker's point of view? How does the speaker reveal the poem's theme?

Visualize

A reader can visualize, or create **mental images,** based on a poet's word choices, including figurative language. Readers can use figurative language to help them create mental images to summarize or deepen their understanding of the poem.

1. **MY TURN** Go back to the Close Read notes and highlight evidence that helps you visualize descriptions or ideas in the poems.

2. **Text Evidence** Use your highlighted text to describe what you visualized.

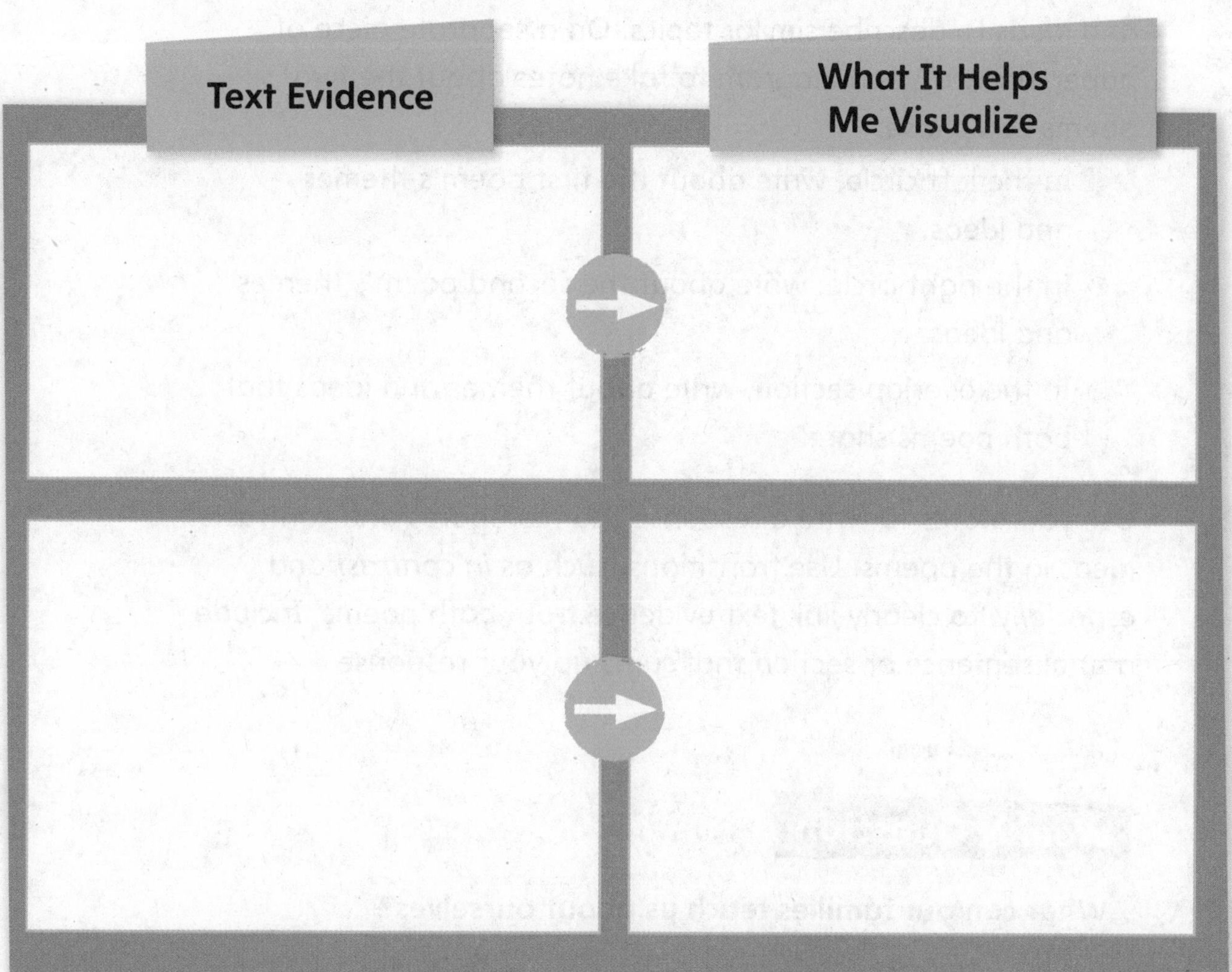

On your own paper, write a short summary of one poem based on what you visualized.

Reflect and Share

Write to Sources In the poetry collection, two different poets describe their thoughts on family. What different themes and ideas do they use? Choose two poems you read this week. Then use specific ideas from the texts to write and support a response.

Compare and Contrast Poems may use different themes and ideas to describe similar topics. On a separate piece of paper, draw a Venn diagram to take notes about the two poems you chose.

- In the left circle, write about the first poem's themes and ideas.
- In the right circle, write about the second poem's themes and ideas.
- In the overlap section, write about themes and ideas that both poems share.

Use your notes to write a response that compares and contrasts ideas in the poems. Use transitions, such as *in contrast* and *especially*, to clearly link text evidence from both poems. Include a final sentence or section that sums up your response.

Weekly Question

What can our families teach us about ourselves?

Academic Vocabulary

Learning Goal

I can develop knowledge about language to make connections between reading and writing.

Figurative language gives words meanings beyond literal definitions. An **idiom** is an expression that cannot be understood from definitions alone. For example, *walk a mile in someone else's shoes* means "try to understand that person's perspective, or way of seeing or thinking about something."

My TURN For each item,

1. **Underline** the idiom or expression that relates to *perspective.*
2. **Explain** the meaning of the idiom or expression.
3. **Confirm** your explanation by researching the idiom online.

Will you read my essay? It could use a fresh pair of eyes.

Explanation: ______________________________

____

Let's look at the big picture before we assign roles for the group project.

Explanation: ______________________________

____

Right now, you can't see the forest for the trees.

Explanation: ______________________________

____

Suffixes *-ous, -eous, -ious*

Suffixes are groups of letters added to a base word to change its meaning. The suffix *-ous* means "full of" or "having." The suffix *-ous* can also appear as *-eous* and *-ious*.

The word *dangerous* means "full of danger."

My TURN Complete the chart by decoding each word, defining it, and identifying the base word from which it is formed.

Word	Definition	Base Word
famous	well-known; having fame	fame
courteous		
envious		
poisonous		

High-Frequency Words

High-frequency words are words that you will see in texts over and over again. Keep in mind that they often do not follow regular word patterns. Read these high-frequency words: *ahead, chance, plural, opposite, wrong, solution*. Look for them in your independent reading.

Read Like a Writer

Writers often use sound devices and figurative language to help create an atmosphere or a feeling in a piece of writing. This atmosphere is called **mood**.

Model! Read the lines from "Spruce."

> A honey-colored melody
> drifts along our narrow street.

words that create a mood

1. **Identify** Malathi Michelle Iyengar uses the words *honey-colored melody drifts along our narrow street.*
2. **Question** How do these words help me understand the mood?
3. **Conclude** The words suggest sweet-sounding music and slow movement. They create a mood of harmony and relaxation.

Reread lines 12 and 13 from "Spruce."

My TURN Follow the steps to analyze the passage. Examine how the author's use of figurative language contributes to mood.

1. **Identify** In "Spruce," Malathi Michelle Iyengar uses the words

   ______________________________.
2. **Question** How do these words help me understand the mood?
3. **Conclude** The words suggest ______________________________

   ____

   The words create a ______________________________

   ______________________________.

Write for a Reader

Rhyme, rhythm, repetition, and onomatopoeia can help create mood.

Poets use figurative language, such as sound devices and sensory details, to create a mood or atmosphere or to emphasize the message in a poem. Sound devices emphasize or connect words. Sensory details help the reader make a mental picture.

My TURN Think about how Davida Adedjouma's and Malathi Michelle Iyengar's use of sound devices creates mood and affects you as a reader. Now identify how you can use sound devices to create a mood to affect your readers.

1. Brainstorm sound devices and examples that you could use to create a joyful, celebratory mood. For example, you could rhyme the words *ring* and *sing*.

2. Write a draft of a poem about a character or experience. Use sound devices and sensory details to create a somber or gloomy mood.

Spell Words with *-ous, -eous, -ious*

Adding the word part *-ous*, *-eous*, or *-ious* as a suffix to a word may require spelling changes. For example, to spell *adventurous*, drop the final *e* before adding *-ous*.

My TURN Read the words. Spell and sort the words by their word part.

SPELLING WORDS

vicious	enormous	humorous	previous
cautious	ridiculous	furious	adventurous
jealous	mysterious	fabulous	precious
courageous	numerous	miscellaneous	suspicious
victorious	curious	obvious	courteous

-ous **-eous** **-ious**

Indefinite and Reflexive Pronouns

Indefinite pronouns do not refer to a particular person or thing. They can be singular or plural. When you use an indefinite pronoun as the subject of a sentence, be sure to use the correct verb form.

Reflexive pronouns reflect the action of the verb back on the subject. Reflexive pronouns end in *-self* or *-selves*.

Indefinite Pronouns

all, another, any, anything, both, each, everyone, few, many, nothing, one, other, several, some, someone

All is well with Papá.

Nothing has been painted yet.

Several play instruments, and **one** claps to the music.

Reflexive Pronouns

myself, himself, herself, itself, yourself, themselves, ourselves

I taught **myself** how to play piano.

You learned about Aunty's history **yourself**.

My TURN Edit this draft by replacing at least four nouns with indefinite or reflexive pronouns.

People in the neighborhood can go to the street fair. The musicians played for the musicians, but people who walked by could also enjoy their music. While at an art booth with her daughter, Susan thinks she sees Susan in an old photo. She and her daughter think the resemblance is striking.

Edit for Capitalization

Learning Goal

I can use elements of opinion writing to write an essay.

Writers use capitalization for abbreviations, initials, acronyms, and organizations.

Original Address	Abbreviated Address
486 West Pine Road, Apartment 202 Dallas, Texas 75001	486 W. Pine Rd., Apt. 202 Dallas, TX 75001

Original Title	Abbreviated Title
Major Emma Wilson	Maj. Emma Wilson

Original Name	Initials
Marcus Lawrence Baker	Marcus L. Baker; M. L. Baker; M. L. B.

Organization Title	Organization Acronym
National Air and Space Administration	NASA

MY TURN Edit the paragraph for correct capitalization. Use three horizontal lines to show which letters should be capitalized.

We went to n.y.c., ny, to visit the building where the united nations meets. We watched a ceremony to celebrate pres. Harry Truman, who helped start the organization. Unicef, the United Nations International Children's Emergency Fund, was also started during Truman's presidency. If you want to visit the United Nations, you should take f.d.r. dr. to 42nd st.

MY TURN Edit a draft of your informational article to use correct capitalization for all abbreviations, initials, acronyms, and organizations.

Punctuate Titles

Facts and details in an opinion essay come from research. When a writer includes facts, he or she must tell where the information came from. To cite, or give credit to, a source, a writer includes the author's name and the title.

Writers use special formatting for different types of titles.

Title Type	Examples		Formatting
book play movie magazine	*Love, Amalia* *The Hermit Thrush* *Bye Bye Plastic Bags* *Cobblestone*	Love, Amalia The Hermit Thrush Bye Bye Plastic Bags Cobblestone	In print: *italics* In handwriting: underline
short story article chapter poem	"The Dog of Pompeii" "The Path to Paper Son" "A Pet for Calvin" from *Dude: Stories and Stuff for Boys* "Artist to Artist"		Quotation marks

Writers also use italics and underline to show emphasis. This formatting is useful when the writer wants to make a strong point.

Original Sentence	Revised Sentence	Emphasis Shows
"What did he just do?" asked Mom.	"*What* did he just do?" asked Mom.	surprise or shock
Keesha, not Jamie, is the team captain.	Keesha, not Jamie, is the team captain.	a correction or clarification
The message is clear: We must save coral reefs.	The message is clear: *We must save coral reefs.*	strong emotion or call to action

My TURN Edit a draft of your informational article to include italics and underlining for titles and emphasis.

Revise by Rearranging Ideas for Clarity

Writers improve word choice and sentence and paragraph structure by rearranging ideas. This helps a reader understand the point the writer is making.

My TURN Read each item. Then revise each sentence.

1. Rearrange ideas to show a clear order of events. Think about what your reader needs to know first so later information makes more sense.

   We watched a film about emperor penguins in Antarctica. Our class is studying penguins around the world.

2. Rearrange subordinate clauses, or less important ideas, so they make sense.

   Penguins, to escape the icy wind, take turns standing at the center of a tightly packed group.

3. Rearrange and revise to use clear, strong nouns and verbs.

   Surviving in cold temperatures is possible because a penguin's blood is warmed up on the way from the feet back to the heart.

My TURN To improve word choice, revise a draft of your opinion essay by rearranging ideas for coherence and clarity.

Revise by Combining Ideas for Clarity

When revising drafts, writers combine ideas to improve word choice. Combining ideas makes the writing more concise, or less wordy, and it clarifies relationships between ideas.

My TURN Read each example. Then revise by combining ideas.

1. Combine sentences with an appropriate transition or linking word.

> I can do fun things. Some things include reading and doing yoga.

2. Combine sentences to show subordinate ideas, or ideas that support the more important thought. Use *because*, *unless*, or *if*.

> I make sure to eat enough protein. Otherwise, I will get too tired.

3. Combine similar ideas to avoid wordiness.

> After I get home I put away the groceries. I check my e-mail. Then I get ready for work.

My TURN Revise a draft of your opinion essay by combining ideas for coherence and clarity.

Participate in Peer Editing

Even expert writers know that it is sometimes difficult to find errors in a paper you have spent a long time writing. Peer editing is when someone of your own experience level reviews your writing. This gives you a chance to make your writing the best it can be.

My TURN Work with your Writing Club. Exchange or collaborate on your essays. Use the checklist to edit each other's writing.

PEER EDITING CHECKLISTS

- ☐ Read your partner's work several times, looking for different things each time.
- ☐ Read once to understand the essay.
- ☐ Read again, stopping to make suggestions.
- ☐ Ask questions about any details you find confusing or out of order.
- ☐ Make suggestions about rearranging, adding, deleting, or combining ideas so they make more sense.
- ☐ Provide possible rewrites when needed.
- ☐ Read again to identify errors in spelling, grammar, or punctuation.
- ☐ Skim the paper from the end to the beginning to find errors.
- ☐ Be respectful of your partner's ideas and hard work.
- ☐ Write at least two comments about parts of the essay that you find especially well written or meaningful.

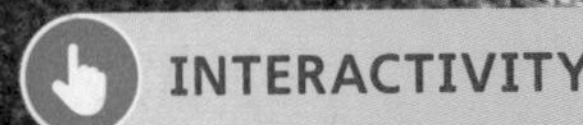

FRANK LLOYD WRIGHT and the Robie House

Frank Lloyd Wright was a widely known and influential architect. He began his career in Chicago at the end of the nineteenth century. Inspired by the earth tones and wide spaces of the Midwest, Wright created a new style of architecture. The Prairie Style he pioneered matches the environment with wide, low roofs and open, flowing living spaces. Long rows of windows let in plenty of sunlight. The wood and brick he used to build each structure echo the natural colors of the prairie.

Wright designed and built fifty Prairie Style homes between 1900 and 1910. One of the most iconic is the Robie House, built in Chicago's Hyde Park neighborhood for local businessman Frederick C. Robie. Robie wanted a home with a large, open living space and natural light.

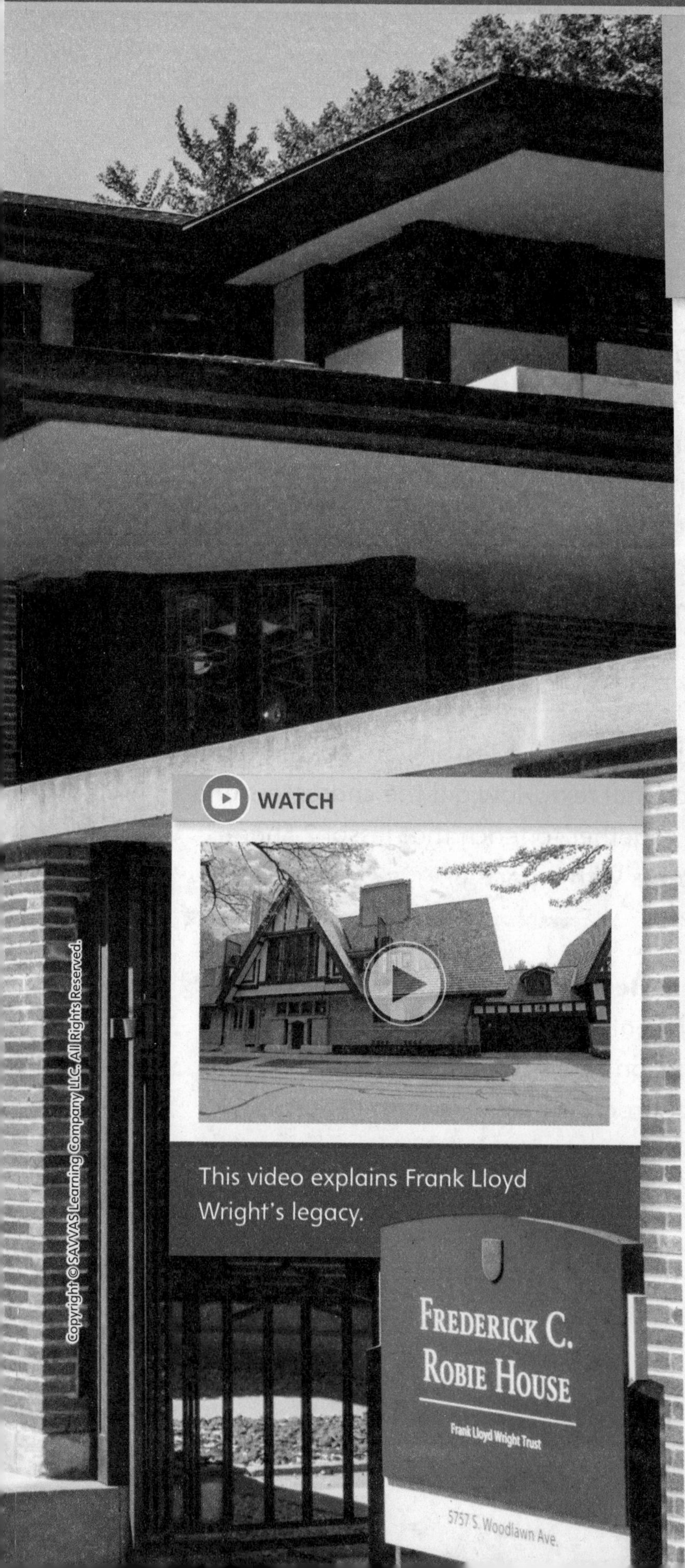

WEEK 5

Weekly Question

How does art reflect people's experiences?

Quick Write How would you express your own experiences through art?

WATCH

This video explains Frank Lloyd Wright's legacy.

Learning Goal

I can learn more about realistic fiction by inferring multiple themes.

Spotlight on Genre

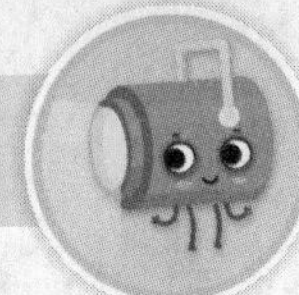

Realistic Fiction

Realistic fiction tells believable stories to entertain readers. **Theme** is the main idea or central meaning of a fictional text. A theme is not usually stated in a text. Instead, readers consider several factors and ask themselves, "What does it all mean?"

- The **characters'** actions and goals can help readers determine theme.
- The **plot** also helps develop a text's theme.
- Theme can be a lesson, a message about life, or a comment on society.
- There can be more than one theme in a text.

TURN and TALK Recall a lesson you learned from a realistic fictional text. How did the characters and plot come together to teach that lesson? Share your thoughts with a partner.

Topic + details = theme!

Be a Fluent Reader Reading with fluency requires practice. Fluent readers read with expression. Realistic fiction often contains dialogue, which is perfect for practicing reading with expression.

When you read dialogue aloud,

- Raise or lower the pitch of your voice to express the emotion of the character.
- Read with excitement when you see an exclamation mark at the end of a sentence.

Theme Anchor Chart

IS a story's central message.

IS NOT usually stated directly in a text.

IS SOMETIMES a lesson, moral, or comment on society.

TO DETERMINE THEME, CONSIDER:

characters' goals

if the characters are successful

how the characters change

key events and how characters respond

the ending and the characters' reactions to it

Meet the Author

Blue Balliett fell in love with art and museums during her childhood in New York City. She studied art history and later became a teacher. The award-winning mystery author currently lives in Chicago's Hyde Park neighborhood, where she writes full time and asks big questions about the world.

Life & Art

Preview Vocabulary

As you read "Life & Art" from *The Wright 3*, pay attention to these vocabulary words. Notice how they connect to the story's theme.

radically **embodies**

indivisible **revolutionary** **ironic**

Read

Before you read, **make predictions** about themes in the text based on the text features and genre. Record your predictions in the chart after the selection. Then follow these strategies as you read this **realistic fiction** story.

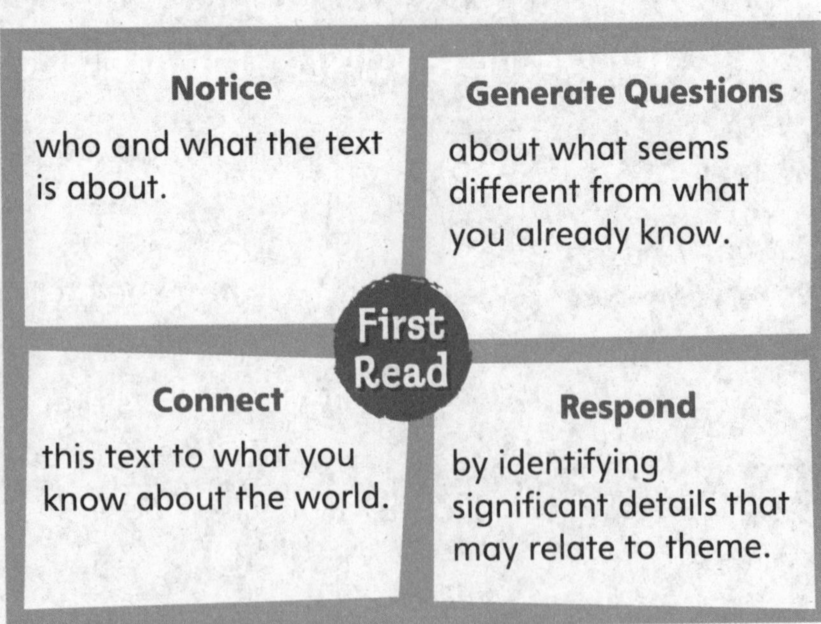

Life & Art

from The Wright 3

by Blue Balliett

AUDIO

ANNOTATE

BACKGROUND

When strange things start happening at a local home designed by architect Frank Lloyd Wright, sixth-grade sleuths Calder, Tommy, and Petra are eager to take the case—and to save the building in the process. Inspired by their teacher's demonstration using broken chalk, the trio sets out to answer the question, *How does something change when it is broken apart?*

Confirm or Correct Predictions

Highlight details that confirm or correct a prediction you made about what the story will be about.

1 "Let's try it." Ms. Hussey picked up a jagged chunk and turned toward the blackboard. She wrote LIFE & ART. The chalk made an ugly double line with each vertical stroke.

2 "Well?" Ms. Hussey had her head on one side. "I'm not really thinking about chalk, you know. I'm thinking about a house that some people see as a piece of art. I'm thinking about what happens when life and art don't mix well. I read about it in the *Chicago Tribune* this morning. Anyone know what I'm talking about?"

3 Calder's hand shot up. "The Robie House?"

4 Ms. Hussey nodded.

5 Tommy swiveled in his seat and studied the faces around him.

6 Calder went on, "My parents said that people in the neighborhood either love it or can't stand it." His pentominoes were lying on his desk, and he now flipped over the L and completed a rectangle made from seven of the twelve pieces.

7 As Calder's fingers moved, the words "life" and "art" began to shift rapidly in his mind. If those seven letters were put in another order, "life art" became "a trifle" or "a filter." Maybe there was a message here. He knew the word "trifle" meant something not too valuable or important, as his Grandma Ranjana had sometimes used that word, and a filter could mean—well, something you looked through or poured stuff through. "Life" plus "art" equaled "a trifle" or "a filter": Calder couldn't wait to tell Petra. She always understood when he discovered new ideas by rearranging the old ones.

LIFE
&
ART

CLOSE READ

Confirm or Correct Predictions

Highlight details that confirm or correct a prediction you made about what will happen later in the story.

8 "Duh."

9 Ms. Hussey frowned. "Who said that? Denise? Tell us what you know about the house."

10 Denise Dodge raised one eyebrow and studied her fingernails.

11 "Who built it, for instance?" Ms. Hussey's tone was crisp.

12 Denise shrugged.

13 Ms. Hussey held the now-crumpled article in front of her with both hands, and Tommy noticed that the newspaper trembled. She said, "Listen carefully. Perhaps I'm wrong."

WRIGHT MASTERPIECE COMING DOWN

14 *In a tragic piece of news for Hyde Park, the University of Chicago, owners of Frank Lloyd Wright's famous Robie House, announced today that the 1910 home will be cut into sections and donated to four great museums around the world: the Museum of Modern Art, in New York City, the*

Smithsonian, in Washington, D.C., the Deutsches Museum, in Munich, Germany, and the Meiji-mura Museum, in Nagoya, Japan. The university cited an impossibly large number of structural repairs as the reason.

15 *Many consider Wright to be the greatest architect of the twentieth century, and his Prairie Style jewel, the home built for Frederick C. Robie, to be a house that radically changed the domestic architecture of the United States.*

16 *The house was owned by three families before 1926, when it was bought by the Chicago Theological Seminary. Affiliated with the University of Chicago and located just steps from the Robie House, the seminary used Wright's building for cafeteria and dormitory space, but allowed the structure to fall into serious disrepair. Wanting the land beneath it for new student housing, the seminary announced in 1941 that the house was going to be demolished.*

17 *It was Frank Lloyd Wright himself who came to the rescue. In an unprecedented move within the architectural community, he put together a committee of world-famous architects and art historians and declared the Robie House to be "a source of worldwide architectural inspiration." The seminary was shamed into keeping it.*

CLOSE READ

Confirm or Correct Predictions

Highlight details that confirm or correct predictions you made about the significance of the Robie House to the story.

radically in an extreme way

CLOSE READ

Infer Multiple Themes

Underline details that help you infer Wright's ideas about his work.

How does this information support one of the main themes of the story?

18 *The building limped on, looking worse and worse, until 1957, when the seminary announced that it was dangerous and would need to be torn down. They called a public meeting and showed completed plans for a new building on that site.*

19 *Wright was then ninety years old, and brandishing his cane, returned to Hyde Park. He had recently completed plans for the Guggenheim Museum in New York City, and he was, by then, a national treasure himself. Describing the Robie House as "one of the cornerstones of American architecture" and commenting that only the kitchen needed improvement, he persuaded William Zeckendorf, a developer, to buy the house from the seminary. Zeckendorf used it for office space and made plans to give it to the National Trust for Historic Preservation. In 1963, however, he changed his mind and deeded it to the University of Chicago, which remodeled much of the interior for office use.*

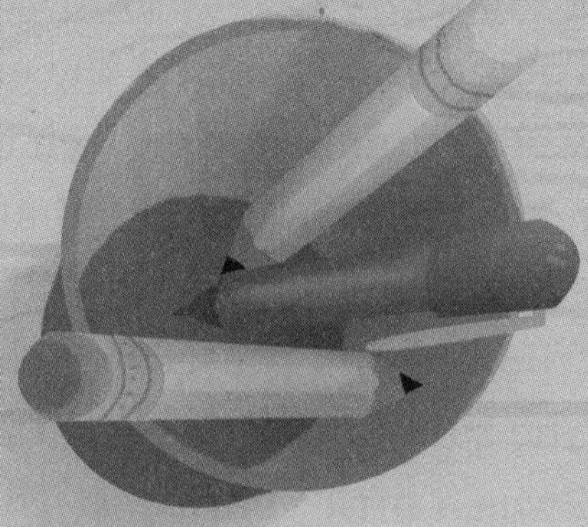

20 *John Stone, president of the university, said today, "It is only after extensive attempts to raise funds, both nationally and internationally, that we have made this painful decision. We have no alternative: The building, in its current state, is a hazard and needs many millions of dollars of renovation both inside and out. With great sadness and reluctance, we pass along a Wright treasure. The university cannot afford to keep it."*

21 *The news has shocked architecture buffs around the world and has left Hyde Park reeling. The Robie House was the only structure Frank Lloyd Wright ever built, during a career that spanned almost seventy years, that he fought to save, and he saved it not once but twice. Many believe that the house embodies his unique spirit and vision in a timeless form. It has come to occupy an almost mystical place in the history of American architecture.*

22 *In a letter to the press, the university defends its decision as "a bold move to provide many millions of people, around the world, with access to Wright's extraordinary work."*

23 *A crew has already begun plans for the job. The actual dismantling of the house will begin on June 21.*

24 *As one Hyde Parker said, "This breaks my heart. Hyde Park weeps."*

CLOSE READ

Infer Multiple Themes

Underline details that show how people react to the university's decision.

How do these reactions help you infer a theme?

embodies symbolizes or represents in a clear way

Confirm or Correct Predictions

Highlight details that confirm or correct your prediction about the importance of Wright's work.

indivisible unable to be split into pieces

revolutionary very different from something that came before

25 Ms. Hussey looked up. For once she didn't ask what the class thought. The tie had fallen off the end of her braid, and her words tumbled over each other: "I felt sick when I read this. A house like that needs light and air, and is one indivisible piece—the idea of carving up the structure and preserving chunks of it in *museums*!" She said "museums" as if it were a dirty word, which was a little confusing. The class knew Ms. Hussey loved to go to museums.

26 Tommy's hand was raised, but just barely. Should he tell the class that his new apartment was right next to one side of the Robie House? Would other kids think that was lucky?

27 Ms. Hussey was pacing again and didn't see Tommy's hand.

28 She went on: "I know all of you have passed it many times—it's only three blocks away. It's long and low, but remember that it's been almost a century since Wright designed it. Things that are normal to us now were revolutionary then, like rooms that flowed into each other; living space that moved easily between inside and outside; a hidden front entrance; deep, overhanging eaves; an attached three-car garage.

29 “Plus, the detail on the interior was extraordinary: Furniture, lamps, ceiling panels, rugs, and window designs all fit together like pieces of a puzzle. There were once 174 art-glass windows in that house, which meant thousands of pieces of colored glass. Amazingly, almost all of the windows are still intact.”

30 Another hand went up, and Tommy’s sank down.

31 “What’s art glass?” someone asked.

32 “It’s what most people call ‘stained glass,’ but Wright didn’t like that label. He described his windows as ‘leaded glass,’ ‘light screens,’ or ‘art glass.’ I like the last term—it somehow fits the man. Wright thought in a geometry that you have to see to understand, and even then it’s hard to figure out what you are seeing.”

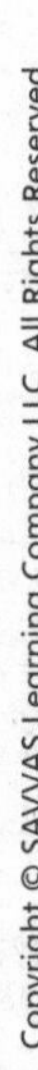

CLOSE READ

Infer Multiple Themes

Underline sentences that summarize a key idea about Wright’s work. Consider how these details support an inference you made about Wright's work.

Infer Multiple Themes

Underline sentences that show how the students react to the threat to Robie House.

How do their reactions help you understand the story's themes?

ironic contrary to expectation

33 Tommy thought Ms. Hussey was hard to figure out, too. Did *she* understand? And was she angry or excited?

34 Their teacher stopped walking and turned toward the class, her mouth in a tight line. "So: Art & Life."

35 Petra Andalee was frowning. "Can't the house just sit there empty until the money comes in?"

36 Ms. Hussey drew a quick breath as if she'd touched something hot. "In an ideal world, yes. In the real world, no. The university probably can't afford to own a piece of property that they aren't able to use, and if part of the house fell on someone walking by, the owner would be held responsible."

37 "Maybe we can visit the place and come up with ideas," Calder suggested.

38 "I wish we could, but they haven't allowed visitors inside for more than a year, and no family has lived there since 1926. This is deeply ironic, of course, since the house was built for children."

39 Ms. Hussey paused, twisting the end of her hair around one finger. The class waited, knowing this meant she was thinking about whether to share something.

40 "Actually," she confided, "I've always wondered about Mr. Wright's focus on play space. At the time he was working on the Robie House, he had just left his wife and six children. And yet here he was, thinking creatively about what would make someone else's kids happy and safe. Maybe it was his way of asking the universe for forgiveness. . . ."

Confirm or Correct Predictions

Highlight details that confirm or correct your prediction about the connections between life and art in the story.

Infer Multiple Themes

Underline words or sentences that tell a message or piece of advice.

41 Tommy picked at a sticker on his desk, careful not to look up. Neither one of *his* dads had said sorry. When Tommy was a baby, his real dad had died in South America—he'd been arrested at a political demonstration and was never seen again. And Tommy's stepfather had started out with a bunch of promises and then broken every one.

42 "Anyway," Ms. Hussey said, her voice businesslike again, "it seems like a crime to destroy such a home, don't you think?"

43 "It doesn't look like a home to me," one of the kids piped up.

44 "Really?" Ms. Hussey said, looking pleased. "Perhaps we have to figure out if the building *is* still a home, and whether a home can exist if it's empty. Or, beyond that, whether a home can also be a piece of art . . ."

45 The class was quiet. Someone sighed. Ms. Hussey looked around, then sighed also. "Okay—maybe it's too much to start an investigation so late in the year. But it's never too late to think. What could we do? Art-home or not, the Robie House has been a part of Hyde Park for as long as you, your parents, or maybe even your grandparents remember. It's just too horrible to think of it being pulled apart."

46 Their teacher sat on the edge of a radiator. She had picked up a round, gray stone that lived on her desk, a rock with two bands of white that crossed neatly on either side. She called it her Lucky Stone, and when she picked it up, the children knew that she was worried or upset. She held it now in both hands, her body a silhouette in the sunshine coming from the window behind her.

CLOSE READ

Vocabulary in Context

Underline the context clues in the sentence that help you understand what *silhouette* means.

Fluency

Read paragraphs 41 through 46 aloud with a partner to practice reading with expression. As you read, pay attention to words spoken by the characters.

Develop Vocabulary

In realistic fiction, authors use precise words to develop believable characters and situations. The characters' actions and ideas give readers clues about the story's themes.

My TURN Complete the chart to identify how the author uses precise words to connect themes in "Life & Art."

Word	How Word Is Used in "Life & Art"	What This Suggests About Art
radically	to explain that Wright changed U.S. architecture	One individual can transform art.
embodies		
revolutionary		
indivisible		

Check for Understanding

My TURN Look back at the text to answer the questions.

1. What details tell you that "Life & Art" is realistic fiction?

2. Is the narrator a character in the story? How do you know?

3. What conclusion can you draw about what Ms. Hussey values based on her ideas about museums? Why does Ms. Hussey think breaking up the Robie House is so "horrible"? Use text evidence.

4. Write a brief argument about whether you think the Robie House should be restored or broken apart. Include reasons and evidence in your claim.

Infer Multiple Themes

A text's **theme** is its central message or meaning. While reading, readers make **inferences**, or figure out information that is not stated directly in the text. Readers combine what they already know with evidence from the text to determine its themes.

1. **My TURN** Go to the Close Read notes in "Life & Art" and underline the parts that help you infer themes.

2. **Text Evidence** Use your underlined text to make and support an inference. Use the chart to organize your ideas.

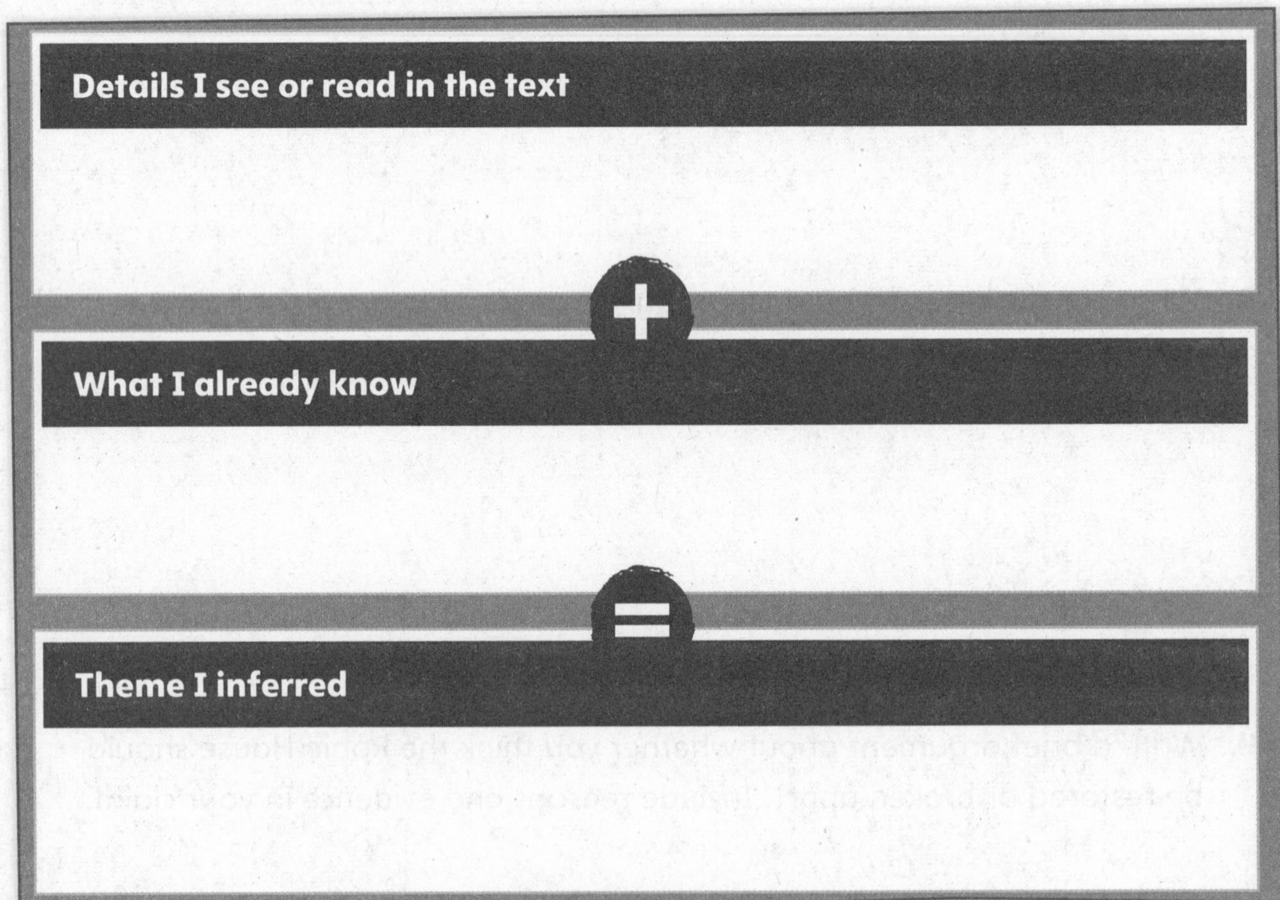

What other themes did you identify? What do the themes have in common?

Confirm or Correct Predictions

Before reading, you previewed parts of the text to **make predictions,** or guesses, about the text. After reading, go back to the text to **confirm,** or make sure, that your predictions were correct.

1. **My TURN** Go back to the Close Read notes and highlight details that helped you confirm or correct your predictions about theme.

2. **Text Evidence** Use your predictions and highlighted text to complete the graphic organizer.

Prediction

=

Evaluate Your Prediction

My prediction is: CORRECT PARTIALLY CORRECT INCORRECT

I know this because

Reflect and Share

Talk About It Consider all the texts you have read in this unit. What experiences did you learn about? How did these experiences affect a character in a story or a speaker in a poem? Use these questions to help you prepare an opinion presentation about how experiences can change people.

Give a Short Presentation To prepare for your presentation, gather and organize your information. On a sheet of paper, write your opinion statement. Then, use the texts in this unit as well as your own observations to find facts, details, and direct quotations that support your opinion. Be sure to include sources.

To give a presentation that communicates your ideas effectively:

- Speak at an appropriate rate and volume.
- Enunciate, or pronounce, your words clearly.
- Employ eye contact with your audience.
- Use formal language, and speak with proper grammar, correct sentence structure, and logical word order.

Weekly Question

How does art reflect people's experiences?

Academic Vocabulary

Learning Goal

I can develop knowledge about language to make connections between reading and writing.

Parts of speech are categories of words. **Nouns** name a person, place, thing, idea, or feeling. **Verbs** can show action, either physical or mental. **Adjectives** describe people, places, things, ideas, or feelings. Words can be used as more than one part of speech, and as a result words can have multiple meanings.

My TURN For each item,

1. **Read** the underlined academic vocabulary word.
2. **Identify** the word's part of speech.
3. **Write** a sentence using the same base word as a different part of speech.
4. **Identify** the new part of speech.

1. The product recall caused stock prices to drop. noun

2. The lawyer filed an appeal with the court after the verdict.

3. The scientist demonstrated how the equipment worked.

Syllable Patterns

A syllable is a word part that contains a single vowel sound. Words with multiple syllables contain different **syllable patterns**. Syllable patterns include closed syllables, open syllables, VCe syllables, vowel teams, *r*-controlled syllables, and final stable syllables. Syllables can also be divided between consonants or between vowels.

Use your knowledge of syllable division patterns or a print or online dictionary to read words with more than one syllable.

My TURN Read the words from "Life & Art." On the line under each word, write the word, and add slashes between each syllable. Use a dictionary to check each word's syllabication.

inspiration

disrepair

developer

geometry

cafeteria

reluctance

impossibly

valuable

prairie

renovation

Read Like a Writer

Point of view is the perspective from which a story is told. The point of view can influence how readers see events. A third-person omniscient point of view can convey the thoughts and feelings of all the characters in a story.

Model! Read the text from "Life & Art."

As Calder's fingers moved, the words "life" and "art" began to shift rapidly in his mind.

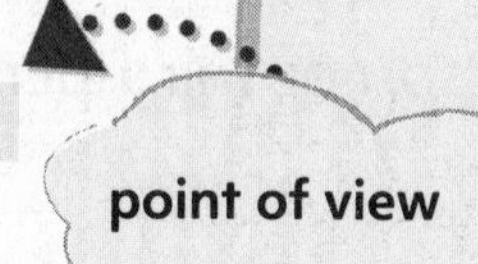

1. **Identify** The narrator tells readers what happens in Calder's mind.
2. **Question** What is the effect of that point of view?
3. **Conclude** It helps readers understand and relate to Calder by knowing his personal thoughts and feelings.

Read the text.

Tommy's hand was raised, but just barely. Should he tell the class that his new apartment was right next to one side of the Robie House? Would other kids think that was lucky?

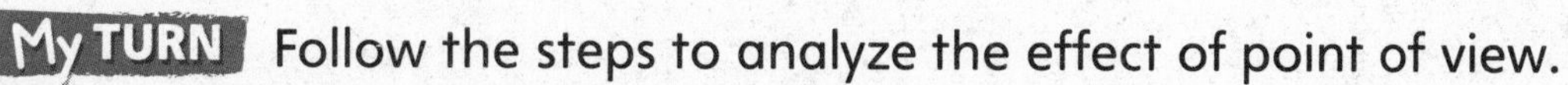

MY TURN Follow the steps to analyze the effect of point of view.

1. **Identify** The narrator tells readers ______________________.
2. **Question** What is the effect of that point of view?
3. **Conclude** It helps readers ______________________

______________________.

Write for a Reader

Elements of craft, such as point of view, help writers shape their stories and influence their audience. Third-person omniscient point of view gives readers access to the thoughts and feelings of many characters in the story. Through this point of view, readers often know more about the characters than any individual character knows. Third-person omniscient point of view is more objective and intimate than first-person or third-person limited point of view.

My TURN Think about how Blue Balliett's choice to use omniscient point of view affects you as a reader. Now identify when you might use omniscient point of view and how it can shape your own writing.

1. If you were writing a story using a third-person omniscient point of view, what details would you include?

2. Write a narrative paragraph about several characters. Use third-person omniscient point of view to help readers understand the thoughts and feelings of the characters.

Spell Words with Syllable Patterns

A syllable is a word part that contains a single vowel sound. **Syllable patterns** can divide words between two vowels, between two consonants, or between a consonant and a vowel. Understanding syllable patterns can help you spell words with multiple syllables.

My TURN Read the words. Spell and sort the words in alphabetical order. After alphabetizing, add a slash between each syllable.

SPELLING WORDS

dispel	indignant	humane	congruent
crusade	confiscate	protest	defiance
selfish	compensate	ignite	supreme
dismal	insistent	diabolic	profile
segment	syntax	museum	impede

Adverbs

Adverbs tell where, when, or how an action happens. A **conjunctive adverb** shows a relationship between ideas within a sentence. It can introduce an independent clause, connect two independent clauses, or link sentences with similar ideas.

Some common adverbs are *additionally, anyway, finally, however, instead, likewise, meanwhile, nevertheless, next, otherwise, similarly,* and *therefore.*

In sentences with two independent clauses, the conjunctive adverb is preceded by a semicolon and followed by a comma.

- Robie House was falling apart; nevertheless, some people wanted to restore it.

In other sentences, commas set off conjunctive adverbs.

- In 1963, however, he changed his mind and deeded it to the University of Chicago.
- Meanwhile, the Wright 3 continued to investigate.

My TURN Edit the draft by using conjunctive adverbs to connect ideas in or between sentences. Remember to add proper punctuation.

Taking apart the Robie House will be difficult. Crews cannot follow their usual routine for demolishing a house. The art glass would be destroyed. Features such as the ceiling panels would be damaged. Workers will use a special technique when dividing the house.

Incorporate Peer and Teacher Suggestions

Learning Goal

I can use elements of opinion writing to write an essay.

A writer may find it difficult to accept criticism from peers or from a teacher. Sometimes it can be hard to hear negative things about something you are proud of. Remember, however, that these editors want to help you make your work as clear, concise, and meaningful as it can be. Consider each change carefully, and use it as an opportunity to improve.

My TURN Use the checklist as you revise based on peer and teacher suggestions.

REVISE BASED ON FEEDBACK

- ☐ Read each comment carefully.
- ☐ Ask questions about comments you find unclear or confusing.
- ☐ First, revise for organization. Rearrange, combine, add, and delete paragraphs, sentences, and details as needed.
- ☐ Look at your word choices. Are there ideas that you can make clearer or more coherent by combining, rearranging, adding, or deleting words?
- ☐ If needed, ask an adult for help with planning or revising your work.
- ☐ Then edit for spelling, capitalization, punctuation, and grammar mistakes.
- ☐ Look up any grammar rules you are unsure about.
- ☐ Read your work one last time, sentence by sentence. Start from the end, and work your way to the beginning. This will help you focus on words rather than ideas.
- ☐ Make final corrections, and prepare the final draft of your essay.
- ☐ If you wrote your essay by hand, make a new, clean version in cursive.
- ☐ Thank your peer editor or teacher for taking the time to read your work.

Publish a Final Draft

Once you have revised and edited your opinion essay, it is time to publish. Publishing your work is an important final step in the writing process. It completes the cycle of writing for a specific task, purpose, and audience. Publishing can mean several things depending on what you wrote, why you wrote it, and who will read it.

My TURN Prepare your writing to be published and presented to an audience.

Publishing

- Reread your writing to make sure it makes sense.
- Revise any ideas or details that are out of place.
- Edit and proofread your final draft to make sure there are no errors.
- Type a final copy of your essay to publish.

Presenting

- Make eye contact with your audience.
- Speak slowly and enunciate your words.
- Speak loudly enough to be heard at the back of the room.
- Present each point clearly.
- Use proper conventions of language to effectively communicate your ideas.
- Use natural gestures as you speak.
- Respond to questions from the audience.

Publish and Celebrate

A writer publishes his or her work after revising and editing it. The writer may choose from many different forms of publishing.

My TURN Complete the items about your writing experience. Use cursive as you summarize your writing.

My favorite thing about writing an opinion essay was

____

____

____

______________________________.

I wrote my favorite opinion essay about ______________ because

____

____

____

______________________________.

The most convincing reasons, facts, and details I included in my essay were

____

____

____

______________________________.

The next time I write an opinion essay, I will

____

____

____

______________________________.

Prepare for Assessment

My TURN Follow a plan as you prepare to write an opinion essay in response to a prompt.

1. **Relax.**

   Take a deep breath.

2. **Make sure you understand the prompt.**

   Read the prompt below. Underline what kind of writing you will do. Highlight the topic you will be writing about.

   Prompt: Write an opinion essay about how other people's experiences have influenced you. Support your opinion with reasons and details from the texts you have read.

3. **Brainstorm.**

   List three topics you could write about. Highlight your favorite.

4. **Plan out your opinion essay.**

   Clearly state your opinion and provide reasons supported by examples, facts, and details.

5. **Write your draft. Remember to include an introduction and a conclusion.**

   Use your own paper to write your essay.

6. **After you finish, revise and edit your essay.**

   Read your essay again to yourself.

Assessment

My TURN Before you write an opinion essay for your assessment, rate how well you understand the skills you have learned in this unit. Go back and review any skills you mark "No."

IDEAS AND ORGANIZATION	Yes!	No
I can brainstorm a topic.	☐	☐
I can clearly state an opinion.	☐	☐
I can provide reasons for an opinion.	☐	☐
I can support reasons with examples, facts, and details.	☐	☐
I can write an introduction and a conclusion.	☐	☐
I can group reasons, facts, and details into paragraphs and sections.	☐	☐

CRAFT		
I can include meaningful and interesting graphic features.	☐	☐
I can use linking words, phrases, and clauses to show logical order.	☐	☐
I can format text to highlight important information.	☐	☐
I can rearrange and combine ideas for clarity.	☐	☐

CONVENTIONS		
I can use rules for capitalization.	☐	☐
I can incorporate italics and underline for titles and for emphasis.	☐	☐

Manage your time! Plan ahead so you have time to plan, draft, revise, and edit your work.

UNIT THEME

Reflections

TURN and TALK

Question the Answers

Read the sentence attached to each selection. Then, with a partner, review the selection and use a separate piece of paper to write a question for each "answer" sentence. Finally, talk to your partner about how the answer relates to the theme, *Reflections*.

WEEK 3

The Carp
The Hermit Thrush

Because of this, Hayate is happy, even inspired, playing music for his family.

BOOK CLUB

WEEK 2

"A Pet for Calvin"

Calvin told his grandma he would know him anywhere.

BOOK CLUB

WEEK 1

from Love, Amalia

She wants Amalia to understand that people must find ways to keep loved ones close, even if they move away.

WEEK 6

BOOK CLUB

WEEK 4

Poetry Collection

This imagery connects all three poems.

BOOK CLUB

WEEK 5

"Life & Art" from The Wright 3

For Calder, the words *life* and *art* could be rearranged to create these two key messages.

BOOK CLUB

Essential Question

MyTURN

In your notebook, answer the Essential Question: How do the experiences of others reflect our own?

Project

WEEK 6

Now it is time to apply what you learned about Reflections in your **WEEK 6 PROJECT: Unsung Heroes**

Unsung HEROES

Activity

Learn more about a person who has had a positive impact on your life. The person can be someone you know, a public figure, or a historical figure. Research the person's childhood, education, career, family, personal life, and accomplishments. Then give a speech about why your state should dedicate a day to this person. Make sure to explain how the person influenced your life in a positive way.

RESEARCH

Research Articles

With your partner, read "The Making of a Holiday" to generate questions you have about the topic. Make a research plan for writing your speech.

1. The Making of a Holiday
2. Awesome Jane Addams
3. You Inspire Me!

Generate Questions

COLLABORATE After reading "The Making of a Holiday," generate three questions you have about the article. Compare questions with a partner to try and answer them. Share any remaining questions with the class.

1. ______________________________

2. ______________________________

3. ______________________________

Use Academic Words

COLLABORATE In this unit, you learned many words related to the theme of *Reflections*. Work with your partner to add more academic vocabulary words to each category. If appropriate, use some of these words when you write your speech.

Academic Vocabulary	Word Forms	Synonyms	Antonyms
demonstrate	demonstrates demonstrable demonstrating	display exhibit show	conceal cover hide
perspective	perspectives perspectively perspectival	outlook point of view position	apathy indifference blindness
recall	recalls recalled recalling	recollect remember reminisce	disremember forget repress
appeal	appeals appealing appellate	allure attractiveness charm	obnoxiousness repulsiveness unpleasantness
confide	confides confided confidence	disclose reveal tell	cloak obscure secret

As I See It

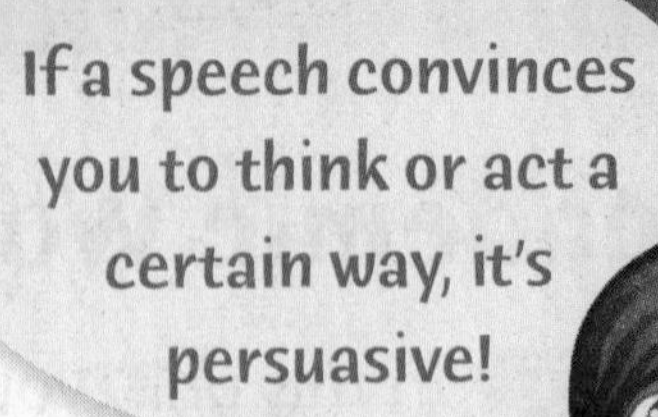

People often write speeches to convince, or persuade, their audience to think or act a certain way. When reading argumentative, or persuasive, speeches, look for

- the claim
- reasons that support the claim
- evidence, such as facts, examples, and quotations, to support the reasons and claim

RESEARCH

COLLABORATE With your partner, read "Awesome Jane Addams." Then answer the questions below about the text.

1. What is the author's claim, or opinion?

2. What is the writer's strongest evidence for the claim? Cite specific facts.

3. Who is the author's intended audience? How do you know?

Plan Your Research

COLLABORATE Before you begin researching heroes, you will need to come up with a research plan. Use the activity to help you write a claim and plan how you will look for evidence for your speech.

Definition	Examples
CLAIMS A claim is a statement that tries to persuade or convince a reader to agree with an opinion. A claim • defines your goal • is specific • is supported with evidence Read the two examples in the right column. One states a claim and one does not. Then, with your partner, write a claim, or opinion statement, for whom you feel deserves his or her own holiday.	• Mae Jemison is a scientist, physician, and astronaut. NO • We should celebrate Mae Jemison's contributions to our country by honoring her in a special way. YES! My claim:
EVIDENCE You can support your claim with evidence, such as • facts • statistics • quotations • examples	**Fact:** Mae Jemison has a degree from Stanford University. **Statistic:** Jemison was the first African American woman in space. **Quote:** "I've been very involved in science literacy because it's critically important in our world today," explained Mae Jemison to CNN. **Example:** She researched bone cells while in space.
List some options for finding evidence for your heroes research project.	

SEARCHING for SOURCES

Libraries have many kinds of **databases**, which provide information on different topics or from different types of sources. Using the **advanced search** option allows you to search many databases at one time. Whichever sources you use, do not **plagiarize**, or copy an author's words without giving credit. Instead, **quote** an author by putting his or her exact words inside quotation marks or **paraphrase** an author by putting information into your own words.

EXAMPLE Mae Jemison, the first African American woman to become an astronaut, inspires Riley to study science. Riley uses the advanced search option on her school library's Web site to search many databases at once.

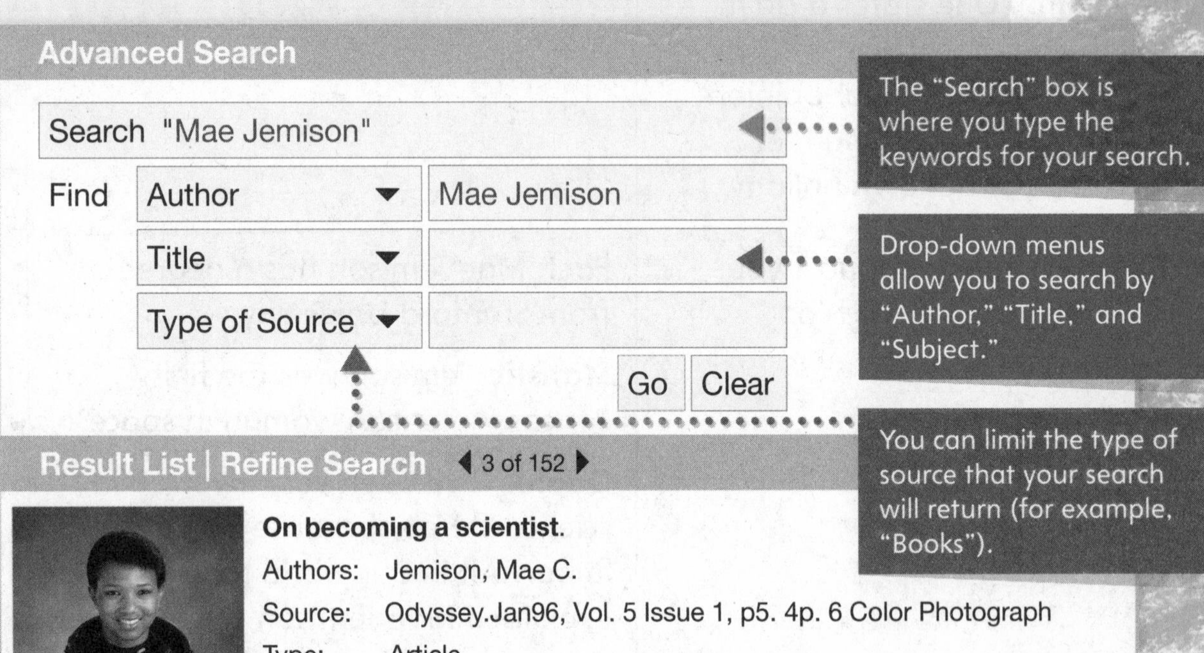

The "Search" box is where you type the keywords for your search.

Drop-down menus allow you to search by "Author," "Title," and "Subject."

You can limit the type of source that your search will return (for example, "Books").

COLLABORATE With your partner, go online to research someone who has had a positive effect on your life. (If you know the person, you can interview him or her and also do online research about aspects of the person's life.) Use the advanced search option on a library's Web site to find different types of sources with relevant information on the person. Take notes and explain how you conducted your search. Then list two of the relevant sources you found.

Advanced search options (keywords, fields) you used:

Title of source:

Type of source:

Title of source:

Type of source:

Write a quotation from one of your sources.

Paraphrase the quotation. Be sure to credit your source to avoid plagiarism.

Discuss your search results. Do you need to change your advanced search options to find more relevant or more specific information?

STAND FIRM and SPEAK OUT

People write **argumentative texts** to convince others to share their point of view. An argumentative speech makes a **claim**. Your claim about setting aside a day to honor a person should include supporting reasons and evidence to convince others to support your proposal.

Before you begin writing, decide on an appropriate audience for your speech. Will you write a speech to deliver to

- your school community?
- your local community?
- a broader community, such as through a video?

After you decide, think of how your audience affects the tone, or attitude, of your speech, including how formal it should be.

COLLABORATE Read the Student Model. Work with your partner to recognize the characteristics of argumentative speeches.

Now You Try It!

Work with your partner to write your argumentative speech. Use the checklist to make sure you include the important aspects of an argumentative speech.

Make sure your speech

- [ ] states a specific claim that can be debated.
- [ ] supports that claim with specific reasons.
- [ ] supports each reason with facts and details from your sources.
- [ ] organizes information in a logical way, such as through order of importance.

Student Model

Mae Jemison: Scientist, Physician, and Astronaut

Highlight the speaker's claim.

Today I am going to share with you information about Mae Jemison, a distinguished scientist, physician, and astronaut. Mae Jemison's accomplishments have inspired students everywhere—including me—to consider careers in the sciences, and that is why we should officially dedicate a day in her honor.

Underline one supporting reason.

Mae Jemison is incredibly inspiring. She worked hard all her life to achieve her dream of being an astronaut. Mae Jemison enjoyed reading about science. She earned a bachelor's degree in chemical engineering at Stanford University. She earned a doctorate degree in medicine at Cornell University. She worked as a medical officer in the Peace Corps. She did medical research in West Africa.

Highlight facts and evidence that support the reason you underlined. Discuss how these support the speaker's argument.

Another reason Jemison is so inspiring is that she became the first African American woman to enter NASA's astronaut training program and fly in space. After completing training, Jemison worked in several roles at NASA before serving as the science mission specialist on the space shuttle *Endeavor*'s 1992 trip into space. She spent eight days in orbit around Earth, running a research experiment on bone cells.

Underline the conclusion that restates the speaker's claim.

Mae Jemison has accomplished much in her life. Many students are inspired by her. For these reasons, I hope you will agree that we should dedicate a day in Jemison's honor.

Bibliography

When you write a text or speech, you must cite your sources. A **bibliography** lists sources in alphabetical order at the end of a text. Different types of sources are cited differently.

Format for a book: Author's last name, author's first name. *Title of book*. Publisher, publication date.

Example: Lassieur, Allison. *Astronaut Mae Jemison.* Lerner Classroom, 2016.

Italicize book titles, magazine or journal titles, and Web site titles.

Format for an article in a scholarly journal: Author's last name, author's first name. "Title of Article." *Title of Magazine*, volume, issue, year, pages.

Example: Chiang, Mona. "Out of This World." *Science World*, vol. 63, no. 5/6, 2006, pp. 24-25.

Use a period after the author's name and after the title.

Format for a Web site: Author's last name, author's first name (if an author is named). "Title of Article or Page." *Title of Container* (organization publishing the Web site), URL. Date of access.

"Date of access" means the date that you visited the Web site.

Example: "Mae C. Jemison (M.D.)." *National Aeronautics and Space Administration*, www.jsc.nasa.gov/Bios/htmlbios/jemison-mc.html. Accessed 4 May 2017.

RESEARCH

COLLABORATE Read "You Inspire Me!" Identify a source from the article. Show how you and a partner would cite this source.

COLLABORATE Read the information given about research sources and answer the questions.

Title of book: *Mae Jemison: Trailblazing Astronaut, Doctor, and Teacher*

Author: Linda Barghoorn

Publisher: Crabtree Publishing Company

Publication date: September 26, 2016

1. Use the information to write a bibliography entry for the source.

The editors of Encyclopedia Britannica. "Mae Jemison: American Physician and Astronaut." *Encyclopedia Britannica*, www.britannica.com/biography/Mae-Jemison. Accessed 28 October 2015.

2. Look at the format of the bibliography entry. What type of source is it? How can you tell?

Add PHOTOGRAPHS and TIME LINES

When you give a speech about a person, you can make your speech stronger by including visual aids, such as photographs and time lines.

Photographs allow your audience to better understand a person's accomplishments as well as particular moments in a person's life.

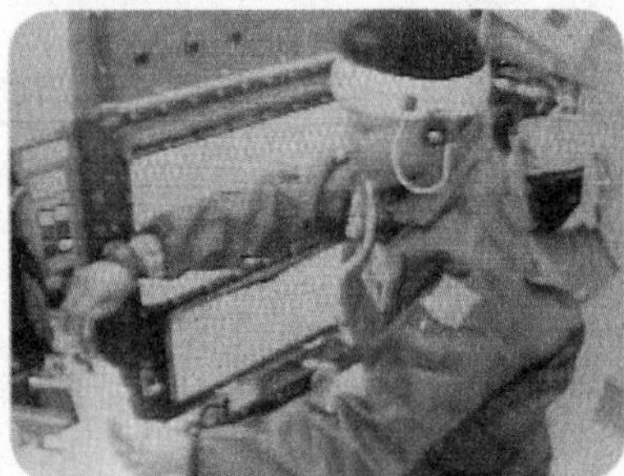

A **time line** shows important events in a person's life, arranged in chronological order and in a visual way.

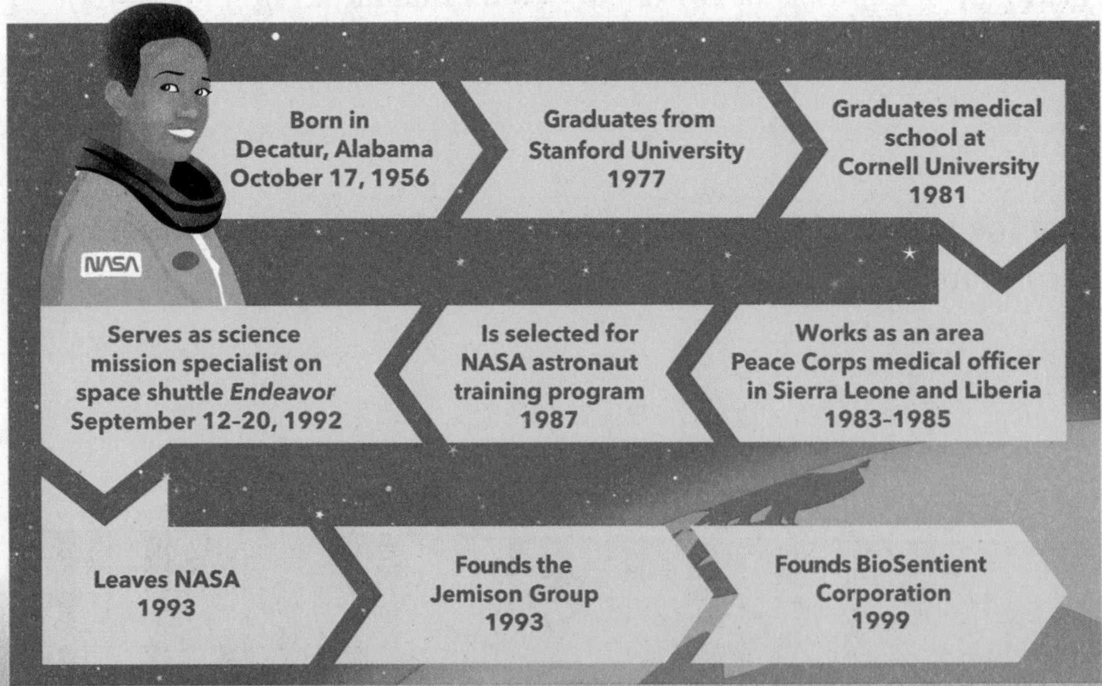

COLLABORATE With your partner, think about photographs that you can display while giving your speech about a person who had a positive influence on your life. Brainstorm which of the person's accomplishments you would like to enhance with a photograph. Then search online and in print sources for compelling photos.

Use online and print sources to find out more about events in the person's life. Then create a time line with your research. After you finish, copy the time line onto poster board or recreate it digitally using presentation software. Display the time line so you can refer to it as you discuss key events during your speech.

Revise

Revise for Clarity Reread your speech with your partner. Have you

- ☐ clearly stated a claim that can be debated and is not a statement of personal preference?
- ☐ developed reasons to fully support your claim?
- ☐ included facts and evidence to fully support your reasons?
- ☐ included only relevant facts and details?

Revise to Combine Ideas

The writers of the speech in the student model realized that parts of it were redundant and choppy. The speech did not always clearly connect supporting evidence to the reasons and claim. In this revision, the writers combined some sentences to emphasize the relationships between ideas. Their revisions make the speech more concise and improve its overall flow.

One reason · is that she

^Mae Jemison is incredibly inspiring. ~~She~~^ worked hard all her life to achieve her dream of being an astronaut.

As a child,

^Jemison enjoyed reading about science. She earned a bachelor's degree in chemical engineering at Stanford

and

University.^ ~~She earned~~ a doctorate degree in medicine at

Soon after graduation, she

Cornell University.^ ~~She~~ worked as a medical officer in the

and

Peace Corps.^ ~~She~~ did medical research in West Africa.

Edit

Conventions Read your speech again. Have you used correct conventions?

- [ ] spelling
- [ ] punctuation
- [ ] complete sentences with subject-verb agreement
- [ ] prepositions and prepositional phrases
- [ ] pronouns and clear antecedents
- [ ] conjunctive adverbs

Peer Review

COLLABORATE Listen while another group practices its speech. Provide feedback on the strength and clarity of the claim, supporting reasons, and evidence. Tell the speakers whether you could hear and understand them, and whether their language was grammatically correct and appropriately formal.

Time to Celebrate!

COLLABORATE It is time to deliver your speech! To give an organized presentation and communicate your ideas clearly

- make eye contact by looking at your audience
- speak at a rate that is easy to understand
- speak at a volume that is appropriate for a large, yet indoor, group
- enunciate, or pronounce words correctly
- use natural gestures, such as hand movements, to point to your visual aids

Now follow these rules to deliver your speech.

Reflect on Your Project

My TURN Think about the argumentative speech you wrote and presented, including the visuals, the speech itself, and your oral delivery. Which parts of your speech do you think are the strongest? Which areas might you improve next time? Write your thoughts here.

Strengths

____

____

____

Areas of Improvement

____

____

____

Reflect on Your Goals

Look back at your unit goals. Use a different color to rate yourself again.

SCALE	1	2	3	4	5
	NOT AT ALL WELL	NOT VERY WELL	SOMEWHAT WELL	VERY WELL	EXTREMELY WELL

Reflect on Your Reading

What was the most interesting fact that you learned from the observations of writers whose selections you read in this unit? Why did you find it interesting?

Reflect on Your Writing

What was the most challenging part of writing an opinion essay for this unit? Explain.

UNIT 4

Liberty

Essential Question

What does it mean to be free?

Watch

"Our Right to Freedom"

TURN and TALK

Which freedom in the video is most important?

SAVVAS realize™

Go ONLINE for all lessons.

- VIDEO
- AUDIO
- INTERACTIVITY
- GAME
- ANNOTATE
- BOOK
- RESEARCH

Spotlight on Historical Fiction

READING WORKSHOP

Infographic: The Underground Railroad

"Keeping Mr. John Holton Alive" from ***Elijah of Buxton*** .... **Historical Fiction**
by Christopher Paul Curtis

Map: The American Revolution

The Scarlet Stockings Spy .... **Historical Fiction**
by Trinka Hakes Noble

Word Puzzle: Our Constitution

from *The Bill of Rights* .... **Informational Text**
by Amie Jane Leavitt

Time Line: The Early Civil Rights Movement

Delivering Justice .... **Biography**
by Jim Haskins

Primary Source: "I Will Go West!"

Ezekiel Johnson Goes West .... **Historical Fiction**
by Guy A. Sims

READING-WRITING BRIDGE

- Academic Vocabulary • Word Study
- **Read Like a Writer • Write for a Reader**
- Spelling • Language and Conventions

WRITING WORKSHOP

Science Fiction

- Introduce and Immerse
- Develop Elements • Develop Structure
- Writer's Craft • Publish, Celebrate, and Assess

PROJECT-BASED INQUIRY

- Inquire • Research • Collaborate

Independent Reading

When you read a lot of assigned and self-selected texts, you build your reading stamina. Building reading stamina means developing your ability to read for sustained periods of time. Read the bullets to learn how to build your reading stamina.

- Choose books wisely. If a book does not hold your attention, consider choosing a different book.
- Pace yourself. Read for enjoyment and monitor your comprehension. Read at a rate that works for you.
- Limit distractions. If possible, choose a location for your independent reading that is quiet and comfortable, where you will not be interrupted.
- Set reasonable goals. Each time you read independently, aim to read a few more pages, or for a few more minutes, than you did last time. Small, achievable goals lead to big successes!

When I read (book title) ________________, I will build my reading stamina by ______________________________________.

Independent Reading Log

Date	Book	Genre	Pages Read	Minutes Read	My Ratings
					☆☆☆☆☆

Unit Goals

Shade in the circle to rate how well you meet each goal now.

SCALE	1	2	3	4	5
	NOT AT ALL WELL	NOT VERY WELL	SOMEWHAT WELL	VERY WELL	EXTREMELY WELL

Reading Workshop	1	2	3	4	5
I know about different types of fiction and understand the elements of historical fiction.					

Reading-Writing Bridge	1	2	3	4	5
I can use language to make connections between reading about fiction and writing fiction.					

Writing Workshop	1	2	3	4	5
I can use elements of fiction to write a science fiction story.					

Unit Theme	1	2	3	4	5
I can collaborate with others to determine what it means to be free.					

Academic Vocabulary

Use these words to talk about this unit's theme, *Liberty: limitation*, *grace*, *noble*, *empower*, and *resist*.

TURN and TALK Read each word. Then read how it is used in a sentence. Use context clues to determine the meaning of each academic vocabulary word. Write your definition and the context clue in the chart. Share your answers with a partner.

Academic Vocabulary	Used in a Sentence	My Definition
limitation	There are many limitations, or restrictions, about driving, such as the driver's age.	A *limitation* is something set within a certain boundary. *Restriction* is the context clue.
grace	The peaceful protestors walked with dignity and grace.	
noble	All the members of the local charity appreciated his noble deeds.	
empower	As the oldest, I like to empower my younger siblings so they can achieve their goals and dreams.	
resist	I resist, or refuse, giving up my rights.	

THE UNDERGROUND Railroad

THE UNDERGROUND RAILROAD did not have actual train tracks or passages in the ground. It was a secret network of routes designed to help enslaved people from the South find safety and freedom.

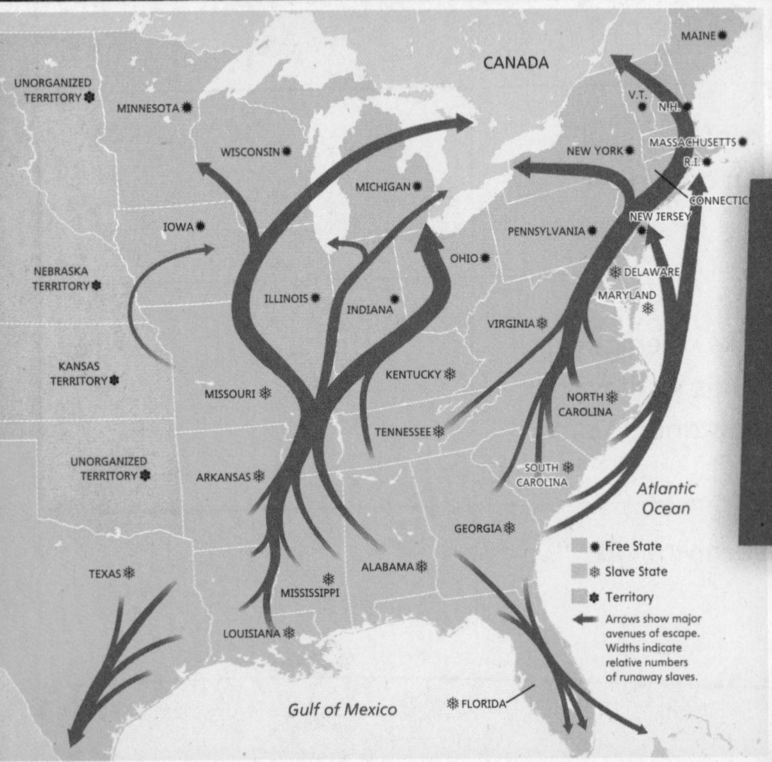

THIS MAP displays the basic routes and networks of the Underground Railroad in the 1800s. Many people who escaped slavery traveled north to Canada.

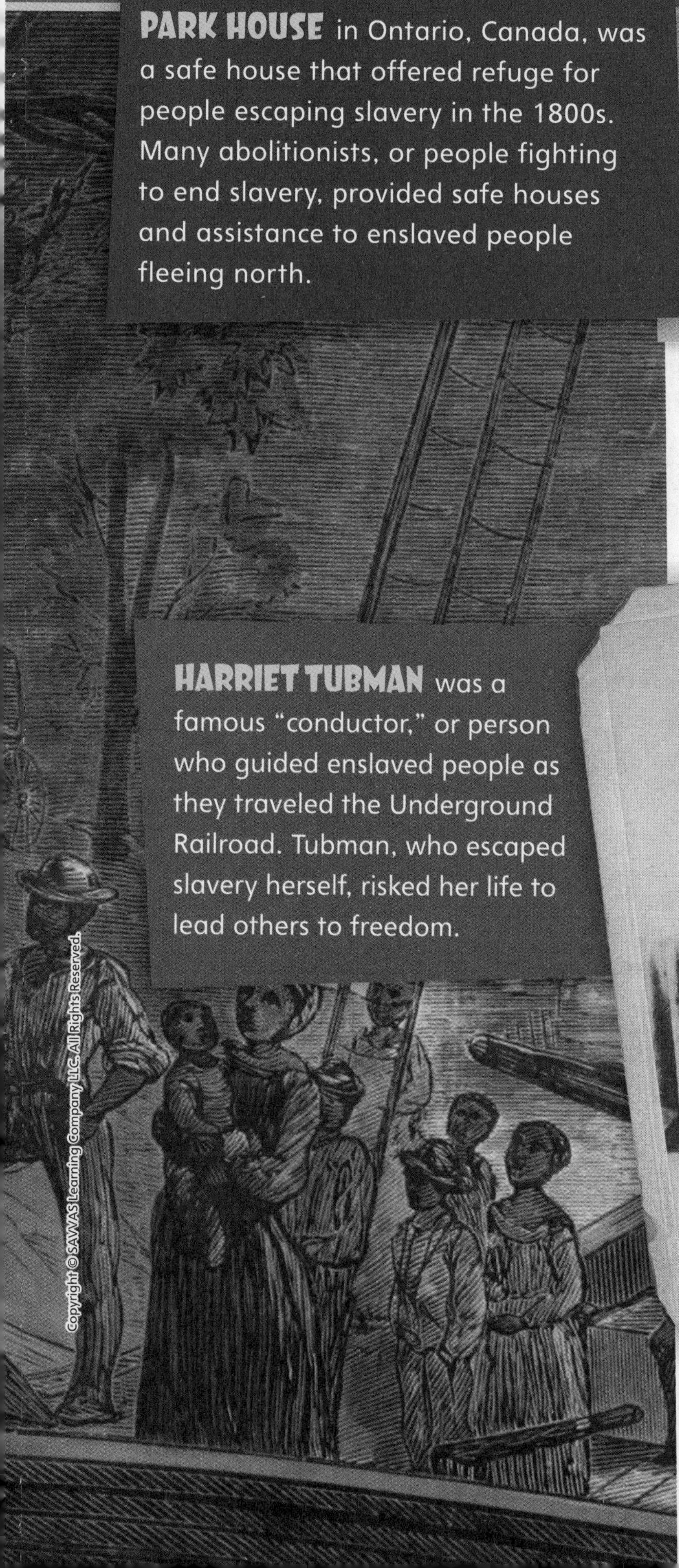

PARK HOUSE in Ontario, Canada, was a safe house that offered refuge for people escaping slavery in the 1800s. Many abolitionists, or people fighting to end slavery, provided safe houses and assistance to enslaved people fleeing north.

WEEK 1

Weekly Question

Why should people work together to help others achieve freedom?

TURN and TALK What kinds of people might have organized and maintained the Underground Railroad?

LC-USZ62-7816

Harriet Tubman (1823-1913)
nurse, spy and scout

HARRIET TUBMAN was a famous "conductor," or person who guided enslaved people as they traveled the Underground Railroad. Tubman, who escaped slavery herself, risked her life to lead others to freedom.

Learning Goal

I can learn more about historical fiction by analyzing characters.

Spotlight on Genre

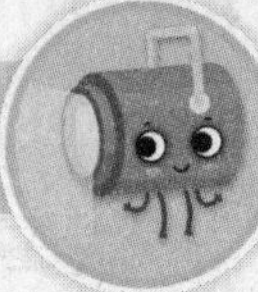

Historical Fiction

Historical fiction tells about events and people from the past. It includes

- **Settings** that describe a time and place in the past
- **Characters** that seem realistic for the setting
- **Plots** that make sense in the setting

Some texts use more than one way of communicating. Examples are

- Fictional text with informational elements, such as primary source news stories
- Persuasive text with illustrations, captions, and video links
- Informational text in a digital format with interactive diagrams and charts

Does the story take place long ago? It might be historical fiction!

TURN and TALK With a partner, discuss why an author might want to use more than one way of communicating when creating historical fiction. Use the chart for ideas. Take notes on your discussion.

My NOTES

Historical Fiction Anchor Chart

Purposes:

- To tell a story about the past
- To entertain and inform

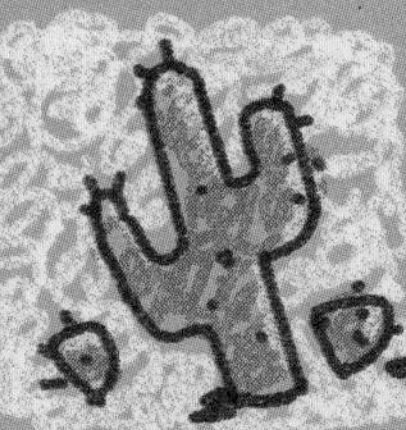

Elements:

- The setting is real and in the past.
- The characters act like real people from the time.

Text Structures:

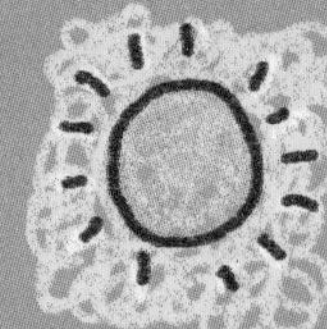

- Chronological order
- Problem and solution

Meet the Author

Christopher Paul Curtis said that when he wrote *Elijah of Buxton*, it was like he and Elijah "became close friends." Although many of Curtis's characters are children, he feels his stories are for everyone. Curtis is also the author of *Bud, Not Buddy* and *The Watsons Go to Birmingham–1963*.

Keeping Mr. John Holton Alive

Preview Vocabulary

As you read "Keeping Mr. John Holton Alive" from *Elijah of Buxton*, pay attention to these vocabulary words. Notice how they provide clues to the characters and events.

endure **ponder** **commotion**
commenced **strapping**

Read

Before you read, use what you know about **historical fiction** to make predictions about the story. Confirm or correct your predictions as you read. Follow these strategies when you read a text for the first time.

First Read

Notice	**Generate Questions**
when and where the story takes place and how characters act.	about the fictional and informational elements in the text.
Connect	**Respond**
this text to stories in history you know about.	by discussing how this text answers the weekly question.

Genre Historical Fiction

Keeping Mr. John Holton Alive

from Elijah of Buxton

by Christopher Paul Curtis

AUDIO

ANNOTATE

BACKGROUND

Eleven-year-old Elijah Freeman lives in Buxton, Canada, a community for people who have escaped slavery in the United States. As the first baby born in Buxton, Elijah has never experienced slavery. While working for Mr. Leroy, who is saving to buy his family's freedom, Elijah begins to learn more about the experiences of his parents and neighbors.

Evaluate Details

Highlight a detail in paragraph 1 that helps you determine a key idea of the author's note.

Author's Note

1 What an interesting, beautiful, hope-filled place the Elgin Settlement and Buxton Mission of Raleigh was and is. Founded in 1849 by a white Presbyterian minister named Reverend William King, the Settlement was first shared by Reverend King, fifteen slaves whom he had inherited through his wife, and six escaped slaves who awaited them. Reverend King felt there was nowhere in the United States that these African-American slaves could truly know liberty, so he purchased a three-mile by six-mile plot of land in southern Ontario on which he and the freed slaves could live. The population of Buxton at its height ranged from an estimated 1,500 to 2,000 escaped and freed people. Though there were a few other settlements of refugees from slavery in Canada at that time, Buxton proved to be the one that thrived. Even into the twenty-first century, several hundred descendants of the original settlers still live in the area, farming the land their ancestors hewed from the once thick Canadian forest.

2 The relative success of Buxton can be attributed to two things: First is the will, determination, courage, and sheer appreciation of freedom that steeled the spines of the newly freed, largely African-American residents. In the face of great opposition by some Canadians, they fought and worked hard to maintain the promise of the North Star. They took themselves from the horrors of southern American slavery into the land of the free, Canada. Every day they awoke

was filled with hardship, every day they awoke was filled with the joy of freedom. In *Legacy to Buxton*, a detailed history of the Settlement, author A. C. Robbins cites a Paul Laurence Dunbar poem to describe these brave people, and I can't think of a more fitting tribute:

Not they who soar, but they who plod
Their rugged way, unhelped, to God
Are heroes; . . .
Not they who soar.

3 The second reason the Buxton Settlement thrived is the set of strict rules that were instituted by Reverend King. People who chose to live within the Settlement's boundaries were required to purchase, with the assistance of very low interest loans, a minimum of fifty acres of land which they had to clear and drain. Their homes had to be a certain size with a minimum of four rooms and were set thirty-three feet from the road. The front of each home was to be planted with a flower garden and the back was to have a vegetable garden or truck patch.

4 Economically, Buxton was fiercely and deliberately self-sufficient and eventually had its own sawmill, potash mill, brickyard, post office, hotel, and school. There was even a six-mile-long tram that carried lumber from Buxton down to Lake Erie, where it was loaded on ships to be sold throughout North America. Buxton's school developed such a sterling reputation that many white families in the area withdrew their children from the local government schools and sent them to the Academy at Buxton instead. Many Native Canadian children also were educated at the school.

Evaluate Details

Highlight details on both pages that help you determine key ideas about the success of the Buxton Settlement.

CLOSE READ

Analyze Characters

Underline text that helps you understand Mr. Leroy's character.

1 A few days later, after supper, one of Mrs. Mae's twins came banging on the door. I answered.

2 "Evening, Eli."

3 "Evening, Eb."

4 "Mr. Leroy told me to come here and tell you not to go di-rect to Mrs. Holton's land tonight."

5 This was peculiar. I was supposed to help him again.

6 "Did he say how come?"

7 Eb said, "Uh-uh, you know Mr. Leroy, he never has much of anything to say. All he said was to tell you to come by the sawmill first."

8 "Thank you, Eb. Tell your ma and pa I asked 'bout 'em."

9 When I got to the sawmill, Mr. Leroy and Mr. Polite were sitting next to a fresh-cut hunk of wood 'bout four foot long and one foot wide.

10 Mr. Polite said, "Here he be. Evening, Eli."

11 "Evening, Mr. Polite. Evening, Mr. Leroy."

12 Mr. Leroy said, "Evening, Elijah. I wants you to look over this here writing 'fore I starts carving it. Mrs. Holton want it to go over her door, and I ain't carving nothing for no one 'less somebody what reads tells me it make sense.

13 "Folks ax you to carve something, then when you do it like they want and someone reads it to 'em and it ain't nothing but jibber-jabber, they say they ain't gunn pay and I done waste all that time. So see if this here's sensical."

14 I could tell Mr. Leroy was mighty worked up 'bout this. That was a whole month's worth of talking for him. He handed me a piece of paper that had rough writing and lots of cross-outs on it. I read, "'These words is done so no one won't never forget the loving memory of my husband John Holton what got whip to death and killed on May the seven 1859 just 'cause he want to see what his family look like if they free. He be resting calm knowing his family done got through. The body won't never endure but something inside all of us be so strong it always be flying.'"

15 I said to Mr. Leroy, "Sir, some of these things *do* need to get changed. How long you gonna let me ponder on this afore I gotta tell you?"

16 Mr. Polite said, "Ponder? Seem to me if you was really some good at reading and writing you wouldn't need no time to ponder nothing. Just change it up 'cause it ain't ringing right to my ear."

17 He turned to Mr. Leroy, "I told you, Leroy, we should've got that little Collins gal. That's one bright child there. This boy ain't too far from being daft."

CLOSE READ

Vocabulary in Context

Context clues are words and sentences around an unfamiliar word that help readers understand the word.

Underline context clues that help you understand the word *daft* in paragraph 17.

endure survive; continue existing

ponder think long and carefully

Analyze Characters

Underline details that tell you about the challenge Elijah faces and how he feels about it.

18 Mr. Leroy said, "Hold on, Henry, the boy say he need some time, I'm-a let him take his time. Mrs. Holton already suffered a lot. She don't need to be suffering no more 'cause of some jibber-jabber what's carved over her door."

19 I showed Ma and Pa the paper Mrs. Holton had writ and they told me it was a great honour to do this, that I had to do the best job I could.

20 Pa said, "You gunn have to help her take some the bite out them words, Elijah. Her pain too fresh to be locking it up so hot in writing."

21 Ma told me, "Poor Mr. Leroy gunn be carving for years to get all that down. But look, baby, some of them words is mine!"

22 I thought on it for the rest of the week. I filled pages and pages in my notebook, working on just the right words for Mrs. Holton. I thought 'bout it when I was supposed to be studying and when I was supposed to be doing chores. It even creeped up on me and made my rock fishing go real unpleasant for both me and the fish. I only chunked four outta twenty. Worst, I sent two of 'em wobbling back into the water with their brains scrambled like eggs.

23 After 'bout a week Mr. Leroy's patience ran out and he said, "I'm starting to agree with Henry Polite. Don't seem like changing some words 'round gunn take all this time. Mrs. Holton been wondering where her sign's at. After your supper, come to the field and have them words ready so's I can get started. And write 'em down clear too."

24 It killed my appetite but I finally got something writ down just after supper. Afore I gave it to Mr. Leroy, I ran over to Mr. Travis's home so he could see if there were any big mistakes. Mr. Travis changed two words, crossed out three, put in some better punctuating, then said, "Admirable job, Mr. Freeman, admirable job."

25 Ma and Pa said it seemed pretty good to them, and when I told the words to Mr. Leroy he didn't do nothing but grunt, which was saying a whole lot for him.

26 It took him a while to carve all the letters in the wood and the day it was finished he showed it to me. It was beautiful!

27 He said, "She real partial to having things done fancy, don't want nothing plain, so I put some decorating on it."

28 In the first three corners of her sign he'd carved a tree, a bird, and some waves. In the fourth corner he put the sun and the moon. He even carved a ribbon to go 'round all the words and you'd have swored it was real. Mr. Leroy let me carry it down to Mrs. Holton's so we could put it over her door.

29 Soon's he drove the first nail into the wood over her door, Mrs. Holton came out to see what the commotion was.

CLOSE READ

Analyze Characters

Underline parts of text that help you understand Elijah's relationships with Mr. Leroy and Mr. Travis.

commotion a loud noise or activity

CLOSE READ

Analyze Characters

Underline a sentence that tells you how Mrs. Holton helps resolve Elijah's conflict.

30 "Good afternoon, Leroy. Good afternoon, Elijah."

31 Me and Mr. Leroy both said, "Afternoon, ma'am."

32 Mr. Leroy told her, "I's sorry, Sister Emeline, I had the boy change them words 'round some. It was too long afore."

33 She stepped outside, looked back up at the sign, and said, "Oh? What it say now?"

34 I read it to her and she smiled and said, "That's just what I wanted it to say, Elijah. Thank you kindly. And thank you kindly, Mr. Leroy, for doing such a good job. I like the way you put them things in the corners, make it look important!

35 "Pardon me for a minute." Mrs. Holton went back inside her home. I figured she was getting some money to pay Mr. Leroy, but when she came back she was holding on to a fancy carved box.

36 She reached into the front of her apron and gave me a whole nickel! She gave me money for coming up with words on a piece a paper!

37 I squozed it tight in my hand and said, "Thank you, ma'am!"

38 But even afore I could slide it down in my pocket I could hear what Ma and Pa would say.

39 I opened my palm and reached the nickel back to Mrs. Holton. I said, "I ain't allowed to take no one's money, ma'am."

40 She wrapped her hand 'round my fingers so the nickel was folded back up in my fist.

41 "Elijah, I insists. If you ain't gunn take it I'm-a throw it out in the yard. I'll tell your ma I made you."

42 That was good enough for me! Ma and Pa would think throwing money away was worst than taking it for doing someone a favour, so I didn't have nothing to worry 'bout!

43 Then Mrs. Holton looked at Mr. Leroy and said, "Sir. This here's for you."

44 She reached the wood box at him.

45 Mr. Leroy wrinkled his forehead for a bit then said, "Sister Emeline, I 'preciate you giving me this here box. It's some fine work. And in light of your loss I'm-a say we's even, but from now on I caint be dealing in nothing but money. Sorry if I'm seeming bold, ma'am, I ain't intending to, but I know with you having someone what was 'slaved down home, you understand."

CLOSE READ

Evaluate Details

Highlight details from the characters' conversation that relate to what you read in the author's note.

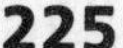

CLOSE READ

Analyze Characters

<u>Underline</u> the conflict that Mr. Leroy faces.

commenced began; started

46 Mrs. Holton said, "I understand. Here. Open the box."

47 Mr. Leroy took the box, pulled the lid off, and both him and me sucked in air like we got dunked in a barrel of cold water.

48 His hands commenced shaking, he busted out in a sweat and looked like his belly was aching him bad. He grabbed ahold of his left arm then whispered, "Mrs. Holton? What this?"

49 Mrs. Holton said, "It's twenty-two hundred dollars in gold, Mr. Leroy. It's what I was gunn buy John Holton with. You need it more'n me now."

50 Mr. Leroy couldn't talk. His legs melted from under him and he ended up in a heap on Mrs. Holton's stoop. He said, "Mrs. Holton, this here'll be my wife and *both* my children. I . . . I . . . I caint turn this down. . . ."

51 "I ain't 'specting you would."

52 She walked over to where he fell and he wrapped his arms 'round her legs like a drowning man holding on to a tree in a flood.

53 He kept on mumbling, "I caint turn it down, I caint turn it down. . . ."

54 It was something terrible to see. In two shakes of a lamb's tail, all the grownedness I'd been showing lately flewed off like ducks off of a pond and I was a fra-gile boy all over again. Seeing someone strong and tough as Mr. Leroy crying made me feel like everything was turned topsy-turvy.

55 Next thing you knowed, all three of us were bawling on Mrs. Holton's stoop. She pulled me in to her and we were a doggone pathetic sight.

56 Mr. Leroy said, "Sister Emeline, I done already save eleven hundred and ninety-two dollars and eighty-five cent. I ain't gunn need all this, but I swear I'm-a pay you back, I swear it. And you ain't never gunn have to worry 'bout no work being done on your land for the rest of your life."

CLOSE READ

Analyze Characters

Underline clues to how Elijah feels about Mr. Leroy's reaction to receiving the gold.

CLOSE READ

Evaluate Details

Highlight details that reveal Mrs. Holton's character.

strapping healthy and strong

57 Mr. Leroy didn't even wipe the tears away. He was crying but started smiling at the same time. "You oughta see my oldest, 'Zekial! He was a big strapping boy when I last seen him four years ago and now he be fifteen and must be big as a oak! Me and him both gunn be at your beck and call, ma'am, I swear it! We gunn pay back every cent! Thank you, thank you. . . ."

58 Mrs. Holton said, "Mr. Leroy, I ain't got no doubt you gunn pay me back, but hearing that Liberty Bell toll when your wife and babies walk into Buxton gunn be near payment enough itself."

59 She sniffed into the 'kerchief she was holding and said, "Elijah, read what them words is to me one more time."

60 I'd toiled on 'em so long I didn't even have to look at the sign above Mrs. Holton's door. I swallowed down some of the looseness in my nose and said what was on the sign:

FOR THE LOVE OF MY HUSBAND,
JOHN HOLTON,
WHO PASSED ON MAY 7TH, 1859,
BUT STILL LIVES. THE BODY IS NOT
MADE TO ENDURE.
THERE'S SOMETHING INSIDE SO STRONG
IT FLIES FOREVER.

61 She said, "That's it, Elijah. Son, you done told the truth."

62 I think all three of us figured the other two waren't gonna quit bawling till we busted up one from the 'nother. Mrs. Holton was the first to untangle herself from the crying party when her two children saw what was going on and commenced bawling too. She kissed me and Mr. Leroy on our heads then closed her door kind of gentle.

63 I was next to leave. It was getting late and I didn't want no trouble from Ma, so I left Mr. Leroy sitting on one of the steps with his face pressed down on that box.

64 I ran all the way home to tell Ma and Pa the good news!

CLOSE READ

Analyze Characters

Underline a detail that shows what Elijah's relationship with his parents is like.

Develop Vocabulary

In historical fiction, authors use specific words to describe character traits and actions. This helps readers understand who the characters are and how others feel about them.

My TURN Complete the chart, listing any characters from "Keeping Mr. John Holton Alive" whom each word might describe. Remember to include real people mentioned in the author's note.

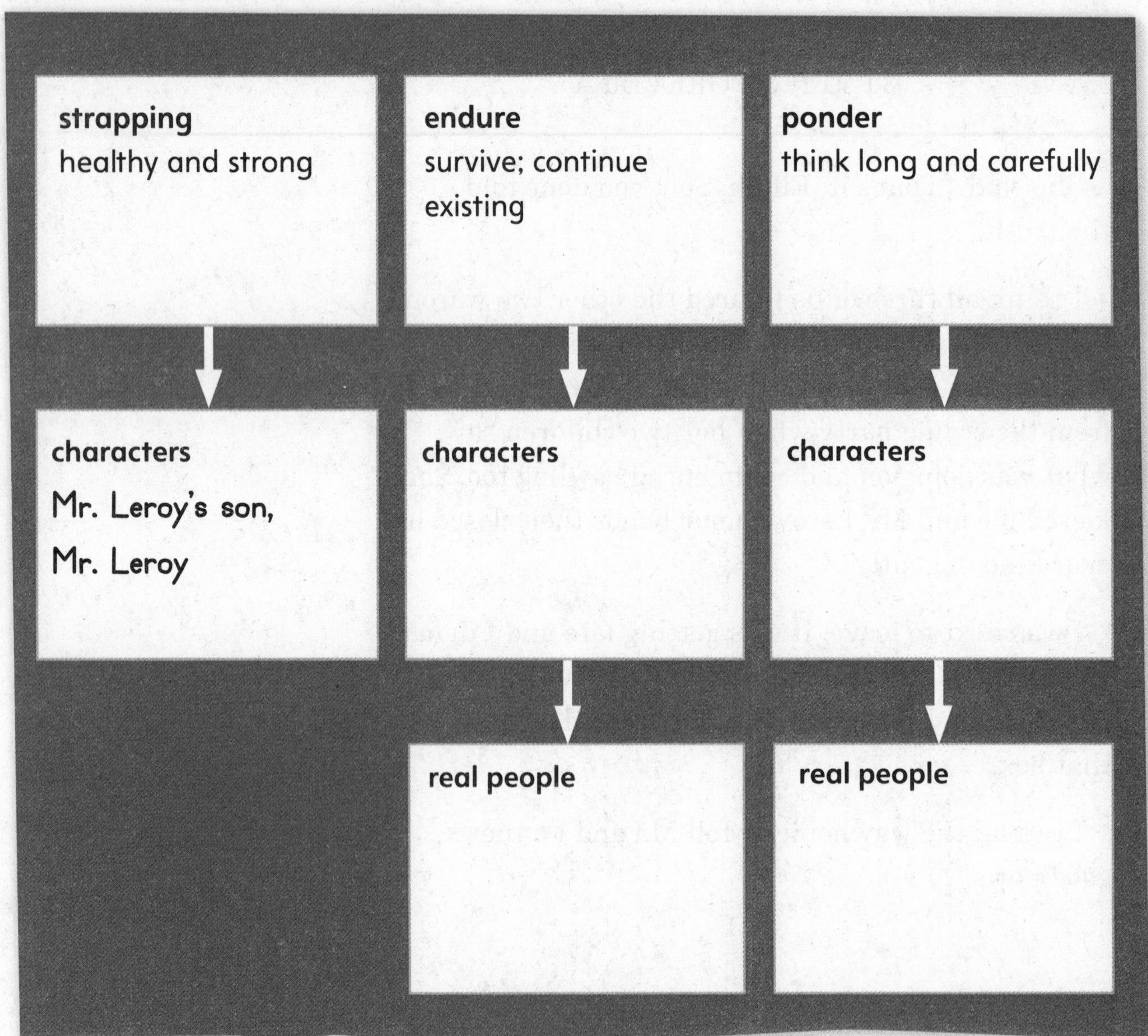

Check for Understanding

My TURN Look back at the text to answer the questions.

1. Identify details from the text that show it is a piece of historical fiction.

2. Evaluate how the author uses language to create the characters of Elijah and Mr. Leroy.

3. Visuals add to the way readers interpret and appreciate a text. Analyze how the images add to the meaning and tone of the text.

4. Do you think Mr. Leroy's reaction to Mrs. Holton's payment affects or changes Elijah? Use text evidence to support your argument.

Analyze Characters

Readers can notice the interactions and conflicts of a main character with other characters. Readers think about how the characters think, feel, and act to analyze the characters' relationships.

1. **My TURN** Go to the Close Read notes in "Keeping Mr. John Holton Alive" and underline the parts that help you understand Elijah's relationships with other characters.

2. **Text Evidence** Use the parts you underlined to complete the organizer. Analyze each character by summarizing how he or she relates to Elijah and using text evidence to illustrate your analysis.

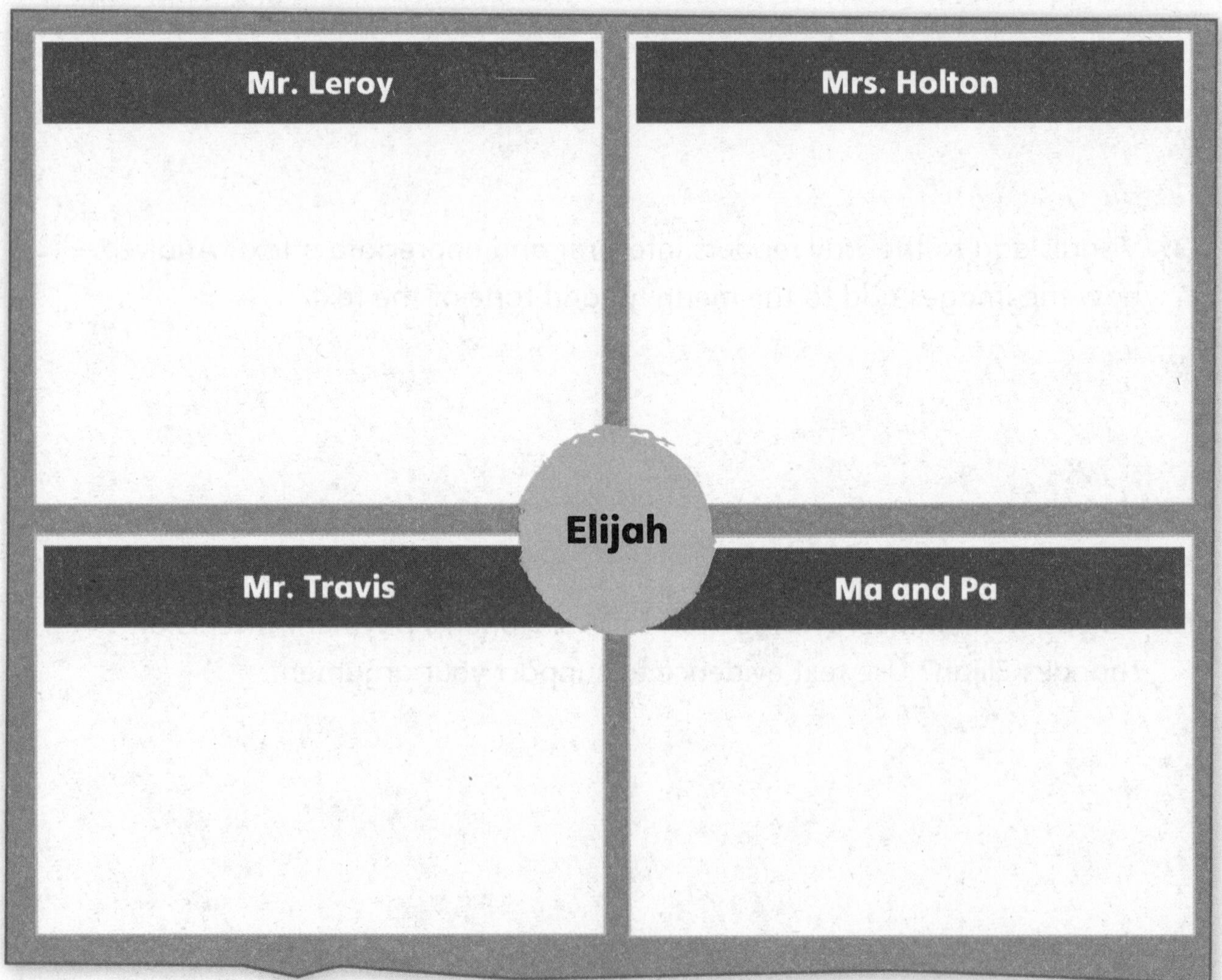

Evaluate Details

To understand characters, readers **evaluate details** as they read and interpret a text. By evaluating details, readers determine key ideas about what characters say, do, and think.

1. **MY TURN** Go back to the Close Read notes and highlight details that help you draw conclusions about characters.

2. **Text Evidence** Use your highlighted text to evaluate details and draw conclusions. Then answer the question.

Details in Dialogue or Description	Related Details from Author's Note	Conclusions
"'you having someone what was 'slaved down home'"	Buxton's residents were freed or escaped African Americans.	

What key idea do your conclusions reveal about Mrs. Holton and other residents of Buxton?

Reflect and Share

Talk About It In "Keeping Mr. John Holton Alive," Mrs. Holton gives money to Mr. Leroy so that he can free his family from slavery. What other stories have you read this week with characters helping other characters? Form an opinion about characters working together to help someone gain freedom.

Ask Relevant Questions During discussion, listen carefully to others' opinions. Then ask questions about those opinions that are relevant, or appropriate, to the topic. Ask questions to

- Discuss specific ideas in the text.
- Request reasons to support the opinion.
- Clarify or support the opinion.

Use these questions to guide your discussion.

What reasons can you give to support your opinion?

Can you tell me more about why you think the text is saying that?

Weekly Question

Why should people work together to help others achieve freedom?

Academic Vocabulary

Learning Goal

I can develop knowledge about language to make connections between reading and writing.

Related words are forms of a word that share roots or word parts but can have different meanings based on how the word is used. Examples are **free, freely,** and **freedom.**

My TURN For each word in the first column,

1. **Use** print or digital resources, such as a dictionary or thesaurus, to find related words.
2. **Choose** a related word and **add** it to the second column.
3. **Write** a sentence using one of the related words.

Word	Related Words	Sentence with Related Word
limitation	unlimited limiting limitless	After a high placement score, Tomas's school choices were practically unlimited.
grace	gratitude gracious ______	
empower	empowered empowerment ______	

Word Parts *pro-*, *com-*, *con-*

Greek and Latin **word parts** often give clues to a word's meaning. For example, the word *promote* contains the Latin or Greek word part *pro-*, which means "forward" or "before." The Latin word parts *com-* and *con-* both mean "with" or "together."

The word *conversation* means "a talk between two or more people." If you know that *con-* means "together," you can use that information to help decode the word and infer the meaning.

My TURN Use advanced knowledge of the word parts as a clue to each word's meaning. Match each word from the Word Bank to the correct meaning. Use a print or digital dictionary to check your answers.

com-, *con-* (with, together) *pro-* (forward, before)

Word Bank

contrast **propel** **compress** **companion** **progress** **community**

1. community ________ a group of people living together in an area

2. ________ forward movement

3. ________ push together

4. ________ a person or thing that goes along with something else

5. ________ to move or push something forward

6. ________ to find differences among two or more things

Read Like a Writer

Writers use language that fits their settings and characters. Sometimes they use dialects, or forms of speech that come from a specific time or place. Dialects may include nonstandard grammar, slang, and unique vocabulary.

Model! Read the text from "Keeping Mr. John Holton Alive."

> Mr. Leroy said, "Evening, Elijah. I wants you to look over this here writing 'fore I starts carving it. ..."

dialect

1. **Identify** Christopher Paul Curtis uses different grammar and vocabulary.
2. **Question** What does the dialect tell me about Mr. Leroy?
3. **Conclude** The dialect reminds me that Mr. Leroy lives a time long ago, and he may not have a formal education.

Reread paragraph 41 from "Keeping Mr. John Holton Alive."

My TURN Follow the steps to analyze the passage. Describe how the author uses dialect.

1. **Identify** Christopher Paul Curtis uses different grammar, such as ______________________, and different vocabulary, such as ____.
2. **Question** What does the dialect tell me about Mrs. Holton?
3. **Conclude** The dialect tells me that ____.

Write for a Reader

Authors use elements of craft, such as informal and formal language, to make characters' speech sound natural and realistic.

My TURN Think about how dialect in "Keeping Mr. John Holton Alive" affects you as a reader. Compare and contrast that dialect with the language used in the poem "Artist to Artist" and the drama *The Hermit Thrush*. Identify how you can use varieties of English to develop realistic characters and settings.

1. What are several words and phrases that are common to your community, region, and time but that people from other places might not understand in the same way?

2. Write a brief dialogue between two characters from your area. Use an appropriate style of language to make the characters sound realistic.

Spell Words with *pro-*, *com-*, *con-*

The word part *pro-* means "forward" or "before." The word parts *com-* and *con-* mean "with" or "together."

My TURN Read the words. Spell and sort the words by their word parts.

SPELLING WORDS

promotion	compress	convene	command
consensus	combine	contingent	provide
complement	protective	companion	projection
congestion	concert	proponent	conclave
protection	provision	concoction	combination

pro-

con-

com-

Adjectives

Adjectives are words that modify, or add to and clarify the meaning of, nouns and pronouns. Adjectives describe people, places, or things by telling *what kind*, *how many*, or *which one*.

An adjective that appears after a linking verb and describes a noun in the subject is a **predicate adjective.** Sometimes words that we think of as nouns are used as adjectives.

Form	Where It Appears	Examples
Descriptive	usually before the word it modifies	fresh-cut hunk of wood
Predicate	after a linking verb	Those words are clever.
Nouns as Adjectives	before the word it modifies	the Buxton settlers

My TURN Add adjectives to improve each sentence.

1. Mr. Leroy was a ______________ man who did not talk very much.
2. Elijah was ______________ that Mr. Leroy asked for his help.
3. It took Elijah a ______________ time to find the ______________ words for the ______________ sign.
4. In the end, Mr. Travis complimented Elijah on his ______________ job.

Organize a Science Fiction Story

Learning Goal

I can use elements of science fiction to write a short story.

A **science fiction** story entertains the reader with a vision of the future.

The **characters** in a science fiction story may be robots or humans who have technology that people do not have today.

The **setting** of a science fiction story differs from the real world. For example, the story might be set in outer space or on Earth in the distant future.

The **plot** of a science fiction story has a problem that is related to the futuristic setting. Like any fiction story, a writer introduces the problem, builds toward a climax, or turning point, and resolves the conflict.

My TURN Write the title of a science fiction story you have read. Draw an illustration to show how the setting, characters, and problem make the story science fiction.

Title

Analyze Characters and Setting

In science fiction, the **characters** may be people, but they may also be made-up creatures or robots. The **setting** may be in the distant future on Earth, on another planet, or somewhere in outer space.

My TURN For each science fiction setting below, name and describe a main character you could write about.

Setting	Character
A dusty planet with several moons, circling a bright red sun	
A luxury cruise ship in space, orbiting a watery planet	
A city on Earth in the year 3155	
A farming community inside a greenhouse dome on Mars	

Analyze Plot

The plot of a science fiction story, like that of any fiction story, begins by introducing the characters and the situation or problem. Events build toward a climax, or turning point. The story ends after the problem is resolved.

My TURN Work with a partner. Read a science fiction short story from your classroom library. Complete the plot diagram.

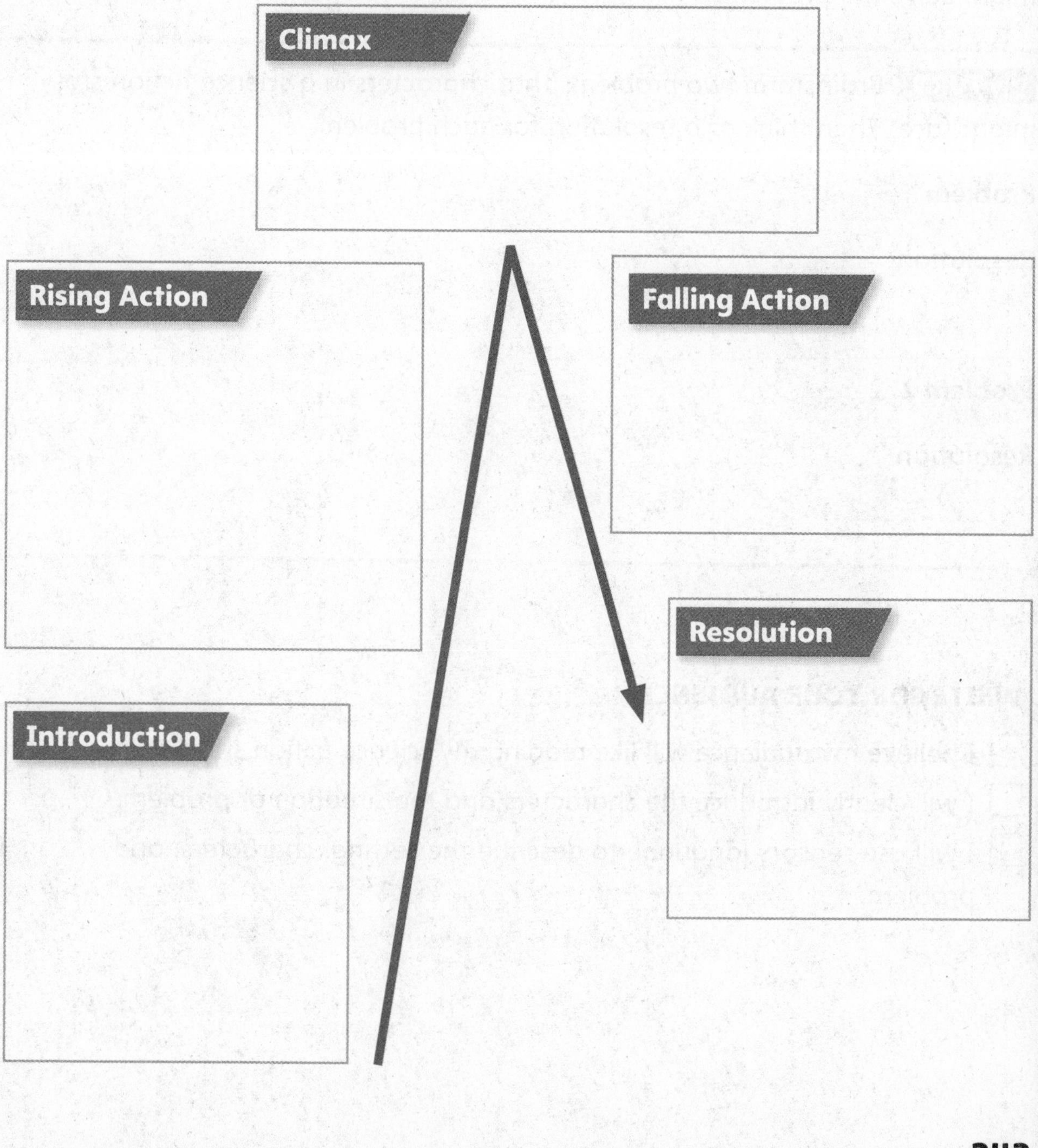

Climax

Rising Action

Falling Action

Resolution

Introduction

Set a Purpose

A writer begins planning a story by thinking about the task, purpose, and audience. The task is what you are asked to do. In this case, the task is to write a science fiction short story. The purpose is your reason for writing. In science fiction, your purpose is to entertain readers. Your audience is your readers.

One way to set an entertaining purpose for a science fiction story is to invent an entertaining problem. Consider how a character using futuristic technology might solve the problem.

My TURN Brainstorm two problems that characters in a science fiction story might face. Then think of a resolution for each problem.

Problem 1 ______________________________

Resolution ______________________________

____

Problem 2 ______________________________

Resolution ______________________________

____

WRITE FOR YOUR AUDIENCE:

- [ ] I believe my audience will like reading my science fiction short story.
- [ ] I will clearly introduce the characters and the situation or problem.
- [ ] I will use sensory language to describe the setting, characters, and problem.

Plan Your Science Fiction Story

Writers sometimes **map** to generate ideas for their stories.

My TURN Use the checklist as you map out ideas for your science fiction story. In your writing notebook, build and complete a story map that resembles this one.

- [ ] Name and describe your main character.
- [ ] Describe the setting.
- [ ] Consider what makes your story a piece of science fiction—technology, space travel, characters who are not from Earth, and so on.
- [ ] Use a problem and resolution you brainstormed to map out the sequence of events.
- [ ] Share your organizer with your Writing Club.

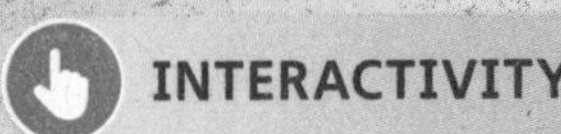
INTERACTIVITY

The AMERICAN REVOLUTION

General George Washington had to face many obstacles in the fight for American independence. In 1777–1778, after a few early victories, one of the most difficult episodes of the war unfolded in Pennsylvania. As a result of Washington's losses there, the British captured the capital city of Philadelphia.

View this map of the area around Philadelphia. Note the locations of important battles.

4

WINTER 1777–1778: Washington settles his army at Valley Forge for the winter. Starvation, disease, and severe cold cause illness and death, but Washington uses the time to better train his soldiers. This enables them to win important victories in the years ahead.

2

SEPTEMBER 1777: Washington is defeated at the Battle of the Brandywine and retreats. The British capture Philadelphia.

Schuylkill River

Valley Forge

Brandywine Creek

Chadds Ford

Wilmington

Delaware River

DELAWARE

MARYLAND

WINTER 1776–1777: Washington surprises and defeats British troops at Trenton and Princeton. This restores confidence in Washington's leadership after defeats in the fall of 1776.

Delaware River

Princeton

Trenton

PENNSYLVANIA

Germantown

Philadelphia

NEW JERSEY

5 miles

Weekly Question

How can ordinary people contribute to a fight for freedom?

TURN and TALK Discuss the map with a partner. Think about the reasons people fought for independence. What freedoms are important to your community? How do people in your community work together to get or to keep those freedoms? Reconsider your own ideas based on what your partner says.

3

OCTOBER 1777: Washington tries to defeat the British occupying Philadelphia, but he is defeated at Germantown.

Learning Goal

I can learn more about historical fiction by inferring multiple themes.

Spotlight on Genre

Historical Fiction

Historical fiction adds imaginary people and events to a real time in history.

- The **purpose** is to entertain with a believable story while informing readers about the past.
- The **characters** can be made-up people or real figures from history.
- The **plot** takes place in the past and combines events that could have occurred with events that really happened.
- The **setting** is a real place and time in the past.

Establish Purpose Before you read historical fiction, ask yourself: *What is my purpose for reading this text?* Historical fiction allows readers to reimagine history. It can entertain and inform.

Did the story happen in the past? Is the time and place real? If so, this fiction is historical.

My PURPOSE ______________________

TURN and TALK Think about a story or novel you read that helped you learn about real past events. Use the anchor chart to decide whether it was historical fiction. Then share your responses with the class.

Historical Fiction Anchor Chart

	Real	Made-up	From the Past
Characters	✓	✓	✓
Events	✓	✓	✓
Time and Place	✓		✓

Meet the Author

Trinka Hakes Noble wanted to be an artist before she wanted to be an author. She has written and illustrated books about everything from pet snakes to families like her own in a time of war.

The Scarlet Stockings Spy

Preview Vocabulary

As you read, pay attention to these vocabulary words. Notice how they provide clues to the characters and theme and help you understand the story.

resembled **suspicious**

relaying **stalking** **solemnly**

Read

Active readers of **historical fiction** establish a purpose for reading. What do you want to gain from reading *The Scarlet Stockings Spy*? Follow these strategies as you read the text for the first time.

First Read

Notice	Generate Questions
times, places, and problems that were a part of history.	about parts that do not match what you already know.
Connect	**Respond**
places and events to other texts you have read.	by marking facts used to support the fictional story.

Genre Historical Fiction

The Scarlet Stockings Spy

by Trinka Hakes Noble

AUDIO

ANNOTATE

Infer Multiple Themes

Underline parts of the text that help you predict a theme, or central message, of the story. Reread "Keeping Mr. John Holton Alive." Compare and contrast themes you find in both stories.

resembled looked like something or someone else

1 In the fall of 1777, Philadelphia sat twitching like a nervous mouse. The British were going to attack, but no one knew where or when. Congress had fled inland to York. The Liberty Bell was secreted to Allentown. Folks thought the year resembled a hangman's gallows and took it as a bad sign. Now, all the church bells were being removed to keep the British from melting them down into firearms. Uncertainty settled over the city like soot. Suspicions skulked through the cobblestone streets like hungry alley cats. Rumors multiplied like horseflies. Spies were everywhere.

2 Some spied for the British, loyal to the king. Others spied for the Patriots, loyal to Washington's army, now camped west of the city. Still other spies were loyal to lining their pockets.

3 But one little spy moved through the streets unnoticed, even though she wore scarlet stockings. Her name was Maddy Rose and she lived with her mother and brother in the Leather Apron District, next to the harbor, where the city's tradesfolk lived and worked in narrow brick row houses.

4 "Maddy Rose," called her mother from the front room, not looking up from her spinning. "Tarry not. Mistress Ross hath need of these linens this morning."

5 Dusty eastern light filtered through the panes of thick glass in their tiny row house on Appletree Alley where the *click*, *clack*, *click* of the flax wheel never stopped from early dawn 'til candlelight.

6 "Yes, Mother," answered Maddy Rose, hurrying to poke up the fire.

7 Each morning, before she went to sew seams for Mistress Ross on Arch Street, Maddy Rose lowered the teakettle over the hearth, then crushed dried raspberry leaves to brew Liberty tea. Since the tea rebellion in Boston, drinking imported English tea was considered disloyal.

8 This morning her mother looked tired, so Maddy Rose added a drop of precious honey. Carefully she carried the only china teacup they owned to her mother, a treasured gift from her father.

9 "Here, Mother dear. This will refresh you."

10 Maddy Rose's mother stopped spinning and gently held her daughter's chin.

11 "You have his strong jaw," she sighed, her eyes glistening softly.

12 Maddy Rose knew her mother was remembering her father, who had fallen at the Battle of Princeton last winter and lay with the others beneath the soil of New Jersey. Many men had gone to the war. Even her brother Jonathan, who was only fifteen, had joined Washington's army to wear the blue coat.

CLOSE READ

Infer Multiple Themes

Underline ways in which the author describes Maddy Rose as a helpful and caring daughter.

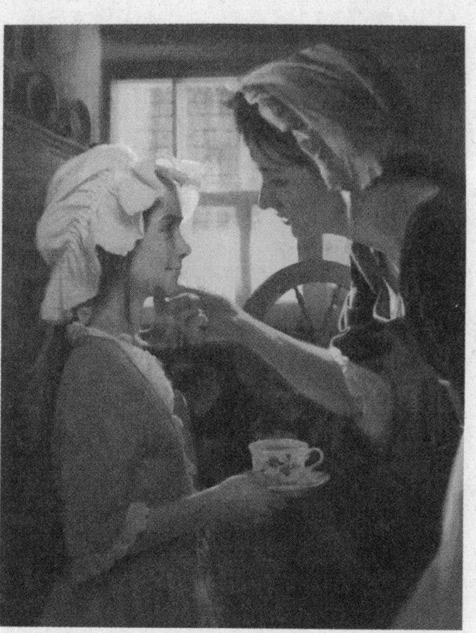

CLOSE READ

Monitor Comprehension

Ask and answer questions about the text with a partner. Highlight evidence that supports the theme of freedom.

13 Outside, on the bustling streets, Maddy Rose marched along to the *rap tap tap* of tinsmiths, blacksmiths, and cobblers. She breathed in the mingled smells of sawdust, pitch, and baking bread as she passed cabinetmakers, coppersmiths, shipwrights, and bakers. She marveled at the swish of the weaver's shuttle, the blurred hands of busy lacemakers and seamstresses, hoping someday she would be as skilled.

14 From their busy shop fronts these hardworking folk traded with the wealthy loyalists, but out the back they gave what they could to the cause of freedom.

15 "Nothing's too good for them who soldier for our country," they all agreed.

16 Maddy Rose agreed too, for she was a Patriot rebel from head to toe in her homespun petticoats, her linsey-woolsey dress and muslin apron, her hand-me-down shoes and woven straw hat. But it was her hand knit scarlet stockings that she valued the most, for their worth was far greater than just warm dry feet.

17 Whenever Maddy Rose strutted by the fine young ladies of Philadelphia in their creamy white stockings and dainty slippers, she'd flounce her skirts and jut out her proud strong chin.

18 "Such poppycock!" she'd cluck to herself. No fancy silks, satins, and brocades imported from London for her. To wear such finery showed loyalty to the king.

CLOSE READ

Infer Multiple Themes

Underline evidence that supports the conclusion that children can play important roles in major events. Compare and contrast how this story and "Keeping Mr. John Holton Alive" deal with similar themes.

19 Maddy Rose was loyal only to Jonathan. No one suspected her of anything, of course. Not this hardworking little seamstress who helped her poor mother by earning threepence. Why, she even hung the wash out every week like clockwork. But that's where Maddy Rose fooled them, for it was her small clothesline, hanging from her third-floor window, that held a secret code.

20 She'd lined her clothesline up perfectly with the harbor, just like when she and Jonathan used to play "Harbormaster." Jonathan pretended to be the harbormaster, cupping his hands like a spyglass, barking out docking and departing orders from an upper window. Maddy Rose scrambled below, playing the harbormaster's assistant, arranging cobblestones, apples, and scraps of wood as though they were real ships. Jonathan always tricked her so there would be a collision, then he'd make loud crashing and exploding sounds 'til they both laughed. It was only a game. But now things were different. The country was at war.

21 So once a week at dusk, using their secret code, Maddy Rose hung out her stockings and petticoats in the same order as the real ships along the wharf. A petticoat was code for a lightweight friendly vessel from the colonies. A scarlet stocking hanging toe up meant a merchant vessel from the islands or foreign port. When the toe hung down, it meant the vessel was suspicious and needed watching. But when the ship was riding low in the water, it meant only one thing—heavy firearms for the British. That's when Maddy Rose would weight that stocking down with a cobblestone.

CLOSE READ

Monitor Comprehension

Think about what you already know about the Revolutionary War. Highlight details in the story that reflect historical facts.

suspicious not to be trusted

22 Jonathan would sneak into the city after dark wearing a disguise, because if a spy were caught, he could be hanged. He'd read her clothesline then steal away through the darkened city to the countryside, relaying the information back to Washington's headquarters, so the Patriots were aware of who might be gunrunners and smugglers for the British.

23 One time Jonathan disguised himself as a crippled beggar with a cane, limping badly. Maddy Rose became worried. But then he flipped into a perfect handstand, balancing on the cane like an acrobat. Oh how she laughed and clapped.

24 Once he saluted her like a puffed up rooster, then did an about-face, tripped on purpose, and fell flat as a flapjack, sending her into gales of laughter.

25 The last time he dressed as a woman, then hiked up his skirts and danced a wild jig in his long johns.

26 "Oh, Jonathan, you silly goat," Maddy Rose giggled from behind her window, then pulled in her clothesline and slept with a smile on her face.

CLOSE READ

Vocabulary in Context

Context clues, or words and phrases around an unfamiliar word, can help readers understand the word.

Underline context clues that help you understand *disguise*.

relaying passing along

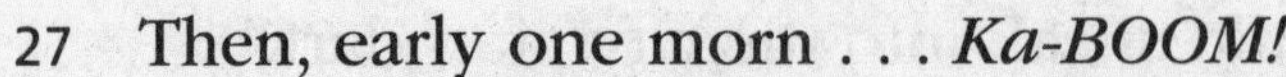

CLOSE READ

Monitor Comprehension

Reread the text. Highlight repeated words that the author uses to set a frightening tone.

27 Then, early one morn . . . *Ka-BOOM!*

28 The battle had started. British and Patriot cannons were blasting each other across Brandywine Creek. The ferocious bombardment was so loud that all of Philadelphia could hear it, even though it was twenty-five miles away. The date was September 11th, 1777.

29 On that same foggy dawn, Jonathan hid in the mist with the Pennsylvania Line, lying low in the barleycorn fields and reedy banks along Brandywine Creek, clutching his musket as cannonballs screeched overhead, waiting for the command to attack the British redcoats on foot.

30 "Cannons!" Maddy Rose cried out as she tore downstairs. "Mother, do you not hear it?"

31 "Aye, child," she answered calmly, trying to spin as usual. "Be brave now. Let's get to thy work."

32 Maddy Rose tried not to think what those thundering cannons meant. She began pounding raspberry leaves as hard as she could. But the harder she pounded, the louder the cannons roared.

33 *Ka-BOOM, BOOM!*

34 She yanked the teakettle from the crane and spun around with the teacup in her hand. Just then . . .

35 *KA-BOOM, BOOM . . . KA-BOOM!!*

36 Maddy Rose jumped . . . and the precious teacup flew from her hand and smashed into a hundred bits and pieces.

37 The blazing cannons kept up their deadly attack, back and forth across Brandywine Creek 'til midday. Then came the command to charge, and the air became thick with the crack of muskets, the hiss of lead balls, and the acrid stench of gunpowder smoke.

38 Maddy Rose's sharp eyes swept over the many ships crowded along the wharf. She memorized their positions, and which would be petticoats, which would be stockings with toes up, or toes down, but on this day she was startled to see that many stockings would need cobblestone weights.

39 Quickly she fetched Mistress Ross's order, but before she left, something made her look across the Delaware toward New Jersey, and her heart nearly stopped! For there, in the middle of the river, hiding among the many moored ships, sat a British man-of-war!

40 "Jonathan must know this!" she gasped.

41 Maddy Rose raced back and set to work. It was the heaviest clothesline she'd ever hung.

CLOSE READ

Infer Multiple Themes

Underline details that support the theme that it is important to be brave during times of danger.

CLOSE READ

Infer Multiple Themes

Underline a part of the author's description that supports the conclusion that Maddy is fearless even though she is in danger.

stalking following closely and in a sneaky way

42 But that night Jonathan didn't come; yet Maddy Rose kept watch for him long into that black night. He didn't come the next night either, or the next, nor the one after that. More and more nights passed, yet she kept looking for him from her window, never losing hope.

43 Then, one night, a shadowy figure stood in Jonathan's place. She snuffed out her candle and peeked over the darkened sill. Who was he? Could it be Jonathan? But when he saw her window go dark he turned to leave.

44 Maddy Rose didn't even stop to think or slip on her shoes. She bounded after him, darting in and out of the shadows between the lampposts, stalking him like a silent cat in her stocking feet through the damp streets.

45 "Jonathan?" she whispered hopefully, shyly touching his cloak. "Is that you?"

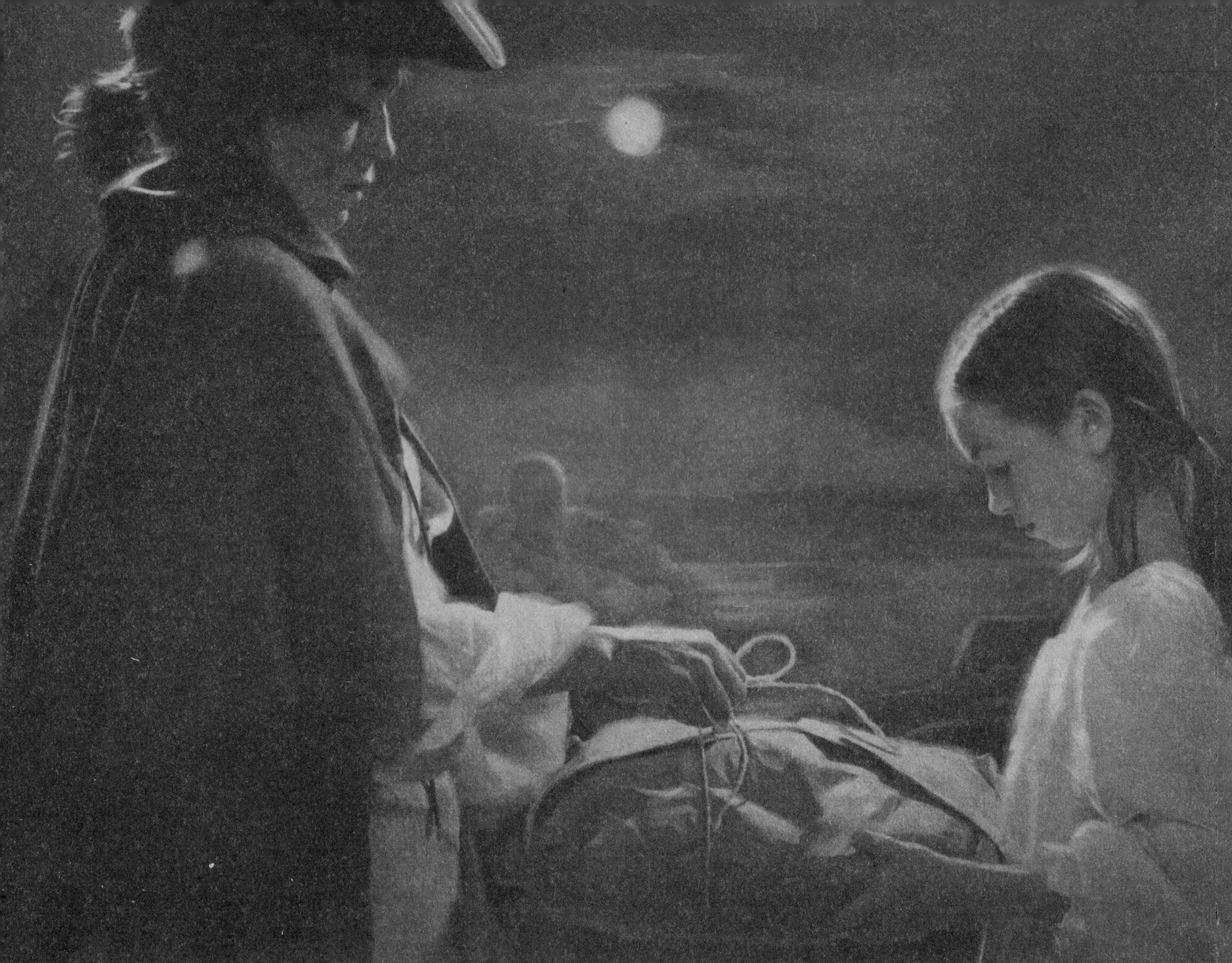

46 The stranger turned and smiled. “I'm Seth,” he answered. “And by the looks of your feet, you must be Little Miss Scarlet Stockings, Jonathan's sister.”

47 “You know him? You know my brother?” she choked. Her face flushed hot and her throat tightened as she waited for Seth's answer.

48 But Seth was silent. Damp night air drifted in from the Delaware River, brushed against Maddy Rose's burning cheeks and seeped into Seth's eyes as he stared hard into the darkness. Then, solemnly, he bowed his head and spoke in a low voice.

solemnly in a sad and serious way

49 "I'm proud to say I did, Miss."

50 Slowly Seth handed her a bundle. With trembling hands, she reached out, and for a few moments they held the bundle together.

51 Then Seth spoke softly. "I know your clothesline code, Miss," he said. "I've come to take Jonathan's place."

52 Maddy Rose nodded slowly as tears spilled from her eyes. She tried to hold up her chin, as her father would have, but it drooped as her bottom lip began to quiver.

53 "We'll not fail, Miss," Seth vowed. "I promise you that."

54 Then he was gone.

55 Back in her darkened room, Maddy Rose slowly untied the bundle. It was Jonathan's blue coat. Tenderly, she let her small fingers explore the blue wool serge until she found it—a stiff dried bloodstain. Then, with her littlest finger, she lightly traced two letters on the pewter buttons—U.S.

56 "Us," she whispered in the dark, ". . . for us, dear brother . . . for all of us."

57 That night, and for many nights to follow, Maddy Rose sat in her tiny room lit by a single candle, threaded her needle and sewed. She was making an American flag from her scarlet stockings, her white petticoats, and her brother's blue coat. And sewn into every one of her stitches was a tear of grief and the clenched fist of defiance.

Monitor Comprehension

Discuss the text with a partner. Highlight details that reveal information about what happened to Jonathan.

Infer Multiple Themes

Underline details about Maddy Rose's behavior that supports a major theme of the story.

CLOSE READ

Monitor Comprehension

Reread paragraph 59 and view the illustration on the opposite page. Highlight details that explain what happened after the events of the story.

58 Through the bleak cold winter that followed, Washington's army retreated to Valley Forge while the British occupied Philadelphia, lock, stock, and barrel. At night the redcoat invaders celebrated with military balls and fancy cotillions. And during the day they patrolled the streets, eyes forward, never noticing a young girl's unmentionables hanging overhead on a small clothesline from a third-floor window.

59 In the spring of 1778 the British left Philadelphia, crossed the Delaware, and were sent running by Washington's army at the Battle of Monmouth in New Jersey. The Patriots of Philadelphia celebrated, flying flags everywhere!

60 But there was one little flag that hung by itself on a small clothesline high over Appletree Alley. And fresh spring breezes traveled from New Jersey and found the little flag and lifted it up high. How proud and strong it flew, just like her father's chin, for it was Maddy Rose's scarlet stockings flag.

61 Many years have passed since the spring of 1778. No one knows for sure what happened to this little flag. But if by chance you found it, in an old trunk or dusty attic or barn loft or musty museum basement, you would notice that one star is bigger than the rest. It sits in a place of honor, at the top of an arch of thirteen stars in a field of blue, the keystone star for Pennsylvania. And if you looked under that star, you would find a musket ball hole.

CLOSE READ

Vocabulary in Context

Underline context clues that help you understand the meaning of the word *musty*.

Develop Vocabulary

In historical fiction, words that help the reader experience sights, sounds, and other details help bring a historical time, place, or event to life.

My TURN Read the vocabulary words. Then use each word to write a sentence that describes something the character Maddy Rose experienced or felt.

Word	Description of an Event or Feeling
resembled	Maddy Rose's mother pointed out that Maddy Rose's jaw resembled that of her father.
suspicious	
relaying	
stalking	
solemnly	

Check for Understanding

My TURN Look back at the text to answer the questions.

1. Identify details about *The Scarlet Stockings Spy* that make it historical fiction.

2. How does the author logically interrupt the sequence of events? What is the effect of this choice?

3. How does the news about Jonathan affect Maddy Rose? How do you know?

4. How does the author's depiction of historical places, events, and battles help you better understand the American Revolution?

Infer Multiple Themes

A text's **theme** is its central message or meaning. While reading, make **inferences**, or figure out information that is not stated directly. Put together what you already know with text evidence to infer the text's theme.

1. **My TURN** Go to the Close Read notes in *The Scarlet Stockings Spy* and underline the parts that help you infer themes. Review "Keeping Mr. John Holton Alive." Compare and contrast how the texts approach similar themes and topics.

2. **Text Evidence** Use your underlined text to infer similar themes in both stories.

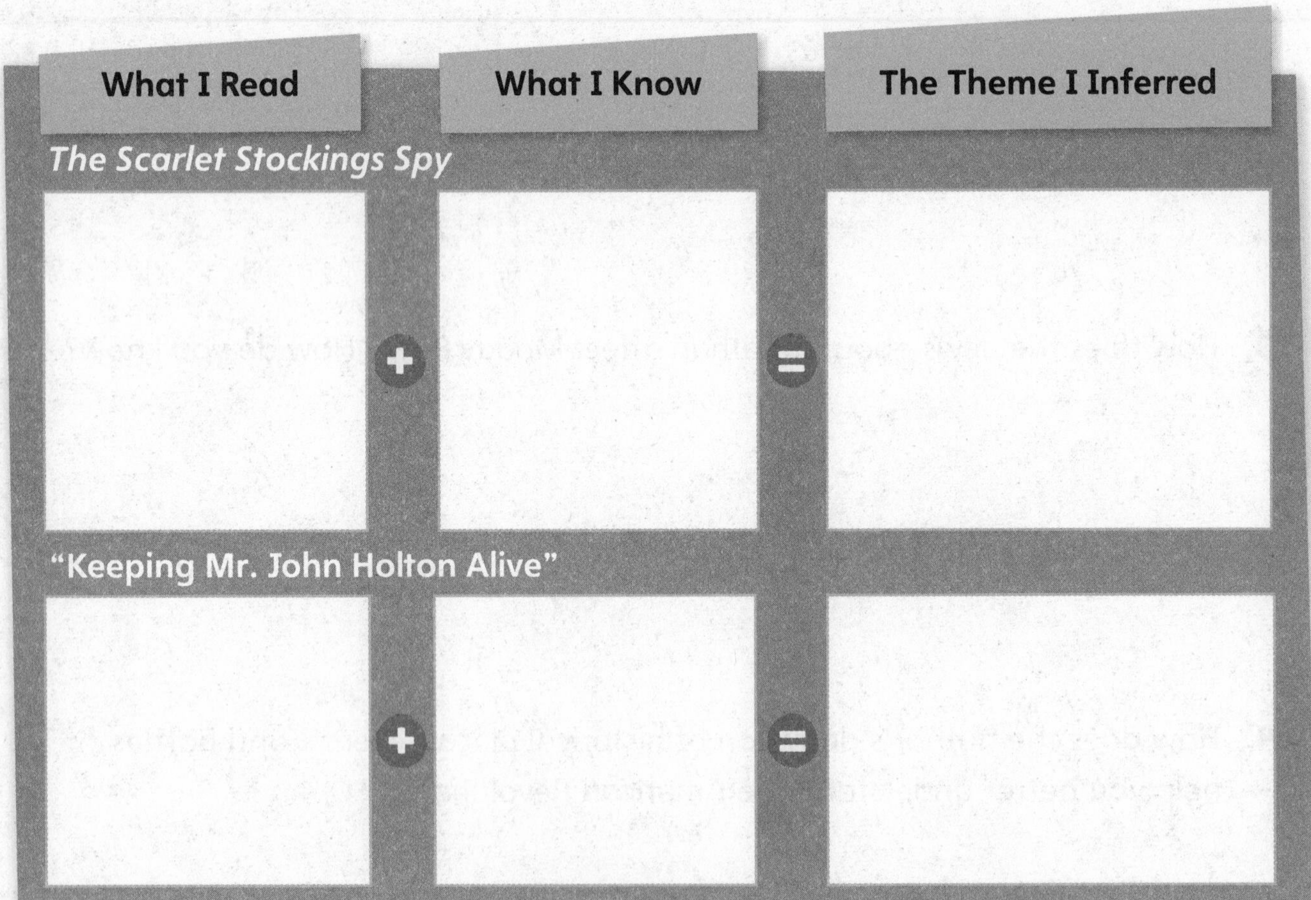

What I Read		What I Know		The Theme I Inferred
The Scarlet Stockings Spy				
	+		=	
"Keeping Mr. John Holton Alive"				
	+		=	

What other themes in *The Scarlet Stockings Spy* did you identify?

Monitor Comprehension

Monitor, or check, your **comprehension** while reading. If you don't understand something, use a fix-up strategy, such as rereading, taking notes, talking to a partner, using background knowledge, or analyzing illustrations.

1. **My TURN** Go back to the Close Read notes and highlight text evidence that you do not understand. Use a fix-up strategy to improve your understanding.

2. **Text Evidence** Use your evidence and fix-up strategies to complete the chart.

	Text Evidence	Fix-up Strategy
Character	"Maddy Rose"	viewed illustrations to confirm who the main character is
Setting		
Events		
Theme		

Reflect and Share

Write to Sources In *The Scarlet Stockings Spy*, "hardworking little seamstress" Maddy Rose spies for the Patriots during the American Revolution. Consider all the texts you have read this week. What other people fought for something they believed in? Was the risk worth it? How did the settings of the stories affect how the characters responded to challenges? Use these questions to help you write an opinion.

Use Text Evidence In opinion writing, include text evidence that directly supports your opinion statement, or claim. Write one sentence that states your opinion about which character who fights for freedom is the bravest. Then gather evidence from the texts to support your claim.

When citing text evidence in your writing, remember to:

- Place quotation marks around direct quotations from a text.
- Include transitions, such as *consequently* and *specifically*, to link your reasons and opinions.
- Explain how the evidence supports your point.
- End your response with a statement or section that restates your opinion.

Weekly Question

How can ordinary people contribute to a fight for freedom?

Academic Vocabulary

Learning Goal

I can develop knowledge about language to make connections between reading and writing.

A **synonym** is a word with the same or similar meaning as another word. An **antonym** is a word with an opposite meaning. Use the relationships between the two words to better understand each word.

My TURN For each sample thesaurus entry,

1. **Read** the entry word. Note that some words have more than one meaning.
2. **Write** two synonyms and antonyms. Pay attention to the part of speech.
3. **Confirm** your synonyms and antonyms using a print or online dictionary or thesaurus.

grace, *n.* **1** a special quality of great worth Synonyms: ______ Antonyms: ______ **2** a charming, stylish appearance and manner Synonyms: ______ Antonyms: ______ **resist**, *v.* to oppose Synonyms: ______ Antonyms: ______	**limitation**, *n.* **1** a boundary that a person or thing cannot go past Synonyms: ______ Antonyms: ______ **2** the act or state of being contained Synonyms: ______ Antonyms: ______

Word Parts *anti-, mid-, trans-*

Greek and Latin **word parts** often give clues to a word's meaning. These word parts often come at the beginning of base words and roots and add meaning:

- *anti-* means "against" or "opposed"
- *mid-* means "middle"
- *trans-* means "across" or "through"

The word part *mid-* added to the base word *day* creates *midday,* which means "in the middle of the day."

If you know that the word part *trans-* means "across" or "through," you can use that information to read the word *translate*. You can confirm its meaning in a dictionary: "to change from one language to another."

My TURN Match each word from the Word Bank to the correct meaning. Use a print or digital dictionary to check your answers.

Word Bank

antibiotic **midnight** **transnational** **antislavery** **midterm** **transaction**

1. medicine that kills harmful germs antibiotic
2. opposed to slavery ______
3. across the nation ______
4. the middle of the term ______
5. a business deal between people ______
6. the middle of the night ______

Read Like a Writer

An author may choose a narrator who is not a character in the story. Third-person limited point of view uses third-person pronouns such as *he, she, it,* and *they* and focuses on just one character. The author reports what all characters do and say but tells the inner thoughts and feelings of only the main character, the protagonist.

Model! Read the text from *The Scarlet Stockings Spy.*

> "Such poppycock!" she'd cluck to herself. No fancy silks, satins, and brocades imported from London for her. To wear such finery showed loyalty to the king.

Maddy Rose's thoughts and feelings

1. **Identify** Trinka Hakes Noble uses the third-person nouns *she* and *herself* and focuses on Maddy Rose.
2. **Question** What is the effect of this point of view?
3. **Conclude** This point of view allows the reader to experience the inner thoughts and feelings of one character in the story.

Read the text.

> "Oh, Jonathan, you silly goat," Maddy Rose giggled from behind her window, then pulled in her clothesline and slept with a smile on her face.

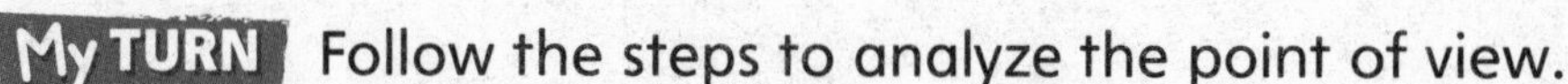

My TURN Follow the steps to analyze the point of view.

1. **Identify** The pronoun ________ identifies the point of view.
2. **Question** What is the effect of this point of view?
3. **Conclude** This point of view allows the reader ____________________

____.

Write for a Reader

Authors carefully select the point of view that will be most effective for a particular narrative. The point of view influences how an author describes events.

My TURN Think about how Trinka Hakes Noble uses point of view in *The Scarlet Stockings Spy* and how it affects you as a reader. Consider how details are revealed or emphasized through the use of third-person limited point of view. Now identify how you can use point of view to shape your story and how your readers experience it.

1. If you were writing a scene containing dialogue, how could third-person point of view give your readers extra insight into one character?

2. Write a conversation in which one of the characters has a secret. Use third-person limited point of view to reveal more than the character says aloud.

Spell Words with *anti-*, *mid-*, *trans-*

The word part *anti-* means "against or opposed." The word part *mid-* means "middle." The word part *trans-* means "across or through."

My TURN Read the words. Spell and sort the words by their word parts.

SPELLING WORDS

transistor	midweek	midnight	transfusion
midpoint	transatlantic	antithesis	midsection
antifreeze	antipathy	transpose	antigravity
translation	midcontinent	transgress	transmission
translucent	transmit	antigen	midstream

anti-

____
____
____
____
____

mid-

____
____
____
____
____
____

trans-

____
____
____
____
____
____
____
____
____

Adjectives

Adjectives describe nouns and pronouns. A **comparative adjective** compares two people, places, things, or groups. A **superlative adjective** compares three or more. Watch for irregular comparative and superlative forms, such as *good, better, best,* and spelling changes in the comparative or superlative form of some adjectives.

Adjectives	Comparative Form + *-er* or *more*	Superlative Form + *-est* or *most*
strong	stronger	strongest
clear	clearer	clearest
noisy	noisier	noisiest
powerful	more powerful	most powerful

Freedom is <u>important</u>.
No struggle is <u>more important</u> than the struggle for liberty.
The <u>most important</u> question is how to protect rights.

My TURN Use comparative and superlative adjectives to write sentences.

1. Comparative adjective using *more*

2. Superlative adjective using *-est*

3. Comparative adjective using *-er*

4. Superlative adjective using *most*

Develop Characters

Learning Goal

I can use elements of science fiction to write a short story.

Writers develop a character by considering how the character would react to a specific problem or situation. In science fiction, as in any fiction writing, characters may be people or animals. However, they may also be made-up creatures or robots.

My TURN Complete the chart to create a character in a science fiction story. Use the details provided to list possible feelings, traits, and actions. Then draw the character.

Character: LMD-180, a robot made for humans; can walk, fly, talk, think, and feel

Setting: Earth, 250 years in the future

Problem: Must show its fearful human family that it wants to help them

Feelings	Traits	Action

Illustration

My TURN In your writing notebook, plan and describe the feelings, traits, and actions of the characters in your own science fiction short story.

Develop Setting

Writers develop a setting by thinking about where and when the events of the story take place. Details of the setting affect the characters and the plot.

My TURN Develop setting details for the story idea provided. Brainstorm ideas in the web. Consider the technology available on the spaceship, what the inside and outside of the spaceship look like, what life is like onboard, what the passengers can see from the windows, and so on.

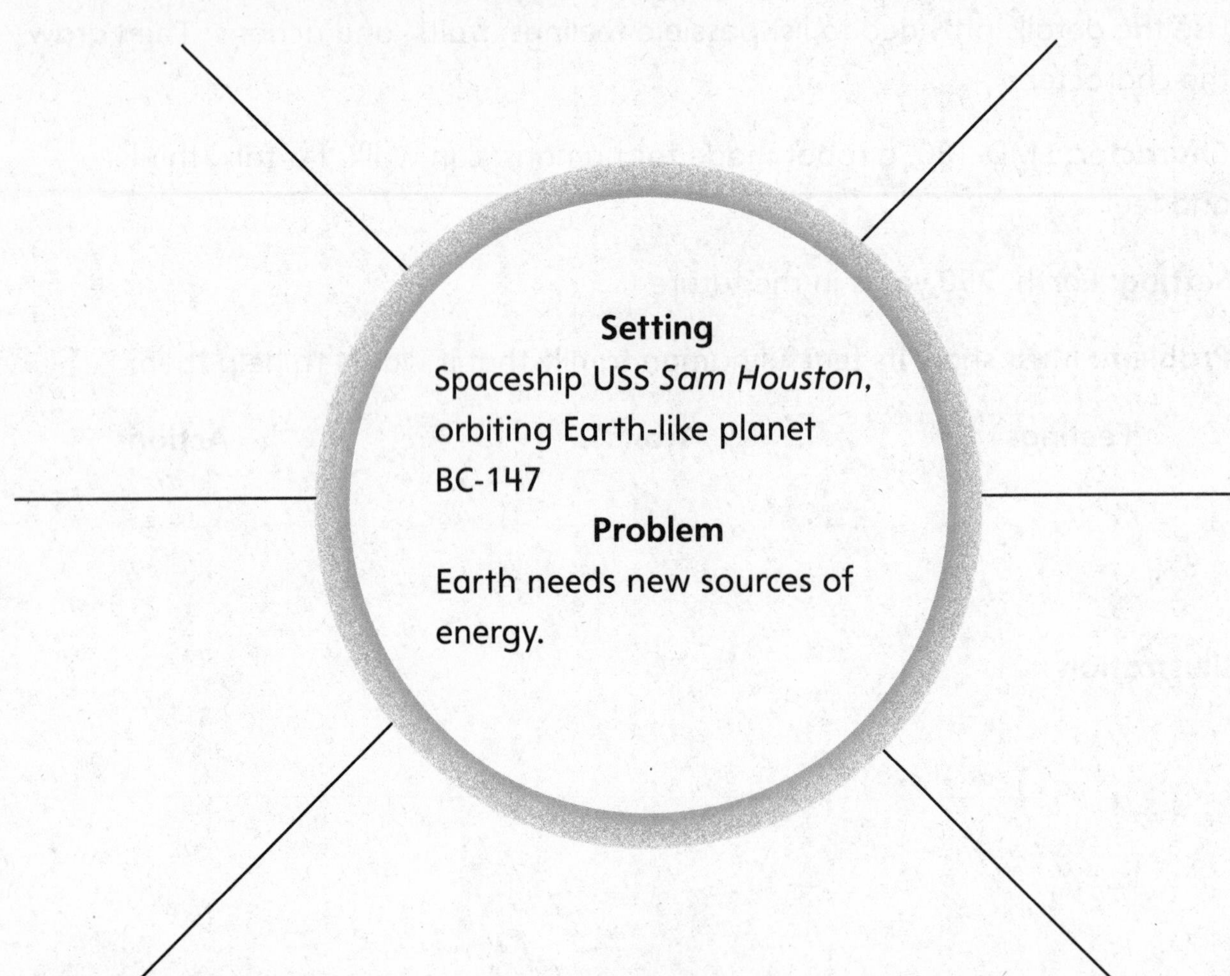

My TURN In your writing notebook, map how the setting affects the problem of your own science fiction short story.

Develop the Conflict

Conflict is the problem or situation that sets a story in motion. There are two main types of conflicts: internal and external.

An **internal conflict** is between the character and himself or herself (for example, a struggle with his or her conscience).

An **external conflict** is between a character and

- another character
- society (for example, a struggle against an unjust law)
- nature (for example, surviving on a mountain during a snowstorm)

A story may use more than one type of conflict.

My TURN Reread a science fiction story from your classroom library. Use the chart to organize details about the conflict and identify it.

Main Character's Goals	Events That Cause Conflict	Opposing Force
Type of Conflict		

My TURN In your writing notebook, identify the conflict the main character will face in your own science fiction short story. Identify the conflict as internal, external, or both.

Develop the Resolution

The climax is the most exciting part of a story. The story ends with a **resolution** that tells what happens to the characters as a result of the climax.

Climax	Resolution
The prince finds Cinderella after searching the entire kingdom.	They lived happily ever after.
Little Red Riding Hood escapes from the wolf with the help of the hunter.	She decides to never travel in the woods alone again.

My TURN Reread a science fiction story from your classroom library. Summarize the main events. Identify the climax. Then describe the resolution.

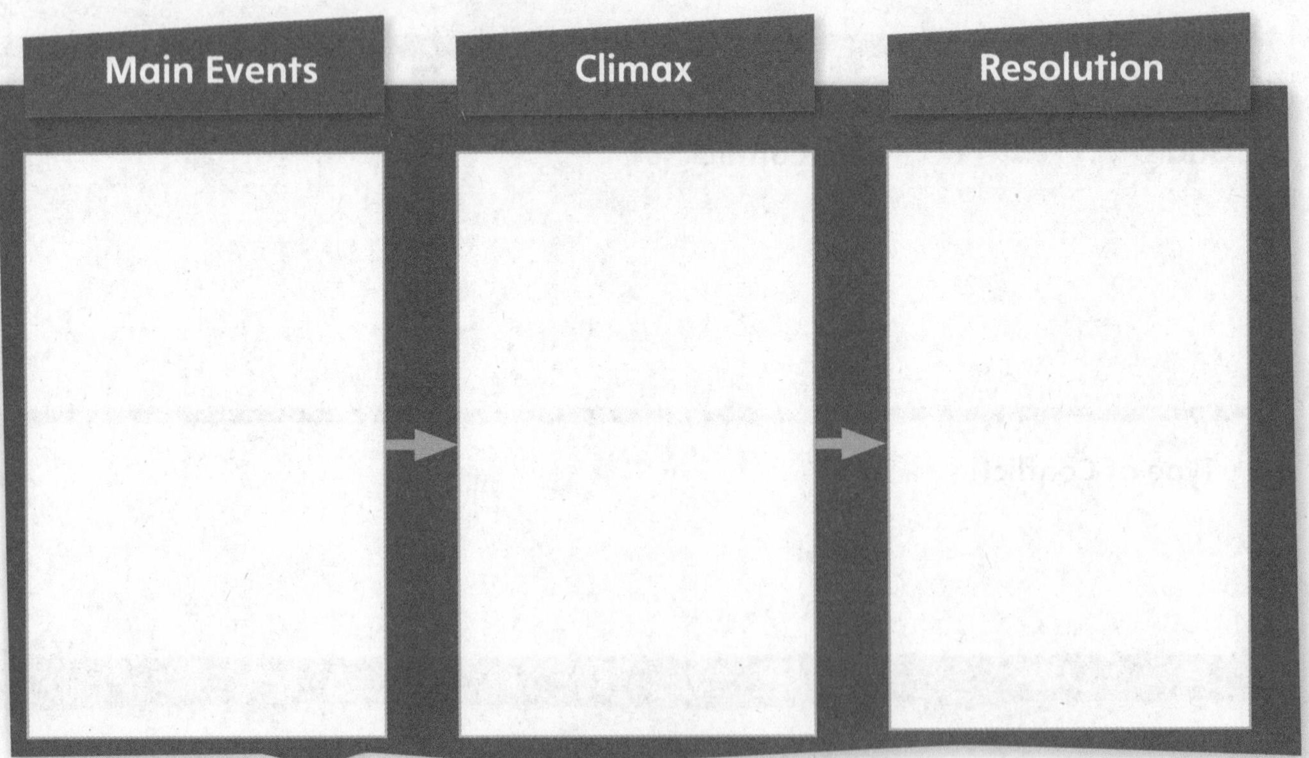

My TURN Plan the plot of your own science fiction short story by developing the climax and resolution of the conflict in your writing notebook.

Develop Dialogue

Dialogue is a written conversation between characters. A writer may use dialogue to develop experiences and events or show the responses of characters to situations in the story. Dialogue allows the characters, not the narrator, to tell what is happening. Dialogue follows rules for punctuating direct speech.

Quotation marks set off dialogue.

"Today we are exploring Lumora," Captain Ruiz announced.

A **comma** separates who is speaking from what is being said.

"There is no air on the planet, so we will have to wear our suits," said Sill.

An **exclamation mark** goes inside the closing quotation mark.

"Ugh!" thought Trox as he rolled his eyes.

A **period** goes inside the closing quotation mark.

He said, "My suit is so uncomfortable."

A **question mark** goes inside the closing quotation mark.

"Well," Sill asked, "do you want to breathe, or not?"

MyTURN In your writing notebook, compose your own science fiction short story using dialogue to develop experiences and events.

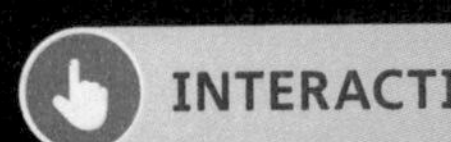

OUR CONSTITUTION

Use the cryptograms to complete each sentence.

A	B	C	D	E	F	G	H	I	J	K	L	M
24	11	8	25	5	15	12	17	19	1	6	14	10
N	O	P	Q	R	S	T	U	V	W	X	Y	Z
7	21	4	20	3	9	13	22	23	16	26	2	18

The first 10 amendments to the Constitution are called

13	17	5		11	19	14	14		21	15		3	19	12	17	13	9

The Bill of Rights was written by

1	24	10	5	9		10	24	25	19	9	21	7

The Bill of Rights has protected the rights of Americans for more than

13	16	21		17	22	7	25	3	5	25		2	5	24	3	9

WEEK 3

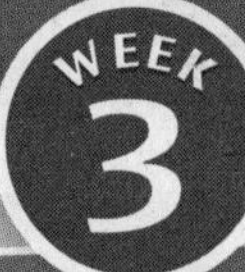

Weekly Question

What can governments do to protect our freedoms?

Quick Write Think about some of the rules at school. How do those rules protect you?

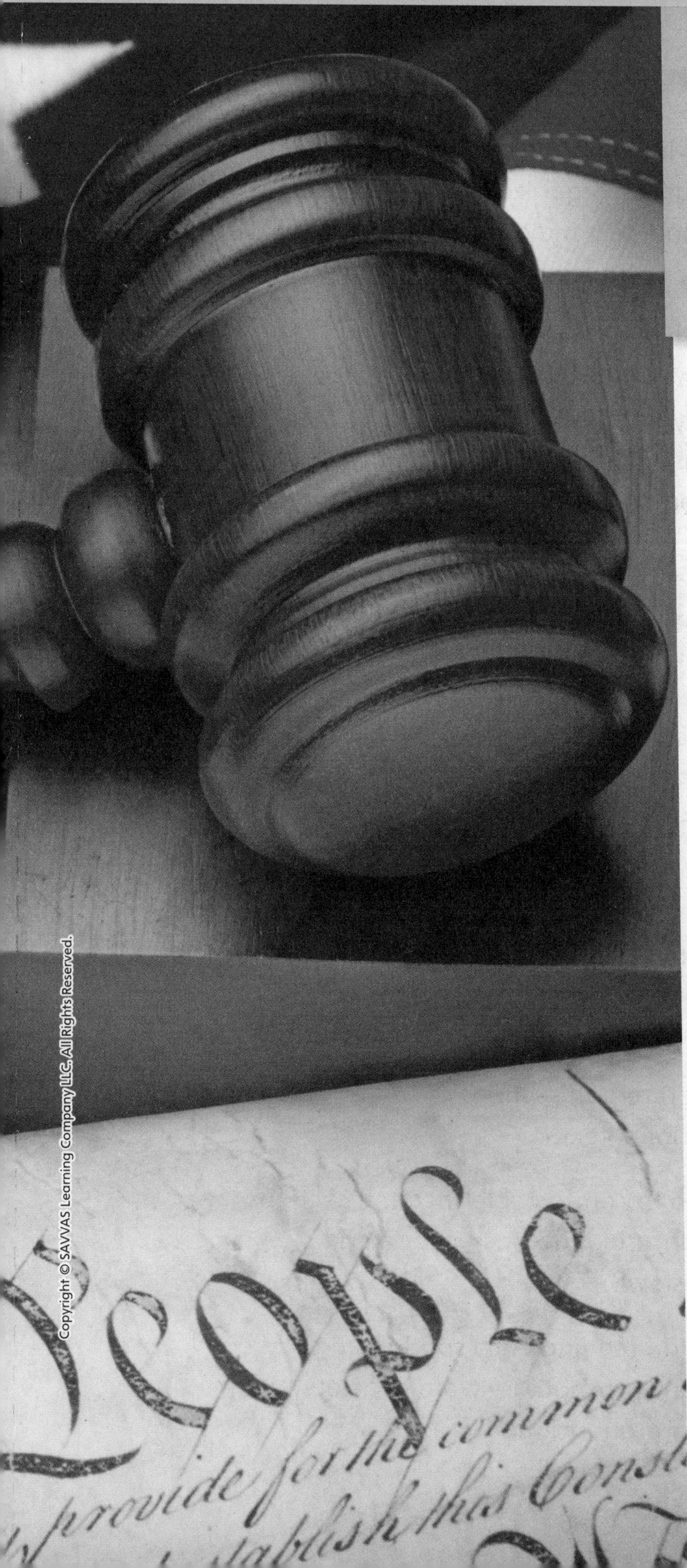

Learning Goal

I can learn about the theme *Liberty* by interpreting text structure in informational text.

Informational Text

A writer of **informational text** will choose a text structure to organize information clearly. Informational text may also include technical vocabulary and such text features as

- A list of the **contents**
- **Titles** for chapters or sections
- **Special type** to show importance
- **Drawings, photographs, diagrams,** or **symbols**
- A **label** or **explanation** for an illustration

TURN and TALK Contrast informational text and historical fiction. Use the anchor chart to help you compare and contrast the genres. Then share your responses with the class.

Look for text features that give information.

Be a Fluent Reader When you read texts aloud, you practice fluency. Fluency is the ability to read a text accurately, with expression, and at an appropriate rate. When you read with appropriate rate, you read neither too fast nor too slow. Reread sections to improve fluency.

When you reread sections of informational text,

- Read at a comfortable speed. If sections are confusing, go back and reread more slowly.
- Focus on reading each specialized or academic vocabulary word accurately with correct pronunciation.

Informational Text Anchor Chart

Purpose:
To communicate facts and information

Text Structures:
Description, chronology, problem and solution, cause and effect, comparison and contrast

Text Features

- Headings and Subheadings
- Table of Contents
- **Boldface** or *Italic* type
- Graphics (charts, diagrams, illustrations, tables, photographs)
- Captions

Meet *the* Author

"'Twas definitely a magical time!" says **Amie Jane Leavitt** about her job shelving beautifully illustrated old books while she was a university student. As a freelance writer, she developed research skills, now one of her favorite parts of writing. She has written many articles and more than 50 books.

from

The Bill of Rights

Preview Vocabulary

As you read *The Bill of Rights*, pay attention to these vocabulary words. Notice how they act as clues to the key ideas.

convention **delegates** **ratification**
petition **violations**

Read

Before you begin, establish a purpose for reading. Active readers of informational text follow these strategies when they read a text the first time.

First Read

Notice	**Generate Questions**
important information, facts, and text features that act as clues to the text structure.	about what you want to understand better.
Connect	**Respond**
this text to other texts you have read about the Constitution.	by marking difficult or confusing parts.

from

THE BILL OF RIGHTS

by Amie Jane Leavitt

AUDIO

ANNOTATE

BACKGROUND

In 1773, Patriots dumped tea into Boston Harbor to protest being taxed for it. The conflict between Britain and the colonies broke out in war in 1775. After the peace treaty, the new nation continued to use the Articles of Confederation adopted during the American Revolution but began work on a Constitution.

CLOSE READ

Interpret Text Structure

Underline a text feature that helps you determine how information is organized.

A New Government

1 Only four years had passed since the end of the Revolutionary War, yet during the hot summer of 1787, leaders of the states were already meeting to discuss a dramatic change in the government. In 1776, during the Revolutionary War, they had written a document called the Articles of Confederation. It explained how the government of the colonies would be organized and how laws would be made. After the war, it became clear that the government described in the Articles would not work for the new nation. It was the responsibility of these leaders—including George Washington, James Madison, Alexander Hamilton, George Mason, and Benjamin Franklin—to agree on how the government of the newly formed United States should be run.

Three patriots lead troops into battle in a painting titled *Spirit of '76* by Archibald M. Willard

Hot Topics

2 The Constitutional Convention lasted from May until September of 1787. During that time, the leaders discussed many important ideas and issues. In their discussions, they sought to answer many questions, such as:

- ★ Who should have more power, the national government or the states?
- ★ How should presidents be elected?
- ★ How should leaders in Congress be elected and how long should they serve?
- ★ Who should have the right to vote?

3 For each of these questions and all the others that were talked about at the convention, there were many different answers and opinions. After much debate, however, a consensus—or agreement—was finally made on many of them. The delegates' final agreement became known as the U.S. Constitution.

The Rights of the People

4 Most of the important questions were agreed upon before the Constitution was finished. Surprisingly, one big question was not: "Should the Constitution protect the rights of the people?"

5 All the leaders at the convention agreed that the rights of people should be protected. After all, a democracy is by definition a government for and of the people. It was because England's King George III abused the rights of the colonists during his rule that they had sought independence during the Revolutionary War. Two opposing groups had strong opinions about why the rights of the people should or should not be in the Constitution.

CLOSE READ

Interpret Text Structure

Underline the text that shows a cause-and-effect relationship between details.

convention a formal meeting of a group with particular interests

delegates people appointed to represent others

CLOSE READ

Interpret Text Structure

Underline sentences that show comparison.

6 One group of leaders, called the Federalists, did not think it was necessary to include a list of rights in the Constitution. In fact, the Federalists feared that by including some rights and not others, the government could actually limit the rights of the people. Another group of leaders, called the Antifederalists, believed the opposite. They felt that if the rights weren't listed in the Constitution, then the government would have the power to take away these rights at any time. By listing them in the Constitution, the rights of the people would be guaranteed and protected.

During King George's rule of the colonies, British sailors would force colonists to serve in the British navy. Called impressment, the practice was one of the ways the king abused individual rights.

7 Most people in the country agreed with the second group of leaders. They remembered what it felt like to have limited rights under King George's rule, and they didn't want that to happen to them again. They wanted a Bill of Rights included in the Constitution.

ratification a formal act of approval or confirmation

8 When the Constitution was sent to the states for ratification, many of the states voiced this opinion. New York, Massachusetts, and Virginia said they wanted a Bill of Rights. They even came up with their own lists of suggestions for the delegates to include. North Carolina and Rhode Island believed so strongly that the Constitution should have a Bill of Rights that they would not approve the Constitution at all unless one was added.

Drafting the Bill

9 Although James Madison was a Federalist, he was also a great writer. Because of this, he was placed on the committee to write the Bill of Rights.

10 Madison looked at many documents when he wrote his list of rights. He wanted to get ideas for what was important to people in his day and in the past. One was the Magna Carta, which was written in England in 1215. Another was the English Bill of Rights, which was written in 1689. He also looked at the lists that were written by some of the states, such as the Virginia Declaration of Rights, written by George Mason in 1776. All of these documents helped Madison come up with a list of rights that he thought would be important to the people of the United States.

Portrait of James Madison, by Gilbert Stuart, 1805

11 By the time Congress met in 1789, Madison had a list of seventeen rights. The leaders in Congress talked about each one. They decided whether each was important or not, and if it was, why it was important. Finally, after talking about the list for the entire summer of 1789, Congress had agreed on twelve amendments to be added to the Constitution.

12 Before anything could be added to the Constitution, though, it had to be approved by the states. The delegates took the list to each of their state legislatures, where the amendments were debated again. In the end, not all twelve amendments were approved—the original amendments 1 and 2 were rejected. The original amendment 3 became amendment 1.

CLOSE READ

Summarize

Highlight information that should be included in a summary of the text.

CLOSE READ

Summarize

Highlight details that summarize the main idea on this page.

13 New Jersey was the first state to approve the ten amendments, and Virginia was the eleventh—the last one needed for ratification. These first ten amendments to the Constitution have been known ever since as the Bill of Rights.

Ratification Dates of the Bill of Rights

STATE	DATE	VOTE
New Jersey	November 20, 1789	Rejected amendment 2
Maryland	December 19, 1789	Approved all amendments
North Carolina	December 22, 1789	Approved all amendments
South Carolina	January 19, 1790	Approved all amendments
New Hampshire	January 25, 1790	Rejected amendment 2
Delaware	January 28, 1790	Rejected amendment 1
New York	February 27, 1790	Rejected amendment 2
Pennsylvania	March 10, 1790	Rejected amendment 2
Rhode Island	June 7, 1790	Rejected amendment 2
Vermont	November 3, 1791	Approved all amendments
Virginia	December 15, 1791	Approved all amendments

One of the two amendments that did not make it into the Bill of Rights was never added to the Constitution. The other was added centuries later—in 1992. It is the 27th Amendment, which states that members of Congress cannot change their rate of pay for the current term.

14 Only 11 states needed to approve the Bill of Rights for it to be ratified. Massachusetts, Connecticut, and Georgia did not vote to ratify the document until 1939, when the Bill of Rights was 150 years old. Vermont had become a state less than a year before ratification—on March 4, 1791.

Freedom to Believe, Speak, Worship, and Assemble

15 Have you ever wondered what it might be like to live in a place where you were only allowed to say, do, and believe things that a government agreed with? Believe it or not, many people today live in places that are like this. The First Amendment in the Bill of Rights gives U.S. citizens the right to speak, write, worship, and assemble without fear of punishment.

Freedom of Speech

16 In October 2010, a woman in China added a comment and retweeted her fiancé's Twitter post. He had written about a Chinese protest against Japan; she had jokingly added the words, "Charge, angry youth." Eleven days later—on the day they had planned to marry—both the woman and her fiancé were arrested. The fiancé was released five days later, but the woman was sentenced to one year in a labor camp. Her crime: disturbing social stability.

Chinese students raised a bronze replica of the Goddess of Democracy, an icon of free speech and democracy, in 2010. The students were marking the 21st anniversary of the Tiananmen Square protests for democracy, which had ended in violence.

17 It is this exact type of situation that the framers of the Constitution feared. They did not ever want the U.S. government to have the ability to limit the things people can say. In order to protect the right to freedom of speech, they included it in the First Amendment to the Constitution:

CLOSE READ

Interpret Text Structure

Underline words in the caption and title that that help you determine the author's purpose for this section.

CLOSE READ

Summarize

Highlight details on both pages that should be included in a summary of the section about freedom of religion.

petition a formal request signed by many people

Amendment I

Congress shall make no law respecting an establishment of religion, or prohibiting the free exercise thereof; or abridging the freedom of speech, or of the press; or the right of the people peaceably to assemble, and to petition the Government for a redress of grievances.

In the 1940s, the Committee for the First Amendment, made up of people who included actors Humphrey Bogart and Lauren Bacall, was established to protest the witchhunt of individuals in Hollywood who were targeted as communists based on their beliefs. Standing in court from left: Danny Kaye, June Havoc, Bogart, and Bacall (seated).

18 Freedom of speech is just one of the rights protected by the First Amendment. Other rights include freedom of religion, freedom to worship, freedom to assemble peacefully, and freedom to make a complaint against the government.

Freedom of Religion

19 One of the reasons early settlers moved from Europe to North America was for freedom of religion. The Pilgrims, for example, were not allowed to practice their religion freely in England. If they did, they faced persecution and sometimes imprisonment. They left their homes and braved the dangers of the New World so that they could worship without fear of punishment. In 1620, they founded Plymouth Colony.

20 Quakers came to Pennsylvania, a colony that William Penn set up for them in 1682. Many Catholics settled in Maryland because Lord Baltimore had founded the colony to protect those who believed in that faith.

21 The First Amendment actually protects several ideas associated with freedom of religion. First, it says: "Congress shall make no law respecting an establishment of religion." This means that the U.S. government cannot make laws about religion. It also means that the government cannot make a "state religion" or say that everyone must follow a certain religion.

22 The second part says: "or prohibiting the free exercise thereof." This simply means that the government cannot keep people from practicing their religion. The Constitution lets people believe in whatever religion they want to, and it protects people who don't want to practice any religion at all. Because the government may not interfere with religious worship, the United States enjoys "separation of church and state."

Freedom of the Press

23 "Freedom of the press" refers to the printing press. It is the freedom to print people's ideas in magazines, newspapers, books, and other forms of media. People in the United States can read different ideas and viewpoints in newspapers or on the Internet. They can listen to news reporters describing events on television. Since things have always been that way in the United States, it may not sound like an important right, but there are many cases where people who have not had this right have suffered.

CLOSE READ

Interpret Text Structure

Underline clues on both pages that help you determine chronological order.

CLOSE READ

Interpret Text Structure

Underline a paragraph that is an example of a description of what happens when there is no freedom of the press.

Vocabulary in Context

Underline context clues around *persecute* in paragraph 25 that help you determine the word's meaning.

Summarize

Highlight the main idea that summarizes paragraph 26.

24 For example, just one month after Adolf Hitler rose to power in Germany, the lives of Germans began to change. It was February 1933, and a fire had broken out in an important government building. Even though no one knew for sure who had started the fire, the Nazis believed it was a group of communists trying to take over the government. Hitler and the other Nazi leaders said they had to act quickly to protect Germany and its people.

25 They changed the country's constitution and took away the civil liberties of the German people. Germans could no longer express their opinions. They could no longer write and print their ideas and beliefs. They could no longer gather in groups. They could no longer talk on the telephone or send mail without the government being able to listen in or read their words. The government could search their houses whenever they wanted and take anything they wanted. These new laws gave the Nazis almost unlimited power. They could now persecute and harm groups of people without technically breaking any German laws.

26 After the Nazis changed their constitution, they used the press to further control the population. People could no longer read any news except what the Nazis wanted them to read. What the Nazis approved was usually false. The way the news was written made the Nazis and their views look good and right, while people from different ethnic, religious, and political groups were portrayed as evil and inhuman. They also controlled what was broadcast over the radio and what was shown at movie theaters. They burned books they didn't agree with, including religious books, and artwork they thought was inappropriate.

In February 1933, arsonists set fire to the Reichstag—the German parliamentary building. Because of this event, the Nazis drastically changed the German constitution and severely limited the rights of the people.

27 These changes helped the Nazis execute their plan of widespread persecution across Germany and the countries they conquered during World War II.

28 The Nazi government hasn't been the only one to try to control the press. Countries such as China, North Korea, Iran, and Vietnam do not allow freedom of the press for their people. Reporters Without Borders has assembled a map that shows what countries have the most and least restrictions on freedom of the press. The people who live in the countries in red and dark orange have very few freedoms to write what they want, and the government controls the information they receive.

29 Although people in the United States have the right to a free press, they do not have the right to print what they know is a lie. This type of writing is called libel, and because it can harm other people, it is against the law.

CLOSE READ

Interpret Text Structure

Underline details that reveal the author's purpose in comparing and contrasting the United States with other countries.

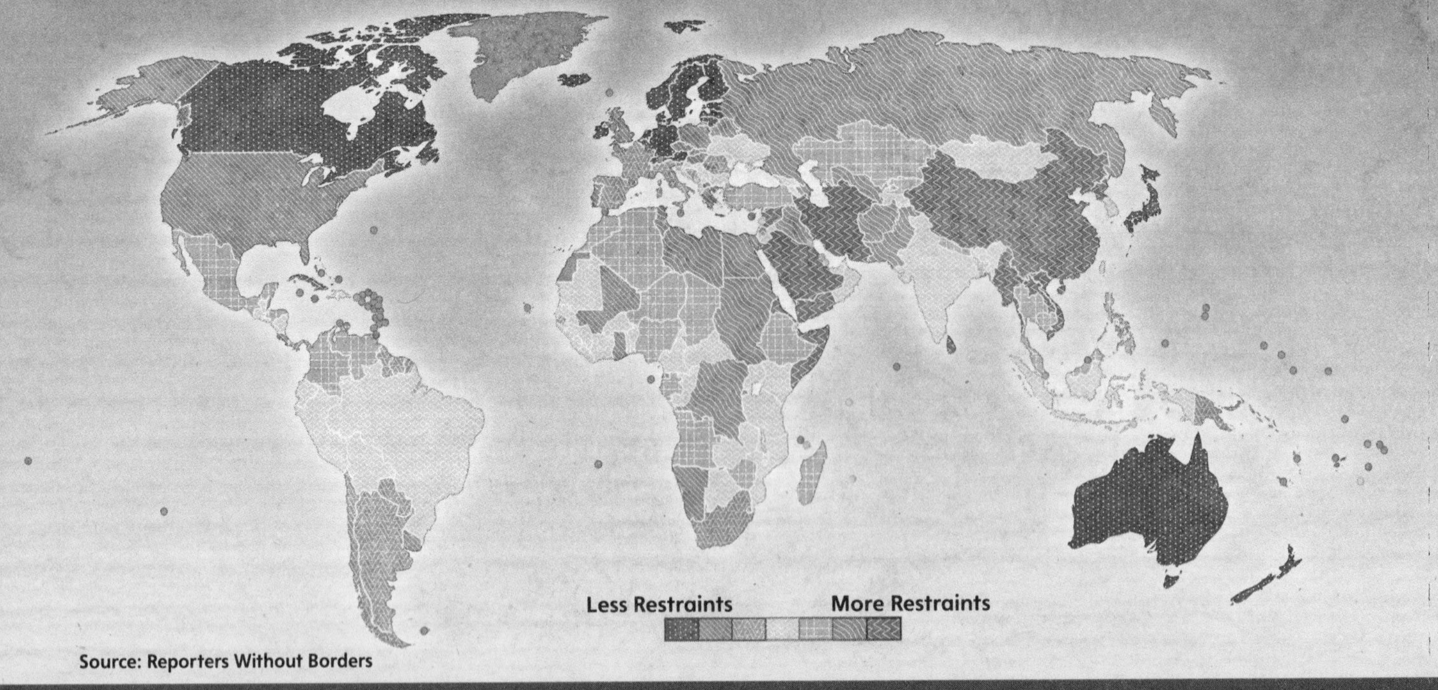

The colors on this map indicate which countries have the least and most restrictions on freedom of the press. If you live in a country that is shaded blue, your government does not limit the information you can read and write. If you live in a country shaded in red or orange, you are severely limited.

CLOSE READ

Summarize

Highlight text features on both pages that summarize each section.

Freedom to Assemble

30 *To assemble* means "to gather in groups." With this freedom, people can get together with other people and talk about ideas. They can protest things they don't agree with—they just have to do so peacefully. Depending on where they want to gather, they may also need to get a permit.

Freedom to Petition the Government

31 If you live in the United States and the government does something you don't like, you can tell the government how you feel. You can write a letter to any leader and express your feelings.

32 In the 1700s, the colonists tried to do this when they disagreed with the laws of King George III. Instead of listening to their grievances, the king passed more

laws to punish the colonists. Since the colonists didn't have any say in what laws were passed—they had no representatives in the British government—there was very little they could do. That was the main reason they fought for their freedom in the Revolutionary War.

33 Today, you can petition the government whenever you want. If you don't like something that has happened in your town, you can go to a city council meeting and speak in front of the leaders. You can also write a letter to the mayor and explain your views. Not only can you write to the leaders of your town, but you can also write or call the leaders of your county, state, or nation.

CLOSE READ

Interpret Text Structure

Underline details that reveal how the author uses structure to organize the text.

You can write to your senator or representative in Congress. Their addresses are available online.

Preservation and Promotion

Global Impact of the Bill of Rights

34 The Bill of Rights, one of the most important documents in the U.S. government, has protected the rights of Americans for more than 200 years. Because it has been so successful, it has been used as the basis for similar bills of rights for other countries and for international law.

International Law

35 Because of the human rights violations that happened during World War II, after the war the leaders of the victorious nations agreed that a Bill of Rights was necessary for all people everywhere. The United Nations was established in 1945 in order to curb warfare and to protect human rights around the

violations acts that disregard an agreement, law, or rule

CLOSE READ

Interpret Text Structure

Underline the solution to the problem in paragraph 35.

The United Nations building is located on the east side of New York's island of Manhattan. Once you enter the United Nations' 18-acre property, you are no longer in the United States but are instead on international soil.

world. In December 1948, the General Assembly of the United Nations agreed on the Universal Declaration of Human Rights. It included 30 groups of rights, such as the following:

- ★ Everyone has the right to life, liberty and security of person.
- ★ No one shall be held in slavery.
- ★ No one shall be subjected to torture or to cruel, inhuman or degrading treatment or punishment.
- ★ Everyone has the right to recognition everywhere as a person before the law.
- ★ No one shall be subjected to arbitrary arrest, detention or exile.
- ★ Everyone is entitled in full equality to a fair and public hearing by an independent and impartial tribunal, in the determination of his rights and obligations and of any criminal charge against him.
- ★ Everyone has the right to leave any country, including his own, and to return to his country.
- ★ Everyone has the right to a nationality.

★ Men and women of full age ... have the right to marry and to found a family.

★ Everyone has the right to own property alone as well as in association with others.

★ Everyone has the right to freedom of thought, conscience and religion.

★ Everyone has the right to freedom of opinion and expression.

★ Everyone has the right to freedom of peaceful assembly and association.

CLOSE READ

Summarize

Highlight information that should be included in a summary of the text.

36 Do some of these rights sound similar to the ones found in the U.S. Bill of Rights? How about the cruel punishment, fair hearing (trial), and freedom of religion, expression, and assembly?

37 This Universal Declaration of Human Rights has helped protect people around the world. However, there are still many countries that refuse to give people basic human rights. The goal of the United Nations is to eventually have every country on earth value the rights of its people more than the power of its own government.

First Lady Eleanor Roosevelt holds a copy of the United Nations Universal Declaration of Human Rights written in Spanish

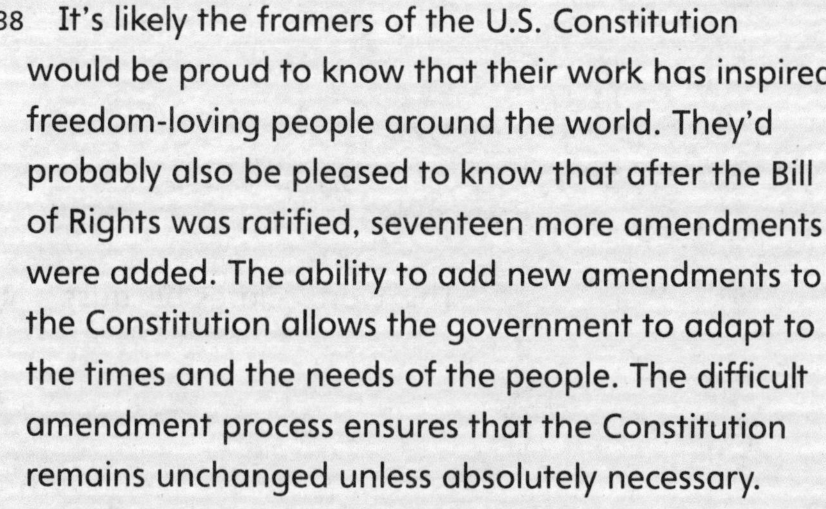
38 It's likely the framers of the U.S. Constitution would be proud to know that their work has inspired freedom-loving people around the world. They'd probably also be pleased to know that after the Bill of Rights was ratified, seventeen more amendments were added. The ability to add new amendments to the Constitution allows the government to adapt to the times and the needs of the people. The difficult amendment process ensures that the Constitution remains unchanged unless absolutely necessary.

Fluency

Read paragraphs 35–38 aloud with a partner to practice reading accurately. Focus on reading each word correctly.

Develop Vocabulary

In this informational text, domain-specific vocabulary relates to U.S. history and the topic of *liberty.* Precise words clarify information and help readers better understand the topic.

My TURN Identify the main idea of *The Bill of Rights.* Then complete the activity. Explain how each word relates to the main idea.

Word Bank

convention **delegates** **ratification** **petition**

convention
This word relates because leaders wanted to agree about the direction of the nation.

This word relates because

Main Idea

This word relates because

This word relates because

Check for Understanding

MyTURN Look back at the text to answer the questions.

1. How do you know that *The Bill of Rights* is an informational text?

2. With a partner, retell details from the text that show differences between the Federalists and the Antifederalists. What was the significance of these groups?

3. Draw conclusions about why the author included the examples of the Chinese woman imprisoned for commenting on a social media post and Germany under the Nazis.

4. Compare and contrast the freedoms that are listed in the Bill of Rights and in the Universal Declaration of Human Rights. How are the documents similar, and why are both important?

Interpret Text Structure

An author chooses a **text structure** that creates a logical order and shows the order of importance of details in the text. The text structure depends on the information provided. Some common structures include comparison and contrast, cause and effect, and chronology. An author may use a single text structure for the entire text or different structures for different sections. To interpret text structure, use transitions as clues.

1. MY TURN Go to the Close Read notes in *The Bill of Rights* and underline the parts that help you interpret, or recognize, its text structures.
2. **Text Evidence** Use the parts you underlined to complete the chart. Then use information in the chart to compare and contrast text structures.

Comparison and Contrast

Transition words: *However, one, another, instead*

Example:

Cause and Effect

Transition words: *Because, then, for, as a result, after all*

Example:

Reread an informational text from your classroom library. Identify transition words to interpret its structure. Then compare and contrast that text's structure with the structure of *The Bill of Rights*. On your own paper, analyze how the text structure contributes to each author's purpose for writing.

Summarize

You can **summarize** ideas in a text to understand what you read. In a summary, briefly restate the main idea and key details in the text, in a clear and logical order. Maintain the meaning of the original text, but use your own words.

1. **My TURN** Go back to the Close Read notes and highlight text that helps you summarize information in a way that maintains meaning and order.

2. **Text Evidence** Use your highlighted text to create a summary of one section of *The Bill of Rights*.

Section	"Freedom of Religion"
Main Idea	
Key Details	
Summary	

Reflect and Share

Write to Sources *The Bill of Rights* outlines freedoms protected by the U.S. government. Consider the texts you have read this week. What have you learned about the freedoms that people want and need? Use examples from the texts you read this week to write and support a response.

Notetaking When interacting with sources, you can take notes to organize and understand facts and details.

Choose two texts that include information about freedoms. Use the questions to take notes on a separate piece of paper:

- Which freedoms are mentioned in the text?
- Which freedoms are protected by the government?
- Which freedoms do people want most?
- Which freedoms do people need most?

Generate and answer your own questions about freedoms to deepen your understanding and gain information. Review your notes and use them to write a brief response on another piece of paper.

Weekly Question

What can governments do to protect our freedoms?

Academic Vocabulary

Learning Goal

I can develop knowledge about language to make connections between reading and writing.

Context clues are the words, phrases, or sentences around an unfamiliar word that can help you determine its meaning. Some types of context clues are synonyms, antonyms, examples, and definitions.

My TURN For each pair of sentences,

1. **Read** the sentences.
2. **Identify** the context clue or clues for each bold word.
3. **Tell** what type of context clue is used.

Sentences	Context Clues	Type of Context Clue
Tariq had only one **limitation**, or restriction. He had to be home by eleven.	restriction	synonym
Sam showed impressive **grace** on the basketball court. Ben, on the other hand, was clumsy.		
We learned to **empower** ourselves. We earned our own money and made decisions without anyone's permission.		
The fifth graders **resisted** changes to the lunch menu. With a petition, students fought to keep them from happening.		

Word Parts *sub-*, *super-*

Latin **word parts** often give clues to a word's meaning. You can confirm a word's origin by looking it up in a dictionary. These word parts often come at the beginning of a word and add meaning: *sub-* means "under" or "near," and *super-* means "above and beyond."

The word part *sub-* added to the base word *way* creates *subway*, which means "an underground way or path."

If you know the meaning of the word part *super-*, you can read the word *supervisor* and confirm its meaning in a dictionary: "someone who is in charge."

My TURN Use your knowledge of word parts to read each word and infer its meaning. Use a dictionary to check your definition. Then write a sentence with the new word.

Word Bank

superstore **supersede** **suburb** **submarine**

1. Meaning: a huge store ______________________

____

2. Meaning: an underwater ship ______________________

____

3. Meaning: an area near a city ______________________

____

4. Meaning: to take the place of something ______________________

____

Read Like a Writer

The author's purpose is his or her reason for writing. Possible purposes include to persuade, to inform, to entertain, and to express.

Model Read the text from *The Bill of Rights.*

Only 11 states needed to approve the Bill of Rights for it to be ratified.

fact about ratification

1. **Identify** Amie Jane Leavitt states a fact.
2. **Question** How does this help me understand her purpose?
3. **Conclude** The fact tells me that the purpose is to inform readers about how many states were needed to ratify the Bill of Rights.

Reread paragraph 35 from *The Bill of Rights.*

My TURN Follow the steps to analyze the text. Describe the author's purpose.

1. **Identify** Amie Jane Leavitt states ____________________
   ____
   ____.
2. **Question** How does the information help me understand her purpose?
3. **Conclude** The information tells me that purpose is ________________
   ____
   ____.

Write for a Reader

One reason authors write is to inform their readers. An author may explain something, give directions, or provide facts and details about a topic.

My TURN Think about how Amie Jane Leavitt's statements reveal her purpose in writing *The Bill of Rights*. Now identify how you can set a purpose to connect with your readers.

1. If your purpose was to inform readers about a topic related to the American Revolution, what topic would you choose? What kind of facts and information would support your ideas?

2. Write an informational passage about a topic, and include supporting details to develop your topic. Make sure your main ideas, facts, and details reveal your purpose for writing.

Spell Words with *sub-*, *super-*

The word part *sub-* means "under" or "near." The word part *super-* means "above and beyond."

My TURN Read the words. Spell and sort the words by their word parts.

SPELLING WORDS

supersonic	supersede	subconscious	subsidiary
subway	supernova	superior	supervisor
superstar	substitute	superintendent	subsequent
subset	supervision	subordinate	subdivision
submarine	submerse	supermarket	superlative

sub-

super-

Coordinating and Subordinating Conjunctions

A compound sentence has two or more independent clauses, or complete thoughts. The independent clauses are connected by a **coordinating conjunction**, such as *and*, *but*, or *or*. A complex sentence has one independent clause and one or more subordinate clauses. A subordinate clause does not express a complete thought. Clauses in a complex sentence are connected by a **subordinating conjunction**, such as *because*, *if*, *then*, *when*, *before*, or *after*. If a subordinate clause appears first in a sentence, use a comma to separate it from the independent clause.

Type and Examples	Use
coordinating *and, but, or*	**Compound sentence:** Federalists thought one way, <u>but</u> Antifederalists disagreed.
subordinating *because, if, then, when, before, after,*	**Complex sentence:** <u>Because</u> he was known as a great writer, he was assigned to work on the document. **Complex sentence:** They revolted <u>when</u> they were taxed unfairly.

My TURN Edit this draft by adding coordinating or subordinating conjunctions to create a compound sentence and a complex sentence.

New York and Massachusetts wanted a Bill of Rights. The outcome was uncertain. Eventually, an agreement was reached. The representatives had talked a long time. They reached a decision.

Organize an Introduction

Learning Goal

I can use elements of science fiction to write a short story.

The beginning of a science fiction short story introduces the characters or narrator and establishes the situation. The introduction makes the reader want to read the rest of the story.

Lira walked in her mother's steps. The imprints of her mother's boots were easy to see. No wind would ever erase them from the surface of this planet. Lira smiled to think how a scientist studying their footprints decades from now would wonder what kind of tech could have made a set of large prints with a smaller set inside. Her smile faded when she remembered what they were setting out to do.

- Immediately introduces two characters
- Introduces the situation the characters find themselves in
- Hooks readers' interest in a problem that promises to move the story forward

My TURN In your writing notebook, develop a draft of the introduction of your science fiction short story. Use the chart to plan your story.

Title		
Hook		
Characters	**Situation**	**Details**

Organize a Sequence of Events

All stories follow an organized **sequence of events**. Most writers use transitions such as *first, then, last,* and *meanwhile* to show the order of events. Sometimes a writer reveals details through a **flashback** to an earlier time. A flashback can clarify details or surprise readers.

My TURN Number the paragraphs to put the story in chronological order. Decide where the flashback best fits into the story.

_______ "Dr. Rand isn't here, but if he knew what the sensor said, he would want a sample of this energy source," she thought. She used her chisel to break off a piece of the rock.

_______ Before she did anything else, Juno checked the display glowing green inside her visor. Her gaze caught on a blinking light. "That can't be right," she thought.

_______ Juno jumped down from the shuttle. The soft red dirt that billowed around her gravity boots was the only evidence that she had just become the first human to set foot on Alpha Terra 8.

_______ The sensor told her that AT8 rocks had energy that could be used on Earth. Juno took out a sample kit. Then she made a decision.

Place this flashback after paragraph _______.

Two weeks ago, Juno had tried to plan for this very situation. "What will I find on AT8, doctor?" Juno had asked. "You may find some new energy sources," Dr. Rand said, "but they might not be safe. If your sensors blink, be very careful."

My TURN In your writing notebook, develop a draft of your own science fiction short story. Use a sequence of events that is organized and clear.

Choose Pacing of Events

A writer uses **pacing** to build events toward a climax, or turning point. Pacing controls how quickly events are presented. Different genres require different pacing. For example, an adventure story builds suspense and excitement by rapidly presenting events to the reader.

Writers can adjust pacing by including more or less detail and description. They can use dialogue to speed up or slow down the events in a story.

My TURN Read the science fiction story. Mark on the line where the pacing of the story falls. Then answer the questions.

"Hold on, now!" Ramon yelled as he tried to maintain control of his speeder. The alarms inside the cockpit seemed to yell back at him. The hoverdrive was about to give out. A wall of the canyon sped toward them. "No, no, no! Pull UP!" he shouted as he pulled on the steering controls.

Gradually ←——————————→ Rapidly

1. What details help you identify the pacing?

2. Did the pacing seem appropriate for the kind of story? Why or why not?

3. If you were the writer, how would you have paced the events?

My TURN In your writing notebook, develop a draft of your science fiction short story. Use appropriate pacing.

Develop the Plot

A writer develops a plot by providing **concrete words and phrases** with **sensory details**. Concrete words and phrases describe events or objects that can be experienced directly. Sensory details appeal to the senses: sight, hearing, taste, smell, and touch.

My TURN Write a sentence based on each idea. Use concrete words and phrases and sensory details. The first example has been completed for you.

1. The planet you can see from your spaceship windows

   The orange sun rose over the glittering, watery planet, briefly blinding me before revealing thousands of small islands.

2. New technology that allows you to time travel

3. The leak in your spacesuit that lets oxygen escape

4. The food you eat while working on your space station

5. The music you hum that is inspired by the stars

My TURN In your writing notebook, develop a draft of your science fiction short story. Use concrete words and sensory details to describe events and experiences.

Select a Different Genre

A writer chooses a genre based on his or her purpose for writing. The major literary genres of poetry, drama, and narrative fiction have several subgenres. This list shows just a few subgenres.

Poetry	Drama, or Play	Narrative Fiction
Narrative Poetry	Comedy	Science Fiction
Lyric Poetry	Tragedy	Realistic Fiction
Free Verse	Historical Drama	Historical Fiction
Epic Poetry	Courtroom Drama	Fables and Folk Tales

My TURN Read the summary of a science fiction story. Choose a different genre and explain to a partner how you could change the story to fit it.

Rix works on a huge space station that delivers supplies all over the galaxy. When he learns that settlers who live on faraway planets need basic supplies, he makes a plan. Rix stocks up his cargo spaceship with machines that will help settlers make food, water, and building materials. He arrives just in time to save a settlement on New Horizon, where he becomes a local hero.

My TURN Identify a topic, purpose, and audience. Then select any genre, and plan a draft by brainstorming your ideas.

The Early CIVIL RIGHTS Movement

MARCH 23, 1951

Farmville, Virginia

Student leaders organized a schoolwide strike to protest conditions for African American students at the county high school.

MAY 17, 1954

Supreme Court

The landmark court case *Brown v. Board of Education* established that school segregation was unconstitutional.

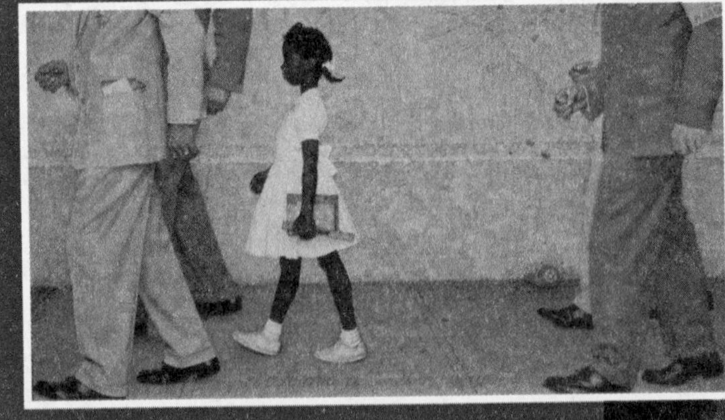

WEEK 4

Weekly Question

What are some things people can do when their freedom is limited?

TURN and TALK What are some ways you can peacefully protest? Discuss this with a partner, and take notes on each other's ideas to share with the class.

AUGUST 28, 1963

Washington, D.C.

One hundred years after the Emancipation Proclamation freed most enslaved Americans, more than 200,000 people gathered to support equal civil rights. At this march, Martin Luther King Jr. gave his famous "I Have a Dream" speech.

AUGUST 6, 1965

Washington, D.C.

The Voting Rights Act of 1965 gave legal protections to voters. It also made it a federal crime to block people from exercising their right to vote. Before the act, some voters were forced to take discriminatory "literacy tests" before voting.

Learning Goal

I can learn more about the theme *Liberty* by explaining relationships between ideas in a biography.

Biography

A biography is the story of a real person's life written by another person.

- The author gives **facts** and **details** to create a portrait of the person's life.
- The author **analyzes** the **relationships** between major events in the person's life.
- The author uses third-person **point of view.**

TURN and TALK Describe how a biography is similar to and different from historical fiction. Use the chart to help you compare and contrast the genres. Take notes on your discussion. Then share your responses with the class.

My NOTES

To compare genres, start with similarities. Then look for differences.

BIOGRAPHY

anchor chart

PURPOSE: To tell the story of a (usually notable) person's life

ELEMENTS of BIOGRAPHY

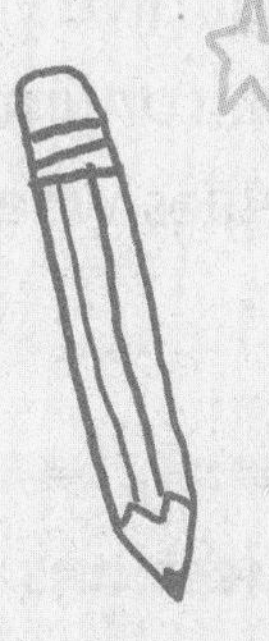

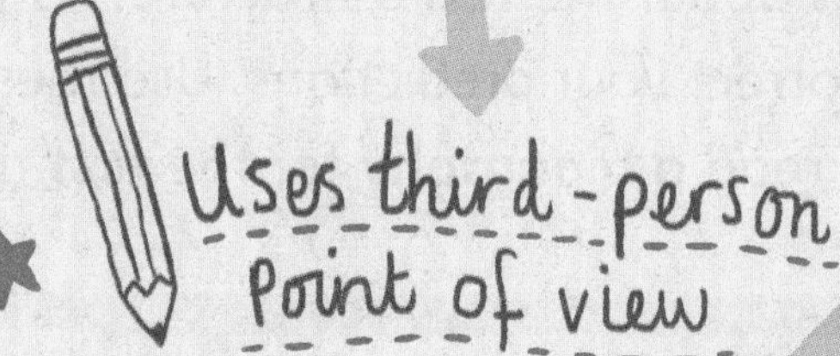

Uses third-person point of view

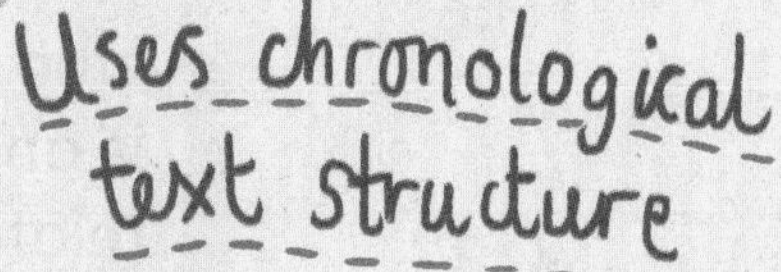

Uses chronological text structure

Shows relationships between the person and other people and events

Is written by another person

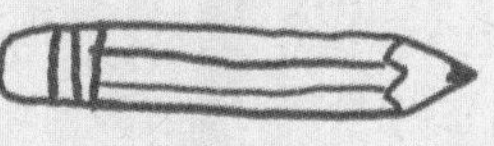

Meet *the* Author

As a child in the segregated South, **Jim Haskins** attended a school that used out-of-date, inaccurate textbooks. He became an elementary school teacher and then a university professor. He made it his mission to write books that would give children an accurate and positive view of African Americans and their accomplishments.

Delivering Justice

Preview Vocabulary

As you read *Delivering Justice*, pay attention to these vocabulary words. Notice how they connect to the topic of civil rights.

segregation **mistreated**
qualified **demonstrators** **sympathize**

Read

Before you read, make predictions and ask questions about the text. Look for transition words that give you clues about the text's structure. As you read, confirm or correct your predictions. Use these strategies when you read a **biography** for the first time.

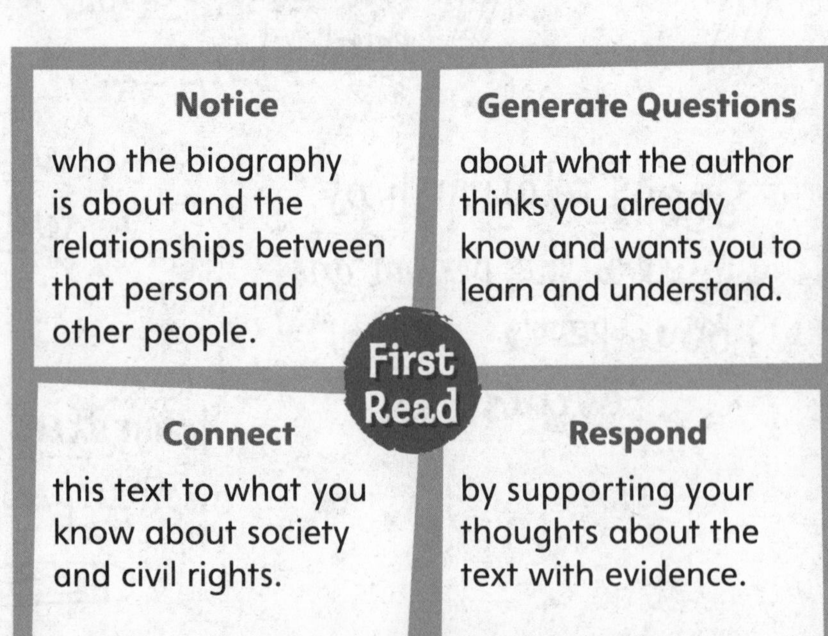

Genre Biography

Delivering Justice

by Jim Haskins

AUDIO

ANNOTATE

Generate Questions

Highlight details that help you ask or answer a question about Westley's relationship with his mother.

Savannah, Georgia, 1932

1 The smell of his grandma's biscuits lured Westley to the kitchen. Westley was excited because today was Thursday, the day he would see his mother. The rest of the week, she worked for a white family just outside Savannah, cooking, cleaning, and taking care of their children. This was her day off.

2 Grandma's friend Old John was sitting at the table. Westley loved listening to the old man's stories. Old John had been born a slave. He had been taken from his mother and had never known her. He was nine—Westley's age—when he and all the slaves were freed in 1865. Westley felt lucky—at least he saw his own mama once a week.

Explain Relationships Between Ideas

Underline details that help you understand inequality in Savannah in 1932.

Easter Shopping at Levy's

3 Once a year, sometime before Easter, Grandma would take Westley downtown to Levy's Department Store on Broughton Street to buy one nice outfit. They used a Levy's charge card and then paid a little bit each month.

4 On one shopping trip, the saleswoman would not serve them until after all the white customers had been helped. Westley had heard the saleswoman politely call the white women customers "Miss" and "Mrs." But she treated his grandma as if she were a child, a nobody.

5 Westley's grandma pretended not to notice. She was polite. But she was also proud. "Come on," she said, "it's time to go home." They left the store without buying a thing.

Segregation

6 Back then, black people weren't treated as well as white people. Most of the time, they were kept segregated from whites. Westley went to a separate school for black children. He had to drink from water fountains marked "Colored." He could not sit and eat at the Levy's lunch counter.

CLOSE READ

Generate Questions

Highlight details that raise questions about how black people were treated in the South.

segregation official separation of groups of people based on a characteristic such as race or gender

CLOSE READ

Generate Questions

Highlight details that help you ask or answer a question about Westley's motivation to work hard.

mistreated treated in an unkind or cruel way

His Grandma's Prayers

7 Sometimes Westley got angry that black people were mistreated and that no matter how hard his mother worked, they were still poor. But his grandma was always there to talk with him. She understood why he was upset, but she didn't want him to have bad feelings about himself.

8 She said that no matter how he was treated, he had no excuse not to "be somebody." She told him again about the day he was born. She said, "I got on my knees and prayed that you would grow up to be a leader of our people."

9 Westley promised himself that he would fulfill his grandma's prayer. He also promised himself that he would work hard so that one day his mother would not have to work in someone else's house.

Voter Schools, 1942

10 Westley knew that many black people didn't vote because they had to pass a test to register. The test was designed to be difficult for black folk to pass. It was intended to keep them from voting.

11 Westley was a member of the Youth Council of the NAACP—the National Association for the Advancement of Colored People. The Youth Council started a special "Voter school" in the basement of a church.

12 With his friend Clifford, Westley talked to everyone, even passersby, about voting. When he found someone who, scared by the test, had never registered to vote, he took them to the voter school. When they felt ready to take the test, Westley went with them to the courthouse and stayed until they were registered. With Westley's help and encouragement, many black people in Savannah became registered voters.

CLOSE READ

Explain Relationships Between Ideas

Underline the central or main idea on this page.

Explain Relationships Between Ideas

Underline details that help you understand the relationship between the students and Westley.

qualified has met the necessary requirements to do or be something

Working as a Mailman, 1949

13 After college and the army, Westley wanted to be a teacher. But because of his membership in the NAACP, no one in Savannah would hire him.

14 So Westley became a mailman. The postal service hired qualified people, regardless of their color. As it turned out, this job suited Westley just fine.

15 "Good morning, Miss Sally Lawrence Jenkins," Westley sang out to a young woman in her garden. "Here's a letter from your sister."

16 Westley liked to address people by their full names. He could trace a person's history in their name. And history was important to Westley. "If you don't know where you've been, how do you know where you're going?" he loved to ask.

At the NAACP Office, February 1960

17 After work, Westley spent long evenings at the NAACP office. One night, he was visited by a group of students who were excited about what was happening in Greensboro, North Carolina. Young black people there had staged a sit-in at a lunch counter in a local store. They had refused to leave until they were served.

18 The students standing in front of Westley wanted to do the same thing at the department stores on Broughton Street. But they needed a leader. Westley remembered how his grandma had been treated at Levy's, and he agreed to help. But first, the students had to be trained. They had to protest without ever using violence, even if the other side did. If they were attacked and they fought back, Westley told them, their cause would be lost.

N.A.A.C.P.

SIT-IN STRATEGY

1 DRESS NEATLY
2 ENTER TOGETHER
3 SIT TOGETHER
4 ORDER POLITELY
5 DO NOT REACT TO INSULTS
6 LEAVE TOGETHER

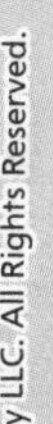

Explain Relationships Between Ideas

Underline details that show a connection between events.

Levy's Lunch Counter

19 After weeks of training, small groups of students made their way downtown, entered the big stores along Broughton Street, and sat down at the lunch counters. The stores refused to serve them. At Levy's, the manager called the police, who arrested the students for breaking the city's segregation laws.

Throwing Down Their Cards

20 Westley called a mass meeting the next Sunday at the Bolton Street Baptist Church. People filled the pews and balconies. Westley opened the meeting with a hymn. All the voices singing together made a thunderous sound. And the mighty noise made people think that perhaps working together, they could really make something happen. Westley spoke about the arrests of the young people at Levy's. He said that things had to change, and he asked if people were ready to fight for their rights.

21 Someone shouted, "I'll never shop at that store again!" Then someone in the balcony threw down a Levy's charge card. Soon, everyone was tossing charge cards into a big pile in the church.

The Boycott Begins March 17, 1960

22 The next morning, Westley led a group downtown. They carried baskets full of charge cards.

23 At Levy's, Westley and his group dumped the baskets of charge cards onto the sidewalk. Then Westley announced that no black people would shop at any store on Broughton Street until they were treated equally.

24 The Great Savannah Boycott had begun!

CLOSE READ

Explain Relationships Between Ideas

Recall what you already know about Martin Luther King Jr. and his role in the civil rights movement. Underline details that show a connection between Westley and Martin Luther King Jr.

Picket Lines

Generate Questions

Highlight evidence that explains why the protesters did not fight back. What question do you have about peaceful protests?

25 Westley and other members of the NAACP organized a picket line every day in front of Levy's. White people yelled and jeered at the protesters and tried to force them off the sidewalk. But day after day, the protesters returned.

Vocabulary in Context

Underline context clues, or words or phrases around an unfamiliar word, to define the word *jeered* in paragraph 25.

demonstrators people who participate in public protests or marches in support of or against something

26 One day a large, burly white man punched one of the demonstrators in the face and broke his jaw. But everyone remembered what Westley had taught them. They didn't yell or fight back, no matter how much they wanted to.

27 Westley organized other protests. There were kneel-ins at the white churches on Sundays and wade-ins at the all-white beach at Tybee. Westley wanted to end segregation everywhere in Savannah—in libraries, theaters, public pools, beaches, and restrooms, as well as at lunch counters.

CLOSE READ

Explain Relationships Between Ideas

Underline details that show a connection between events.

Talking About Peaceful Change

28 Large meetings were held every Sunday at different churches. Protesters talked about their activities; some gave fiery speeches. The meetings became so popular that no church was big enough to hold everyone who wanted to get in.

29 For a year and a half, no one from the black community shopped on Broughton Street.

30 Westley walked down the street and started counting: One, two, three, four, five GOING OUT OF BUSINESS signs. The white storeowners couldn't stay in business without black customers.

31 When he delivered mail to white people, Westley told them how much he loved Savannah. He wanted the city to be a better place for everyone. They respected Westley. They saw how peaceful and committed to change the protesters were. Little by little, more and more white people began to sympathize with the protesters.

sympathize feel or express concern, compassion, and support for someone

Desegregation Without Violence

32 White people in the community who supported Westley asked what they could do to end segregation and stop the boycott. Together, leaders from the white and black communities worked out a plan. Each evening after delivering the mail, Westley organized a group of students to sit in at a different kind of business or facility the next day. The theaters would be first, then the restaurants, then the library, and on down the line until every business had been desegregated.

33 Sometimes angry crowds would gather, or white people would leave in protest when the black students arrived. But most of the white and black leaders stuck together. The mayor made sure that all the signs marking separate facilities for blacks and whites at City Hall, the courthouse, health department, and hospital were taken down. City officials took the segregation laws off the books. Unlike desegregation efforts in other cities and towns in the South, there was very little violence in Savannah.

CLOSE READ

Generate Questions

Highlight a detail that helps you understand how Savannah handled desegregation efforts. What question do you have about desegregation?

Explain Relationships Between Ideas

Underline details on this page that show a relationship between two important events.

Justice Delivered

34 On a Sunday in September 1961, Westley greeted the hundreds of people who arrived at a downtown Savannah church. Inside, their voices joined together to sing out, "We are Soldiers in God's Army." When the song ended, Westley stood in front of the crowd. He saw his mother sitting in the front row. He saw students who had been arrested. He saw faces beaming with pride. Then he announced in a loud clear voice, "We have triumphed!"

35 Savannah was the first southern city in the United States to declare all its citizens equal, three years before the federal Civil Rights Act made all segregation illegal. People, both black and white, saw Westley as Savannah's hero. He had kept the protest disciplined and peaceful, even in the face of violence. Modestly, he would say, "I was just doing what every black American should be doing."

36 Westley Wallace Law delivered more than just the mail to the citizens of Savannah; he delivered justice, too. His grandma's prayers had been answered.

Develop Vocabulary

In a biography, an author uses words that are specific to the historical time in which the subject of the biography lived. These words can help readers better understand connections between events in the person's life.

My TURN Complete the sentences to show the connections between the vocabulary words from *Delivering Justice*.

Demonstrators and **sympathize** are connected because

the words and actions of the Savannah demonstrators caused some white people to sympathize with their cause

.

Segregation and **mistreated** are connected because

.

Qualified and **segregation** are connected because

.

Mistreated and **demonstrators** are connected because

.

Check for Understanding

My TURN Look back at the text to answer the questions.

1. Identify details that show this text is a biography.

2. Evaluate how the author creates a logical structure in the text.

3. Compare the ways African Americans and white people were treated in Savannah in 1941 to the ways they were treated in late 1961.

4. Do you think Westley's influence helped eliminate segregation in Savannah? Use evidence to support your argument.

Explain Relationships Between Ideas

One way the author of a biography can show the **relationships** between major ideas in the life of a person is to use a **problem-and-solution** structure in the text.

1. **My TURN** Go to the Close Read notes in *Delivering Justice* and underline the parts that help you explain relationships between problems and solutions in the text.

2. **Text Evidence** Use the parts you underlined to complete the organizer and answer the question. Use text evidence to describe events that lead from the problem to the solution.

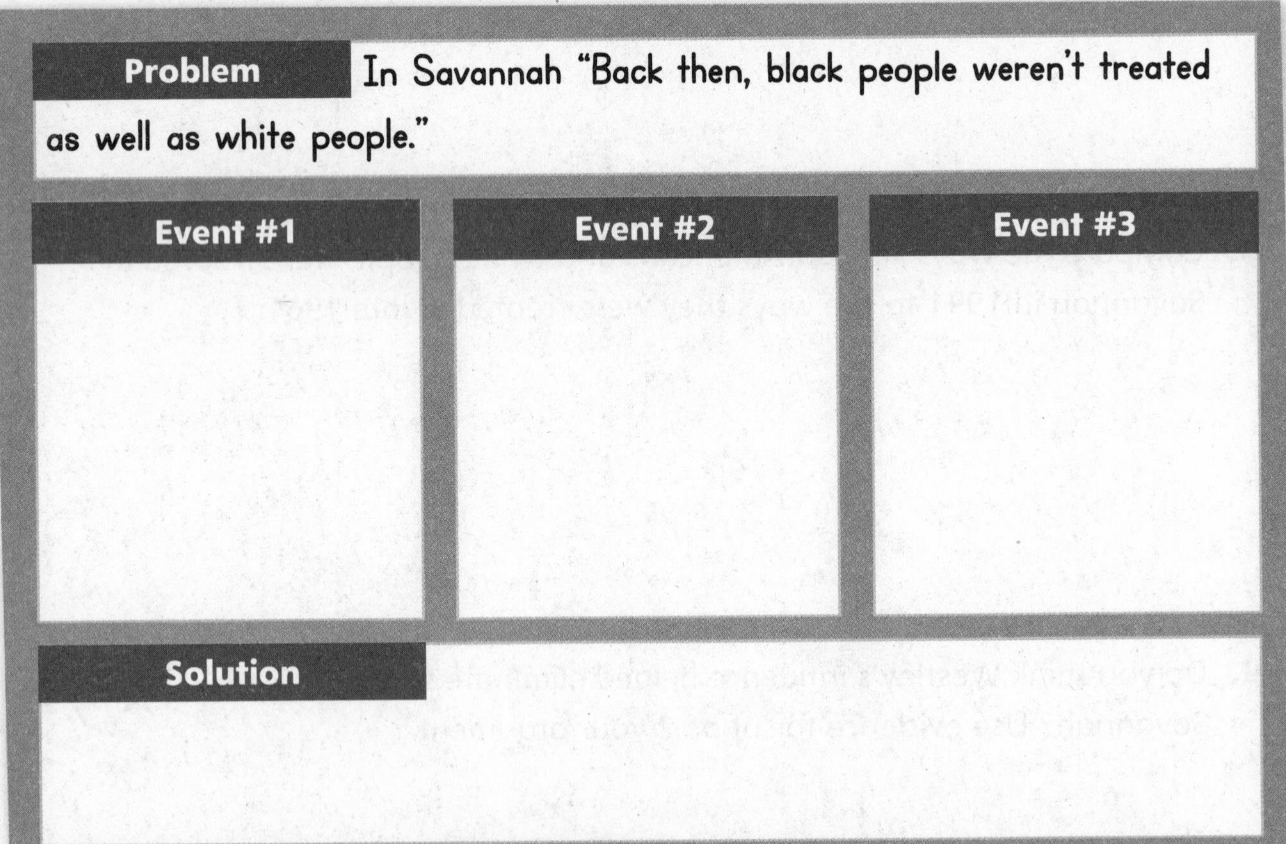

Explain Relationships How did the idea of equality relate to the idea of segregation in Savannah?

Generate Questions

Asking **questions** before, during, and after reading will help you identify key details and better understand relationships between major events in a text. The text may directly state answers to the questions, or you may be able to infer answers from details in the text.

1. **My TURN** Go back to the Close Read notes and highlight text evidence that helped you ask and answer questions about *Delivering Justice.*

2. **Text Evidence** Use your evidence and your inferences to complete the chart and support your responses.

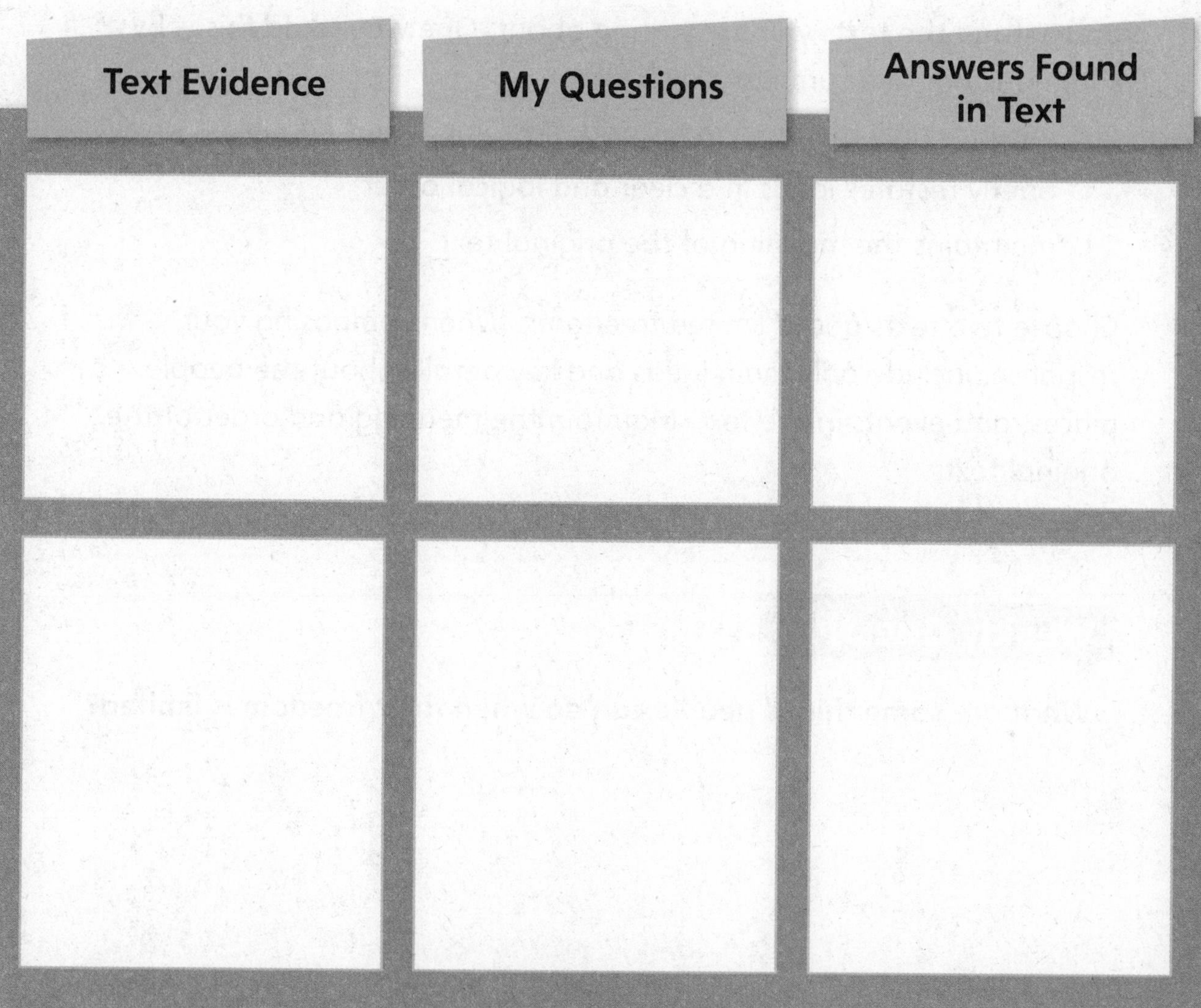

Text Evidence	My Questions	Answers Found in Text

Reflect and Share

Write to Sources In *Delivering Justice*, Westley leads nonviolent protests against segregation in Savannah, Georgia. Consider all the texts you have read this week. What other unfair situations have you read about? How did people react to these situations? How do characters in each story interact? Use these questions to write and support a response.

Summarize Texts When writing a response, it is important to understand the texts you are writing about. One way to do this is by summarizing. In a summary, a reader

- includes only the main ideas and most important details
- briefly restates ideas in a clear and logical order
- maintains the meaning of the original text

Choose two texts about limited freedoms. When composing your response, include only main ideas and key details about the people, places, and events in the text. Maintain the meaning and order of the original texts.

Weekly Question

What are some things people can do when their freedom is limited?

Academic Vocabulary

Learning Goal

I can develop knowledge about language to make connections between reading and writing.

Adages and **proverbs** are traditional sayings about common observations or truths. "The early bird gets the worm," for example, is an adage that means whoever arrives first has the best chance to succeed.

My TURN

1. **Read** each adage.
2. **Match** the academic vocabulary word with the adage or proverb that best relates to the word's definition.
3. **Choose** an adage or proverb, and **write** a new sentence that uses the saying and its related academic vocabulary word.

Word Bank

limitation **grace** **noble** **empower** **resist**

1. You can't teach an old dog new tricks. ______
2. It is better to give than to receive. ______
3. Better safe than sorry. ______
4. Do unto others as you would have them do unto you. ______
5. Where there's a will, there's a way. ______

My Sentence ______

Word Origins

English contains many roots that come from Greek, Latin, and other languages. The roots *graph*, *micro*, and *tele* are of Greek origin. Print and digital resources can help you determine a word's origin. To form English words, roots are combined with prefixes, suffixes, or other roots.

My TURN Define each word. Then identify the word's root and its origin to complete the chart. Confirm your answers in a print or digital dictionary.

Word with Root	My Definition	Root and Word Origin
biography	writing about a real person	*bio;* Greek for "life" *graph;* Greek for "to write, written"
microwave		
predict		
telephone		

High Frequency Words

High-frequency words are words that you will see in texts over and over again. Keep in mind that they often do not follow regular word patterns. Read these high-frequency words: *actually, adjective, especially, experience, similar, workers*. Look for them in your independent reading.

Read Like a Writer

Authors use specific graphic features, including illustrations, to further explain information in a text.

Model! Review the illustration that goes with paragraphs 17 and 18 of *Delivering Justice*. Then read the text.

> [T]he students had to be trained. They had to protest without ever using violence, even if the other side did. If they were attacked and they fought back, Westley told them, their cause would be lost.

information further explained by the illustration

1. **Identify** The illustration shows Westley teaching students a list of sit-in strategies.
2. **Question** How does the illustration help me better understand Jim Haskins's statement that "students had to be trained"?
3. **Conclude** The specific strategies shown in the illustration emphasize both the danger and seriousness of the cause.

Reread paragraph 19 and review its nearby illustration.

My TURN Analyze the illustration and the text.

1. **Identify** the illustration shows ______________________________ ______________________________.
2. **Question** How does the illustration help me better understand Jim Haskins's statement that "the stores refused to serve them"?
3. **Conclude** The ______________________________ in the illustration emphasizes ______________________________ ______________________________.

Write for a Reader

Authors can use illustrations and other graphic features to give more detail than the text alone does.

My TURN Think about how the illustrations in *Delivering Justice* affect you as a reader. Now identify how you can use illustrations to provide more detail to your own readers.

1. If you were trying to draw a person acting bravely in a difficult situation, what details would you include in the illustration?

2. Draw an illustration to accompany a text about the topic. The illustration should add more detail about the topic.

Spell Words with Greek Roots

Greek Roots form the basis of many English words. For example, combining the roots *tele* and *graph* creates *telegraph*, a word that means "to send messages or words somewhere far away." It also refers to the machine that "writes" these messages in two distant places.

My TURN Read the words. Spell and sort the words in alphabetical order.

SPELLING WORDS

graph	homograph	monograph	television
telephoto	telepathy	telecast	microcosm
microbiology	microchip	microbe	graphics
telemetry	seismograph	holograph	televise
bibliography	graphite	topography	microwave

Correlative Conjunctions

Coordinating conjunctions (*and*, *but*, *for*, *nor*, *or*, *so*, and *yet*) join words, phrases, and clauses. (I walked to the store and bought a book.) **Correlative conjunctions,** which come in pairs, require parallel structure. For example, if a noun appears after the first correlative conjunction, a noun must appear after the second.

Correlative Conjunctions	Parallel Structure
both . . . and	Both Jenna and Steven play baseball.
either . . . or	Let's either play a game or swim in the pool.
neither . . . nor	Neither the rain nor the snow will stop the mail.
not only . . . but also	We brought not only the food but also the drinks.
whether . . . or	I did not know whether to call or e-mail her.

My TURN Edit this draft by using pairs of correlative conjunctions to join independent clauses in a parallel structure.

African Americans living in Savannah decided that their rights would be recognized. Their protests would continue. Physical violence could not stop African Americans living in Savannah from working for civil rights. Hurtful words could also not stop them. Westley helped African Americans register to vote in Savannah. Clifford did too.

Edit for Prepositions and Prepositional Phrases

Learning Goal

I can use elements of science fiction to write a short story.

A **preposition** is a word that introduces a prepositional phrase, which modifies another word or element in the sentence. The **prepositional phrase** begins with a preposition and ends with a noun or a pronoun called the **object of the preposition**.

Jack, Darius, and Nora set up a robot repair stand in Jack's front yard in the shade of the oak tree.

The verb must agree with the subject of the sentence, not the object of a prepositional phrase.

Incorrect: The fleet of ships are moving fast.	Fleet is the subject, but the verb are incorrectly agrees with ships, the plural object of the prepositional phrase.
Correct: The fleet of ships is moving fast.	The verb is correctly agrees with fleet, the singular subject of the sentence.

My TURN Underline each prepositional phrase. Highlight the subject of each sentence. Then edit for subject-verb agreement.

A group of space pirates are about to board the ship! If we don't act fast, our ships full of cargo is going to be lost. At the last minute, the crews in the landing module makes a daring rescue. After a brief battle, the last of the pirate ships speed away.

My TURN Edit your science fiction short story to have subject-verb agreement in sentences with prepositional phrases.

Edit for Irregular Verbs

To form the past tense of a regular verb, a writer adds *-ed*. A writer uses the past participle plus *has*, *have*, or *had* to show action that began in the past.

Present Tense Verb	Past Tense Verb	Past Participle
act	acted	acted
play	played	played
want	wanted	wanted
jump	jumped	jumped

An **irregular verb** has a different form for the past tense and the past participle.

Present Tense Verb	Past Tense Verb	Past Participle
do	did	done
take	took	taken
write	wrote	written
grow	grew	grown

My TURN Write the correct form of the irregular verb in each sentence.

1. Yesterday, Tru (past tense of *grow*) ____________ the first head of lettuce on the International Space Station.

2. She (past tense of *write*) ____________ her notes in the computer system, but when the system malfunctioned, everything was lost.

3. Without her notes, the botanists in the Sector 4 greenhouse will never know how to do what Tru and her team have (past participle of *do*) ____________.

My TURN Edit your science fiction short story to have correct use of the past tense of irregular verbs.

Edit for Collective Nouns

A **collective noun** names a group of persons or things. A collective noun is singular in form, but it refers to a group or collection.

Common collective nouns include *group, set, band, flock, gang, collection, pack, bunch, team, herd, family, pair, clump, pack,* and *crew.*

Use a **singular verb** and a **singular pronoun** when you use a collective noun to mean the group as a whole.

The **flock** flies south to its winter home. ◀······· Together the birds are flying to the same place.

Use a **plural verb** and a **plural pronoun** when you use a collective noun to mean each individual in the group.

The **flock** sleep in their nests. ◀··············· Each bird in the flock has its own nest, but all the birds are sleeping.

My TURN Edit the paragraph to have subject-verb agreement with collective nouns.

The crew of rowers work together. The group move as if it were connected to one brain. Together the team glide across the pond with precision and grace.

My TURN Edit your science fiction short story to have correct use of collective nouns.

Edit for Subordinating Conjunctions

A conjunction connects words, phrases, and sentences.

Subordinating conjunctions connect an independent clause and a subordinate clause. A **subordinate clause** does not express a complete thought by itself. A subordinate clause joined with an **independent clause** creates a **complex sentence.** Some common subordinating conjunctions include *because*, *if*, *then*, *when*, *before*, and *after.* If a subordinate clause comes first in a sentence, use a comma to separate it from the independent clause.

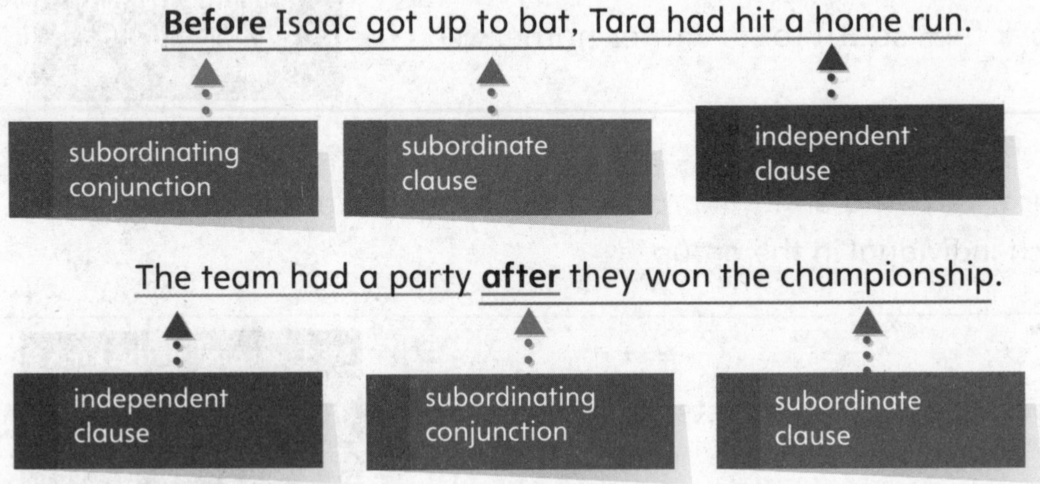

My TURN Edit the paragraph to have correct use of subordinating conjunctions.

> Hummingbirds seem to be hovering in air. They are actually flapping their wings more than 80 times per minute. Look closely. You can see each movement the bird makes.

My TURN Edit your science fiction short story to have correct use of subordinating conjunctions in complex sentences.

Edit for Punctuation Marks

Commas can be used to:

- separate items in a series
- set off an appositive phrase
- combine independent clauses to form a compound sentence
- combine independent and subordinate clauses to form a complex sentence
- set off spoken text in quotations from the speaker's name
- set off an introductory element or yes or no from the rest of a sentence
- set off a direct address
- set off a question within a sentence

Quotation marks are needed for:

- dialogue and direct quotations
- titles of articles, short stories, and poems

My TURN Edit the dialogue to correctly use commas and quotation marks.

Who wants to go swimming this afternoon? asked Julie.

I want to go but I have to go to the store said Lucy.

Julie Sam Marcus and I can help you and then go to the pool! exclaimed Morris.

Morris my friend you are the best said Lucy with a smile.

Sam held up an article called Swimming the Backstroke.

I want to try out all the techniques he said.

My TURN Edit your science fiction short story to have correct use of commas and quotation marks. Discuss your edits with your Writing Club.

INTERACTIVITY

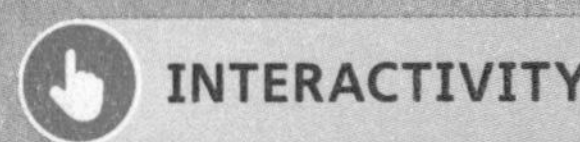

from "I Will Go West!"

words by Joseph L. Eldridge, music by J. P. Barrett

By 1875, when this song was published, westward expansion was in full swing. Railroad track was being laid faster than ever before, and the railroad was connecting people to areas of the United States that had been expensive and difficult to access. At the same time, life in cities was becoming more and more crowded and unpleasant. Farmland on the frontier was readily available. What contrasts between city and country life does the song reveal?

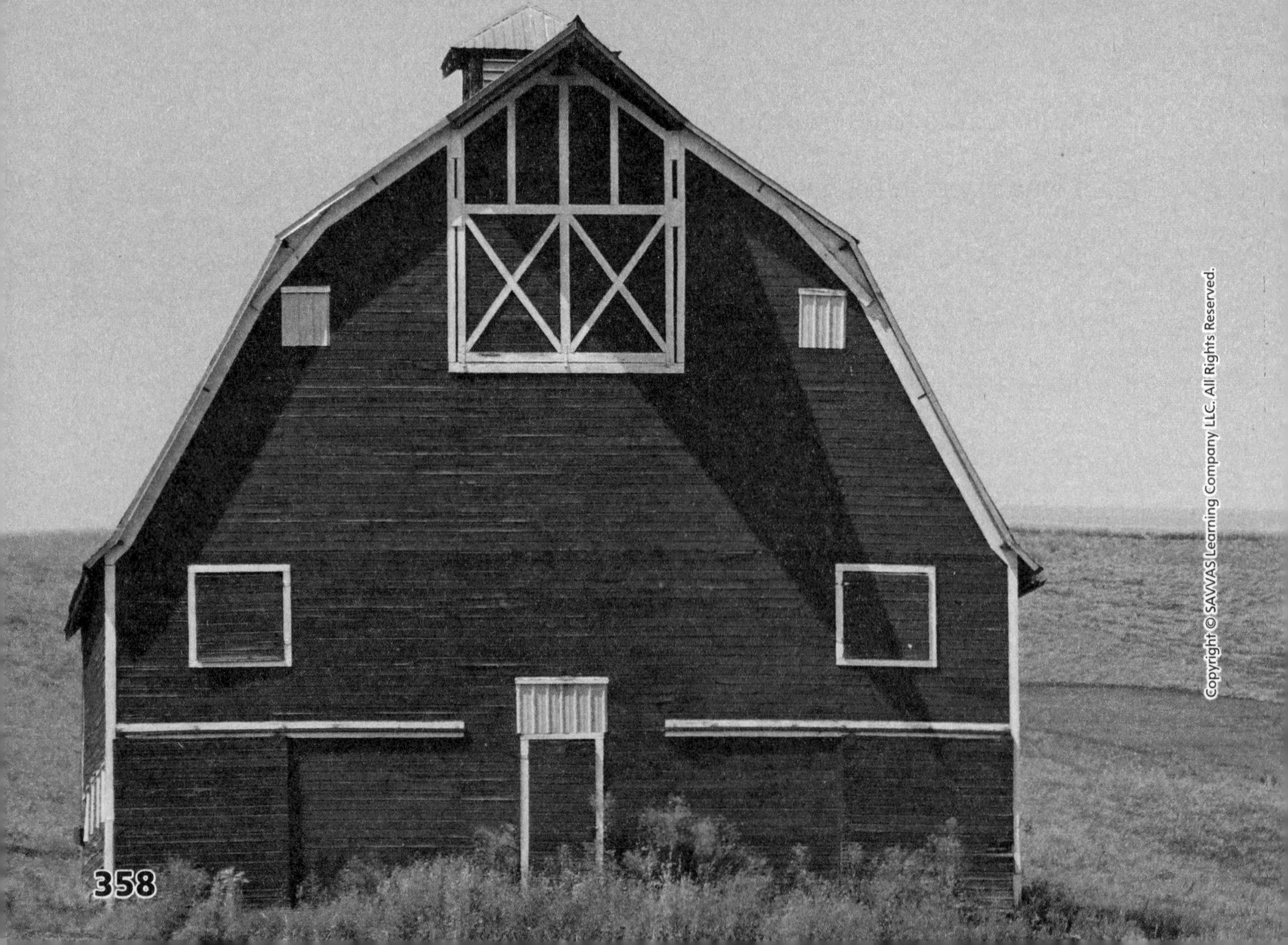

1 Oh! times are tough, amazing rough,
Expenses are alarming,
I will go West, it's far the best,
Try my luck at farming.

2 For the idea, of staying here
To just earn your gruel,
Makes me feel sad and sometimes mad
'Tis so awful cruel.

3 Now it's no use, I've stood abuse
I'll take all with dear Mary,
Settle down in a country town,
Farm it on a prairie.

4 My barns replete with corn and wheat,
Lots of milk and butter,
T'would be a shame, to here complain
Or a murmur utter.

Weekly Question

How can going to a new place give a person new opportunities?

TURN and TALK Think about stories, movies, or events from your own life in which someone moved away to achieve a goal. How was the new place different? What made the new place special? Explain your ideas to a partner and ask questions about your partner's ideas.

Learning Goal

I can learn more about historical fiction by explaining author's purpose.

Spotlight on Genre

Historical Fiction

Historical fiction is a story about a real time and place in history.

- **Characters** can be real or imagined and often have a conflict or problem to solve.
- Authors of historical fiction use **descriptive details,** or vivid language, to present people, places, and events in history.
- **Novels, short stories, movies, plays**, and **graphic novels** can all be historical fiction.

Establish Purpose Readers of historical fiction set a purpose, or reason, for reading. The purpose could be for enjoyment. It could also be to learn about a certain time period or person in history.

If it's set in the past, it's historical fiction!

TURN and TALK With a partner, discuss different purposes for reading historical fiction. For example, you may want to be entertained with a story about the past. Use the anchor chart to set a purpose. Take notes on your discussion.

My NOTES

Historical Fiction Anchor Chart

Characters

- Are real or imagined people from history
- Use authentic, but made-up, dialogue

Details

- Include historically accurate facts
- Include fictional descriptions

Voice

- Reflects the historical time and place
- Helps readers personally connect with historical events

Theme

- Is meaningful to readers today

Meet *the* Author

Guy A. Sims began writing in eighth grade for his elementary school newspaper. His passion for writing grew stronger in adulthood. Different settings, including cities and towns, inspire him to write. In fact, a lot of his stories take place in or near his home of Philadelphia.

Ezekiel Johnson Goes West

Preview Vocabulary

As you read *Ezekiel Johnson Goes West*, pay attention to these vocabulary words. Notice how they connect to western migration.

provisions **terrain**
settlement **bandits** **oblige**

Read

Use what you know about **historical fiction** to make predictions about the story and characters. Confirm or correct your predictions after you read. Follow these strategies when you read historical fiction.

First Read

Notice	**Generate Questions**
how the images add to the meaning and beauty of the text.	about what the author thinks you already know and wants you to learn and understand.
Connect	**Respond**
this text to another historical fiction story you have read.	by talking about the graphic novel with a partner.

Genre Historical Fiction

EZEKIEL JOHNSON GOES WEST

by Guy A. Sims

GOLD STAR STAGE CO.

AUDIO

ANNOTATE

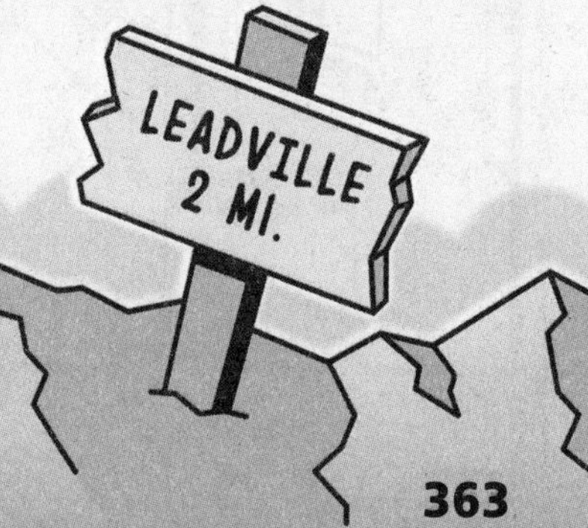

CLOSE READ

Explain Author's Purpose

Underline text evidence that helps you determine that the author is writing a piece of historical fiction. Consider how the images add to the meaning of the text.

CLOSE READ

Make Inferences

Highlight evidence that helps you infer that Ezekiel is trying to improve his life.

CLOSE READ

Explain Author's Purpose

Underline details the author uses to show Ezekiel's character as hardworking.

CLOSE READ

Explain Author's Purpose

Underline text evidence that shows the central message the author wants to share.

Explain Author's Purpose

Underline evidence in the text and consider details in the images that show that the author and illustrator want to inform as well as entertain readers.

What's that say? Read it.

Gold Star Coach Company through routes from St. Louis to Oro City, Colorado, and connect to points west, southwest, and northwest....

19

CLOSE READ

Make Inferences

Use the illustrations to make an inference about Ezekiel.

Highlight details in the text that support your inference.

CLOSE READ

Explain Author's Purpose

Underline evidence that supports the idea that people move to find new opportunities.

provisions materials or supplies

This here ticket will get you as far as a small settlement east of Oro City, Colorado. It's about a two-week trip, so you best pack enough provisions. Coach leaves from here 5 A.M. sharp. You miss it, no refunds.

27

CLOSE READ

Make Inferences

Highlight details about the journey west. Make an inference about why this information is important.

terrain an area of land and its surface features

CLOSE READ

Make Inferences

Highlight text evidence on both pages that helps you make an inference about skills that were needed in the West.

CLOSE READ

Explain Author's Purpose

How do the author and illustrator work together to create a tone of excitement?

Underline details that support your explanation.

CLOSE READ

Explain Author's Purpose

Underline details that show that living in the West in the 1860s required creativity and skill.

CLOSE READ

Make Inferences

Highlight details that help support the inference that the trade Ezekiel taught himself in St. Louis will help him survive in the West.

CLOSE READ

Make Inferences

Highlight details that help you infer that Ezekiel has some doubts about the settlement.

settlement a place or region that is settled

CLOSE READ

Vocabulary in Context

Use **context clues**, including the story's graphics, to determine the meaning of the phrase *cooped up*.

Underline context clues that support your definition.

CLOSE READ

Explain Author's Purpose

Underline details that help you explain why the author chose to present the settler's story.

bandits enemies or outlaws

CLOSE READ

Make Inferences

Highlight text evidence that supports your inference about why the author included the settler's story.

CLOSE READ

Explain Author's Purpose

Underline details in the text that show how the author shows the passage of time.

CLOSE READ

Make Inferences

Highlight text that helps you infer what Ezekiel's request was.

oblige earn gratitude; do a favor for

CLOSE READ

Vocabulary in Context

Underline context clues on this page that help you define *grub*.

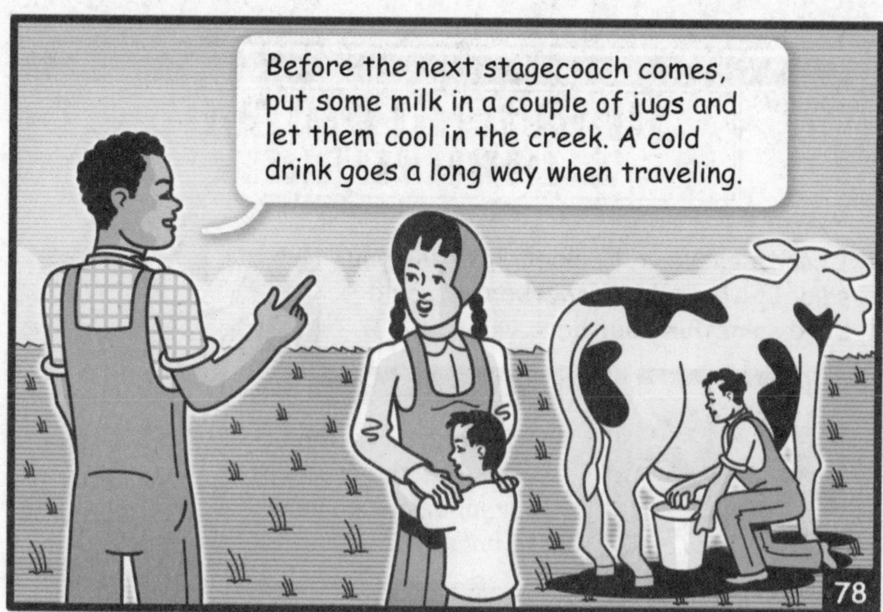

CLOSE READ

Explain Author's Purpose

How does the author show that Ezekiel has become a leader of the settlement?

Underline details in the text that support your explanation.

CLOSE READ

Make Inferences

Highlight details that support the inference that people wanted to start new lives by settling in the West.

CLOSE READ

Explain Author's Purpose

How do the words and pictures work together to show how Ezekiel achieved his dream?

Underline details in the text that support your response.

...and my dream came true.

87

Develop Vocabulary

In historical fiction, authors use specific words to help readers visualize the people, places, and events in a story.

My TURN Demonstrate your understanding of the words and their meanings from *Ezekiel Johnson Goes West.* Complete each sentence in the chart two different ways.

If a person needs **provisions**, he or she needs . . .	supplies.
She described the rocky **terrain** as . . .	
They reached the **settlement**, or . . .	
He wanted to **oblige** his new neighbors by . . .	
The **bandits** crept up to the campsite and . . .	

Check for Understanding

My TURN Look back at the text to answer the questions.

1. What details make *Ezekiel Johnson Goes West* a piece of historical fiction?

2. How do the author and illustrator use the setting to influence the plot?

3. Compare and contrast Ezekiel and Amos. What traits make Ezekiel special?

4. Think about other historical fiction stories you have read. How does presenting the story of Ezekiel Johnson as a graphic novel affect your understanding of the time period?

Explain Author's Purpose

An **author's purpose** is his or her reason for writing. Authors may write to inform, to persuade, to entertain, or to express. In historical fiction, an author uses informative details about history to entertain readers. The illustrator of a graphic novel has an additional purpose of adding meaning and beauty to a text.

1. **MyTURN** Go to the Close Read notes in *Ezekiel Johnson Goes West* and underline the parts that help you understand the author's and illustrator's purposes.

2. **Text Evidence** Use the parts you underlined to complete the organizer. In the center circle, explain the author's and illustrator's purposes.

Make Inferences

When an author does not state details directly, you must **make inferences** about characters, events, or the author's purpose or message. To make an inference, combine evidence in the text with what you already know.

1. **My TURN** Go back to the Close Read notes and highlight text evidence that helps you make inferences about why the author included specific historical details in *Ezekiel Johnson Goes West*.

2. **Text Evidence** Use your evidence to complete the chart and support your response.

What I Read

+

What I Know

=

My Inference

Reflect and Share

Talk About It In *Ezekiel Johnson Goes West*, the main character leaves Missouri to start a new life. What other texts have you read where characters follow their dreams? Do you know anyone who left home to pursue an opportunity? Use these questions to express an opinion about the characters' choices. Be sure to connect your personal experiences to your opinion.

Describe Personal Connections When giving an opinion, make sure to use accurate information to support your views. Think about your own life and what you have in common with the topic, characters, or other parts of a text. Include descriptions of these personal connections in your opinion. Choose two texts you read this week to discuss in a small group.

- Pay attention to your partners' expressions and gestures to understand how they feel about the connections they share.
- Listen to comments and questions about the topic.

Use these sentence starters to guide your responses:

I can tell by your expression that you feel . . .

Ezekiel wanted different opportunities because . . .

Weekly Question

How can going to a new place give a person new opportunities?

Academic Vocabulary

Learning Goal

I can develop knowledge about language to make connections between reading and writing.

Parts of speech are categories of words. The way a word functions in a sentence determines its part of speech. A **noun** names a person, place, thing, idea, or feeling. A **verb** can show physical or mental action. An **adjective** describes people, places, or things.

My TURN For each sentence,

1. **Read** the underlined academic vocabulary word or its related form.
2. **Identify** the word's part of speech.
3. **Write** your own sentence using the same base word as a different part of speech. Write the part of speech in parentheses after your answer.

Sentence	Part of Speech	My Sentence
As an African American cowboy, he had to fight against many <u>limitations</u>.	noun	She wanted to limit her toddler's access to electronic devices. (verb)
The hostess showed style and <u>grace</u> at her dinner party.		
Preserving the rain forests is a <u>noble</u> cause.		
Helen <u>empowered</u> her younger sister's dreams of becoming a doctor.		
He <u>resisted</u> the temptation of a second dessert.		

Latin Roots *audi, rupt, scrib, spec*

Latin roots are the basis for many words in English. Knowing the origin of words and word parts can help you define unfamiliar words. You can use a dictionary to confirm the origins of words and word parts.

For example, the Latin root *rupt* means "burst." Knowing the Latin root *rupt* can help you define words with this root, such as *abrupt*, which means "relating to an unexpected or surprise action."

My TURN Read the chart. Add two related words for each root.

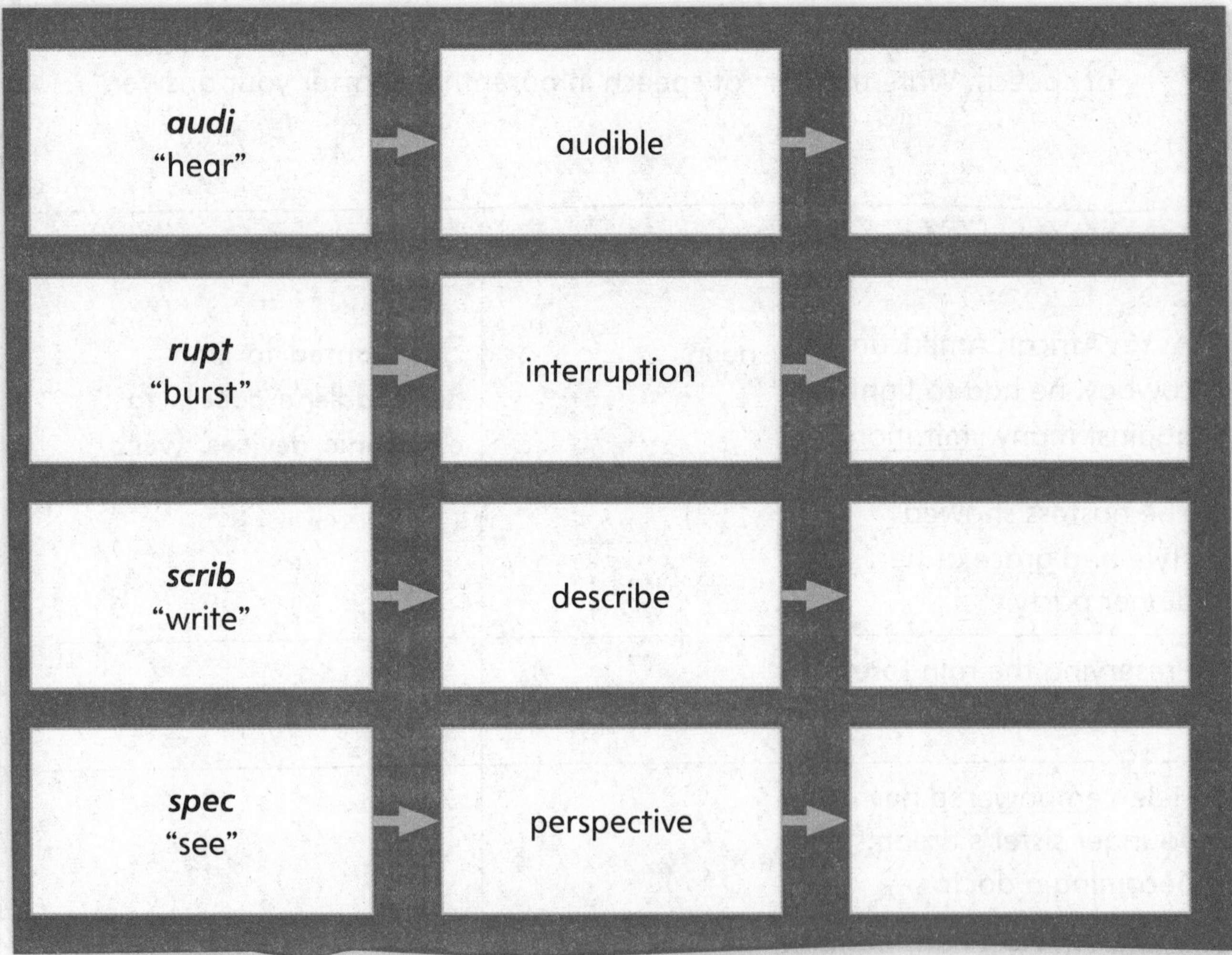

Root	Related word	Related word
audi "hear"	audible	
rupt "burst"	interruption	
scrib "write"	describe	
spec "see"	perspective	

Read Like a Writer

Adages and proverbs are figurative language. They are traditional sayings about common truths. For example, the proverb "Don't judge a book by its cover" means you should not judge someone or something based on appearance. An adage is a very old saying. For example, "When in Rome, do as the Romans do" means you should behave as others do.

Model! Read the text.

> Obadiah decided to stay in Missouri instead of going west. "Better safe than sorry," he told Ben.

proverb

1. **Identify** Obadiah says, "Better safe than sorry."
2. **Analyze** What does the proverb tell me about the story?
3. **Conclude** The proverb tells me that Obadiah plays it safe.

Read the text.

> Joe laughed at Jesse's sculpture. "Hey! Beauty is in the eye of the beholder!" she said.

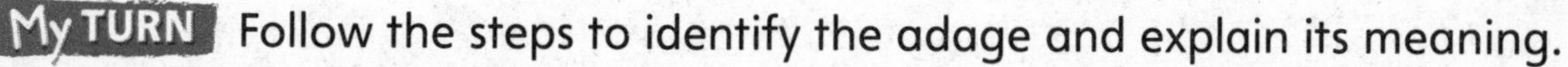

My TURN Follow the steps to identify the adage and explain its meaning.

1. **Identify** Jesse says ______________________________, which means ______________________________.
2. **Analyze** What does the adage tell me about the situation?
3. **Conclude** The adage tells me that ______________________________ ______________________________.

Write for a Reader

Adages and proverbs are common sayings that express general, widely accepted truths. They often convey advice, warnings, or wisdom beyond their actual words. An adage is a very old proverb.

MyTURN Think about how the use of adages and proverbs affects you as a reader. Now identify how you can use adages and proverbs to entertain and connect with your own readers.

1. If you were trying to offer encouragement to someone, what adage or proverb would you use?

2. Write a dialogue that includes at least one adage or proverb.

Spell Latin Roots *audi, rupt, scrib, spec*

Many words in English are formed from Latin roots. The root *scrib*, which means "write," is sometimes spelled as *script*.

My TURN Read the words. Spell and sort the words by their Latin roots.

SPELLING WORDS

retrospective	prospect	inspection	script
audio	audit	scribble	rupture
disruptive	speculate	auditory	auditorium
inscription	bankrupt	disruption	transcribe
audience	audition	spectator	spectacle

audi

rupt

scrib

spec

Capitalization

Abbreviations, initials, acronyms, and organizations follow special rules for capitalization.

Type of Capitalization	Examples
abbreviations	addresses: St., Rd., Ave., Ct., Apt.
	states: TX, FL, IL
initials	Franklin D. Roosevelt, C. S. Lewis, W. E. B. DuBois
organizations	Federal Bureau of Investigation, United Nations, American Medical Association
acronyms	GIF, NATO

My TURN Edit this draft by using proper capitalization for abbreviations, initials, acronyms, and organizations. Write three underlines (≡) beneath each letter that should be capitalized.

In 1775, the second continental congress established the United States postal service. In 1963, the Zone Improvement Plan, or zip, created codes to allow mail to travel more easily. The hottest U.S. post office can be found in Death Valley, ca, at 328 Greenland blvd. Megan j. Brennan was appointed the first female postmaster general in 2015.

Revise by Adding and Deleting Ideas for Clarity

Learning Goal

I can use elements of science fiction to write a short story.

A writer revises drafts by **adding ideas** to clarify details that are vague, missing, or unclear.

> **because the heat made the boxes seem heavier**
> Whitney hated moving in the summer.^

A writer revises drafts by **deleting ideas** that are distracting, misleading, or unnecessary. This makes the story clear and coherent. It improves word choice.

> Whitney packed up her living room first. ~~She was tired of her old couch.~~ Then she packed up the dining room.

MyTURN Revise the paragraph. Add an idea from the bank to make the paragraph clearer. Delete distracting or unnecessary ideas.

> Joo-won packed the tools he would need. His spacesuit was uncomfortable. He put the blowtorch in a special pocket on the front of his spacesuit. What would he find when he surveyed the damage to the ship? He must fix any panels that had been damaged.

Idea Bank

by the asteroids	**The ship had panels on the outside.**

MyTURN Revise a draft of your own science fiction short story by adding and deleting ideas for clarity. Check to be sure your word choice has improved.

Edit for Indefinite Pronouns

Indefinite pronouns do not always refer to a specific person or thing. Some singular indefinite pronouns include *somebody, anyone, everybody,* and *no one*. Some plural indefinite pronouns include *few, several, many,* and *others*.

A **singular indefinite pronoun** needs a singular verb. If the sentence includes another pronoun, that pronoun must be singular.

> **Everyone wants** to travel safely to the outer planets.
>
> **Everyone wants his or her** ship to have working equipment.

A **plural indefinite pronoun** needs a plural verb. If the sentence includes another pronoun, that pronoun must be plural.

> **Few leave** Earth without learning the basic rules of space safety.
>
> **Few leave their** planet without learning how to survive.

My TURN Edit the paragraph for subject-verb agreement with indefinite pronouns.

> Several sensors on the ship blinks its lights to tell passengers when it is time to put on breathing masks. If this happens, everyone need to put on their mask immediately. If something cause problems with the sensors, a crew member will warn passengers.

My TURN Edit your science fiction short story for subject-verb agreement with indefinite pronouns.

Publish and Celebrate

A writer publishes his or her work by making it available to an audience. Publishing includes printing, posting, e-mailing, presenting, or talking about your work.

My TURN Answer the questions about your writing experience. Write legibly in cursive.

My best story idea was ____
____
____
____
____.

My favorite characters to write about were __________________________
because ____
____
____
____.

The best setting I developed was ____________________________________
____
____
____
____.

When I write another science fiction short story, I will ______________
____
____
____
____.

Prepare for Assessment

My TURN Follow a plan as you prepare to write a science fiction short story from a prompt.

1. **Relax.**
   Take a deep breath.

2. **Make sure you understand the prompt.**
   Read the prompt. Underline what kind of writing you will do. Highlight the topic you will be writing about.

   Prompt: Write a science fiction short story about people in a future society who are fighting against limitations on their freedom.

3. **Brainstorm.**
   Brainstorm three story ideas. Choose your favorite.

4. **Plan your short story.**
   Create a sequence of events that unfolds naturally.

5. **Write your draft on your own paper.**
   Remember to create a clear situation and an entertaining conflict.

6. **After you finish, revise and edit your story.**
   Look for errors in grammar and punctuation.

Remember to correctly punctuate dialogue between characters.

Assessment

My TURN Before you write a science fiction short story for your assessment, rate how well you understand the skills you have learned in this unit. Go back and review any skills you mark "No."

Ideas and Organization	Yes!	No
I can create and develop characters in a science fiction story.	☐	☐
I can create and develop the setting of a science fiction story.	☐	☐
I can map a sequence of events.	☐	☐
I can introduce the situation and the conflict my characters experience.	☐	☐
I can write a resolution for the story's conflict.	☐	☐
Craft		
I can develop the plot of a science fiction story with sensory details and concrete language.	☐	☐
I can use dialogue to provide details and description in a story.	☐	☐
I can use transitions to logically develop a sequence of events.	☐	☐
I can use appropriate pacing to develop the story.	☐	☐
I can add and delete ideas for clarity.	☐	☐
Conventions		
I can follow rules for subject-verb agreement with prepositional phrases, collective nouns, and indefinite pronouns.	☐	☐
I can use irregular verbs and subordinating conjunctions.	☐	☐
I can punctuate with commas and quotation marks.	☐	☐

UNIT THEME

Liberty

TURN and TALK

Connect to Theme

In this unit, you learned many new words to talk about *Liberty*. With a partner, go back into each text. Find a sentence that best illustrates the academic vocabulary word. Be prepared to explain why you chose that sentence.

WEEK 3

from The Bill of Rights

limitation

WEEK 2

The Scarlet Stockings Spy

grace

WEEK 1

"Keeping Mr. John Holton Alive" from Elijah of Buxton

noble

resist

WEEK 4

BOOK CLUB

WEEK 5

empower

BOOK CLUB

Essential Question

My TURN

In your notebook, answer the Essential Question: What does it mean to be free?

WEEK 6

Project

Now it's time to apply what you learned about freedom in your **WEEK 6 PROJECT, What It Means to Be Free.**

What It Means to Be FREE

Activity

The word *freedom* means different things to different people. Conduct a survey to find out what freedom means to friends, family members, and others. Then create your own project, such as a speech or a poster, to show what you think it means to be free.

Research Articles

With your partner, read "Experiencing Freedom." Then develop a plan to complete your project. To do this, make a list of the tasks that need to be completed. Assign a person to each task. Make sure you assign the tasks evenly so that responsibilities are shared equally.

1. **Experiencing Freedom**
2. **You Can Quote Me!**
3. **Thomas Paine's Legacy**

Generate Questions

COLLABORATE Read "Experiencing Freedom" and generate three questions about the article. Compare questions with a partner. Answer any you can before sharing them with the class.

1. ______________________________

2. ______________________________

3. ______________________________

Use Academic Words

COLLABORATE In this unit, you learned many words related to the theme of *Liberty*. Work with your partner to add more academic vocabulary words to each category. If appropriate, use these words when you create your project on the meaning of freedom.

Academic Vocabulary	Word Forms	Synonyms	Antonyms
limitation	limitations limit limited	restriction control barrier	freedom advantage permission
grace	graceful disgrace gracefully	elegance smoothness charm	clumsiness awkwardness roughness
noble	nobility nobleman nobles	moral selfless principled	selfish immoral corrupt
empower	empowered empowers empowering	permit encourage authorize	limit forbid discourage
resist	resistance resisting resisted	fight struggle oppose	comply agree consent

Information, Please!

People create informational texts to teach readers about a particular topic. When you read an informational text, recognize:

- a main idea with a clear structure
- facts and other supporting details based on research
- text features that support the facts in the text

COLLABORATE With a partner, read "You Can Quote Me!" Then answer the following questions about the text.

1. What is the main idea of the article?

2. In what way is the article an example of informational text?

3. In what way is the article *not* an example of informational text?

Plan Your Research

COLLABORATE Before you begin creating your project, you will survey people to find out what the term *freedom* means to them. Use the chart to plan who you will survey and what questions you will ask.

When you conduct a survey, you ask people questions. Usually, you ask the same questions of each person.

Dylan and Jin are conducting a survey about pet ownership. They wrote several questions. Then they chose two questions that were most clearly about their topic.	• Do you have a pet? • Do you have any siblings? • Have you ever been to the zoo? • Which animal would you most like to have for a pet?

My interview questions about what freedom means:

When you conduct a survey, try to talk with people who have different backgrounds and experiences.

Hector and Marlena are conducting a survey about freedom. They can ask four people. Underline people who could provide an interesting mix of answers.	• 12-year-old boy, born in this country • 64-year-old man, living in another country • 34-year-old man, born in this country • 72-year-old woman, moved here last year • 24-year-old woman, moved to another country

With your partner, list some people you could survey for your project.

SURVEY SAYS

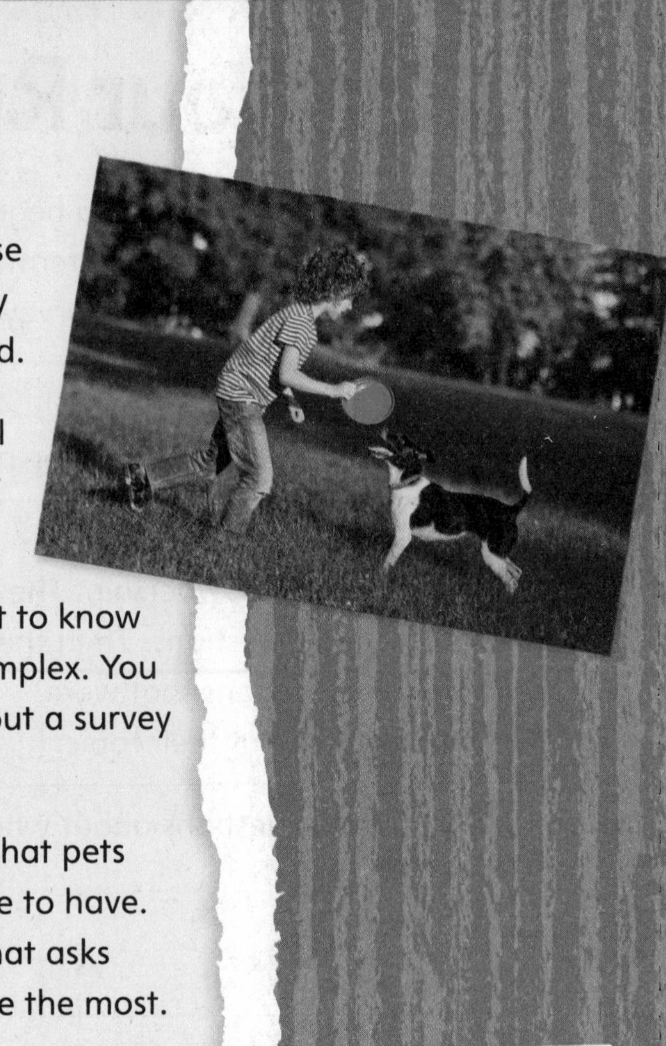

When you **conduct a survey,** you ask people for information about a topic. Investigators use surveys to learn what people do or think. They also use surveys to learn more about the world.

You can conduct a survey that asks for factual information, or you can conduct a survey that asks for people's opinions.

EXAMPLE: Factual Information You want to know how many pets live in your apartment complex. You ask one person in each apartment to fill out a survey that asks for this information.

EXAMPLE: Opinions You want to know what pets the students in your grade would most like to have. You ask ten students to fill out a survey that asks them to name the five pets they would like the most.

Oliver is conducting an opinion survey to learn people's thoughts about politics and government. He will generate formal questions.

Question 1: What issues would you like your U.S. representative to focus on?
Question 2: What candidate do you support for U.S. representative in the next election, and why?

Mya is conducting a factual survey to find out how households in her town spend money. She will generate formal questions.

Question 1: About how much money did you spend on housing last month?
Question 2: Do you spend more money on transportation or recreation each week?

COLLABORATE With your partner, generate a list of formal questions that you could ask people about the meaning of freedom.

Interview Questions

1.

2.

3.

Now carry out your survey and gather relevant information. Record people's responses. Remember that you can use e-mail, video conferencing, and phone calls to get in touch with people who do not live near you.

Person	Response

Briefly summarize the data you collected. In what ways are the responses alike? In what ways are they different? Were you surprised by anything anybody said? Talk to your partner about these questions.

Collect Your DATA

Once you have your survey responses, you and your partner can choose a format for your project. Remember that you will be creating an informational text based on your survey results. You will be reporting what people say about freedom and what freedom means to them. You will not be giving your own opinion about freedom.

Some possible formats for your project include:

- a speech for you and your partner to read aloud
- a poster with images in addition to text
- a television broadcast

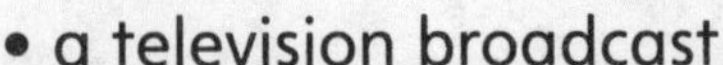

Now You Try It!

Discuss the checklist with your partner. Follow the steps as you create your project.

Make sure your project

- ☐ has a clear focus on a single topic.
- ☐ is organized in a logical way.
- ☐ includes facts and other supporting details.
- ☐ is based on the survey you created.
- ☐ ends with a brief conclusion.

Student Model

The Best Pets: A Speech

My fellow Americans, there are many important issues before us today: war and peace, jobs and the environment, and much more. But today, I want to talk about an issue that is overlooked: the question of what animals make the best pets.

I asked people to name their favorite pets. I also asked them why they chose them. Two people who answered my survey said the best pets were dogs. They liked that dogs would come when you called. "My dog is very loyal," my brother explained.

More people chose cats. These people liked that cats did not take up as much of your time. "You never have to walk a cat," my neighbor pointed out.

I got other responses, too. One person chose a cockatoo, which is a kind of bird. Another chose a lizard called a gecko. My grandmother said a ferret, but she added that ferrets sometimes bite. "Most ferrets are still wild animals," she explained.

I am not here to tell you what pet to get, if you need a pet. But you should listen to the reasons in my speech. They will help you choose an animal that is best for you!

Underline the topic.

Highlight details that show the facts are based on survey results.

Underline details that show the author is reporting the facts, not his or her opinions.

Highlight the conclusion.

Sources

Writers use two kinds of sources: **primary sources** and **secondary sources**. Primary sources are the words of people who were part of an event or witnessed it directly. Secondary sources are the words of people who did not experience the event themselves. Credible sources, whether primary or secondary, are sources that can be trusted. A source must include facts that support its opinion or central idea.

Primary Source Jaden goes to a new amusement park on the first day it is open and writes an essay for school about her experiences. Jaden's essay counts as a primary source because she was actually at the park. It is a credible source.

Secondary Source Soren writes an essay for school about the opening of an amusement park in the 1950s. Soren's essay counts as a secondary source because he was not at the park on the first day it opened. Soren's essay is credible if he used sources that can be trusted. Did he cite facts and information from a reliable book or Web site? If so, his essay is credible.

RESEARCH

COLLABORATE Read "Thomas Paine's Legacy." Identify the article as a primary source or a secondary source. Underline "Primary Source" or "Secondary Source" and explain your choice.

Primary Source

Secondary Source

COLLABORATE Read the excerpt from a TV news broadcast and answer the questions.

NEWS ANCHOR PAT MURPHY: Today, we're talking about pets. The demand for therapy dogs has been rising, so more and more people are training their own pets to help. Dr. Diana Nataro is a veterinarian who has been training therapy dogs for ten years. Tell me about these pets, Dr. Nataro.

DR. NATARO: A therapy dog is one that is trained to comfort people who are sick. In the last ten years, I have trained and paired more than fifty therapy dogs with patients who need them. Through my research I have found that therapy dogs can lower anxiety and blood pressure in patients.

MURPHY: Truly remarkable. Let's hear from local resident Alan DeSilva. Alan was recently visited by a therapy dog during a lengthy hospital stay.

ALAN DESILVA: In the hospital, I felt bored and tired. Then I met Spike. Whenever Spike visited the hospital, I instantly brightened. I looked forward to his visits, and I always felt happier and calmer after my time with him.

MURPHY: Thank you, Alan. Dr. Nataro, what advice can you give pet owners who would like to train their pets to become therapy animals?

DR. NATARO: You can enroll your pet in a training class to become a therapy pet, but first, just nurture your pet to be calm and kind.

1. Is this news broadcast a primary source or a secondary source? Explain.

2. Is this news broadcast a credible source? Explain.

Do AS I SAY!

A number of online tools can help you create your own survey. Your teacher can help you find some of these tools. You may be able to use these survey tools to ask people your survey questions, especially if the people do not live near you.

You can adapt survey forms online to generate your questions. Adjust the question types to fit the information and responses you need. You may wish to review survey forms and sample surveys before you create your own questions. Remember to keep your own opinions and biases—or preferences and prejudices—out of the survey questions.

When you create your own survey, be sure to

- Use clear, specific language
- Break down complicated ideas into multiple questions
- Ask about only one thing per question
- Avoid "leading" or biased questions

QUESTIONS RESPONSES

Pet Survey

Thank you for participating in our survey. We are researching which pets people prefer and why. Please complete this quick survey. Your answers will be anonymous.

What is your favorite pet?

- dog
- cat
- bird
- lizard
- other

Multiple choice

Choose your question type.

Type your specific question.

COLLABORATE With your partner, review the steps of conducting a survey: generate questions, create the survey, distribute the survey to people, collect responses, and combine data. Then discuss your data.

Experiment with using online survey tools to add to or change the questions you asked in your original survey.

- Clarify or revise questions that are vague or wordy.
- Clarify or revise complicated questions into separate questions.
- Clarify or revise leading or biased questions.
- Decide if you should conduct a new survey.

New or Revised Questions

1.

2.

3.

4.

5.

Revise

Informational Text Reread your work with your partner. Make sure your project is an example of informational text. Have you included

- ☐ a clear statement of your subject?
- ☐ facts about your topic?
- ☐ information based on your survey?
- ☐ a brief conclusion?

Revise for Clarity

Be as clear as possible when writing informational text. Make sure that your audience will understand exactly what you are trying to say. The writers of the speech earlier in this lesson realized that they had not been entirely clear in some places. They went back and changed a few sentences so their intentions were clear to their listeners.

eight
To prepare for this speech, I asked ^ people to name their favorite pets. I also asked them why they chose ~~them~~.
^ those particular animals

These people liked it that cats did not take up as much of your time.
^ as a dog does

Edit

Conventions Read your work again. Have you used correct conventions?

- ☐ spelling
- ☐ punctuation at the ends of sentences
- ☐ capital letters for proper nouns
- ☐ quotation marks for quoted material
- ☐ clear, precise language

Peer Review

COLLABORATE Exchange your project with another team. Read their work carefully and thoughtfully. Identify characteristics of an informational text as you read. Tell the other team the strong points of their work and what areas, if any, they can improve. Be specific in your explanations.

Time to Celebrate!

COLLABORATE Prepare to present your project. If you are using multimedia, create your video, audio, or other media before class and have it ready to share. If you are presenting orally, practice ahead of time. Practice using eye contact, conventions of language, and a natural speaking rate and volume.

Finally, share your project with the whole class. How did your classmates react to your presentation? List some of their reactions here.

Reflect on Your Project

My TURN Think about your project and your presentation. Which parts do you think were strongest? Which parts needed improvement? How might you make changes for next time? List your ideas here.

Strengths

Areas of Improvement

Reflect on Your Goals

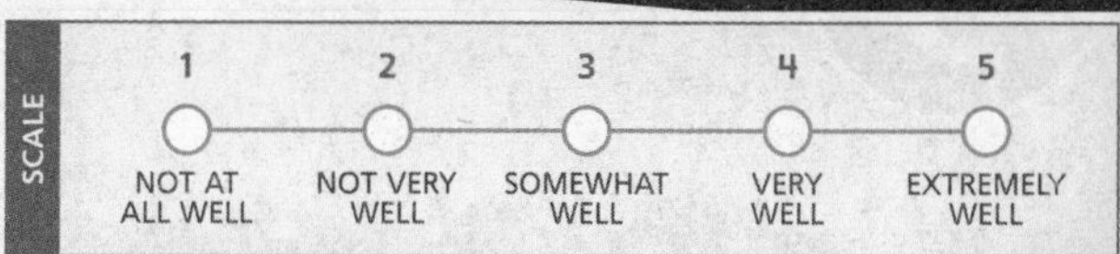

Look back at your unit goals. Use a different color to rate yourself again.

Reflect on Your Reading

Think about the books that you chose and read on your own during this unit. What did you find most interesting about these books? What did you enjoy the most?

Reflect on Your Writing

Think about your writing during the whole unit. What improvements have you made in your writing?

Systems

Essential Question

How do elements of systems change?

Watch

"The Changing Earth"

TURN and TALK

What changes do you see on Earth?

SAVVAS realize™

Go ONLINE for all lessons.

- VIDEO
- AUDIO
- INTERACTIVITY
- GAME
- ANNOTATE
- BOOK
- RESEARCH

Spotlight on Informational Text

READING WORKSHOP

Infographic: Who Are Geologists?

from *Rocks and Fossils* .... **Informational Text**
by Richard Hantula

Poem: The Water Cycle

from *Earth's Water Cycle* .... **Informational Text**
by Diane Dakers

Video: How Volcanoes Work

"The Dog of Pompeii" .... **Historical Fiction**
by Louis Untermeyer

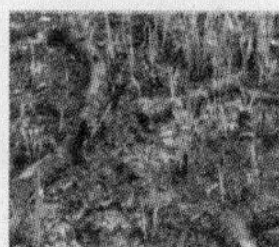

Diagram: Waste Is a Problem

"Let's Talk Trash" and "It's Time to Get Serious About Reducing Food Waste, Feds Say" .... **Informational Texts**
by USDA | by NPR

Map: How People Influence Natural Systems

People Should Manage Nature .... **Argumentative Text**
by Lee Francis IV

READING-WRITING BRIDGE

- Academic Vocabulary • Word Study
- **Read Like a Writer • Write for a Reader**
- Spelling • Language and Conventions

WRITING WORKSHOP

- Introduce and Immerse • Develop Elements
- Develop Structure • Writer's Craft
- Publish, Celebrate, and Assess

Poetry

PROJECT-BASED INQUIRY

- Inquire • Research • Collaborate

Independent Reading

In this unit you will read assigned texts with your teacher. You will also self-select texts to read independently.

Follow these steps to evaluate and respond to books you read on your own.

Step 1 Ask yourself:

- Who is the audience?
- Is the text informative, persuasive, or entertaining?
- What new vocabulary in the text helps me understand the topic?
- How does the author's craft add to the meaning of the text?
- How do the chapters or sections fit together to provide structure to the text?

Step 2 As you read, highlight and underline ideas and details that will help you evaluate the quality of the text.

Step 3 After reading, write a summary or a book review. Include details that will help a classmate decide whether to read the same text. Share your evaluation with your classmate.

Independent Reading Log

Date	Book	Genre	Pages Read	Minutes Read	My Ratings
					☆☆☆☆☆

Unit Goals

Shade in the circle to rate how well you meet each goal now.

SCALE	1	2	3	4	5
	NOT AT ALL WELL	NOT VERY WELL	SOMEWHAT WELL	VERY WELL	EXTREMELY WELL

Reading Workshop	1	2	3	4	5
I know about different types of informational texts and understand their structures and features.	○	○	○	○	○

Reading-Writing Bridge	1	2	3	4	5
I can use language to make connections between reading and writing.	○	○	○	○	○

Writing Workshop	1	2	3	4	5
I can use elements of poetry to write a poem.	○	○	○	○	○

Unit Theme	1	2	3	4	5
I can collaborate with others to explore how elements of systems change.	○	○	○	○	○

Academic Vocabulary

Use these words to talk about this unit's theme, *Systems*: *disturb*, *cycle*, *impact*, *composed*, and *engineer*.

TURN and TALK Read the words and definitions. Complete each sentence with the correct vocabulary word. Read your sentences aloud with a partner and discuss why you chose each word.

Academic Vocabulary	Definition
disturb	interfere with or interrupt something
cycle	a sequence of events that occurs regularly
impact	a strong effect on something; to hit with force
composed	formed by putting together
engineer	a person who plans and builds a machine

Example

Earth's surface is ___composed___ of three kinds of rock.

1. An earthquake can ________ the seafloor.

2. The ________ of lightning striking sand can create fulgurite.

3. The four seasons happen every year in a ________ .

4. The scientist and ________ worked together.

Who Are GEOLOGISTS?

Geologists are scientists who study rocks and soil to learn more about life on Earth. A geologist's job includes writing reports about scientific findings, creating maps, and collecting and analyzing rock samples. Geologists can work in more than twenty different careers, including seismology, volcanology, and hydrogeology. Geologists can work in a variety of settings, such as the outdoors, a school, an office, or a laboratory.

Facts That Rock!

- The oldest rock found on Earth is said to be about 4.4 billion years old.
- Basalt is the most common volcanic rock.
- Rocks melt at temperatures between 1,100 and 2,400 degrees Fahrenheit.
- There are three types of rocks:

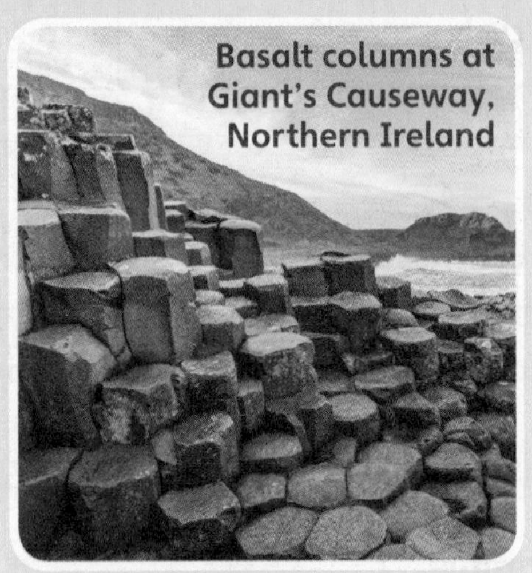
Basalt columns at Giant's Causeway, Northern Ireland

Igneous

Sedimentary

Metamorphic

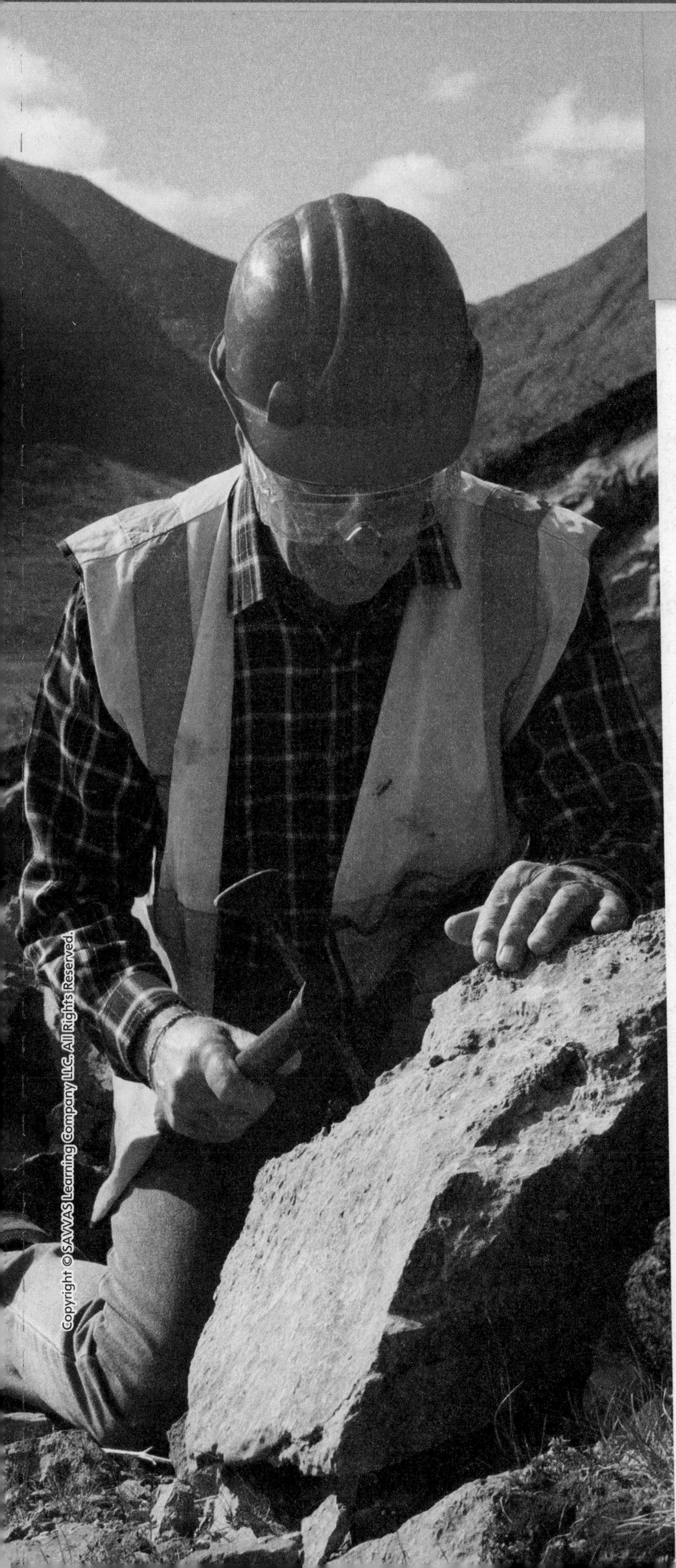

WEEK 1

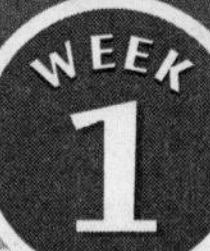

Weekly Question

How do rocks form and change over time?

Quick Write What can people learn from digging into Earth?

Learning Goal

I can learn more about informational text by identifying main ideas and details.

Spotlight on Genre

Informational Text

Informational texts inform or explain information about the natural or social world and include textbooks, newspapers, and magazines.
Informational texts contain

- **Facts**
- **Domain-specific vocabulary,** or words related to a specific topic
- **Text features,** such as graphics, captions, and sidebars
- **Titles, headings,** and **subheadings** that show how information is organized

TURN and TALK Think about an informational text you have read. Use the anchor chart to help you describe the text to a classmate. How do you know it is informational? What elements does it include? Take notes on your discussion.

My NOTES

The purpose of informational text is in the name– to inform!

Informational Text Anchor Chart

Informational Text = Fact-based

Features:

- **Table of contents:** a list of sections at the beginning of a text
- **Index:** a list of subjects in alphabetical order with page references; appears at the end of a text.
- **Glossary:** a list of defined words
- **Visuals**
  - graphs • diagrams • infographics • maps • photos • illustrations

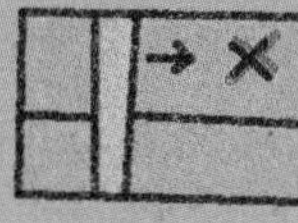

- Captions, sidebars, and labels
- Bold, *italic*, or highlighted words

Meet *the* Author

Richard Hantula writes to inform young readers about the world. Many of his books focus on social studies and science topics. He has written biographies about innovators, such as Thomas Edison. He has also written books about rocks, space, and the science behind soccer.

from

Rocks and Fossils

Preview Vocabulary

As you read the excerpt from *Rocks and Fossils*, pay attention to these vocabulary words. Notice how they connect to the main idea and details of the text.

minerals **particles**

deposits **erosion** **principles**

Read

Before you begin, establish a purpose for reading. Follow these strategies to read an **informational text** for the first time.

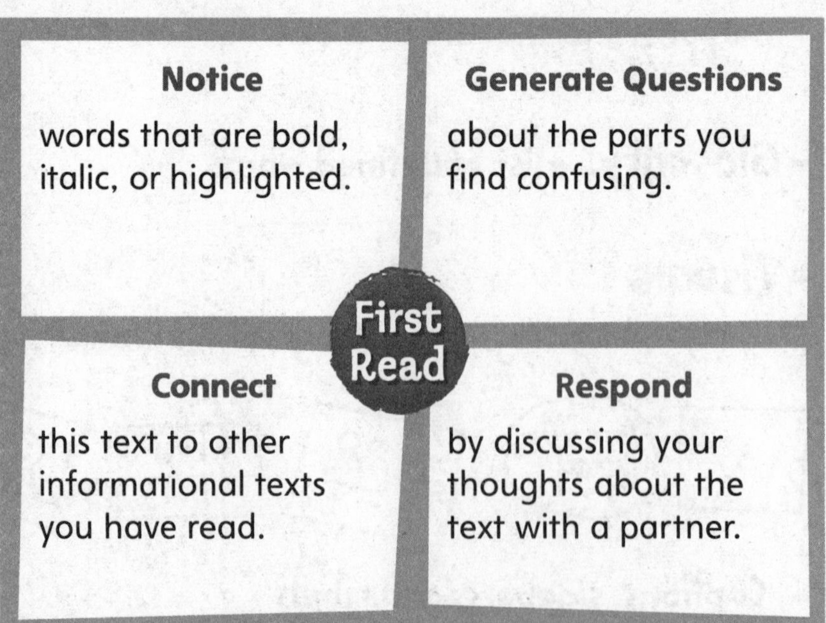

Genre Informational Text

from Rocks and Fossils

by Richard Hantula

AUDIO

ANNOTATE

BACKGROUND

Rocks and Fossils discusses not only the rocks we see on Earth's surface but also the many different processes that have created, moved, and shaped that surface for millions of years. The text explains how thousands of different minerals and three different types of rock were formed, and how we use them now.

Identify Main Idea and Details

Underline a sentence that helps you determine a main idea of the text. Then underline details that support the main idea.

minerals solid substances made of one or more simple chemicals

particles very small pieces of matter

ROCKS AND MINERALS

1 All rocks are solid and hard, but they come in an amazing variety of sizes, shapes, colors, and textures. They are all composed of mixtures of materials, usually (but not always) including substances called minerals. Some are made almost entirely of one mineral. Limestone is an example. It is composed mainly of the mineral calcite. Most rocks, however, are mixtures of two, three, or more minerals.

2 The word *mineral* is sometimes used for all sorts of substances. For example, many vitamin pills contain not only vitamins but also minerals. Workers in the mining industry often use the word *mineral* for any material taken from the earth. They may call oil, gravel, coal, and copper ore minerals.

3 The term *mineral*, however, is usually used more narrowly by scientists who study Earth and its rocks. These experts are known as geologists. For geologists, a mineral is a solid substance made of one or more simple chemicals called elements. Each element has its own specific type of atoms. Atoms are particles that constitute the building blocks of matter. In each mineral, atoms are combined in a particular way. They form a regular pattern called a crystal. Many geologists insist on one more thing before they call a substance a mineral. They require that it not be formed from living things.

Mineral Medley

4 More than four thousand minerals have been discovered on Earth. Color, hardness, and weight are some of the ways in which they differ. A key reason that minerals differ is that they are made of different elements. That is not the only reason, however. How the elements' atoms are arranged in a crystal is also important. Combining the same atoms in different ways will produce different crystals, and the results will be different minerals. For example, atoms of carbon that are joined together in one way make diamond. Putting them together in a different way makes graphite. Graphite is black and quite soft. Diamond is transparent and is the hardest substance found in nature.

Both diamond (*left*) and graphite (*right*) are made of carbon, but they are very different minerals. Graphite is soft, is black or gray in color, and has a metallic sheen. Diamond, formed under high pressure and temperature, is extremely hard.

5 A few minerals are plentiful in Earth's crust. This rocky top layer, especially the portion under the continents, is the part of the planet we know best. More than 98 percent of the continental crust is made up of just eight elements. The most common ones are oxygen and silicon. Minerals containing these two elements are found almost everywhere. One mineral, feldspar, makes up more than half of the continental crust. Feldspar is actually a group of related minerals. All feldspars contain not only oxygen and silicon but also aluminum plus another element. Quartz is the next most common mineral. It is silicon dioxide. The name means it is made up of two atoms of oxygen for every atom of silicon.

CLOSE READ

Make Connections

Highlight evidence that helps you make a connection to what you already know about how minerals form.

Make Connections

Highlight details that help you make connections to what you already know about gemstones.

Identify Main Idea and Details

Underline a detail that helps explain the value of gemstones.

Two of these four gemstones, ruby (*upper left*) and sapphire (*upper right*), consist primarily of the hard mineral known as corundum. Ruby's red color comes from the presence of a small amount of chromium. Green emerald (*lower left*) is made mainly of the mineral beryl. Topaz (*lower right*) tends to be white or light-colored.

Prized Minerals

6 Gemstones are minerals that can be cut and polished to have an attractive look. They are durable and highly prized. After they are cut and polished, they are known as gems. Gems tend to be valued highly because they are not only beautiful but also so hard that they resist being scratched. Diamonds are the hardest of all, and they are especially prized. Beautiful, durable, and rare gemstones, such as emeralds and rubies, are said to be precious. Gemstones that meet only one or two of these three criteria are usually known as semiprecious. Jade and zircon are examples of semiprecious stones.

7 Ores make up another group of prized minerals. An ore contains a valuable metal or another substance. For a mineral to be called an ore, it must be present in one place in amounts, or deposits, large enough to make mining worthwhile.

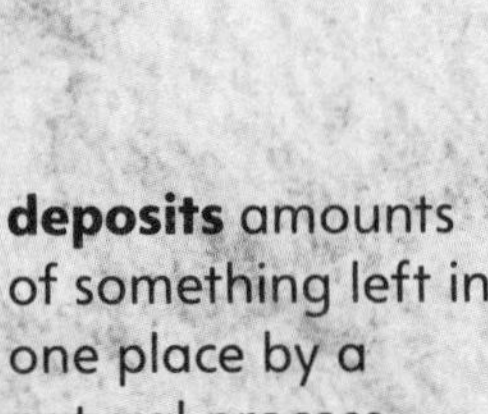

deposits amounts of something left in one place by a natural process

Nonmineral Rocks

8 While most rocks on Earth contain minerals, as defined by geologists, some do not. Coal is one example. It is a rock that was formed from the remains of dead plants. Two more examples are obsidian and pumice, which come from volcanoes. They are glassy and lack a crystal pattern.

ROCK TYPES

9 There are three basic types of rocks—igneous, sedimentary, and metamorphic. Each type is formed in a different way. A rock's makeup reflects the way it was formed. Rocks also carry other clues about their history. These clues may reveal when a rock was formed. They may also give hints as to what conditions were like when the rock was formed. There may even be clues about events that have occurred right up until the present. Clues found in rocks can help scientists learn about the history of Earth.

Igneous Rocks

10 Most rocks in Earth's crust are igneous. They began as hot liquid material called magma. Magma usually is found at depths where it is much hotter than on the surface. This heat is how igneous rocks got their name. *Igneous* comes from a Latin word that means "fire." If magma gets cool enough, it turns solid and becomes igneous rock.

11 There are many kinds of igneous rocks. Each type is determined by how it was formed. Another factor is what its original magma was made of.

CLOSE READ

Make Connections

Highlight details that help you connect to other information you have read about rocks.

Identify Main Idea and Details

Underline text that helps you identify an important detail about different types of rocks that supports a main idea.

Identify Main Idea and Details

Underline phrases in the caption that support a main idea of the section "Intrusive Igneous Rocks."

Intrusive Igneous Rocks

12 If magma cools slowly, it turns into one type of igneous rock. This can happen when magma moves to a part of the crust with a somewhat lower temperature. For example, magma might be pushed closer to the surface through a crack. The magma intrudes, or inserts itself, into the crack. The new rock that forms when the magma cools is called intrusive rock. Since the magma cools slowly, there is plenty of time for crystals to grow. As a result, the crystals in intrusive rocks tend to be large.

13 Although formed underground, some intrusive rocks later end up on the surface. If you look at such a rock, you can see in it large bits or particles called grains, which contain one or more crystals. The most common sort of intrusive rock on the surface is granite. It contains feldspar and quartz, along with a little mica and tiny bits of other minerals. It is very hard. Its color tends to be gray or whitish, but some kinds are pinkish or even other colors. The colors depend on the minerals that make up the granite. Another common intrusive rock, gabbro, is darker in color.

This towering rock face in Yosemite National Park in California is made of granite. It was formed by intrusion of magma, which solidified and later was left behind when surrounding rock was worn away.

Extrusive Igneous Rocks

14 If magma cools down fast, it turns into a different type of igneous rock. This happens when magma comes out onto the surface. It may come out through an opening called a vent in a volcano. It may also come through a crack, or fissure, in the ground. Magma that flows onto the surface is called lava. The temperature on the surface is much lower than in the crust, and the lava cools quickly. Since the magma is pushed out, or extruded, onto the surface, igneous rocks made in this way are called extrusive. They are also sometimes called volcanic rocks. Extrusive rocks tend to have tiny grains. If they cool very quickly, they may even lack grains. They may look smooth like glass.

Vocabulary in Context

Context clues are words and sentences around an unfamiliar word that help readers understand the word.

Underline context clues to find the meaning of *extruded*.

A highway passes by the edge of a rock formation of hardened lava.

15 The most common extrusive rock is basalt. It is dark-colored. Its ingredients are similar to those of the intrusive rock gabbro, but basalt and gabbro look different. It is much easier to see grains or crystals in gabbro. Because basalt comes from fast-cooling lava, its grains are very tiny. Many of the rocks brought back to Earth from the Moon are basalt. They were probably formed in the same way as Earth's basalt rocks—lava poured out onto the surface from below and cooled.

16 Another sort of extrusive rock is rhyolite. It is light-colored and has the same minerals as the intrusive rock granite. When certain kinds of lava cool very rapidly, the result is a glassy black or darkish rock called obsidian. Obsidian forms sharp edges when broken.

CLOSE READ

Make Connections

Highlight details in the text and text features that show a connection between pumice's form and its use in the world.

17 Sometimes lava contains air bubbles. It may seem like foam. If the lava is very thick, like molasses, the bubbles can't escape before it hardens into a rock. This rock is called pumice. It is full of spongelike holes and is lightweight. Some kinds of pumice can even float on water.

The so-called Giant's Causeway on the coast of Northern Ireland consists of thousands of columns of basalt that were formed some 60 million years ago when an extrusive lava flow quickly cooled.

18 Air also plays a role in another sort of igneous rock. Some volcanoes throw powdery dust, or ash, into the air. If the ash piles up, it may turn into a soft rock known as tuff.

Putting Igneous Rocks to Work

Since ancient times, people have made buildings and monuments from hard, durable granite. It can be polished, so it is also used as a decorative stone. Granite is often used today to make floor tiles and kitchen countertops.

Obsidian is shiny and sharp-edged. For ages, it has been used to make jewelry, mirrors, and cutting tools. Even today, doctors use obsidian scalpels because they are so sharp.

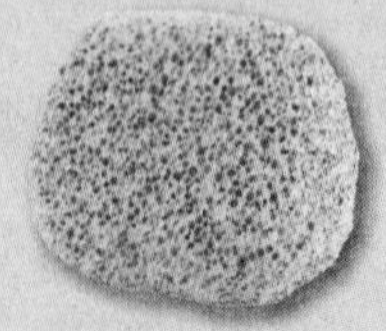

Lightweight pumice makes a good decorative stone. Ground-up pumice is an ingredient in some types of concrete. Pumice is an abrasive and is good for grinding, cleaning, or polishing surfaces. Pumice is also used to make cosmetics and soaps.

Sedimentary Rocks

19 Most of the rocks on Earth's surface are sedimentary rocks. They were formed from sediment, or material that settles in an area. It might be sand, mud, dust, little stones, or the remains of dead plants and animals. The material may be deposited by water, wind, or even moving ice (as in a glacier). As more and more of the material piles up, its weight generates enormous pressure at the bottom of the sediment. Here the sediment material is squeezed tightly together and slowly turns into solid rock, a process that may take thousands, or even millions, of years.

Identify Main Idea and Details

<u>Underline</u> details about sedimentary rocks that help support a main idea of the text.

These rock strata in Capitol Reef National Park in Utah were originally formed over millions of years when the area was at the bottom of a sea. Later, uplift of land and erosion resulted in the formations that exist today.

20 Sediment sometimes settles on the seafloor. Sediment is also deposited on the bottoms of other bodies of water, such as lakes, and on the floors of swamps. Accumulations of sand in beaches and dunes may eventually be transformed into sedimentary rock if conditions are right.

21 Sedimentary rocks can tell scientists a lot about the past. The rocks' makeup carries clues about the conditions that existed when the rocks were created. Sediment tends to be laid down in layers, or strata. This layering helps scientists identify neighboring areas of rock that were formed at the same time.

erosion a slow process of being worn away

22 Sedimentary rocks also give clues about life in the distant past. These clues usually involve fossils, which are remains or traces (such as tracks or burrows) of ancient living things. Fossils often form part of the materials found in sedimentary rock.

Make Connections

Highlight a detail that helps you make a connection to your own experience.

Putting Sedimentary Rocks to Work

When trying to list the most useful sedimentary rocks, coal may be the first thing that comes to mind. There are, however, many others. Sedimentary rocks are the source of such fossil fuels as oil and natural gas. Conglomerate and other sedimentary rocks play a major role in the construction industry. Limestone is used to make cement. Shale is also sometimes used to make cement, as well as bricks. Limestone and sandstone are important building stones. There are many examples outside the construction industry as well. Gypsum is used as an ingredient in making various products, such as plaster of paris, pottery, and cake icing. Rocks containing phosphate are used to make fertilizer. Rock salt is a primary source of salt, which is an essential component of our diet and is also used for many purposes. (Salt is also produced through the evaporation of seawater.)

Types of Sedimentary Rocks

23 Sedimentary rocks can be divided into three types. They are called clastic, chemical, and organic (or biological). The basic difference between these types is the way they were formed. This results in differences in appearance.

24 *Clastic* comes from the Greek word *klastos*, meaning "broken." Clastic rocks are made from broken pieces of other rocks. For example, sand grains are tiny bits of rock. If these bits are squeezed together long and hard enough, the result is the clastic rock called sandstone.

25 The bits of material in silt or mud are extremely tiny. If they are pressed tightly enough together to form a rock, the result is shale or mudstone. Shale and mudstone are rather soft and have finer grains than sandstone.

CLOSE READ

Identify Main Idea and Details

Underline a sentence about chemical rocks that summarizes paragraph 27.

26 Clastic rocks may contain rock pieces that are bigger than sand grains. The pieces may even be as big as boulders! Smaller bits of material help to cement these pieces together. If the pieces have spent a long time in moving water, they will have rounded edges. The same is true of pieces that have been moved and tumbled a lot among other rocks. Sedimentary rocks containing such smooth-edged pieces are called conglomerates. If the original rock pieces were simply piled up at the foot of a mountain, however, their edges will be sharp. The sedimentary rock containing them is called breccia.

27 Chemical rocks contain principally material that was carried or dissolved in water. Under certain conditions, the material settles on the bottom of the body of water, where it may form solid crystals. Another way dissolved material may separate, or precipitate, from water is to be left behind when the water evaporates. Examples of rocks formed by precipitation from water include rock salt (halite), rock gypsum, a few types of limestone, and most of the world's important iron ore deposits. In caves, stalactites and stalagmites are formed from minerals in dripping water. Stalactites look like icicles and extend from the roof of a cave. Stalagmites are deposits that build up from the floor.

Sandstone can sometimes take rather impressive shapes and sizes.

CLOSE READ

Identify Main Idea and Details

Underline a main idea that summarizes how metamorphic rocks form.

You can see some of the variety of sedimentary rocks in these examples. Conglomerate (*left*) is a clastic rock containing rock pieces that tend to be smooth or rounded. The pieces in breccia (*center*), a different sort of clastic rock, are sharp edged. Some limestones (*right*) contain an abundance of fossils.

28 Organic rocks form mainly from the remains of living things. Among the types of remains that may end up in organic rocks are plants, shells, bones, and the skeletons of tiny living organisms called plankton. Lignite and bituminous coal, for example, develop from ancient plant remains. Limestone comes mainly from the shells of tiny creatures living in reefs or on the sea bottom. Chalk is a soft type of limestone.

Metamorphic Rocks

29 The word *metamorphism* means "change of form." Metamorphic rocks are rocks that have changed as a result of being subjected to new conditions. These conditions may involve increased heat, increased pressure, or exposure to fluids containing substances that can help alter the rock's makeup. (For example, hot water sometimes carries certain chemicals, such as carbon dioxide, that may dissolve material in the rock, cause chemical reactions, or promote the formation of crystals.) Most often the new conditions involve heat and/or pressure that bakes the original rock. However, the combined effect must not be so great as to cause the original rock to melt. If the original rock melts, it becomes magma. When it cools, the new rock is considered igneous rather than metamorphic.

30 Metamorphism changes any kind of rock—igneous, sedimentary, or metamorphic—into a new metamorphic rock. Metamorphic rocks have some things in common. They are usually harder than the original rock. Also, they contain crystals. The kinds of changes that happen in metamorphism depend on the makeup of the original rock and on the conditions the rock undergoes. Metamorphism may alter the rock's crystal pattern or texture, for example, or it may change the original minerals into different ones.

Contact and Regional Metamorphism

31 When scientists talk about metamorphism, they commonly have in mind effects caused by heat or pressure. There are two chief ways such metamorphism can take place. One is called contact metamorphism. This can occur when a bit of rock comes into contact with hot flowing magma or lava. The amount of rock affected is small. Contact metamorphism can happen at the surface, since hot lava appears there. Usually, however, the conditions causing it are found somewhere deep underground.

32 Another way rock changes is called regional metamorphism. Large amounts of rock are exposed to high pressure or heat below the surface. This kind of metamorphism can happen, for example, below a mountain range, whose weight subjects the rock below it to high pressure. High pressure and heat can also occur as a result of major rock movements. The outer layer of Earth is broken up into a number of large slabs called tectonic plates. Some are under continents, and some are under oceans. Forces from deep below the plates cause them to move slowly.

CLOSE READ

Identify Main Idea and Details

Underline details in the text that give you clues about the main idea of the section "Contact and Regional Metamorphism."

Make Connections

Highlight details that help you understand how metamorphic rocks move and change over time.

In some places, plates slip past each other. In some places, they bang into each other. The edge of one plate may be pushed under another, exposing rocks at the edge to the high heat that exists deep below. One way or another, rocks in a large region are exposed to enough heat and pressure to undergo change.

Some metamorphic rocks are foliated. They appear to be made of layers. Some are not foliated. This gneiss in Bayerischer Wald National Park in Germany (*left*) is an example of a foliated rock. The fractured quartzite in the Negev Desert in Israel (*right*) is unfoliated.

Foliation

33 Because of the pressure they undergo, the crystal grains in regional metamorphic rocks are often arranged in parallel stripes or flat sheets. This is called foliation. In a way, it is like the grain pattern in wood. Schist and gneiss are common regional metamorphic rocks that show obvious foliation. They form under high pressure and at high temperatures, and they have coarse grains. Slate forms from the sedimentary rock shale under more moderate conditions. It has fine grains and can easily be split into sheets. Marble usually forms from limestone. It has an even texture and lacks foliation.

34 Foliation ordinarily does not occur in contact metamorphic rocks. The most common contact rock called hornfels, for example, lacks foliation. Instead, it has grains to form even texture.

Getting to the Surface

35 Most metamorphic rocks are formed deep underground, so it may seem strange that they are often found on the surface. How does this happen? Sometimes forces within Earth lift up sections of buried rock.

36 Metamorphic rocks also can reach the surface as a result of erosion, when rock and soil that cover metamorphic rocks are worn away. Thanks to these natural processes, many metamorphic rocks are available for a variety of purposes. Scientists value these rocks because they carry clues about their origins. They reveal what conditions are like deep within Earth's crust.

CLOSE READ

Identify Main Idea and Details

Underline the main idea of the text feature. Then underline details about marble that support the main idea.

Putting Metamorphic Rocks to Work

Marble has a smooth texture, and the best-known type is white. Marble is also easy to carve, compared with many other rock materials. Because of features like these, it has been used for centuries to make statues and impressive buildings, such as the Lincoln Memorial in Washington, DC, with its seated statue (*right*) of Abraham Lincoln, the sixteenth president of the United States. Another well-known marble building is the ornate Taj Mahal in Agra, India.

Slate is another important construction rock. It is used as a finishing stone for buildings and as a material for roofing tiles and pool tables. Schist and gneiss are also used as building stones.

Anthracite, a hard, black coal formed from bituminous ("soft") coal by metamorphic processes, is an important fuel.

Identify Main Idea and Details

Underline details in the text and text features that help you determine the main idea of this section.

ROCK CHANGES

Constant Activity

37 With rocks, change is always going on. New rocks are constantly being created on Earth. Right now, metamorphism is occurring all over the world. Hot lava is cooling into new igneous rock. Sediments are hardening into new sedimentary rock.

Horseshoe Bend in Arizona vividly shows the power of erosion. The Colorado River has carved a spectacularly curvy path through the rock.

38 Meanwhile, many old rocks are undergoing various kinds of changes. Some may gradually wear away, or erode. Others may be broken up by the growth of tree roots. Some may slowly break up as a result of weathering. Weathering includes various processes. Rocks may be eaten away by chemicals, such as acid in rainwater or in substances from living creatures. Rocks may also be slowly broken down by changes in temperature, by freezes and thaws.

39 Movement on Earth's surface is another major cause of change in rocks. Glaciers, rivers, and landslides move rocks from one place to another.

Mount Belukha, located near Russia's border with Kazakhstan, is the highest peak of the Altai Mountains. The movement of mountain glaciers can drag rocks from one place to another.

In the process, the rocks are knocked around and break up. Alternatively, they may end up in a place where conditions, such as temperature and pressure, are quite different. Movements below the surface of Earth also cause change. Rocks may be affected by the flow of magma from one place to another. The movements of the tectonic plates lift up land in some places, creating mountains, and cause land to sink in other areas. Earthquakes involve sudden movements of huge masses of rock. Some rocks may be altered by the new conditions they end up in. Some may be destroyed by the shock of the quake.

The Rock Cycle

Earth is more than 4 billion years old. For virtually this entire time, it has consisted of more or less the same amount of matter. (Meteorites and other objects coming from space have added some, but the amount is small.) As we have seen, rocks are constantly undergoing change. At the same time that old rock is being destroyed, new rock is being created. The old rock is recycled to make new rock. Scientists call this process the rock cycle.

CLOSE READ

Make Connections

Highlight words or phrases that connect to an earlier idea in the text.

Make Connections

Highlight words and phrases in the text that connect to information in the diagram.

41 To see how the process works, start at any part of the cycle and follow it step by step. Let's begin with hot magma. Suppose the magma moves into a cooler underground region or erupts onto the surface. It then cools off and forms igneous rock. Underground igneous rock may be brought to the surface. It might be carried there by movements in Earth's crust. It might end up there because the rock and soil above it were worn away. Igneous rock can even form on the surface, when lava cools. No matter how it gets there, igneous rock on the surface undergoes erosion and weathering. These processes slowly break it down into tiny pieces. The pieces may be carried away, perhaps to the sea. When a lot of this material collects as sediment in one place, the pressure on the lower part of the sediment may be great enough to turn it into sedimentary rock. If the sedimentary rock happens to undergo high heat and pressure underground, it turns into metamorphic rock. The metamorphic rock may come into contact with very hot magma; it may be crushed between tectonic plates. It might be pushed deep into Earth, where it is extremely hot. Any of these events could make the metamorphic rock melt and become magma. Then, the cycle can begin again.

The Rock Cycle

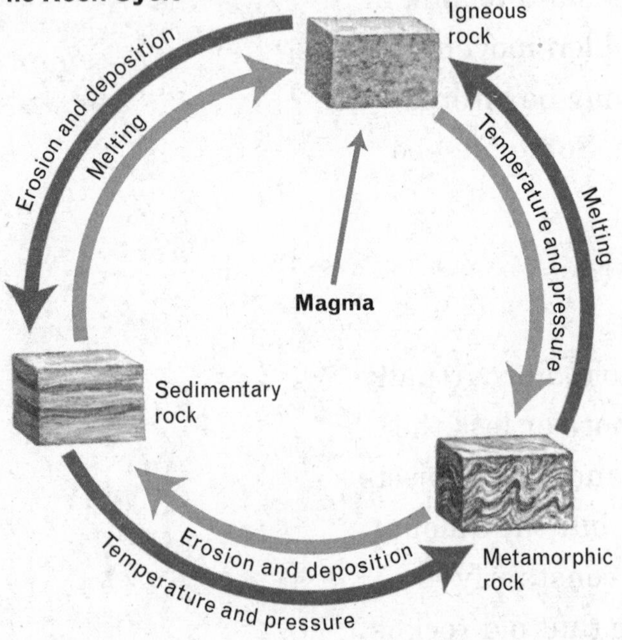

The three basic types of rock—igneous, sedimentary, and metamorphic—are interrelated. Rock of each type can be turned into one of the other types. Scientists call this interrelationship the rock cycle.

CLOSE READ

Identify Main Idea and Details

Underline words and phrases the author repeats that help support the main idea of the section "Rock Changes."

42 Actually there is more to the cycle. Rock of each type can be turned into one of the other types. Rock of each type can also be turned into new rock of the same type. Any rock exposed to sufficient heat and pressure can melt. This means that, under the right conditions, igneous and sedimentary rock can be turned directly into magma. When the magma cools, new igneous rock results. Also, erosion and weathering can affect any type of rock, not just igneous. Thus, under the right conditions, metamorphic and sedimentary rock may be broken down to form sediment. This sediment may accumulate and may eventually form new sedimentary rock. In addition, sedimentary rock is not the only type that can undergo metamorphism. Under the right conditions, igneous and metamorphic rock can also be changed into new metamorphic rock.

Layers Upon Layers

43 Sediment usually accumulates on a flat surface. As conditions change over time, the sediment may change in content or in the rate at which it is deposited. When sedimentary rock eventually forms, these differences in sediment give the rock a layered look. The layers, or strata, can be easily seen when something exposes them to view. For example, erosion by a river may create a canyon in whose walls sedimentary layers are visible. Road builders cutting through rock also may expose sedimentary strata.

These rock strata have been shaped into a vertical position by forces within the Earth.

Identify Main Idea and Details

Underline details that help you understand relationships among layers of rock.

44 The thickness and makeup of the strata in a particular area can tell geologists much about what happened there in the past. The strata's makeup may include not only minerals but also fossils of ancient living creatures. Scientists often find similarities between certain strata in different parts of the world. This may mean the strata were formed at the same time. By studying such strata and fossils found in them, geologists sometimes can discover what conditions were like over a wide area of the world at that time.

Two Basic Principles

principles general theories or facts

45 A couple of basic principles guide geologists in their work. One is called superposition. This is the idea that in a stack of rock layers, the higher strata tend to be younger than the lower ones. So as you go lower, you go farther back in time.

46 Another basic principle is called original horizontality. This means that when sediments were originally laid down, they formed flat layers approximately parallel to the surface of Earth.

47 Although these two principles are helpful, geologists usually need more information to understand a series of layers. Over millions of years, many events might interfere with sedimentary strata. For example, a flow of magma might make its way into the layers.

48 Another possible event is an earthquake, which might cause a break in the strata, shifting one section in one direction and a neighboring section in the opposite direction. Such a break, or fracture, is known as a fault.

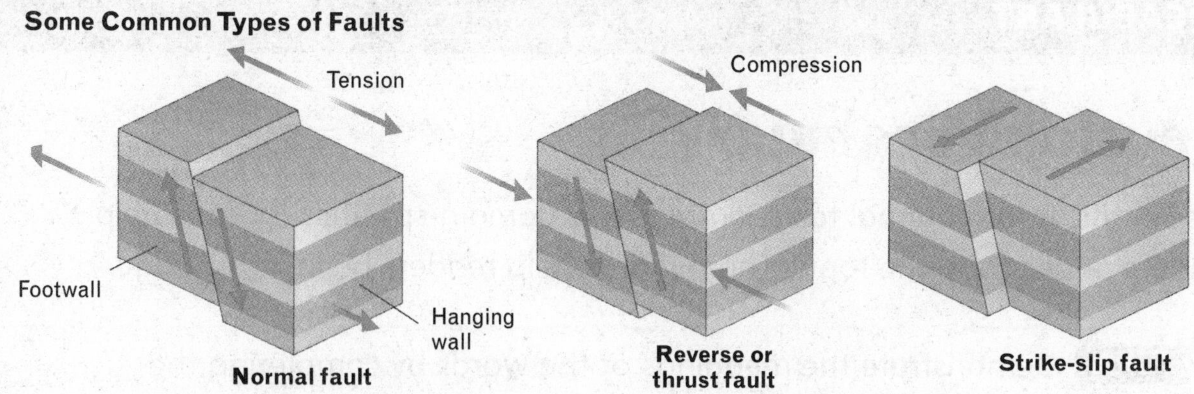

Forces in the Earth's crust can cause movement of rock along a fault, which is commonly at an incline. Faults are classified by the direction of this movement. In a normal fault, the blocks of rock on each side of the break are pulled apart by tension forces, and the block overlying the break—called the hanging wall—moves downward relative to the other block—the footwall. If compression forces are involved, however, the blocks are pushed together, and the hanging wall moves upward relative to the footwall. In this case, the fault is called a reverse fault if the inclination, or dip, is greater than 45°; it is a thrust fault if the dip is 45° or less. In a strike-slip fault, the movement is horizontal.

49 Also, pressure within Earth might cause the layers to tilt or even bend into a fold. The layers are no longer horizontal—a telltale sign of movement, according to the principle of horizontal originality.

Need for Caution

50 Geologists need to be cautious when they draw conclusions. It is possible for powerful forces within Earth to shift older strata on top of younger strata. In that case, the principle of superposition does not apply. An unconformity is another factor that can complicate the job of "reading" history from a series of layers. An unconformity is a gap in the series where some layers seem to be missing. The layer above the unconformity is much younger than the layer below it. There are various possible reasons for such a gap. One is that the missing layers were eroded away before new strata were laid down. Another possibility is that environmental conditions changed and, for a certain period, no sediment was deposited.

CLOSE READ

Identify Main Idea and Details

Underline details that help clarify why geologists must use caution.

Develop Vocabulary

In scientific informational texts, authors use domain-specific words to help readers understand the topic. These words help readers build knowledge.

My TURN Demonstrate the meanings of the words by completing the sentences. Make connections between the pairs of words that help you understand rocks and the rock cycle.

1. **Minerals** and **deposits** are connected because

____

____

____.

2. **Deposits** and **erosion** are connected because

____

____

____.

3. **Erosion** and **particles** are connected because

____

____

____.

4. **Deposits** and **principles** are connected because

____

____

____.

Check for Understanding

My TURN Look back at the text to answer the questions.

1. Explain how you know that this is informational text.

2. When and why does the author use text features in *Rocks and Fossils*? Describe one use and say how it affects readers.

3. Compare and contrast the ways igneous and sedimentary rocks are formed.

4. As the text explains, the rock cycle is more complicated than the circle diagram suggests. To expand on the diagram, explain how igneous rock can change into sedimentary rock and how metamorphic rock can change into igneous rock.

Identify Main Idea and Details

The **main idea** is the most important idea about the topic. An author explains the main idea with supporting evidence, including facts and other details. The reader may have to infer the main idea from information the author provides. A text may have more than one main idea.

1. **My TURN** Go to the Close Read notes and underline the parts that help you understand a main idea and the details that support it.

2. **Text Evidence** Use the parts you underlined to complete the chart. Identify a main idea and three supporting details.

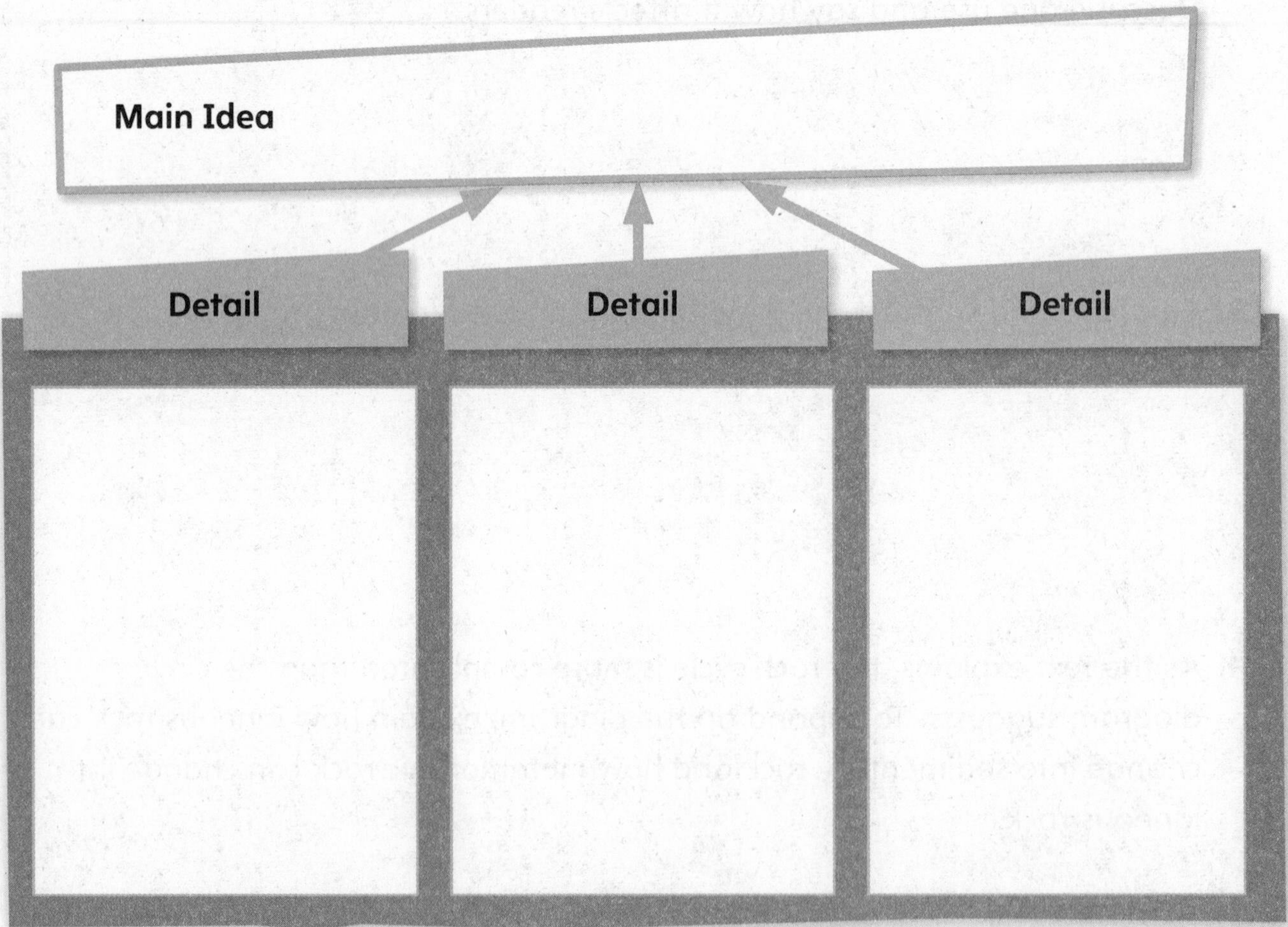

TURN and TALK Discuss another main idea of the text. What details support the idea?

Make Connections

While reading informational text, readers **make connections** to what they know from reading other texts, from personal experiences, and from their understanding of the world.

1. **MY TURN** Go back to the Close Read notes and highlight evidence that helps you make connections to your own experience, to other texts you have read, and to a rock's use in the world.

2. **Text Evidence** Use your highlighted text to complete the graphic organizer.

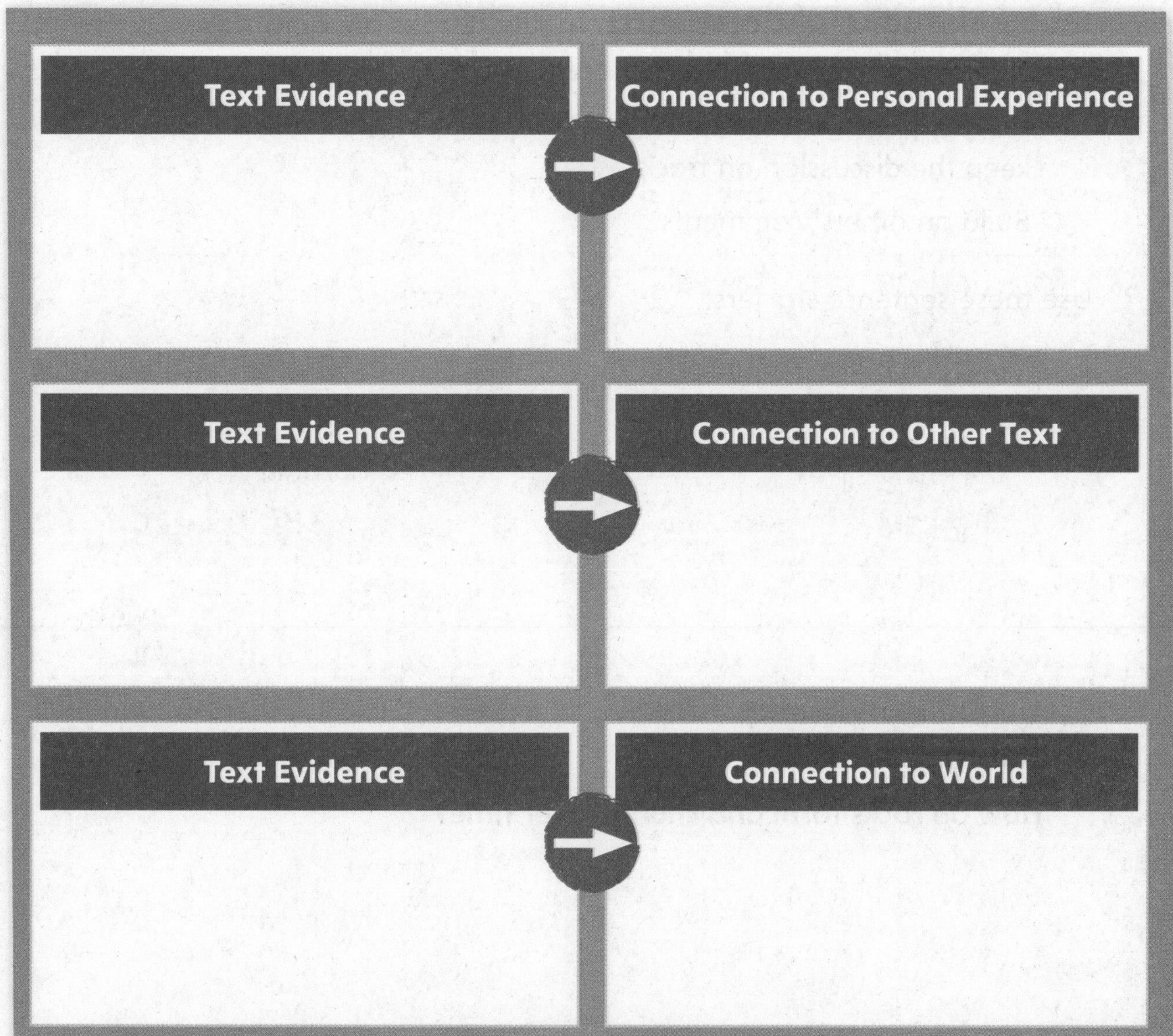

Reflect and Share

Talk About It A system is a group of items or processes that regularly and consistently interact with one another. Consider all the texts you have read this week. What other geological processes did you learn about? How do these processes form a system? Use these questions to discuss how geological processes are related.

Make Thoughtful Comments In any discussion, only make comments that are related to the topic.

- Discuss specific, important ideas that are on topic. This will keep the discussion on track.
- Build on others' comments.

Use these sentence starters:

Another point about that is . . .

Your comment made me remember that . . .

Weekly Question

How do rocks form and change over time?

Academic Vocabulary

Learning Goal

I can develop knowledge about language to make connections between reading and writing.

Adding a prefix or suffix to a base word creates a **related word** and often changes the base word's part of speech. For example, adding affixes to the verb *vary* forms new words, such as the noun *variety* and the adjective *various*.

My TURN For each row in the chart,

1. **Read** the sentence.
2. **Use** context clues to **define** the academic vocabulary word.
3. **Add** affixes to create new words. Consult a print or digital reference if you need help.

Sentences	Meaning of Boldface Word	Word Forms with Affixes
Moving water can **disturb** sediment under the surface.	interfere with	disturbed, disturber, disturbance, disturbingly
In the rock **cycle**, new rock is formed with recycled old rock.		
Magma erupting to Earth's surface causes an immediate **impact**.		
Rocks are **composed** of minerals and other materials.		

Consonant Changes

Consonant changes can affect how a letter in a word is pronounced. The final consonant sound in the word *music*, for example, is the sound *k*. After adding the ending *-ian*, the sound changes to the sound *sh* in *musician*.

The letter *t* in the word *erupt* spells the sound *t*. However, changing the word to *eruption* changes the sound *t* to the sound *sh*.

My TURN Read words with consonant changes. Then complete the chart by writing the correct pronunciation of each word. If necessary, use a print or digital resource to confirm your answers.

Word	*k* sound or *t* sound?	Word with Consonant Change	Change in Pronunciation
construct	*t* sound	construction	*t* sound to *sh* sound
direct		direction	
electric		electrician	
pediatric		pediatrician	
react		reaction	

Read Like a Writer

Authors of informational text often include print features such as headings, subheadings, captions, and graphics to clarify and structure their ideas.

Read the text from *Rocks and Fossils*.

heading

ROCK TYPES

There are three basic types of rocks—igneous, sedimentary, and metamorphic.

1. **Identify** Richard Hantula uses the heading ROCK TYPES.
2. **Question** What does this text feature tell me about the text?
3. **Conclude** It tells me this part of the text will describe rock types.

Read the text.

ROCK CHANGES

Constant Activity

With rocks, change is always going on. New rocks are constantly being created on Earth. Right now, metamorphism is occurring all over the world.

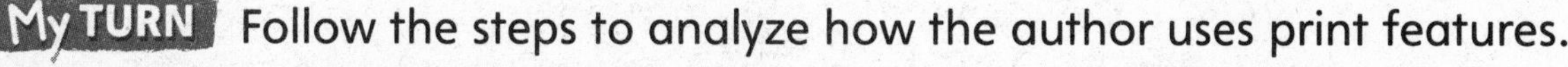

My TURN Follow the steps to analyze how the author uses print features.

1. **Identify** Richard Hantula uses a ______________ and a ______________.
2. **Question** What do these text features tell me about this section?
3. **Conclude** The text features tell me ______________________________

____.

Write for a Reader

Authors of informational text use elements of craft, such as print features, to achieve specific purposes. Headings, subheadings, captions, and graphics can produce specific effects.

My TURN Think about how Richard Hantula's use of text features in *Rocks and Fossils* affects you as a reader. Now identify how you can use print features to influence your own readers.

1. Think about a topic that interests you, such as a type of animal, a sport, a book series, or a game. If you were writing to inform others about this topic, what text features might you use?

2. Write a short passage about this topic. Use text features to clarify or emphasize your ideas.

Spell Words with Consonant Changes

Consonant changes affect how a word is spelled. For example, you drop the final *e* in *coordinate* when you add the ending *-ion* to make *coordination*. When the word is changed to *coordination*, the *t* spells the sound *sh*.

My TURN Read the words. Find the related word pairs with consonant changes. Sort and spell the words of each related pair side by side.

SPELLING WORDS

isolation	politician	frustration	politics
music	hesitate	elect	election
clinician	selection	hesitation	coordinate
select	frustrate	mathematics	coordination
mathematician	musician	clinic	isolate

coordinate	coordination

Commas and Semicolons in a Series

A series is a list of three or more items, which may be words or phrases. A **comma** is used after each item in the series except the last item. However, sometimes an item in a list contains its own comma. To avoid confusion, these items are separated with a **semicolon**.

I carried water, snacks, and a first-aid kit.

commas

I carried a bottle of water, a pack of fruit snacks, and a certified first-aid kit.

I carried water, which was required by the tour guide; snacks, which were recommended; and a first-aid kit, in case of injuries.

semicolons

My TURN Edit this draft by placing commas and semicolons in the correct places in each series.

The word *mineral* can be defined as a solid substance part of vitamin pills or materials from Earth. The three types of rock are igneous which starts underground as magma sedimentary which is formed from settled material and metamorphic which changes under new conditions. Some fossil fuels are oil coal and natural gas.

Analyze Poetry

Learning Goal

I can use elements of poetry to write a poem.

Poetry is the arrangement of words in lines with rhythm, or a regularly repeated accent. Lines often rhyme. A poet chooses language to create a mental image or express thoughts or feelings. The purpose of a poem is often to give pleasure to the reader.

There are three major kinds of poems.

Narrative Poetry	Tells a story
Lyric Poetry	Includes expressions of emotions, descriptions of nature, or both
Epic Poetry	Involves a long narrative in an elevated style about the adventures of characters who are important to the history of a nation or race

MY TURN Use a poem you have read to answer the questions.

Title ______

How do you know this is a poem? ______

______

What images or feelings does the poet want to express? ______

______

Does the poem rhyme? ______

What kind of poem is it? ______

How do you know? ______

What Poetry Sounds Like

Poems have **rhythm,** or a pattern of stressed (') and unstressed (˘) syllables. Rhythm may be regular, following a specific pattern, or irregular. The poet can use rhythm to create a specific mood.

Many poems have **rhyme,** or words that have the same ending sound.

˘ ' ˘ ' ˘ ' ˘ '
Dawn's cool, pale hands —a mother's —smooth

˘ ' ˘ ' ˘ ' ˘ '
Night's weary brow —calm, hush, and soothe.

Read a poem aloud to better hear its rhythm and rhyme.

My TURN Annotate the poem. Underline rhymes. Use ' and ˘ to show stressed and unstressed syllables. State whether the rhythm is regular or irregular. The first line has been done for you.

˘ ' ˘ ˘ ' ˘ ˘ ' ˘ ˘ '
I watch the rain rush its way down from the sky.

I can't comprehend, so I have to ask why.

It has to be bliss to be up there so high,

So why do you flee with your thunder and cry?

Rhythm Pattern: ____________________

What Poetry Looks Like

A poem usually follows a particular **form.** Most forms can be used with the three basic kinds of poetry—narrative, lyric, and epic.

Form	Looks Like	Sounds Like
Quatrain	Has four lines with a similar rhythm	Rhymed or unrhymed
Example		
To be rich, I thought, Oh how nice. Then I wondered—would I be happy, though? My love and friendships could be the price I pay to watch my prosperity grow.		
Form	**Looks Like**	**Sounds Like**
Haiku	Has three lines of five, seven, and five syllables	Unrhymed
Example		
The music left me With a sigh it crept away I must earn it back		
Form	**Looks Like**	**Sounds Like**
Blank Verse	Lines of ten syllables	Syllables alternate unstressed and stressed; unrhymed
Example		
The rainbow's edge was pressed against the sky. I only saw one half before a cloud Cut off its arc and kept it safely tied To Earth so I could find its pot of gold.		

My TURN Work with a partner. Read a poem from your classroom library. Describe the poem's form.

Brainstorm Ideas

While a poet may write about any subject or try to create any message, many poems follow themes such as nature, beauty, love, heroism, childhood, or self-reflection.

My TURN Brainstorm poem ideas based on each theme. Write or draw to show the subject of each idea for a poem.

Theme: The beauty of nature

Poem Idea:

Theme: Growing up

Poem Idea:

WRITE FOR YOUR AUDIENCE:

- ☐ I believe my audience will like reading my poem.
- ☐ I will use language that creates mental images and strong feelings in my readers.
- ☐ I will choose a form for my poem that fits with the feelings I want readers to have.
- ☐ I will enjoy writing this poem.

Plan Your Poetry

Writers **freewrite** to generate ideas for their poetry.

My TURN Follow these steps as you freewrite ideas for your poem.

THINK

- Use the general theme you chose to write about during brainstorming.
- Think about feelings, ideas, actions, events, people, or places that you connect with that theme.
- Think of rhyming words, and experiment with different rhythms.

WRITE

- Write until the timer goes off.
- Do not stop to cross out ideas you do not like.
- Do not stop to edit your spelling or punctuation.

REVIEW

- At the end of the freewrite, review your ideas.
- Highlight or underline the ideas you like best, and use them when you write your poem.

SHARE

- Discuss your ideas with your Writing Club.

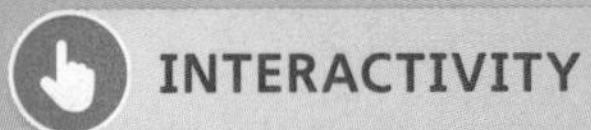

The WATER CYCLE

Water flows from sea to sea.
in a series that occurs repeatedly.

Rising from Earth, invisible to the eye
Creating feathery clouds in the sky.

Twisting and turning, changing form
Developing into a dangerous storm!

Thunder rumbles like the banging of tin,
a torrent of raindrops quickly begins.

Winter welcomes bone-chilling breezes,
Temperatures drop and water freezes.

The result of ice crystals falling to the ground—
blankets of snow all around.

Warmer weather fends off the shivers
As melting runoff fills the rivers.

In ponds and lakes and oceans and then . . .
The water cycle continues again.

WEEK 2

Weekly Question

What can cause water to change form?

TURN and TALK With a partner, discuss items you would need to be prepared for different weather conditions related to the water cycle. For example, you might need a shovel to clear a path for walking after snowfall.

Learning Goal

I can learn more about informational text by interpreting text features.

Spotlight on Genre

Informational Text

An **informational text** gives factual information about a topic. Its purpose is to inform or explain using text and visuals. Informational texts include

- Multiple **text structures**
- **Text features**, or additional information that is separate from the main body of text
- **Academic vocabulary**, or words that often appear in academic texts

Establish Purpose The purpose, or reason, for reading informational text is often to learn more about the world. Before you begin, set a purpose for reading this week's text, *Earth's Water Cycle*.

A text is informational when it gives facts about people, places, and things.

TURN and TALK With a partner, discuss different purposes for reading this week's text. For example, you might want to examine the author's use of text features. Review the anchor chart. Take notes on your discussion.

My PURPOSE

Text Features

Anchor Chart

Lists
- Table of contents
- Glossary
- Index

Visuals
- Diagrams
- Charts
- Tables
- Graphs
- Maps
- Photographs
- Illustrations

Titles
- Headings
- Subheadings

Text
- Captions
- Labels
- Sidebars

Meet *the* Author

Diane Dakers began her career as a journalist. She used to write, edit, produce, and report stories on culture in Canada, specifically art. Her stories appeared on news channels and in newspapers and magazines. Today, she is a well-known children's fiction and nonfiction author.

from

Earth's Water Cycle

Preview Vocabulary

As you read *Earth's Water Cycle*, pay attention to these vocabulary words. Notice how their placement in the text helps you interpret text features.

abundant **substance**

condenses **altitude** **trickles**

Read

Before you begin, **make predictions** about what you will learn in the informational text based on the genre and text features. Record your predictions in the chart after the selection. Follow these strategies as you read.

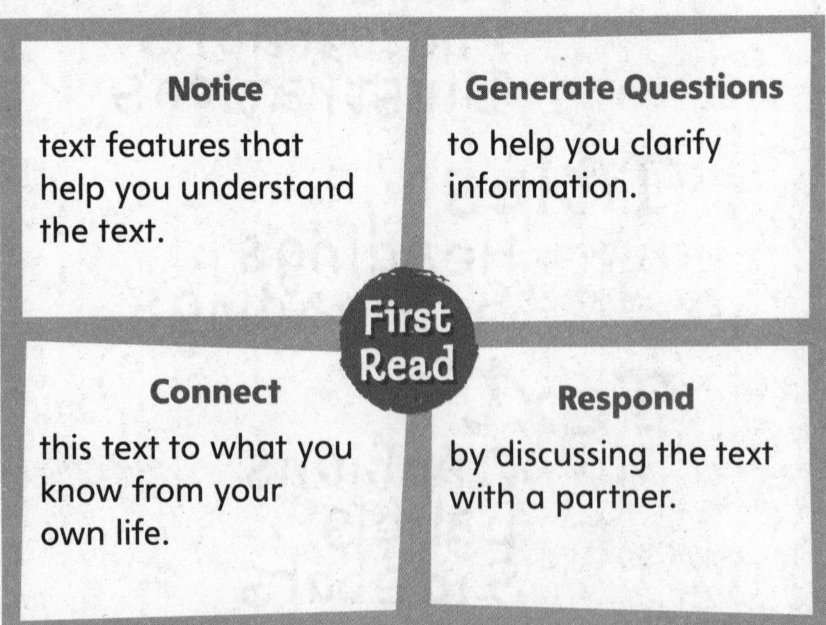

from EARTH'S WATER CYCLE

by Diane Dakers

AUDIO

ANNOTATE

BACKGROUND

Water is everywhere. It is on Earth in rivers, oceans, and glaciers. It is above Earth in the atmosphere and clouds. It is under Earth as groundwater. The water cycle describes the way water changes and moves through the three states of liquid, gas, and solid.

Water, Water, Everywhere

Interpret Text Features

Underline text features that are used to group and separate information.

Photos can often better illustrate information than words alone. Underline information in the caption that the photograph shows.

abundant existing in large amounts; plentiful

1 Water is all around us. About 70 percent of Earth is covered with water. Look at a photo of the planet from space. All the blue parts are water. That's why Earth is sometimes called the "blue planet." Water is the most abundant, or plentiful, substance on Earth, and one of the most important.

Water World

2 About 97 percent of all the water on Earth is contained in five oceans—the Atlantic, Pacific, Indian, Arctic, and Antarctic. Ocean water is salt water. Only about 3 percent of the planet's water is fresh water. That's the kind of water that people and animals drink.

3 About two-thirds of Earth's fresh water is not available to drink because it is frozen as ice in the Arctic and in Antarctica. Just one-third of all fresh water is found in rivers and lakes and underground. This adds up to only about one percent of all the world's water being available as drinking water.

This photo from space shows Earth's western hemisphere. It also dramatically illustrates why we call our world, which is 70 percent covered with water, the "blue planet." The clouds that swirl around the planet are also filled with water. They play a major role in Earth's weather patterns and in the water cycle.

4 Water is the only substance on Earth that naturally exists in three states—solid, liquid, and gas.

5 Solid water takes the form of ice or snow. In addition to the ice and snow around Earth's North and South Poles, glaciers and icebergs are made of solid water.

6 Liquid water is what fills our oceans, lakes, rivers, and streams. Water also soaks into the ground, where gravity pulls it deeper and deeper. The underground water is called groundwater.

7 Water exists as a gas in our air. In this form, it is called water vapor. Up to four percent of our air is made of gaseous water, or water vapor. This amount varies from day to day, and place to place.

CLOSE READ

Confirm or Correct Predictions

Highlight a detail that you could use to confirm or correct a prediction about the water cycle.

substance a physical material

Earth's North Pole is covered with floating sea ice over the Arctic Ocean.

CLOSE READ

Confirm or Correct Predictions

Highlight text that you can use to confirm or correct a prediction about water vapor.

8 You can't see water vapor, or smell it, or taste it, but sometimes you can feel it. On a hot, muggy day, it is the water vapor that makes the air feel humid, clammy, or "damp." Another way you can tell that liquid water has turned into water vapor is to hang wet laundry on the clothesline. Eventually, the laundry is no longer wet. That's because the liquid water has turned into vapor and escaped into the air.

9 The only time you can "see" water vapor is when a lot of it collects in one place and starts to cool. At that point, water vapor turns into steam. For example, when a tea kettle boils, a tiny cloud of steam comes out of the spout. That's because the hot water in the kettle quickly turns to vapor, collects in a small area, and immediately begins to cool. The steam is actually a collection of tiny water droplets floating in the air.

The steam coming out of this tea kettle is actually a tiny cloud of water droplets. It forms when water vapor from within the kettle comes into contact with cooler air outside of the kettle.

Cycles Make the World Go 'Round

10 A cycle is a pattern of related processes or events that happens over and over again. Like a circle, a cycle has no beginning and ending. It just keeps going and going and going. . . .

Cycles of Life

11 Every day, our planet performs many cycles. In fact, every day is a cycle, and so is every year. One very obvious cycle is the changing of the seasons. This cycle occurs as Earth orbits, or travels around, the Sun. Spring, summer, fall, winter. That's a cycle that happens over and over again, year after year.

The Water Cycle

12 Some of Earth's cycles are quite complicated. The water cycle, for example, has many steps. Powered by energy from the Sun and by gravity, water is in constant motion. As a natural substance that cannot be created or destroyed, all the water that exists on the planet moves through its three states, cycling from Earth to the sky and back to Earth—again and again in a never-ending cycle.

The raindrops falling in this pond may have been part of an ocean wave just a few weeks ago.

CLOSE READ

Interpret Text Features

Underline details in a text feature that help you interpret how water changes over time.

The Never-Ending Cycle

Interpret Text Features

Underline a sentence that supports your understanding of the water cycle diagram.

condenses to make or become more close; compact

13 After a rainfall, water sits in a puddle. The puddle water eventually evaporates into the air, where water vapor cools, condenses, and collects into droplets and forms clouds, until it rains again. That's a super-simple version of the water cycle. The path of that puddle water is part of a never-ending cycle that is constantly moving all the water on our planet, from the sky to the Earth, and back to the sky. The cycle includes not only bodies of water, the land, and the sky, but also all of Earth's plants and animals. Let's look at the water cycle one step at a time, beginning with the biggest water source on the planet—the oceans.

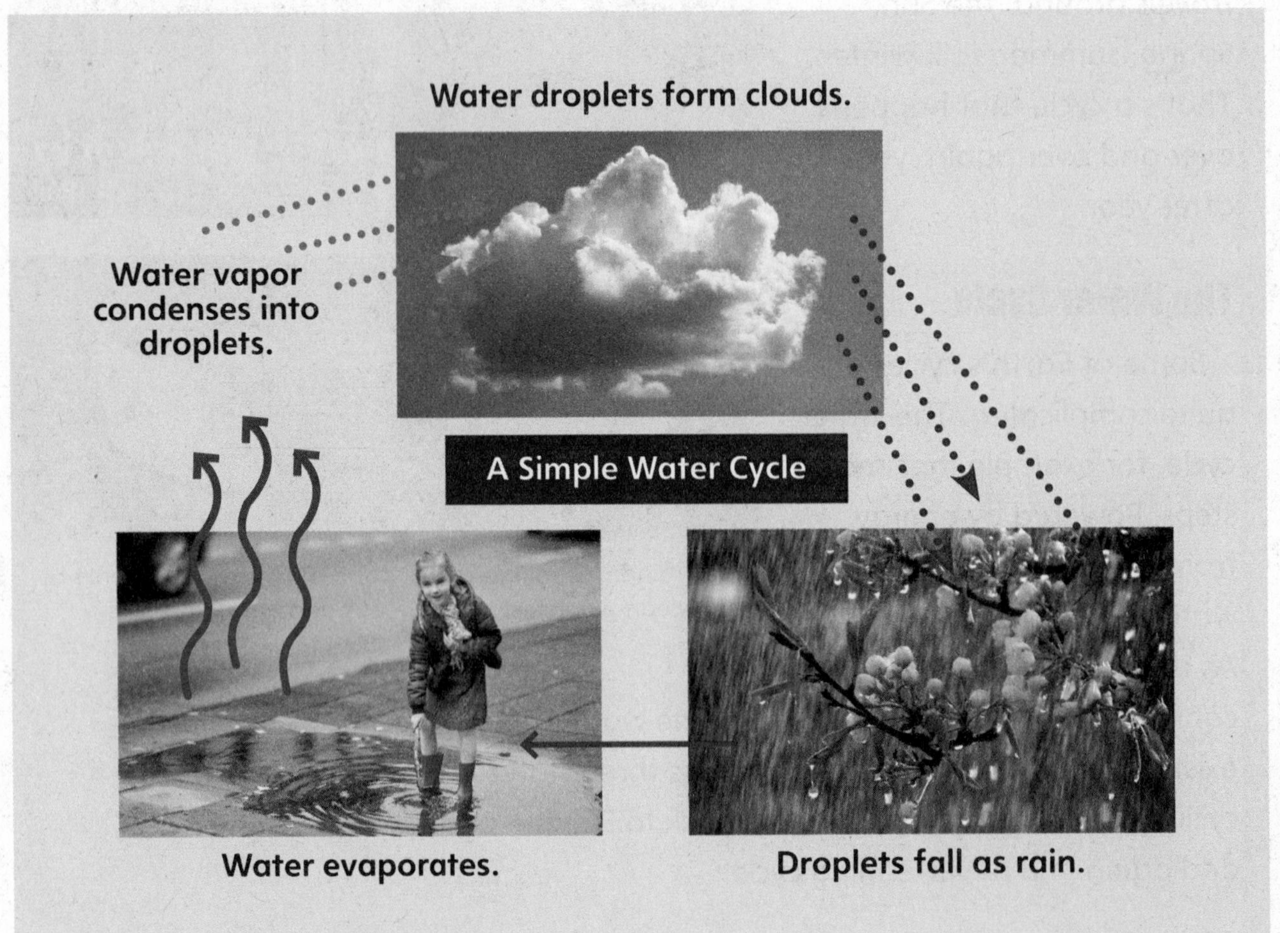

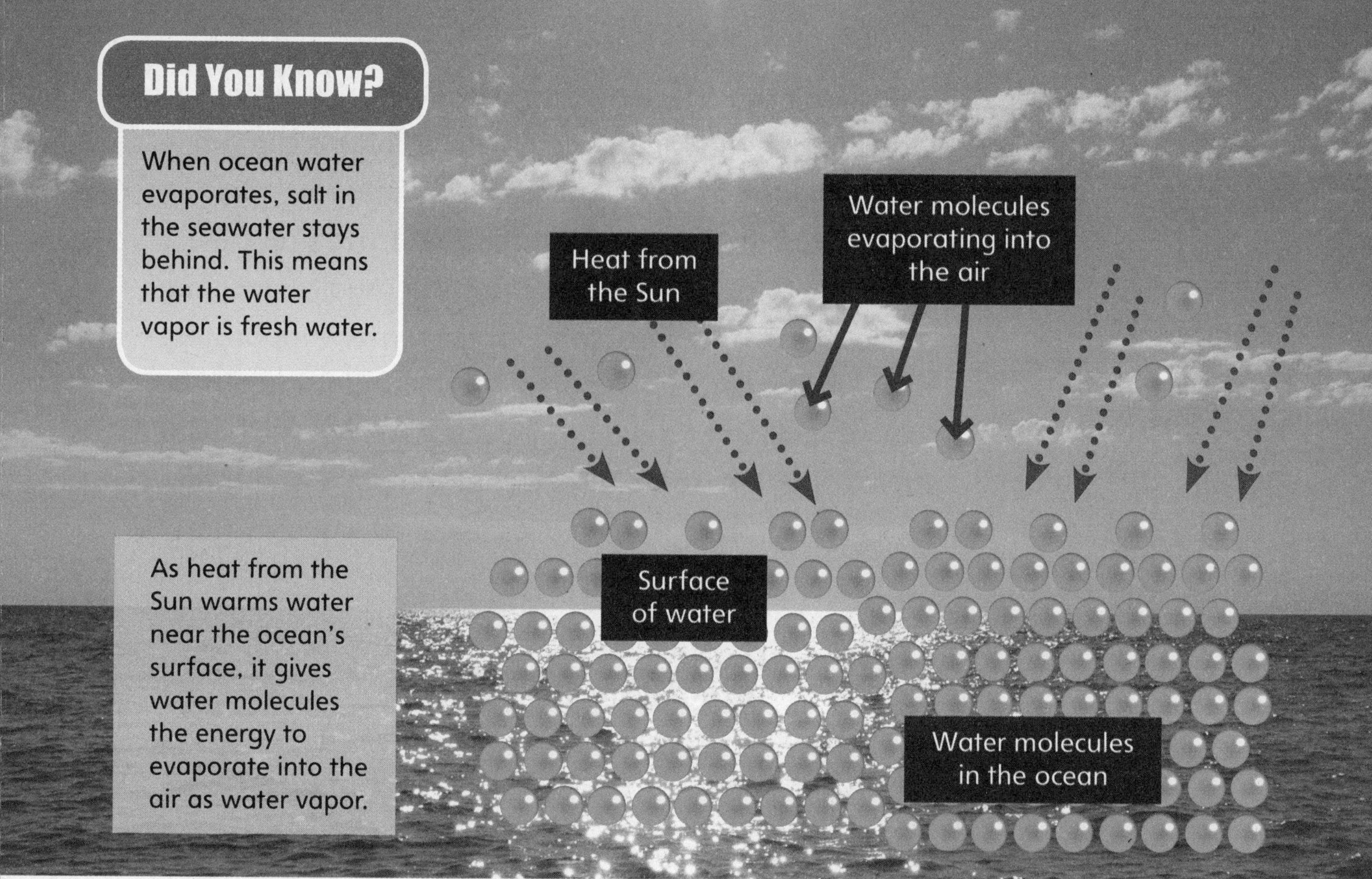

Into the Air

14 All the water that exists on Earth has been here for millions of years. Even though water changes states, most of it is, and has always been, contained in liquid form in the world's oceans. The surface area of Earth's oceans is vast, so it absorbs a huge amount of sunlight every day.

15 The energy in that sunlight warms the seawater near the surface, giving water molecules the energy they need to escape, or evaporate, into the air. The warmer the air, the warmer the water, and the more liquid converts to gas, or water vapor. This step in the water cycle is evaporation, and it also happens in lakes, rivers, and other freshwater bodies.

CLOSE READ

Confirm or Correct Predictions

Highlight details that confirm or correct a prediction you made about evaporation.

CLOSE READ

Interpret Text Features

Underline information in a text feature on these pages. Interpret how it helps you understand the main ideas of the text.

16 This isn't the only way that liquid water becomes water vapor, though. Remember that plants contain a lot of water, too! A plant takes in water from the soil through its roots. The water then travels up the stem and to all parts of the plant, eventually reaching the leaves. From there, some of the water evaporates through small holes, or pores, on the underside of the leaves, moving into the air. This process, by which water travels from the roots throughout the plant and then evaporates through the leaves, is called transpiration.

The small pores on the underside of a plant's leaves are called stomata. Each leaf has thousands of stomata. Water vapor is released through these holes during transpiration.

17 From Ice to Vapor

Water may also change into water vapor through a process called sublimation.

18 Even in ice, water molecules are in constant motion. They just move more slowly when water is in its solid state. Still, some of the molecules at the surface of ice will eventually escape. During sublimation, some of the molecules change from snow or ice directly to water vapor, without melting into water first. When it's windy, or when the Sun is shining, sublimation happens faster. This is why, on bitterly cold, bright sunny days, ice often disappears from sidewalks and highways.

19 Sublimation also happens in your freezer! Look at a tray of shrunken ice cubes that have been left in the freezer for a really long time. They have shrunk because of sublimation. There is no liquid water in the ice tray, but the ice cubes are smaller. That's because the water molecules in the ice have transformed directly into water vapor.

20 In the opposite process, water vapor changes directly into ice, such as snowflakes or frost, without first becoming a liquid. This process, called deposition, also occurs when temperatures are very cold.

During deposition, water vapor comes into contact with a cold window pane and changes to frost, creating these beautiful patterns.

What Goes Up Must Come Down

21 Once water vapor is in the air, wind moves it around and lifts it high into the sky. Thanks to the wind, water vapor can travel a long way from where it started! As the vapor rises, it cools and forms tiny droplets of water. This transformation from water vapor to liquid water is called condensation.

CLOSE READ

Vocabulary in Context

Context clues are words and phrases that help a reader understand an unfamiliar word. Context clues appear in or around the unfamiliar word.

Underline context clues that help you define *transformed*.

Confirm or Correct Predictions

Highlight details in the caption that confirm or correct your prediction about how clouds form.

altitude position of height

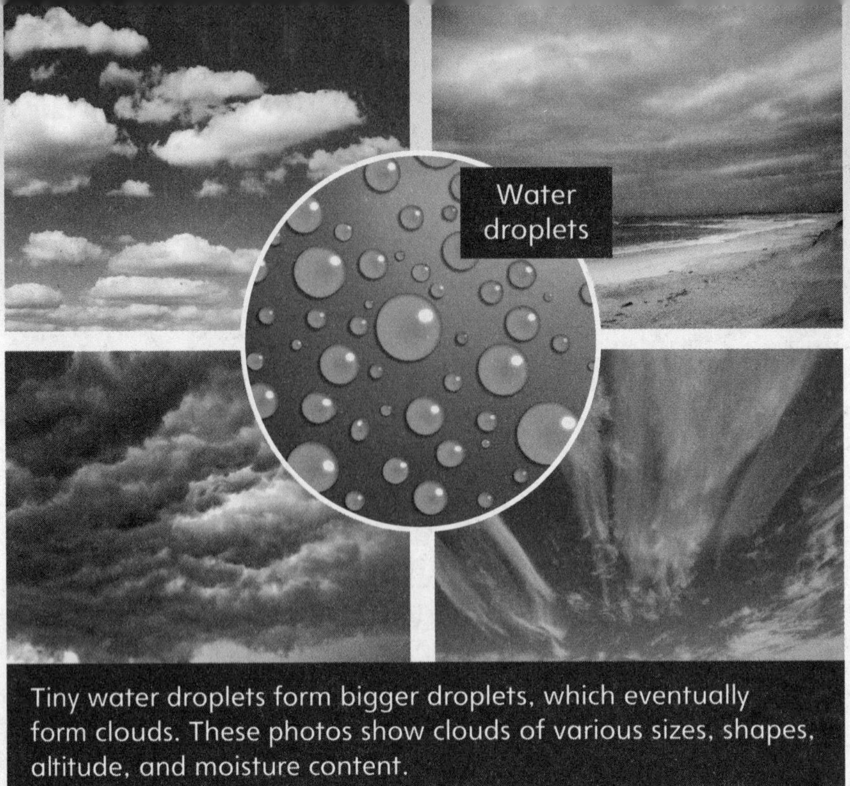

Tiny water droplets form bigger droplets, which eventually form clouds. These photos show clouds of various sizes, shapes, altitude, and moisture content.

22 High in the chilly sky, droplets bump into each other and join together to form bigger droplets. They also form around dust, pollen, and other particles that attract the water droplets. These particles help water vapor condense faster.

23 When billions of these droplets join together, they form clouds. Eventually, the water droplets become too heavy to stay in the air. Gravity pulls them toward Earth, and they fall as rain.

24 If the temperature in the cloud is below the freezing point of water, the vapor in the air forms ice crystals instead of water droplets. These tiny ice crystals bond together to form larger crystals. When these crystals become too heavy to stay in the cloud, they fall as snow. Under some weather conditions, rain and partially melted snow may become a slushy, wintery mix. In other conditions, water may freeze into ice pellets, sometimes called sleet. These pellets make tapping or "hissing" sounds as they hit objects on the ground.

Dew Drops

Sometimes, when you get up in the morning, you see water droplets on the grass or on spider webs. Those drops are called dew. Dew is formed by the condensation of water vapor in the air. When the air cools down at night, some of that water vapor condenses and becomes liquid water. In the morning, the water has collected into the little droplets you see.

CLOSE READD

25 Ice may also strike the ground in the form of hail. Hail usually occurs during warmer times of the year, when thunderstorms carry droplets high into the atmosphere. There, the temperatures are cold enough for droplets to join together as they freeze and form hailstones. The size depends on how much water freezes around it before it falls to the ground. We sometimes hear hail banging on cars and roofs during the summer!

26 The various forms of rain and ice crystals falling from the sky are all types of precipitation, the name of this part of the water cycle.

Confirm or Correct Predictions

Highlight details in the text feature that confirm or correct a prediction you made about how dew forms.

A photo of precipitation in the form of ice crystals bonded together in larger crystals out of supercooled water droplets—better known to most of us as snow!

Interpret Text Features

Underline part of a text feature that supports your understanding of water runoff.

Use this example to interpret the role of runoff in the water cycle.

trickles flows or falls in drops

Underground Water

27 Once water has fallen back to Earth as precipitation, it has to go somewhere before it starts to evaporate and begin the cycle all over again. This step in the cycle is called collection.

28 Because 70 percent of our planet is covered with water, most of the precipitation ends up back in those bodies of water—oceans, lakes, rivers, and streams. Some, though, falls onto land.

29 In certain regions, the water trickles down hillsides, mountains, and slopes until it runs into a river or lake. This water is called runoff, and sooner or later it finds its way back to an ocean.

30 About 20 percent of water that falls to Earth soaks into the ground. It seeps through the top layers of soil and is pulled deeper by the force of gravity.

Making Sense of Cycles

Clouds come in different sizes, shapes, and colors, and they can be found at many different altitudes, or heights. For example, fog is a cloud that is close to the ground. The size and shape of a cloud may depend on temperature and wind in the sky, as well as how high the cloud is. Based on facts and pictures in this book, think about why certain clouds might be different colors and shapes. What do you think makes some clouds thin and wispy, and others heavy looking, and some almost completely white and others very dark?

The water in this spectacular waterfall in Norway started out as precipitation falling to Earth and collecting into small mountain streams. As shown here, those streams flow into larger rivers, which eventually find their way to the sea.

Watering the Animals

All animals, including humans, need water to survive. Many animals get it by drinking fresh water or by eating plants, which contain water. Water constantly circulates throughout an organism, bringing nutrition and energy to every organ and cell in every part of the body. It eventually leaves the organism and returns to the water cycle. Humans and other mammals sweat, which releases water into the air—and, therefore, into the water cycle. Mammals and other types of animals, even insects, also urinate, which releases liquid water into the water cycle. Fish take in and get rid of water through their gills. Other animals, such as frogs and lizards, absorb and release moisture through their skin. Every type of animal has to get rid of waste material somehow, and they all do it in different ways!

CLOSE READ

Confirm or Correct Predictions

Highlight details that confirm or correct a prediction that you made from reading the heading of the text feature.

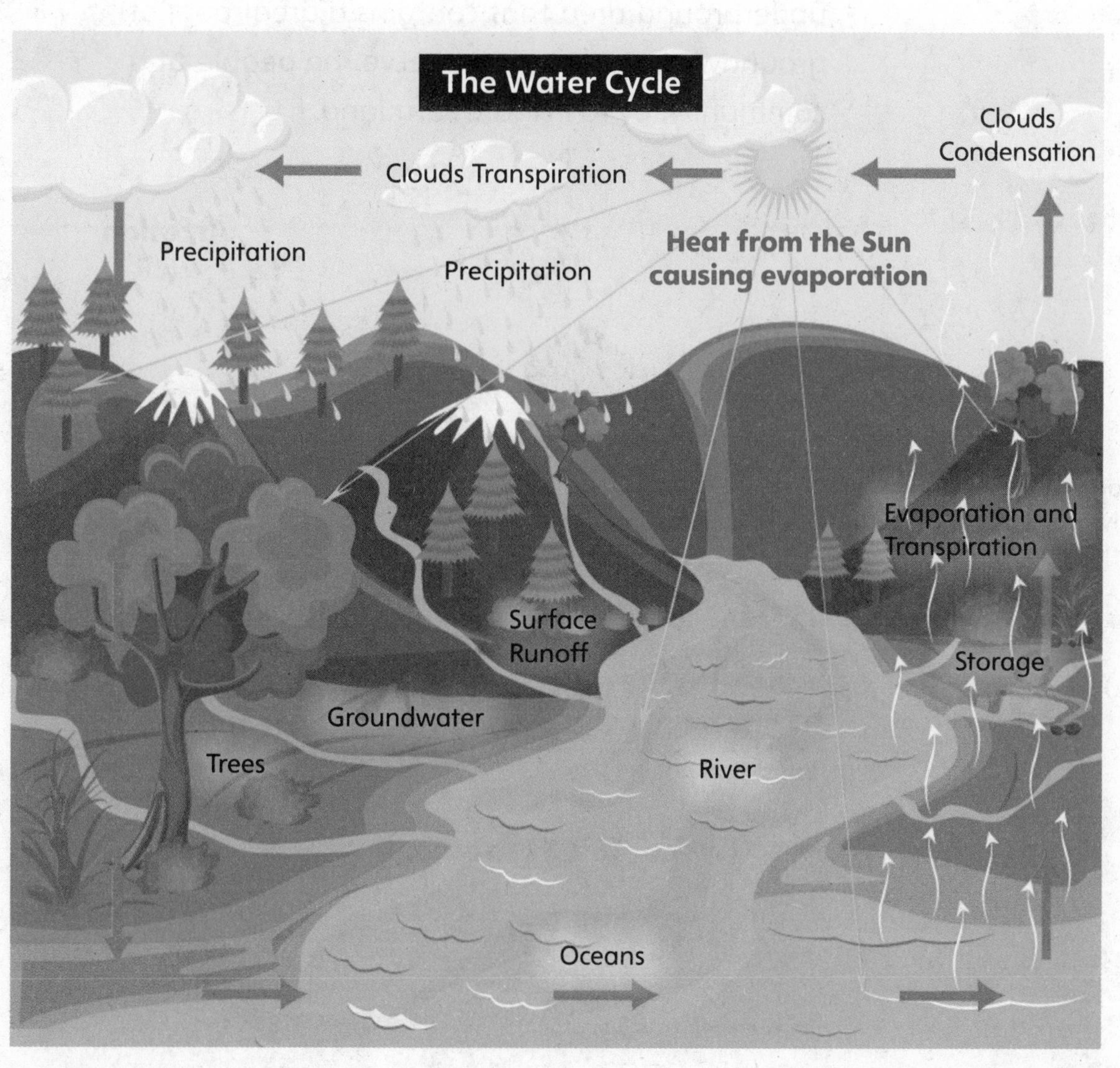

Interpret Text Features

Underline words and phrases that help you interpret the water table diagram.

31 Eventually, the water reaches a level called the water table. The depth of the water table varies from location to location. Above the water table, the underground water trickles around rocks, stones, and sand, flowing downward.

32 Below the water table, every crack, pore, and air pocket in the ground is completely filled with water. This area is called the saturated zone, because it is saturated with, or full of, groundwater.

33 This is a source of drinking water for many people around the world. They dig wells, searching for an aquifer in the saturated zone. An aquifer is an underground area that contains a great deal of groundwater—enough to serve the people of a community, or to irrigate farmland.

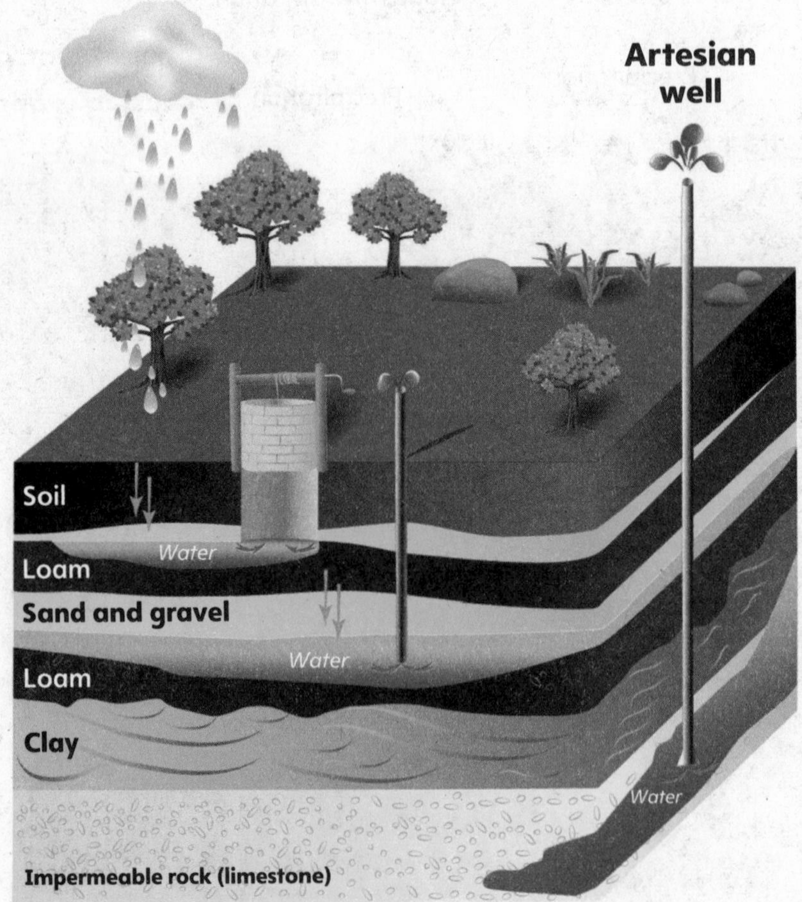

This diagram shows how groundwater collects below the surface.

In Hot Water

The deeper underground that groundwater goes, the hotter it gets. Sometimes groundwater is pulled so deep into Earth's crust that its temperature can reach the boiling point. In some places, this water then returns to the surface in pools called hot springs. Sometimes, a cold spring feeds into the same pool. This cools down the water, so people can enjoy soaking in the hot spring. Sometimes, people add cooler water to control the heat. In other cases, as the hot water circulates back to the surface, it naturally cools down again, making the hot spring a suitable temperature for human relaxation.

CLOSE READ

Interpret Text Features

Underline details that support your understanding of how mammals use hot springs.

It's not only people who enjoy soaking in hot springs. In Japan, macaque monkeys warm up in hot springs during the cold, snowy winter.

Develop Vocabulary

In informational text, authors use words related to a subject, such as science. Understanding domain-specific words helps readers become more familiar with the subject.

My TURN Complete the word web. In each circle, write a sentence using the vocabulary word.

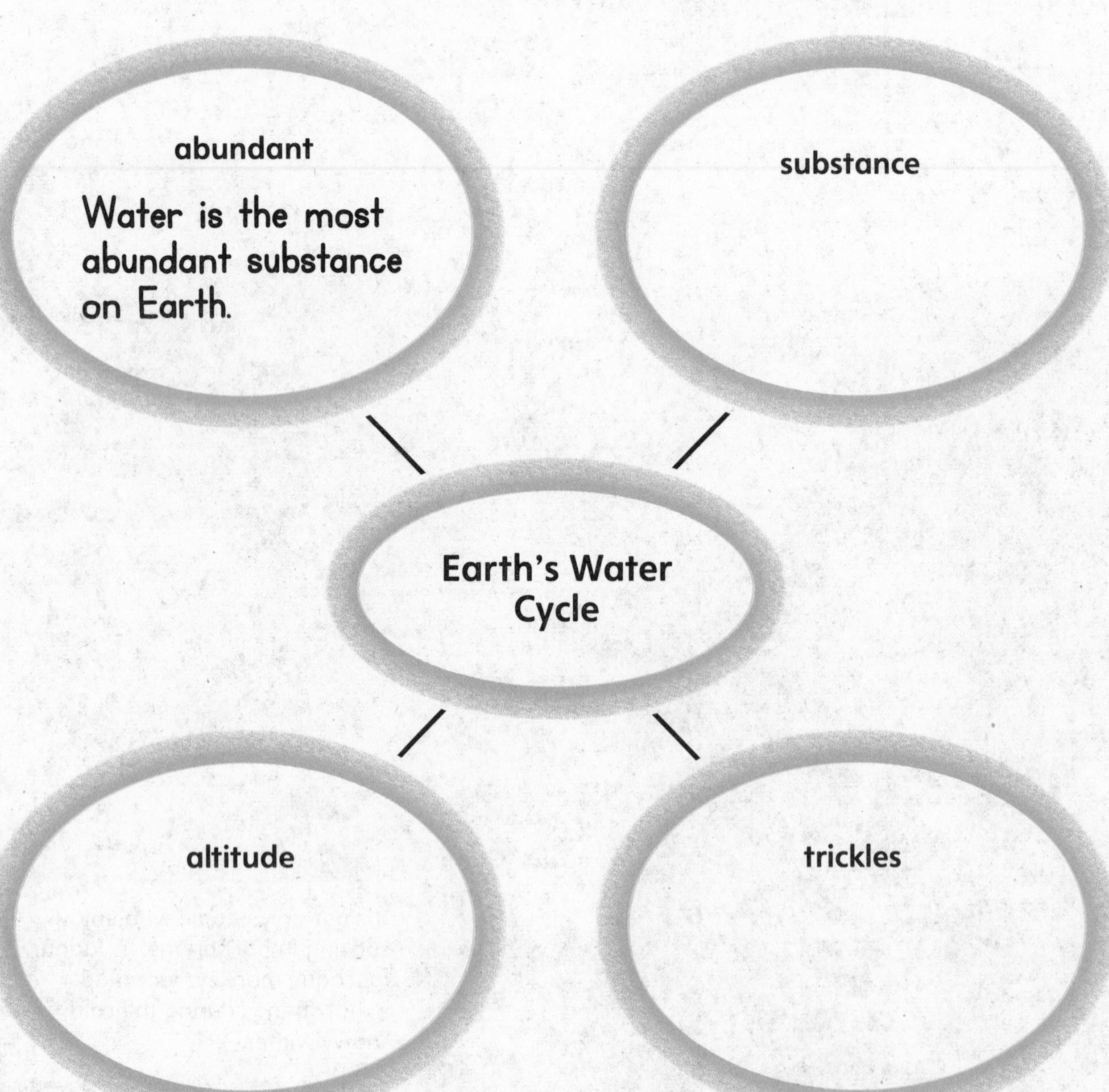

Check for Understanding

My TURN Look back at the text to answer the questions.

1. What details make *Earth's Water Cycle* an informational text?

2. Evaluate the strategies the author uses to explain the water cycle.

3. Draw conclusions about why the water cycle is so important to life on Earth.

4. Why is it important to avoid polluting water? Use details from the text to defend your opinion.

Interpret Text Features

Text features provide additional information to help readers understand a subject. They include graphic features, such as photos, time lines, and diagrams. They also include print features, such as sidebars, headings, and captions.

1. **My TURN** Go to the Close Read notes in *Earth's Water Cycle* and underline details that help you interpret text features.

2. **Text Evidence** Use the parts you underlined to complete the chart. Provide an example of each type of feature, and explain how it helps you better understand the text.

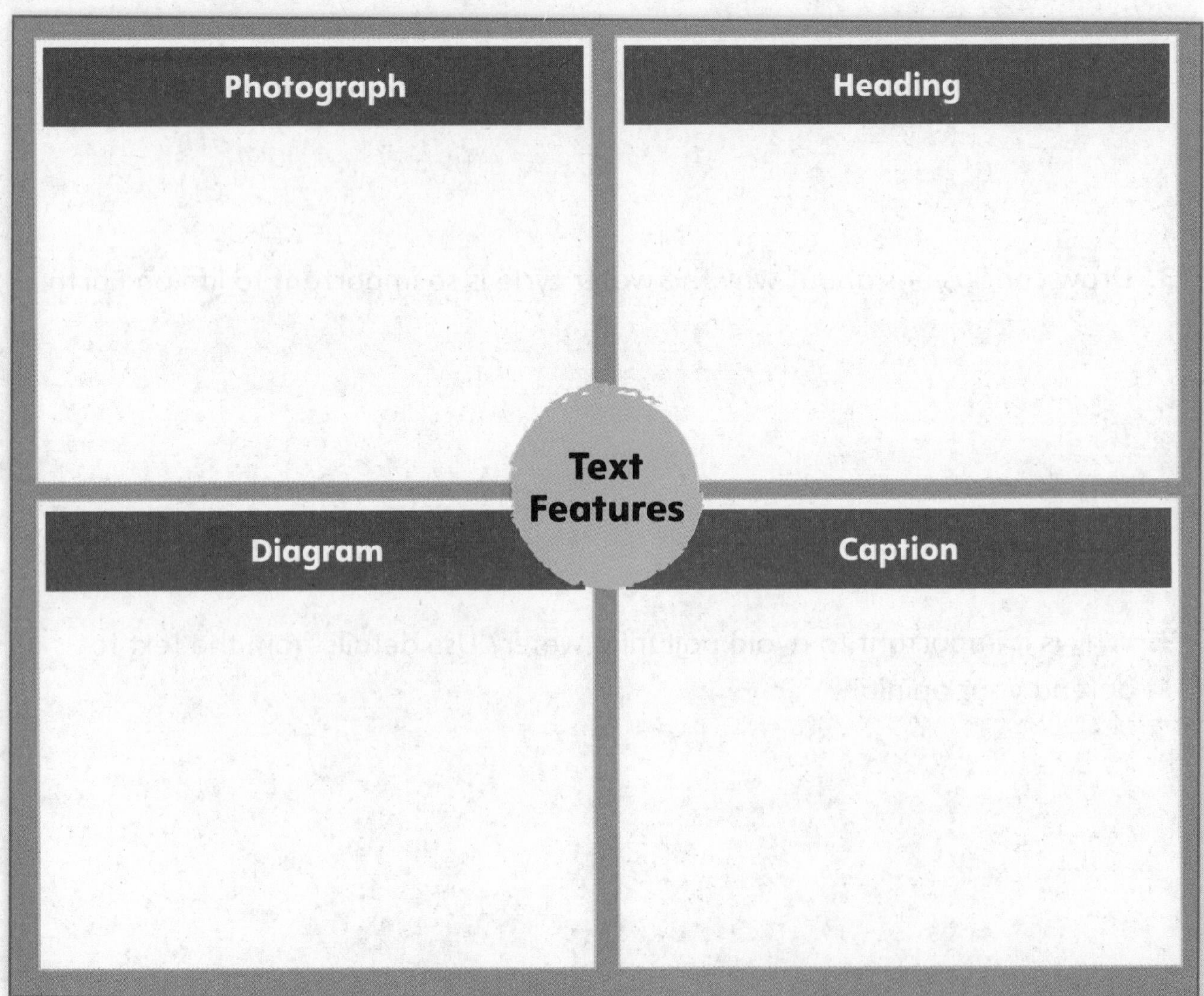

Confirm or Correct Predictions

Before you read, make predictions about what the text will be about. Preview text features, such as photographs, headings, diagrams, and sidebars. As you read, **confirm or correct** your predictions.

1. **My TURN** Go back to the Close Read notes and highlight evidence that helps you make predictions about the text.

2. **Text Evidence** Use your highlighted text to confirm or correct your predictions, and use evidence to support your responses.

Heading

My Prediction:

Text Evidence:

Confirmed or Corrected:

Diagram

My Prediction:

Text Evidence:

Confirmed or Corrected:

Sidebar

My Prediction:

Text Evidence:

Confirmed or Corrected:

Reflect and Share

Write to Sources Consider the texts you've read this week. How have they informed you about systems in nature? What causes water to change form? Explain what you learned and how it may influence your everyday life.

Use Text Evidence When writing about informational texts, include text evidence that directly supports your response. Choose two texts you read this week, and identify text evidence from each. Use these questions to evaluate the evidence:

- Does this information clearly support my answer?
- Is there information that better supports my response? If yes, then I need to review my annotations and notes.

Add evidence as needed. Finally, on a separate sheet of paper, write a short paragraph that explains what you have learned from each text. Remember to use quotation marks around any direct quotations from the texts.

Weekly Question

What can cause water to change form?

Academic Vocabulary

Learning Goal

I can develop knowledge about language to make connections between reading and writing.

A **synonym** is a word that has the same meaning as another word. An **antonym** has an opposite meaning.

My TURN For each word,

1. **Read** the definition.
2. **Write** a synonym and an antonym.
3. **Use** a print or digital resource, such as a thesaurus, as needed.

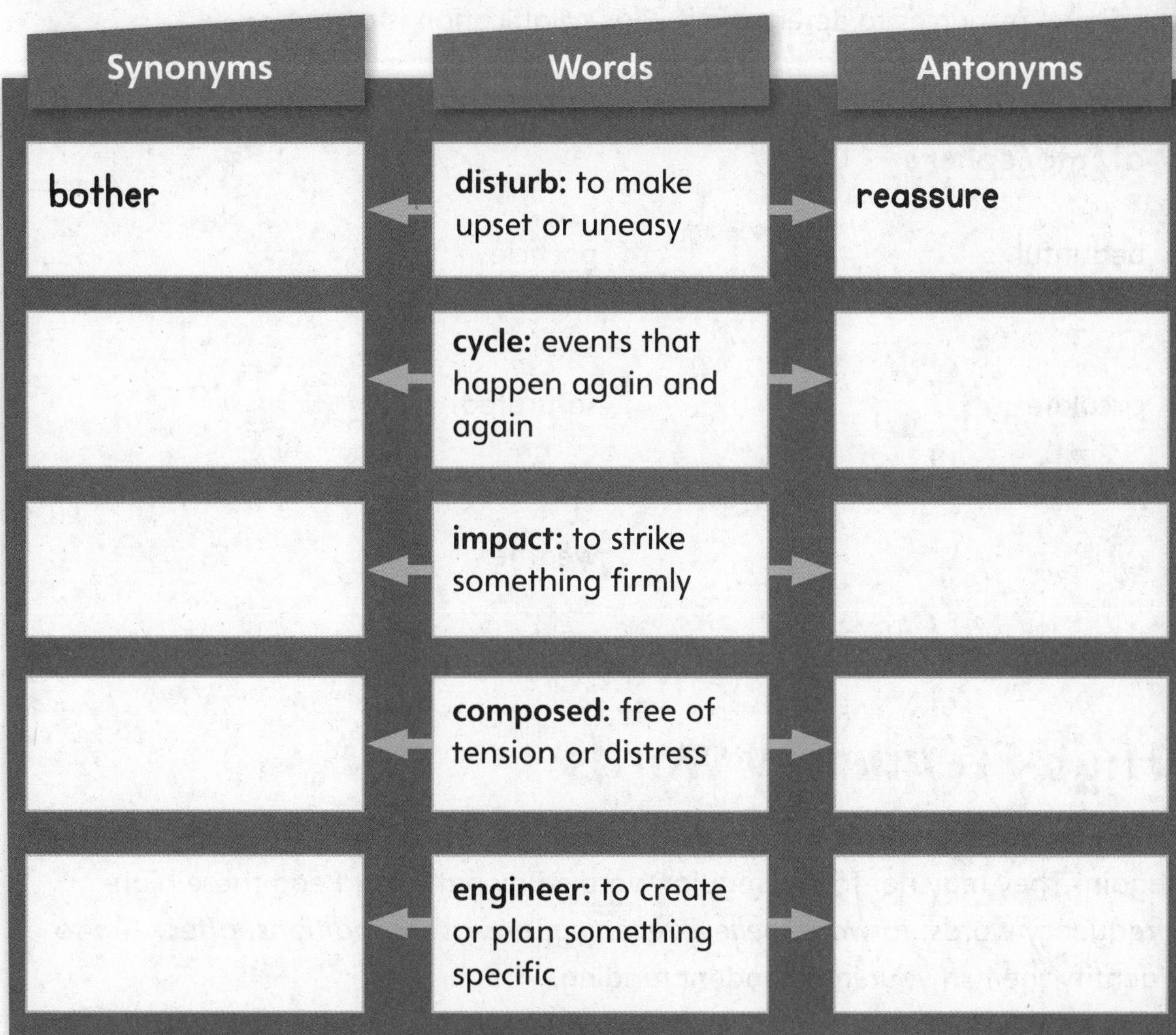

Synonyms	Words	Antonyms
bother	**disturb:** to make upset or uneasy	**reassure**
	cycle: events that happen again and again	
	impact: to strike something firmly	
	composed: free of tension or distress	
	engineer: to create or plan something specific	

Syllable Patterns

A syllable is a word part that contains a single vowel sound. To read multisyllabic words, divide syllables according to **syllable patterns**. Some familiar syllable patterns include vowel teams; VCe syllables; open syllables and closed syllables, such as V/CV and VC/V; final stable syllables, such as syllables ending in *-le*; and *r*-controlled syllables.

Syllables can be divided between consonants or between vowels.

My TURN Use your knowledge of syllable division patterns to read each word. On each line, write the word with slashes between the syllables. Then use print or digital resources to determine if your syllabication is correct.

atmosphere at/mo/sphere	evaporate ________
beautiful ________	particle ________
circulate ________	saturated ________
cycle ________	weather ________

High-Frequency Words

High-frequency words are words that you will see in texts over and over again. They may not follow regular word study patterns. Read these high-frequency words: *forward, believe, evening, exercise, conditions, affect.* Try to identify them in your independent reading.

Read Like a Writer

Authors use different text structures to organize support for their main idea and achieve their purpose for writing. For example, description is a text structure that lists and explains information such as facts, characteristics, and examples.

Model! Read the text from *Earth's Water Cycle*.

> Fish take in and get rid of water through their gills. Other animals, such as frogs and lizards, absorb and release moisture through their skin.

examples

1. **Identify** Diane Dakers uses "gills" and "skin" as examples of body parts through which animals get rid of water.
2. **Question** How does the structure achieve the author's purpose?
3. **Conclude** Diane Dakers's use of examples helps me understand information about animals.

Reread the second sentence in paragraph 14.

My TURN Analyze how the author uses text structure.

1. **Identify** Diane Dakers uses ______________________________ ______________ as ______________________________.
2. **Question** How does the text structure achieve her purpose?
3. **Conclude** Diane Dakers's use of ______________ helps me understand ______________________________ ______________________________.

Write for a Reader

Authors often use the text structure of description to achieve their purposes for writing. With description, informational texts use adjectives to describe the topic. They provide facts, examples, and qualities that inform readers.

Text structures organize facts to help readers understand a topic.

My TURN Think about how Diane Dakers's use of description as the text structure in *Earth's Water Cycle* affects you as a reader. Now identify how you can use that text structure to influence your own readers.

1. If you were using description as the text structure, how would you organize information?

2. Write an informational paragraph. Use description as the text structure to organize information for your readers.

Spell Words with Different Syllable Patterns

A syllable is a word part that contains a single vowel sound. **Syllable patterns** can divide words between two vowels, between two consonants, or between a consonant and a vowel. Understanding different syllable patterns can help you spell words.

My TURN Read the words. Spell and sort the words by their number of syllables.

SPELLING WORDS

contact	trifle	medium	radiate
alligator	obstacle	variable	strategy
escalator	miracle	idea	finish
classical	icicle	studio	dutiful
innocent	struggle	stadium	arthritis

two syllables

____

____

____

____

three syllables

_______________ _______________

_______________ _______________

_______________ _______________

_______________ _______________

_______________ _______________

_______________ _______________

_______________ _______________

_______________ _______________

_______________ _______________

four syllables

____

____

____

Commas and Introductory Elements

When you address a person directly, use a **comma** to set off the name. Use one comma when the name begins or ends a sentence, and use two commas when the name is in the middle of a sentence.

Asa, look at the fog.

I can't see across the street, Dad.

Fog, Asa, is a cloud near the ground.

Introductory words and phrases, such as *yes*, *no*, *as usual*, and *well*, at the beginning of a sentence are followed by a comma.

Yes, I learned about fog in science class.

Use a comma in a sentence that has a statement followed by a question.

Fog is droplets of water vapor, isn't it?

My TURN For each item, put commas in the correct places.

1. What is a cumulus cloud Mom?

2. A cumulus cloud Kim looks puffy and round at the top.

3. No I don't think it will rain this afternoon.

4. Your father predicted that earlier didn't he?

5. Ron what did you learn about how dew forms?

See Like a Poet

Learning Goal

I can use elements of poetry to write a poem.

Poets find creative ways to express what they see in the world. A poet carefully chooses words that show exactly what he or she sees, thinks, senses, or feels. Because poems have few words, each word must help accomplish the poet's goals.

Poet's Goal	Precise Word Choices
To tell about light	*shine, gleam, glow, glitter, glint, incandescent, radiant, sunlit, luminous, brilliant*
To tell about time	*generation, season, fate, progress, eternity, era, span, instant, fleeting, lifetime*
To tell about importance	*essential, heavy, serious, urgent, significant, extraordinary, powerful, notable*
To tell about beauty	*dazzling, exquisite, divine, radiant, magnificent, captivating, breathtaking, delightful*
To tell about happiness	*bliss, cheerful, glee, enjoyment, smile, twinkling, bright, light, playful, sunny*

My TURN On your own paper, rewrite the lines of the poem. Replace the vague words in boldface with precise language that provides more emotion or description. Rewrite other parts of the poem as needed to make sense with your changes.

The **happy little** daffodil
Moved her **pretty** petals **with the wind.**
She **said** good morning to the **little** bee
Who **flew** too near her head.

My TURN In your writing notebook, develop a draft of your poem. Use precise words and sensory details.

Use Rhythm and Rhyme

Rhythm is a regularly repeated accent. Poets use patterns of stressed (ˈ) and unstressed (˘) syllables to create rhythm. Reading a poem aloud can help you identify the rhythm. Poets can play with the rhythm of some common words, such as *over* and *ever,* by removing letters to change their number of syllables (*o'er* and *e'er*).

˘ ˈ ˘ ˈ ˘ ˈ ˘ ˈ
And then the purple haze of dusk

˘ ˈ ˘ ˈ ˘ ˈ
Spread o'er the land and sea.

Rhyme in poetry usually refers to lines that end with the same sound. Rhyming words may not have the same spellings. Read aloud the poem to hear the rhymes.

The animals will go on through
The gates that lead right to the zoo.

My TURN Complete the poem by writing two additional lines. Create a regular rhythm and make each line rhyme with the line before it.

Where will the rain in the summertime fall?

What will you do when the thunderstorms blow?

My TURN In your writing notebook, develop a draft of your poem. Experiment with rhythm and rhyme.

Use Personification

Personification is a figure of speech in which human traits are given to animals, inanimate objects, or abstract ideas. Some common traits include speech, intelligence, actions, and emotions.

Animals	Inanimate Objects	Abstract Ideas
The cat sang loudly after he caught the feather.	The lock of hair knew just where to lie.	Twilight spread her dark cloak over the hills.

Personification can make poetry lively.

The young raindrop left his cloud,
Excited to be on his own—free.
He aged on his way to Earth,
Learning what it meant to be lonely.

My TURN Brainstorm human traits to give to each animal, object, or idea. Include verbs you would use to describe his or her actions.

A parrot	A beach towel	Spring

My TURN In your writing notebook, develop a draft of your poem to include personification.

Use Simile and Metaphor

Figurative language gives words meaning beyond their everyday definitions. **Simile** and **metaphor** are two types of figurative language that compare unlike things.

A **simile** uses *like* or *as* to compare unlike things.

Jana runs as gracefully **as** a gazelle.

That girl swims **like** a fish.

A **metaphor** does not use *like* or *as*. The similarity is implied.

He was a riddle.

They arrived with an army of lawyers.

My TURN Write a simile and a metaphor that compare things from Category 1 with things from Category 2.

Category 1		Category 2	
a person	the moon or stars	a color	a piece of technology
an animal	a place	a holiday	a landmark

1. Simile

2. Metaphor

My TURN In your writing notebook, develop a draft of your poem. Include a simile and a metaphor to creatively compare unlike things.

Use Interjections

Interjections are words that express feelings. When an interjection expresses a strong feeling, it is followed by an exclamation mark.

Wow! I can't believe we won.

When an interjection does not express a strong feeling, it is followed by a comma.

Well, let's pack our bags.

My TURN Insert an interjection from the word bank into each sentence. Use correct punctuation.

Word Bank

Ah	Ha	Oh	Wow
Alas	Hey	Oops	Yeah
Eww	No	Well	Yes

_______ the day is done and I have so much yet to see and do.

_______ tomorrow is a new chance to succeed where today I failed.

My TURN In your writing notebook, compose a poem that uses interjections to add interest. Share your poem with your Writing Club.

Because interjections are informal, try not to overuse them in your writing.

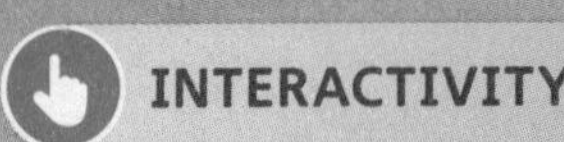

How VOLCANOES Work

Volcanoes erupt on land, on the ocean floor, and under ice caps. While the eruptions are harmful, they also create new mountains and islands, as well as fertile soil.

Watch

Watch the video to learn more about volcanoes.

Ninety percent of Earth's volcanoes rest on the seafloor of the Pacific in an area called the Ring of Fire. The world's largest active volcano is Mauna Loa in Hawaii.

WEEK 3

Weekly Question

How can Earth's changes affect where and how we live?

Quick Write Choose a feature of Earth, such as volcanoes, oceans, or atmosphere. Think about how the feature changes over time. How does that change affect people?

▲ Many volcanoes go through long quiet periods between eruptions. In 1980, Mount St. Helens in Washington erupted after 123 years of inactivity.

Learning Goal

I can learn more about the theme *Systems* by analyzing plot and setting in historical fiction.

Historical Fiction

Historical fiction is realistic fiction that takes place in the **past**.

- Most **characters** are fictional but act like people from that time period.
- Sometimes characters are **real historical people** whom the author places in made-up situations.
- The **point of view** can be first person or third person.
- The **setting** is a real time and place. It is what makes this genre historical fiction.
- The **plot** mixes fact with fiction.

TURN and TALK With a partner, discuss how historical fiction is similar to and different from informational text. Use the chart to help you compare and contrast the genres. Take notes on your discussion.

My NOTES

To compare and contrast, start with what makes the genres similar.

HISTORICAL FICTION

ANCHOR CHART

PURPOSE: To tell a REALISTIC story set in a PAST time and place

Characters: REAL or MADE-UP

SETTING: A real place and time in the past

TEXT STRUCTURE: Usually chronological

POINT OF VIEW: First- or third-person

Meet *the* Author

Louis Untermeyer's mother read him many stories and poems, including some about historical figures. He used the texts as raw material for bedtime stories he told his brother. Later, he wrote poems, essays, and short stories, many for children, and collected the poems of others in anthologies.

The Dog of Pompeii

Preview Vocabulary

As you read "The Dog of Pompeii" from *Best Shorts: Favorite Short Stories for Sharing*, pay attention to these vocabulary words. Notice how they connect to elements of plot and setting.

comrade **custom**

coaxed **revived** **heed**

Read

Before you begin, establish a purpose for reading. You may want to learn more about ancient Pompeii. You could also read to distinguish fact from fiction in the text. Follow these strategies when you read **historical fiction**.

First Read

Notice

the setting and how the author develops the historical time period.

Generate Questions

about how this text applies to the theme, *Systems*.

Connect

this text to what you already know about the ancient city of Pompeii.

Respond

by discussing the text's relationship to the theme, *Systems*.

Genre Historical Fiction

The Dog of Pompeii

by Louis Untermeyer

AUDIO

ANNOTATE

CLOSE READ

Analyze Plot and Setting

Underline details that introduce the setting of the story.

1 Tito and his dog Bimbo lived (if you could call it living) under the city wall where it joined the inner gate. They really didn't live there; they just slept there. They lived anywhere. Pompeii was one of the gayest of the old Roman towns, but although Tito was never an unhappy boy, he was not exactly a merry one. The streets were always lively with shining chariots and bright red trappings; the open-air theaters rocked with laughing crowds; sham battles and athletic sports were free for the asking in the great stadium. Once a year the emperor visited the pleasure city, and the fireworks and other forms of entertainment lasted for days.

2 But Tito saw none of these things, for he was blind—had been blind from birth. He was known to everyone in the poorer quarters. But no one could say how old he was; no one remembered his parents; no one could tell where he came from. Bimbo was another mystery. As long as people could remember seeing Tito—several years at least—they had seen Bimbo. The dog never left his side. He was not only a watchdog, but mother and father to Tito.

3 Did I say Bimbo never left his master? (Perhaps I had better say "comrade," for if anyone was the master, it was Bimbo.) I was wrong. Bimbo did trust Tito alone exactly three times a day. It was a custom understood between boy and dog since the beginning of their friendship, and the way it worked was this:

4 Early in the morning, shortly after dawn, while Tito was still dreaming, Bimbo would disappear. When Tito awoke, Bimbo would be sitting quietly at his side, his ears cocked, his stump of a tail tapping the ground, and a fresh-baked loaf of bread—more like a large round roll—at his feet. Tito would stretch himself, Bimbo would yawn, and they would breakfast.

5 At noon, no matter where they happened to be, Bimbo would put his paw on Tito's knee, and the two of them would return to the inner gate. Tito would curl up in the corner (almost like a dog) and go to sleep, while Bimbo, looking quite important (almost like a boy), would disappear again. In a half-hour he would be back with their lunch. Sometimes it would be a piece of fruit or a scrap of meat; often it was nothing but a dry crust. But sometimes there would be one of those flat, rich cakes, sprinkled with raisins and sugar, that Tito liked so much.

CLOSE READ

Analyze Plot and Setting

Underline a detail that helps you understand how Tito and Bimbo's relationship affects the events of the plot.

comrade a companion who shares in a person's activities and who is that person's equal

custom an accepted, repeated way of behaving or doing things

Make Inferences

Highlight details that help you make an inference about what Tito's life would be like without Bimbo.

Vocabulary in Context

A **context clue** is a word or phrase around an unfamiliar word that helps readers determine the unfamiliar word's meaning.

Underline context clues around the word *villa* in paragraph 9 to determine its definition.

6 At suppertime the same thing happened, although there was a little less of everything, for things were hard to snatch in the evening with the streets full of people.

7 But whether there was much or little, hot or cold, fresh or dry, food was always there. Tito never asked where it came from, and Bimbo never told him. There was plenty of rainwater in the hollows of soft stones; the old egg woman at the corner sometimes gave him a cupful of strong goat's milk; in the grape season the fat winemaker let him have drippings of the mild juice. So there was no danger of going hungry or thirsty. There was plenty of everything in Pompeii if you knew where to find it and if you had a dog like Bimbo.

8 As I said before, Tito was not the merriest boy in Pompeii. He could not romp with the other youngsters or play hare-and-hounds and I-spy and follow-your-master and ball-against-the-building and jackstone and kings-and-robbers with them. But that did not make him sorry for himself. If he could not see the sights that delighted the lads of Pompeii, he could hear and smell things they never noticed. When he and Bimbo went out walking, he knew just where they were going and exactly what was happening.

9 As they passed a handsome villa, he'd sniff and say, "Ah, Glaucus Pansa is giving a grand dinner here tonight. They're going to have three kinds of bread and roast pigling and stuffed goose and a great stew—I think bear stew—and a fig pie." And Bimbo would note that this would be a good place to visit tomorrow.

10 Or "Hmm," Tito would murmur, half through his lips, half through his nostrils. "The wife of Marcus Lucretius is expecting her mother. She's airing all the linens; she's going to use the best clothes, the ones she's been keeping in pine needles and camphor, and she's got an extra servant cleaning the kitchen. Come, Bimbo, let's get out of the dust!"

11 Or, as they neared the forum, "Mmm! What good things they have in the marketplace today! Dates from Africa and salt oysters from sea caves and cuttlefish and new honey and sweet onions and—ugh!—water buffalo steaks. Come, let's see what's what in the forum." And Bimbo, just as curious as his comrade, hurried on. Being a dog, he, too, trusted his ears and nose more than his eyes, and so the two of them entered the center of Pompeii.

CLOSE READ

Make Inferences

Highlight a detail that helps you make an inference about why Bimbo is excited to enter the center of the city.

12 The forum was the part of town to which everybody came at least once during the day. Everything happened there. There were no private houses; all was public—the chief temples, the gold and red bazaars, the silk shops, the town hall, the booths belonging to the weavers and the jewel merchants, the wealthy woolen market. Everything gleamed brightly here; the buildings looked new. The earthquake of twelve years ago had brought down all the old structures; and since the citizens of Pompeii were ambitious to rival Naples and even Rome, they had seized the opportunity to rebuild the whole town. Hence there was scarcely a building that was older than Tito.

13 Tito had heard a great deal about the earthquake, although, since he was only about a year old at the time, he could hardly remember it. This particular quake had been a light one, as earthquakes go. The crude houses had been shaken down, and parts of the outworn wall had been wrecked, but there had been little loss of life. No one knew what caused these earthquakes. Records showed they had happened in the neighborhood since the beginning of time. Sailors said that it was to teach the lazy cityfolk a lesson and make them appreciate those who risked the dangers of the sea to bring them luxuries and to protect their town from invaders. The priests said that the gods took this way of showing their anger to those who refused to worship properly or failed to bring enough sacrifices to the altars. The tradesmen said that the foreign merchants had corrupted the ground and it was no longer safe to traffic in imported goods that came

CLOSE READ

Vocabulary in Context

Underline context clues to determine the definition of *bazaars* in paragraph 12.

Analyze Plot and Setting

Underline details that show how the cultural setting of ancient Pompeii contributes to the rising action of the story.

CLOSE READ

Analyze Plot and Setting

Underline a detail that suggests that the setting might be dangerous. Analyze how the setting contributes to the rising action of the plot.

from strange places and carried a curse upon them. Everyone had a different explanation and everyone's explanation was louder and sillier than his neighbor's.

14 People were talking about it this afternoon as Tito and Bimbo came out of the side street into the public square. The forum was crowded. Tito's ears, as well as his nose, guided them to the place where the talk was loudest.

15 "I tell you," rumbled a voice that Tito recognized as that of the bath master, Rufus, "there won't be another earthquake in my lifetime or yours. There may be a tremble or two, but earthquakes, like lightning, never strike twice in the same place."

16 "Don't they?" asked a thin voice Tito had never heard before. It had a high, sharp ring to it, and Tito knew it as the accent of a stranger. "How about the two towns in Sicily that have been ruined three times within fifteen years by the eruptions of Mount Etna? And were they not warned? And does that column of smoke above Vesuvius mean nothing?"

17 "That?" Tito could hear the grunt with which one question answered another. "That's always there. We use it for our weather guide. When the smoke stands up straight, we know we'll have fair weather; when it flattens out, it's sure to be foggy; when it drifts to the east—"

18 “Very well, my confident friend,” cut in the thin voice, which now sounded curiously flat. “We have a proverb: ‘Those who will not listen to man must be taught by the gods.’ I say no more. But I leave a last warning. Remember the holy ones. Look to your temples. And when the smoke tree above Vesuvius grows to the shape of an umbrella pine, look to your lives!”

19 Tito could hear the air whistle as the speaker drew his toga about him, and the quick shuffle of feet told him that the stranger had gone.

20 “Now what,” said Attilio, the cameo cutter, “did he mean by that?”

21 “I wonder,” grunted Rufus. “I wonder.”

CLOSE READ

Make Inferences

Highlight details that help you make an inference about the stranger’s purpose in the story.

Vocabulary in Context

What is the definition of *keen* in paragraph 22? Underline context clues around *keen* to help you determine the word's meaning.

Make Inferences

Highlight evidence that helps you make an inference about how Tito experiences the changes that occur in Pompeii in this scene.

22 Tito wondered, too. And Bimbo, his head at a thoughtful angle, looked as if he were doing a heavy bit of pondering. By nightfall the argument had been forgotten. If the smoke had increased, no one saw it in the dark. Besides, it was Caesar's birthday, and the town was in a holiday mood. Tito and Bimbo were among the merrymakers, dodging the charioteers, who shouted at them. But Tito never missed his footing. He was thankful for his keen ears and quick instinct—most thankful of all for Bimbo.

23 They visited the open-air theater; then went to the city walls, where the people of Pompeii watched a sham naval battle in which the city, attacked from the sea, was saved after thousands of flaming arrows had been burned. Though the thrill of flaring ships and lighted skies was lost to Tito, the shouts and cheers excited him as much as anyone.

24 The next morning there were two of the beloved raisin cakes for his breakfast. Bimbo was unusually active and thumped his bit of a tail until Tito was afraid he would wear it out. Tito couldn't imagine whether Bimbo was urging him to some sort of game or was trying to tell him something. After a while he ceased to notice Bimbo. He felt drowsy. Last night's late hours had tired him. Besides, there was a heavy mist in the air—no, a thick fog rather than a mist—a fog that got into his throat and made him cough. He walked as far as the marine gate to get a breath of the sea. But even the salt air seemed smoky.

25 Tito went to bed before dusk, but he did not sleep well . . .

26 He awoke early. Or rather, he was pulled awake, Bimbo doing the pulling. The dog had dragged Tito to his feet and was urging the boy along. Where, Tito did not know. His feet stumbled uncertainly; he was still half asleep. For a while he noticed nothing except the fact that it was hard to breathe. The air was hot and heavy, so heavy that he could taste it. The air, it seemed, had turned to powder, a warm powder that stung his nostrils and burned his sightless eyes.

CLOSE READ

Analyze Plot and Setting

Underline sensory details that help describe the setting and suggest that the climax of the story is near.

27 Then he began to hear sounds, peculiar sounds. Like animals under the earth. Hissings and groanings and muffled cries. There was no doubt of it now. The noises came from underneath. He not only heard them—he could feel them. The earth twitched; the twitching changed to an uneven shrugging of the soil. Then, as Bimbo half pulled, half coaxed him along, the ground jerked away from his feet and he was thrown against a stone fountain.

coaxed persuaded someone to do something by words or actions

Make Inferences

Highlight details about the setting that help you make inferences about how the tension will reach a climax.

revived brought back to consciousness

28 The water—hot water!—splashing in his face revived him. He got to his feet, Bimbo steadying him, helping him on again. The noises grew louder; they came closer. The cries were even more animal-like than before, but now they came from human throats. A few people began to rush by; a family or two, then a group, then, it seemed, the whole city of people. Tito, bewildered though he was, could recognize Rufus's voice as he bellowed like a water buffalo gone mad.

29 It was then that the crashing began. First a sharp crackling, like a monstrous snapping of twigs; then an explosion that tore earth and sky. The heavens, though Tito could not see them, were shot through with continual flickerings of fire. Lightning above was answered by thunder beneath. A house fell. Then another. By a miracle the two companions had escaped the dangerous side streets and were in a more open space. It was the forum. They rested here awhile; how long, the boy did not know.

30 Tito had no idea of the time of day. He could feel it was black—an unnatural blackness. Something inside, perhaps the lack of breakfast and lunch, told him it was past noon. But it didn't matter. Nothing seemed to matter. He was getting drowsy, too drowsy to walk. But walk he must. He knew it. And Bimbo knew it; the sharp tugs told him so. Nor was it a moment too soon. The sacred ground of the forum was safe no longer. It began to rock, then to pitch, then to split. As they stumbled out of the square, the earth wriggled like a caught snake, and all the columns of the Temple of Jupiter came down. It was the end of the world, or so it seemed.

Make Inferences

Highlight evidence that supports an inference you made about the purpose of the stranger in the story.

31 To walk was not enough now. They must run. Tito, too frightened to know what to do or where to go, had lost all sense of direction. He started to go back to the inner gate; but Bimbo, straining his back to the last inch, almost pulled his clothes from him. What did the dog want? Had he gone mad?

32 Then suddenly he understood. Bimbo was telling him the way out. The sea gate, of course. The sea gate—and then the sea, far from falling buildings, heaving ground. He turned, Bimbo guiding him across open pits and dangerous pools of bubbling mud, away from buildings that had caught fire and were dropping their burning beams.

33 New dangers threatened. All Pompeii seemed to be thronging toward the marine gate, and there was the chance of being trampled to death. But the chance had to be taken. It was growing harder and harder to breathe. What air there was choked him. It was all dust now, dust and pebbles as large as beans. They fell on his head, his hands—pumice stones from the black heart of Vesuvius! The mountain had turned itself inside out. Tito remembered what the stranger had said in the forum two days ago: "Those who will not listen to man must be taught by the gods." The people of Pompeii had refused to heed the warnings; they were being taught now, if it was not too late.

heed pay attention to; listen to

34 Suddenly it seemed too late for Tito. The red-hot ashes blistered his skin; the stinging vapors tore his throat. He could not go on. He staggered toward a small tree at the side of the road and fell. In a moment Bimbo was beside him. He coaxed, but there was no answer. He licked Tito's hands, his feet, his face. The boy did not stir. Then Bimbo did the thing he least wanted to do. He bit his comrade, bit him deep in the arm. With a cry of pain, Tito jumped to his feet, Bimbo after him. Tito was in despair, but Bimbo was determined. He drove the boy on, snapping at his heels, worrying his way through the crowd, barking, baring his teeth, heedless of kicks or falling stones.

35 Sick with hunger, half dead with fear and sulfur fumes, Tito plodded on, pursued by Bimbo. How long, he never knew. At last he staggered through the marine gate and felt soft sand under him. Then Tito fainted.

CLOSE READ

Analyze Plot and Setting

Underline the story's turning point, or the climax. Analyze how the setting influences the events.

Analyze Plot and Setting

Underline the outcome of Bimbo's actions, the falling action of the plot.

36 Someone was dashing sea water over him. Someone was carrying him toward the boat.

37 "Bimbo!" he called. And then louder, "Bimbo!" But Bimbo had disappeared.

38 Voices jarred against each other. "Hurry! Hurry!" "To the boats!" "Can't you see the child's frightened and starving?" "He keeps calling for someone!" "Poor child, he's out of his mind." "Here boy, take this!"

39 They tucked him in among them. The oarlocks creaked; the oars splashed, the boat rode over the toppling waves. Tito was safe. But he wept continually. "Bimbo!" he wailed. "Bimbo! Bimbo!"

40 He could not be comforted.

41 Eighteen hundred years passed. Scientists were restoring the ancient city; excavators were working their way through the stones and trash that had buried the entire town. Much had already been brought to light—statues, bronze instruments, bright mosaics, household articles, even delicate paintings that had been preserved by the ashes that had taken over two thousand lives. Columns were dug up, and the forum was beginning to emerge.

42 It was at a place where the ruins lay deepest that the director paused.

43 "Come here," he called to his assistant. "I think we've discovered the remains of a building in good shape. Here are four huge millstones that were most likely turned by slaves or mules, and here is a whole wall standing, with shelves inside it. Why, it must have been a bakery! And here's a curious thing—the skeleton of a dog!"

44 "Amazing!" gasped his assistant. "You'd think a dog would have had sense enough to run away at that time. What is that flat thing he's holding between his teeth? It can't be a stone."

45 "No, it must have come from this bakery. Do you know, it looks to me like some sort of cake, hardened with the years. And bless me, if those little black pebbles aren't raisins! A raisin cake almost two thousand years old! I wonder what made him want it at such a moment?"

46 "I wonder," murmured his assistant.

CLOSE READ

Analyze Plot and Setting

Underline details that show the resolution of the story. Analyze how the setting affects the outcome.

Make Inferences

Highlight evidence that supports an inference about Bimbo's loyalty to Tito.

Develop Vocabulary

Concrete words refer to things people can touch. In historical fiction, authors often use vivid, precise words to describe characters and their actions. These words give readers mental images to connect with the story.

My TURN Complete the chart to identify how the author uses precise words to describe the relationship between Tito and Bimbo in "The Dog of Pompeii."

Word	Mental Image	Clues About Relationship
comrade	two people walking together, smiling, and talking	Normally a person is the "leader" of his/her dog, but Tito is more like Bimbo's friend than his leader.
custom		
coaxed		
revived		

Check for Understanding

My TURN Look back at the text to answer the questions.

1. What details from "The Dog of Pompeii" show that it is historical fiction?

2. Analyze how the author makes Bimbo into a main character in the story.

3. Retell the events of the story. Be sure to maintain meaning and logical order.

4. Data from natural disasters help scientists develop early warning systems that allow people to get to safety. How might the people of Pompeii have benefited from a better early warning system?

Analyze Plot and Setting

In historical fiction, the plot is influenced by the setting when the setting focuses on the events or culture of a particular time and place.

1. **My TURN** Go to the Close Reading notes in "The Dog of Pompeii" and underline parts that help you analyze how the setting affects the plot.

2. **Text Evidence** Use text evidence to analyze how the setting influences the events.

Setting

Rising Action

Climax

Falling Action

Resolution

How does the historical setting influence the plot?

Make Inferences

When an author does not state every detail about the plot, setting, or characters directly, readers must make inferences. To make an inference, readers combine what they already know with evidence from the story.

1. **My TURN** Go back to the Close Read notes and highlight evidence that helps you make inferences about the how Bimbo helps Tito.
2. **Text Evidence** Use your highlighted text to complete the chart, and use evidence to support your inferences.

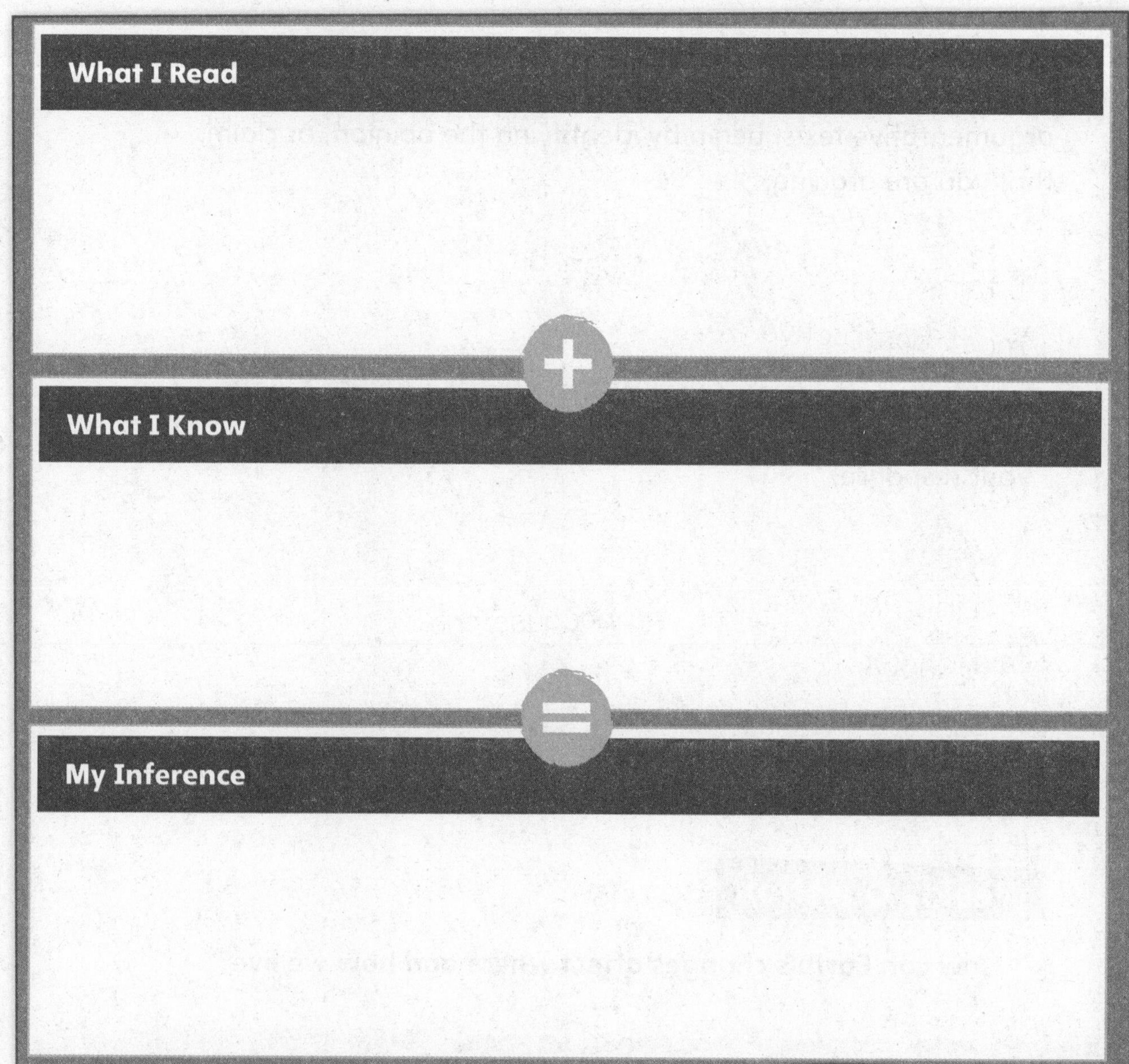

Reflect and Share

Write to Sources In "The Dog of Pompeii," movement of the tectonic plates below Earth's crust causes a volcanic eruption that separates Tito and Bimbo forever. What other texts describe how systems in nature affect people? On a separate sheet of paper, state an opinion about which system in nature can be most destructive. Use examples from more than one text to support your response.

State and Support an Opinion When writing argumentative texts, begin by identifying the opinion, or claim, that you are arguing.

I think ______ can be the most destructive.

Use facts, details, and evidence from texts to support your response.

I think ______ because the text shows ______.

Weekly Question

How can Earth's changes affect where and how we live?

Academic Vocabulary

Learning Goal

I can develop knowledge about language to make connections between reading and writing.

Words and sentences around an unfamiliar word that can give clues to the word's meaning are called **context clues.** You can use context clues to determine the definition of a multiple-meaning word.

My TURN For each item,

1. **Read** the sentence.
2. **Determine** the meaning of the bold word as it is used in the sentence.
3. **Underline** the context clues and the correct definition of the bold word.

1. Many natural processes, such as the repetition of seasons or the phases of the moon, happen in a **cycle**.

A. a wheeled vehicle

B. to ride a wheeled vehicle

C. events that happen again and again

2. Beethoven was completely deaf when he **composed** his Ninth Symphony, one of the most well-known pieces of music in the world.

A. made up of

B. free of tension or distress

C. wrote or created something

3. Cody liked building things as a child, but he did not design real machines until he became an **engineer** many years later.

A. a person who drives a train

B. to create or plan something specific

C. a person who designs and builds engines

Multisyllabic Words

Many words are **multisyllabic**, or contain more than one syllable. Many multisyllabic words contain common syllables, which include *-tion*, *-ize*, *-ance*, *-ist*, *-ly*, *pro-*, and *con-*. Recognizing syllable patterns, such as V/CV, VC/V, and VCe, in multisyllabic words makes them easier to read.

The word *ambitious* in paragraph 12 of "The Dog of Pompeii" has three syllables: am/bi/tious. The syllables divide with the common pattern VC/CV and before the suffix *-tious*.

My TURN Read each multisyllabic word from "The Dog of Pompeii." Then divide each word using your knowledge of syllable division patterns. To determine if your syllabication is correct, use a print or digital dictionary.

Word	Divided by Syllables
protect	
explanation	
recognize	
scientists	
continually	

Read Like a Writer

Denotation is the literal, or dictionary, meaning of a word. **Connotation** is the feelings or ideas that the word brings to a reader's mind. When authors choose to use a certain word, they often intend for the word's connotations to convey a particular feeling or idea. This may be called a "shade of meaning."

Model! Read the text from "The Dog of Pompeii."

> The streets were always lively with shining chariots and bright red trappings; the open-air theaters rocked with laughing crowds. . . .

words with positive connotations

1. **Identify** Louis Untermeyer uses the words *lively*, *shining*, *bright red*, *rocked*, and *laughing*.
2. **Question** How do the connotations convey shades of meaning?
3. **Conclude** The words' positive connotations convey that Pompeii was an energetic city, and its citizens liked to have fun.

Reread the first two sentences of paragraph 29.

My TURN Follow the steps to analyze how the author uses shades of meaning.

1. **Identify** Louis Untermeyer uses the words ______________________________ .
2. **Question** How do the connotations convey shades of meaning?
3. **Conclude** The words' ______________ connotations convey ______________________________ .

Write for a Reader

Authors can use literal language, or a word's denotation, for the purpose of stating something directly and clearly. They can also use elements of craft, such as connotation, to convey meanings without stating them outright for the purpose of expressing feelings.

My TURN Think about how Louis Untermeyer's use of shades of meaning in "The Dog of Pompeii" affects you as a reader. Now identify how you can use denotation and connotation to influence your own readers.

1. What literal language could you use to describe a sad situation directly?

2. What language could you use to describe a sad situation without directly stating it?

3. Compose a literary paragraph about an imaginary sad situation. Use words with unhappy connotations to show readers that the situation is sad.

Spell Multisyllabic Words

Multisyllabic words have more than one syllable. Recognizing syllable patterns and knowing common syllables such as *-ment*, *-ial*, *-ate*, and *in-* makes multisyllabic words easier to spell.

My TURN Read the words. Spell and sort the words by the number of syllables, using multiple sound-spelling patterns.

SPELLING WORDS

harmonica	literature	humiliate	curiosity
elementary	ravioli	tuxedo	stationery
miniature	cafeteria	cylinder	certificate
mosaic	probability	intermediate	amateur
definition	environment	centennial	punctuation

three syllables

____

____

____

____

four syllables

____

____

____

____

____

____

____

____

____

____

five syllables

____

____

____

____

____

Title Punctuation

When writing the title of a book, movie, play, or magazine, **underline** it. When typing these titles, **italicize** them. The titles of stories, articles, poems, and chapters within books are enclosed in **quotation marks**.

Title Type	Examples		Formatting
book	A Wrinkle in Time	*A Wrinkle in Time*	In handwriting: underline In print: *italics*
movie	The Wizard of Oz	*The Wizard of Oz*	
play	Hamlet	*Hamlet*	
magazine	Cricket	*Cricket*	
short story	"The Dog of Pompeii"		Quotation marks
article	"Farewell to the Enchanted City"		
poem	"Mending Wall"		
book chapter	"The First Day of School"		

Italics and underlining can also be used for emphasis: I can't *believe* that Bimbo stayed behind. Their separation was heartbreaking.

My TURN Edit this draft by underlining or adding quotation marks to titles. Underline emphasized text.

One of my favorite books is Charlotte's Web. I knew I would love it as soon as I finished the first chapter, Before Breakfast. I cried so much when Charlotte dies near the end.

Choose Line Breaks

Learning Goal

I can use elements of poetry to write a poem.

A poet chooses where to break each line in a poem. Line breaks affect rhythm and pacing, which are best understood when a poem is read aloud.

An **end-stopped line** ends with the actual line of text.

> The breeze, rippling the grass, begs not to stop; ← end of line
> It presses on, to find my hair, a stream, a treetop.

A **run-on line** does not end with punctuation. Instead, the line ends where the rhythm and rhyme make sense for it to end.

> She runs, never deciding where; a game ← end of line
> With goals that have and need no focused aim.

In this example, the reader should pause after *where*, not after *game*.

My TURN Read the text aloud. Insert a slash (/) between words to show the best places to break the lines. Explain why you chose to break the lines as you did.

In my dream, stardust glittered in my hair. The glow of the moon shimmered ev'rywhere. I laughed as I floated up, up; I know there are so many places I could go. Sailing the skies had tired my heavy head. I awoke in the downy warmth of bed.

Explanation: ______________________________

____

My TURN In your writing notebook, compose a poem. Choose line breaks to achieve the rhythm and pacing you want.

Develop Stanzas

A poet can break thoughts into lines and groups of lines into **stanzas**. Like paragraphs in a story, stanzas often organize thoughts into groups.

The emperor looked down his regal nose
At his subjects displayed for him in rows.
He thought as he sneered, "How nice for all these
To worship me on lowly peasant knees."

The first stanza introduces the subject of the narrative poem.

Alas for the proud king, once thought so grand.
He hadn't a clue that his own heavy hand
Would mean that his people would soon rebel,
Cut short his rule, and put him in a cell.

The poet begins a new stanza to describe what will happen to the emperor.

The poet breaks the stanzas evenly so each has four lines, a regular rhythm, and complete rhyming patterns.

My TURN Draw a horizontal line between lines of the poem below to show where to break the stanzas.

One afternoon our treehouse became
A ship circling Earth on a whim.
It could go anywhere we might name:
Mars, ocean, or volcano's rim.
But today we packed water and grapes
To eat as we journeyed to space.
We pushed the cockpit's buttons and shapes.
Blast off on our thrilling moon race!

My TURN In your writing notebook, compose a poem. Use stanzas to organize your thoughts.

Develop Poetry with Punctuation

When poets use punctuation, they get to break some rules. In poetry, punctuation creates rhythm and separates ideas. A poet can choose to use no punctuation at all. Each choice creates a specific effect.

Type of Punctuation	Purpose	Example
Dash, semicolon, period	To create a long pause or to end a complete thought	The telltale high squeak— The patter of tiny feet; A mouse on the floor.
Comma	To create a short pause between continuing thoughts	She ran in heels, kept her balance. No luck— She missed the boat, the hour had struck.
No punctuation	To run ideas together or to keep the reader from pausing	Light drifts Down the streetlamp Dripping onto pavement Glossing across my shoes to find The city

My TURN Read the poem aloud with a partner. Choose punctuation to insert, and discuss where it should go to create rhythm.

The wind made a desert of my eyes nose and mouth
My canteen long empty Life where is my river
My stream between the rocks my trickle in a ditch?
Forget such small thinking Life where is my ocean?

My TURN In your writing notebook, compose a poem. Use punctuation to create pauses and other rhythms.

Develop a Rhyme Scheme

The pattern of rhyme in a poem is called the **rhyme scheme**. Understanding the rhyme scheme can help you identify the kind of poem you are reading. Each rhyming sound is given a letter of the alphabet, starting with *a*. All lines with the same rhyme are labeled with the same letter.

Example

Along the wall	a
Daffodils stood tall	a
The flowers grew	b
In yellows of every hue	b

Example

On the old gray stones	a
The roses clung	b
Their deep red tones	a
Spoke every tongue	b

My TURN Choose words from the word bank to complete the poem. Use each word once. Label the rhyme scheme.

Word Bank

cello **Sally** **valley** **yellow**

Deep in the ______________ ________

In a house painted ______________ ________

Lives a woman named ______________ ________

Who loves playing the ______________. ________

My TURN In your writing notebook, compose a poem. Create a rhyme scheme.

Rewrite for Precise Meaning

Because a poet usually accomplishes his or her goals with just a few words, he or she must choose each word carefully to have the biggest possible impact.

When rewriting, the poet considers the connotation of each word. Connotation is a word's emotional, imaginative, or traditional meaning. Words can have positive or negative connotations. For example, the word *thrifty* has a positive connotation, while the word *stingy* does not.

My TURN Rewrite the poems. Adjust the feeling by replacing the underlined words with words that have different connotations. Use a thesaurus and a dictionary if needed.

Change to positive feelings about winter

The winter wind grated against the door

We feared a foot of snow, maybe more.

Change to negative feelings about the rabbit

The rabbit hopped around the yard.

Nibbling on every cabbage and chard.

My TURN In your writing notebook, compose a poem. Choose words with precise connotations. Use a thesaurus to find synonyms.

My TURN Identify a topic, purpose, and audience. Then select any genre, and plan a draft by mapping your ideas.

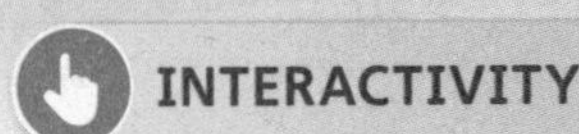

WASTE Is a PROBLEM

A plastic bag is useful for storing a sandwich, but it becomes useless once the sandwich is eaten. After you throw the bag away, it gets dumped into a landfill. Biodegradable waste, such as a banana peel, will naturally break down and nourish the soil. Nonbiodegradable waste, including plastic, takes years to decompose and creates many problems in our environment.

The Problems

- Landfills produce air pollution.
- Waste contaminates the groundwater.
- Hazardous chemicals get into soil, which can harm plants and food.
- Landfills produce greenhouse gases, including methane, which traps heat in the atmosphere.
- Waste emits odor.
- Waste is harmful to animals and their habitats.

Weekly Question

How do human actions create and change cycles?

TURN and TALK With a partner, discuss different ideas to reduce the amount of waste your school produces. Consider a recycling program or a school garden where food compost can be used to improve the soil.

Transfer facility

Learning Goal

I can learn more about informational text by comparing and contrasting authors' points of view on a topic.

Spotlight on Genre

Informational Text

Informational texts explain topics using facts and details. Writers can use visuals, including text features, and text structures to organize and support their ideas. Digital texts are often informational and include links, videos, and other media.

- **Information** is grouped into sections.
- **Titles, headings,** and **subheadings** emphasize central ideas and help the reader navigate.
- **Text and visuals,** such as infographics, work together to develop main ideas and details.

Textbooks, newspaper and magazine articles, and recipes are all informational texts!

TURN and TALK There are different types of informational text. Read the chart and think about the different types of informational texts you have read. Discuss each with a partner. Take notes.

My NOTES

TYPES of INFORMATIONAL Texts ANCHOR CHART

PURPOSE: To explain and inform

ARTICLES

- Provide updates on current events and interests
- May include text features, such as headings and photos

PROCEDURAL TEXTS

- Show steps in a process
- include instructions, recipes, and game rules

NARRATIVE NONFICTION

- based on real people and events
- includes biographies and autobiographies

EXPOSITORY TEXTS

- include textbooks, encyclopedia entries, and dictionaries
- often have navigational text features, such as indexes

Meet the Author

About the USDA
USDA stands for the United States Department of Agriculture, which oversees farming and food. Grocery stores and restaurants have to meet USDA food standards before selling food to customers. The USDA manages nationwide nutrition programs, such as the National School Lunch Program, which provides healthful, low-cost lunches to children each school day.

Let's Talk Trash and It's Time to Get Serious About Reducing Food Waste, Feds Say

Preview Vocabulary

As you read the infographic and interview, pay attention to these vocabulary words. Notice how they help you compare and contrast ideas.

edible **compost**
conscious **manufacturer** **contamination**

Read

Before you begin, make predictions using what you know about structures used in infographics and interviews. Follow these strategies to compare and contrast.

First Read

Notice text and images that help you make predictions.

Generate Questions about ideas that challenge what you already know.

Connect ideas by comparing and contrasting details in both accounts.

Respond by telling a classmate which account was more effective.

Genre Informational Media

Let's Talk Trash Infographic

from U.S. Department of Agriculture (USDA)

It's Time to **Get Serious About Reducing Food Waste**, Feds Say

from National Public Radio (NPR)

AUDIO

ANNOTATE

BACKGROUND

Currently the United States is home to more than 320 million people, and the population is growing every day. Each person produces 4.3 pounds of garbage daily, and much of it is food. What is the impact of these habits? How can we reduce the amount of food we waste? The USDA and NPR examine these important questions. See SavvasRealize.com to access the audio link to the NPR interview.

Compare and Contrast Accounts

Underline details on both pages that help you compare the texts' accounts of how much uneaten food is wasted each year.

Vocabulary in Context

A **context clue** is a word or phrase that surrounds an unfamiliar word.

Underline the words, phrases, and images that help you define *consumers* based on context clues.

edible safe to eat

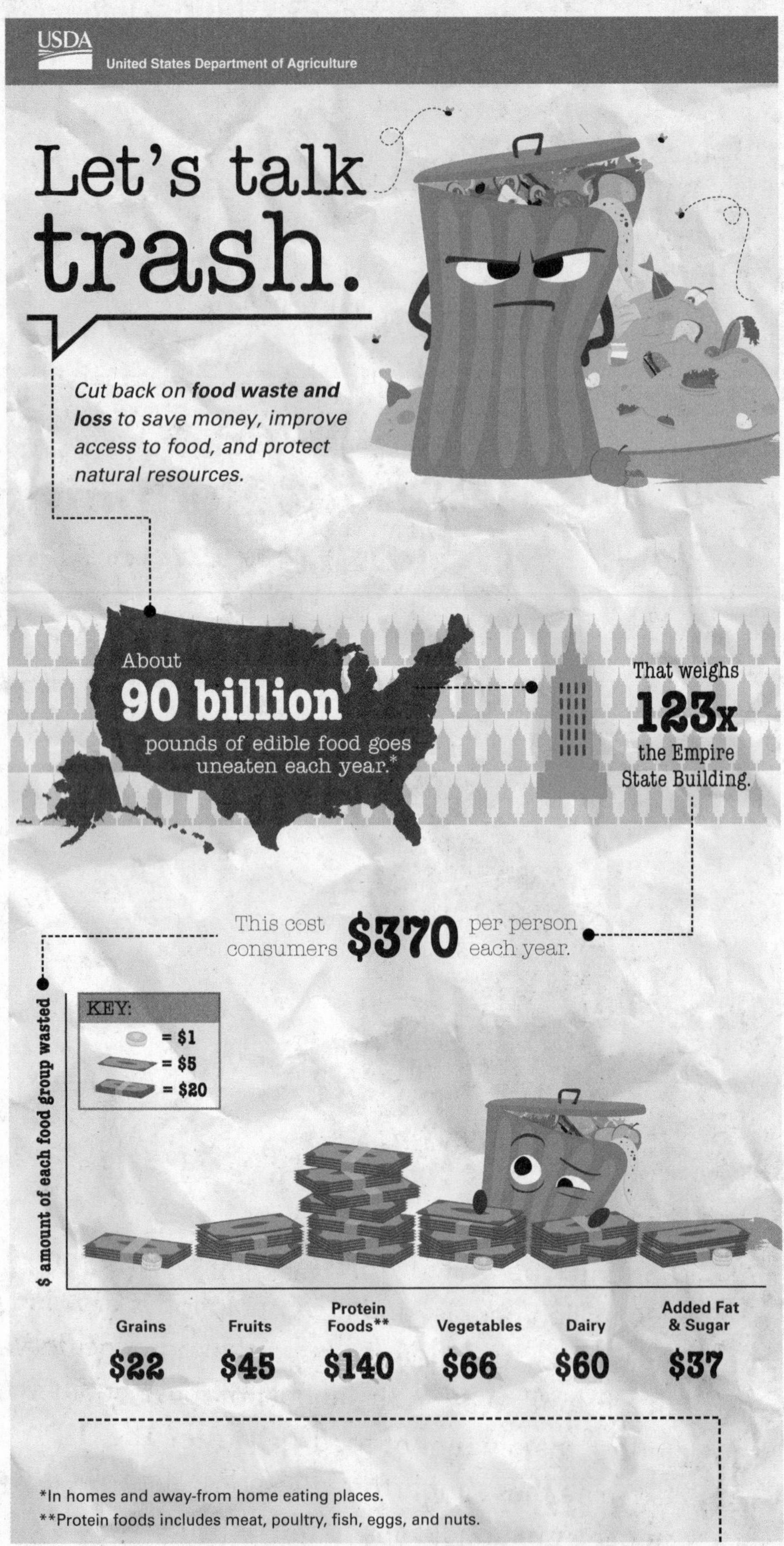

Reduce **wasted food** in your home with simple shopping, storage, & cooking practices.

WHAT YOU CAN DO

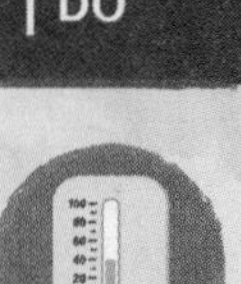

Plan & Save

Plan your weekly menu and make a grocery list. Does the list include food that you already have at home? Buy only what you need and stay within your budget.

Be Food Safe

Shop refrigerated or frozen foods just before checking out. Transport items that spoil easily in a cooler or thermal bag and refrigerate or freeze within two hours of shopping.

Check for Quality

The dates on a food package help the store determine how long to display the product for sale. It can also help you to choose a product at its best quality.

Set Storage Reminders

Track storage times for different foods using The FoodKeeper Application. This tool will remind you when foods are near to the end of their storage date.

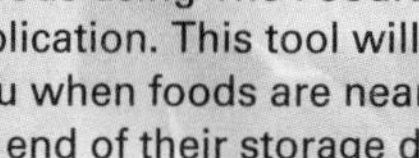

Be Organized

Foods are less likely to go bad when you use the older items first. Keep your pantry and refrigerator clean and organized so you can see what needs to be eaten first.

Re-purpose

Give leftovers a makeover when you reuse them in recipes. Add broccoli stems to a salad or blend overripe fruit into a low-fat smoothie. Freeze extra food.

Donate

Many shelters, food banks, and faith-based organizations will accept food donations to feed others who need a meal.

Recycle & Compost

Instead of throwing out food, create a compost bin. Don't have a yard? Your city may help you find composting or recycling options that are right for you.

Sources:
All sources are available at
ChooseMyPlate.gov/lets-talk-trash.

Center for Nutrition Policy and Promotion
USDA is an equal opportunity provider and employer.
September 2015

Monitor Comprehension

Reread the text. Highlight details from the infographic that help you understand how recycling and organizing can reduce waste.

How can background knowledge help you understand the text?

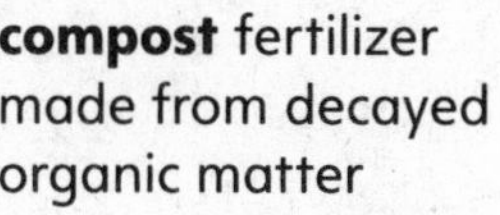

compost fertilizer made from decayed organic matter

It's Time to **Get Serious About Reducing Food Waste,** Feds Say

from National Public Radio (NPR)

Compare and Contrast Accounts

Underline facts about food waste that differ from those in the infographic.

1 RENEE MONTAGNE, HOST: And here's a startling number about a preventable loss. The average American family throws away a quarter of the food it buys each year. And in hopes of changing that, the U.S. Department of Agriculture and the Environmental Protection Agency have announced the first-ever national goal for reducing food waste. NPR's Allison Aubrey reports.

2 ALLISON AUBREY, BYLINE: The USDA estimates that America wastes 133 billion pounds of food a year. Now, to get a sense of how much that is, Agriculture Secretary Tom Vilsack says think of a certain Chicago skyscraper.

3 TOM VILSACK: It's enough to fill 44 Sears Towers.

4 AUBREY: The Sears Tower is now called the Willis Tower, but you get the point. It's a lot.

5 VILSACK: And basically it ends up, for the most part, in landfills.

6 AUBREY: Where it rots and creates methane, a powerful greenhouse gas linked to climate change. And given how much water and energy it takes to produce food, the effects of food waste are even greater. To make Americans more conscious of this problem, Vilsack along with the EPA and partners including grocery stores and food banks, have joined together to announce a new national goal.

conscious aware of an issue or idea

7 VILSACK: Basically challenge the country to reduce food waste by 50 percent by the year 2030.

8 AUBREY: Vilsack says there are lots of ways to make this happen. Farms and grocery stores can scale up efforts to donate food, and in our own homes, lots of us can make simple changes that may help. Given our current habits, the typical American household tosses out $1,500 worth of food every year. Here's Dana Gunders of the Natural Resources Defense Council.

9 DANA GUNDERS: It's like walking out of the grocery store with four bags of food, dropping one in the parking lot, and not even bothering to pick it up at all. And that's crazy.

10 AUBREY: Gunders says a lot of what we toss out is still OK. We tend to take sell-by dates on food a little too seriously.

CLOSE READ

Compare and Contrast Accounts

Underline a detail in the text that is also supported in the infographic.

Compare and Contrast Accounts

Underline information about expiration dates that is not represented in the infographic.

manufacturer a company that creates items by hand or by machinery

11 GUNDERS: A lot of people misunderstand expiration dates.

12 AUBREY: The dates stamped on food are really a manufacturer's best guess as to when a product is at its freshest. So . . .

13 GUNDERS: Often the products can be eaten days, weeks, even months after those dates.

14 AUBREY: Take eggs, they're usually good for weeks after the sell-by date. And you can actually test them. Put them in a bowl of water and if they sink to the bottom, they're still good. Gunders says even food that looks bad may be OK.

15 GUNDERS: Most vegetables that wilt can be soaked in a bowl of ice water, and that will crisp them up.

16 AUBREY: And that milk that's gone a little sour? It's actually safe to use in your pancake or biscuit batter.

17 GUNDERS: I had no idea, but actually cooking with sour milk is delicious. It substitutes for buttermilk.

18 AUBREY: Now, don't go overboard here. Foods like meat and poultry have higher risks of contamination. If they smell bad or look off, it's probably best just to toss them in the trash. Allison Aubrey, NPR News.

CLOSE READ

Monitor Comprehension

Highlight details that help you determine the relationship between expiration dates and health issues. If you are having trouble, ask questions and reread the text to find answers.

contamination the process of infection

Develop Vocabulary

In informational texts, authors use domain-specific vocabulary to develop and discuss ideas. These words help readers better understand complex topics.

My TURN Write the meaning of each vocabulary word. Then use each word in a sentence that explains its connection to trash or food waste.

Word	Definition	Sentence Related to Trash or Food Waste
compost	fertilizer made from decayed organic matter	Compost bins reduce the amount of food people throw away.
conscious		
manufacturer		
contamination		

Check for Understanding

MyTURN Look back at the texts to answer the questions.

1. What details make both texts informational?

2. How does the creator of the infographic make the data relevant and interesting to a wide audience?

3. What inference can you make about American food waste based on the comparisons to the Empire State Building and Willis Tower?

4. How should people use the sell-by dates on food? Synthesize information from both texts.

Compare and Contrast Accounts

To **compare and contrast** means to tell how two or more things are alike and different. When readers read multiple sources on the same topic, they compare and contrast the accounts from those texts. An **account** is how an author presents his or her point of view on the topic.

1. **My TURN** Go to the Close Read notes in both texts. Underline the parts that help you compare and contrast the accounts of how much uneaten food there is in America.

2. **Text Evidence** Use the parts you underlined to fill in the chart. Then analyze your findings by completing the sentences.

"Let's Talk Trash"	"It's Time to Get Serious About Reducing Food Waste, Feds Say"
Uneaten Food 90 billion pounds of food go uneaten each year, or 123 times the weight of the Empire State Building.	**Uneaten Food**
Expiration Dates	**Expiration Dates**

Analysis: An important similarity in the accounts is that

______________________________.

An important difference in the accounts is that

______________________________.

Monitor Comprehension

When readers read a complex text, they check their comprehension to make sure they understood what they read. You can use a variety of fix-up strategies, such as rereading, annotating, reviewing images, asking questions, or using background knowledge, to adjust and clarify your understanding.

1. **My TURN** Go back to the Close Read notes and highlight evidence that helps you monitor your comprehension of the texts.
2. **Text Evidence** Use your highlighted text to explain how you used each fix-up strategy to understand the texts.

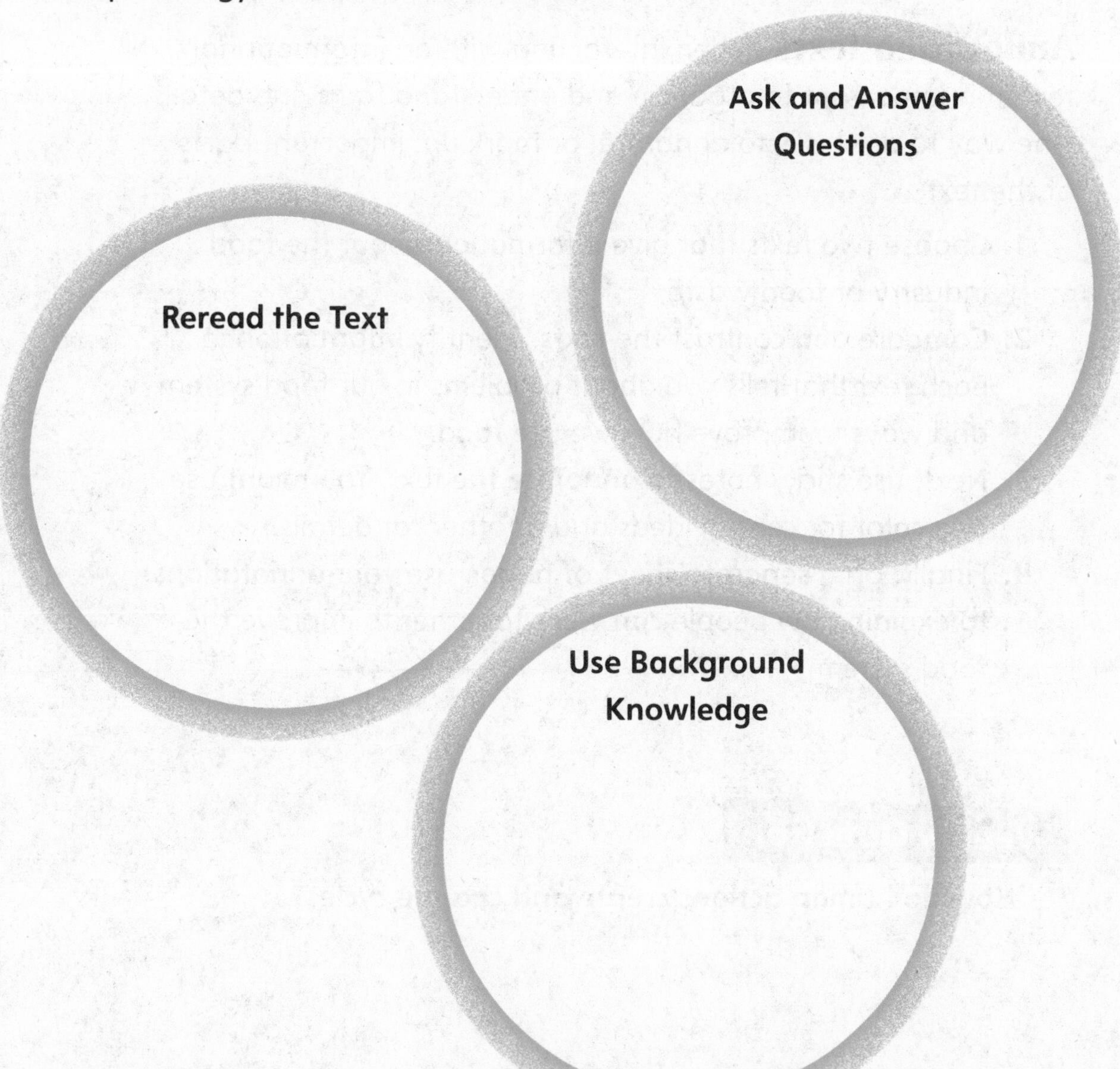

Reflect and Share

Write to Sources Consider the texts you have read this week. What do they say about how the food system works in our society? Analyze the texts by comparing and contrasting the problems and solutions they present. Use specific ideas from the texts to write a short informational paragraph about how people can work together to improve how we use food.

Annotating Texts When interacting with an informational text, it is important to organize and understand facts and details. One way to do this is to annotate, or mark up, important parts of the text.

1. Choose two texts that give information about the food industry or food waste.
2. Compare and contrast the texts. Identify information in each text that tells you about problems in our food system and ways to improve how we use food.
3. Next, use sticky notes to annotate the text. You might use one color for central ideas and another for details.
4. Finally, on a separate sheet of paper, use your annotations to explain how people can work together to improve the food system.

Weekly Question

How do human actions create and change cycles?

Academic Vocabulary

Learning Goal

I can develop knowledge about language to make connections between reading and writing.

Analogies compare two things that have something in common. Through analogies, readers expand their vocabulary and find connections between words.

My TURN For each analogy,

1. **Identify** the relationship between words in the analogy.
2. **Write** the missing word on the line. There can be more than one answer.
3. **Explain** the comparison in the analogy.

Calm is to **disturb** as ______________________ is to edible.

____

____

Cycle is to bike as drive is to ______________________.

____

____

Composed is to verb as composition is to ______________________.

____

____

Hit is to **impact** as ______________________ is to waste.

____

____

Schwa

The **schwa,** or *uh*, sound is the most common sound in English. Any vowel can create this sound. The schwa sound often appears in the unstressed syllable of a word.

For example, the academic vocabulary words *cycle, composed,* and *engineer* all have a syllable with a schwa sound.

cy/**cle**	**com**/posed	eng/**i**/neer

My TURN Read each word from "Let's Talk Trash." Next to each word write the word with slashes between each syllable. Then write the syllable or syllables with the schwa *(uh)* sound. Use a dictionary to check your work.

Word	Syllabication	Syllable(s) with Schwa Sound
protect	pro/tect	pro
edible		
consumer		
examine		
amount		
grocery		
vegetable		

Read Like a Writer

Authors use graphic features for specific purposes. An infographic shows information, usually statistics, using words and visuals.

Model! Look at the graphic feature from "Let's Talk Trash."

1. **Identify** The infographic shows how heavy the wasted food is. The author's purpose is to inform.
2. **Question** How does the graphic achieve the purpose?
3. **Conclude** The graphic helps readers visualize the amount of wasted food by connecting it to a well-known building.

Reread the part of "Let's Talk Trash" about the amounts of different food groups wasted every year.

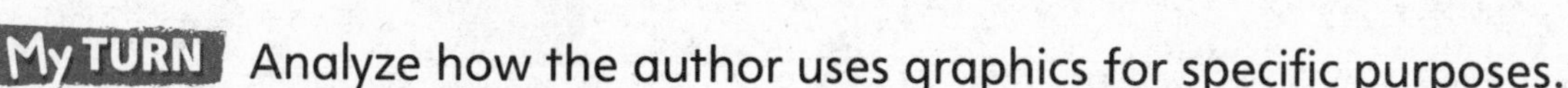

My TURN Analyze how the author uses graphics for specific purposes.

1. **Identify** The USDA uses ______________________ to ______________________.
2. **Question** How does the graphic achieve the author's purpose?
3. **Conclude** The graphic helps readers understand ______________________ ______________________ by ______________________ ______________________.

Write for a Reader

Writers use graphic features to present their ideas and draw in readers. For example, infographics can sometimes convey information more clearly than words alone do.

My TURN Think about the graphic features the USDA used in "Let's Talk Trash." Now identify how you can use graphic features to inform your own readers about a topic.

1. Choose a topic that interests you. What type of graphic feature would best showcase your topic and your knowledge?

2. Create an infographic about your topic. Be sure to emphasize information that supports your purpose.

Spell Words with Schwa Sounds

The most common sound in English is the **schwa,** or *uh,* sound. The schwa sound can be spelled by any vowel.

My TURN Read the words. Spell and sort the words in alphabetical order.

SPELLING WORDS

jewel	tropical	bulletin	terrific
kingdom	pajamas	carnival	celebrate
gasoline	universal	illustrate	independent
consolidation	ordinary	elegant	celery
garage	humidity	census	experiment

Quotation Marks with Dialogue

In **dialogue**, or words that are spoken between people in a narrative, a person's exact words are a direct quotation. Direct quotations begin with capital letters, end with the appropriate punctuation marks, and are enclosed in **quotation marks.**

A comma separates who is speaking from what is said. In interrupted quotations, the words that tell who is talking may be followed by a comma or by end punctuation.

Shannon asked, "Do you want to start a recycling club?"

"It sounds like fun," Dev agreed, "but it needs a name."

"I have an idea," Anna announced. "How about Green Warriors?"

"Perfect!" Shannon answered.

My TURN Edit this draft by adding quotation marks to direct quotations and changing or correcting punctuation as needed.

You want us to start composting? her mother asked.

It's good for the environment Sofia argued and it will give us all-natural fertilizer for the garden.

Mom shrugged okay she said.

Thanks Sofia replied I'll look for bins online.

Use Poetic License

Learning Goal

I can use elements of poetry to write a poem.

Writers can use poetic license, or decide not to follow traditional writing rules, to achieve a purpose.

A writer might use incomplete thoughts to create a sense of urgency.

> We left the canoe behind. Would it be there when we got back? Don't know. Can't wait any longer.

Because punctuation creates rhythm, a poet might use it unconventionally.

> Tunneling deep, below the hill—when at last!
> There, gleaming in the yellowed lantern's light,
> A mountain of gold, and gems, and treasure vast.

My TURN Read the poem aloud. Then answer the question.

> Spring—politely—asked to be a guest
> On the boughs of my apple tree.
> In return—she asked a finch to nest
> So that I could listen to its chee-chee.
> Weary from making the world turn green,
> Spring rested in my tree for weeks;
> Until the apples had a bright red sheen,
> Then she arose and gave Fall her seat.

How does the poet break the rules of writing, and what is the effect?

Try a New Approach

Sometimes, despite a writer's or poet's best efforts, a piece of writing needs to be completely rethought. This may mean revising or rewriting whole sections. It might also mean changing the genre.

A writer chooses a genre based on his or her task, audience, and purpose for writing. Some examples of genres include realistic fiction, argument, informational text, poetry, news article, or persuasive speech. If your genre does not match your purpose, do not be afraid to try a new approach. Ask for help from a partner or teacher, if needed.

My TURN Read the poem. Choose a different genre into which to rewrite the poem. Explain your choice.

Mother Earth's oceans are deep and vast
And have millions of creatures amassed.
But in the middle of the blue
Lurks a danger they cannot swim through.

Its name alone is ominous.
A mass of plastic—it's villainous.
The Great Pacific Garbage Patch.
There, unlucky creatures meet their final match.

We must act and try to pick up the pace
To remove this stain on our mother's face.
Some say it's as large as the U.S.A.
Can we save her before it's too late?

New genre ______

Why did you choose the genre you did?

______

Edit for Subordinating Conjunctions

Subordinating conjunctions connect an independent clause and a subordinate clause. A subordinate clause does not express a complete thought. When a subordinate clause is joined to an independent clause, it creates a **complex sentence**. Some common subordinating conjunctions include *because*, *if*, *then*, and *when*. If a subordinate clause appears first in a sentence, use a comma to separate it from the independent clause.

When it was her turn, Isla stepped up to the microphone.

subordinating conjunction

subordinate clause

independent clause

She got over her fears **because** success was important to her.

independent clause

subordinating conjunction

subordinate clause

My TURN Edit this draft to connect the subordinate clauses to independent clauses to make complex sentences. Insert commas as needed.

When Zosia and Tommy get to the summit. They will be able to see for miles. Because the trek was more difficult than they had planned. They had to stop many times to rest. They made it to the top of the mountain. After a lot of hard work. If they make this climb again. They will take a different route.

Edit for Adjectives

A **comparative adjective** compares two people, places, or things. Most comparative adjectives end in *-er*. Use *more* with longer comparative adjectives instead of adding an ending.

A **superlative adjective** compares more than two people, places, or things. Most superlative adjectives end in *-est*. Use *most* with longer superlative adjectives instead of adding an ending.

Some adjectives, such as *good*, *bad*, *little*, and *much*, have irregular comparative and superlative forms that do not use *more* or *most* or an ending.

Adjective	Comparative	Superlative
tall	taller	tallest
important	more important	most important
little	less	least

My TURN Edit the poem for the correct forms of comparative and superlative adjectives.

As I gaze upon this beautifulest morning,
I look forward to a more better day.
When everyone is more kind to each other,
In everything they do and say.

My TURN Edit a draft of your poem for correct forms of comparative and superlative adjectives.

Edit Titles and Show Emphasis

Use quotation marks when you refer to the titles of poems, articles, chapters, or short stories. Use italics or underlining when you refer to the titles of longer works, such as books, plays, movies, or magazines.

You can also use italics or underlining to show emphasis. This formatting is useful when you want to make a strong point and cannot rely on words alone to make the meaning clear.

My TURN Edit the poem by underlining for emphasis. Then tell what you would title the poem. Use correct formatting for the title.

The silvery cat leapt upon the sill.

The happy birds on the branch were no match for this hunter's skill.

But on they sang, unaware of the threat. Away, away! He snarled, so fierce.

You would be in such trouble if this glass weren't here.

I would name this poem

____.

My TURN Edit a draft of your poem to use italics or underlining for emphasis.

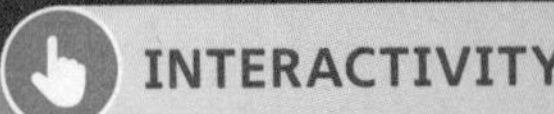

How PEOPLE Influence NATURAL SYSTEMS

SAN FRANCISCO, CALIFORNIA Fresh water from the Sacramento and San Joaquin Rivers flows into a delta and then into San Francisco Bay. There it mixes with salt water from the ocean. This mix of water creates an ecosystem called an estuary. Scientists explore how human activities, such as shipping and farming, affect the fish and wildlife that live in the estuary.

WEEK 5

Weekly Question

How much should people try to influence natural systems?

CHICAGO, ILLINOIS Chicago is known for its frigid and snowy winter months. The city pours salt on icy roads to prevent accidents. Road salt keeps people safe, but it has negative impacts on the environment. When snow and ice melt, salt drains into sewers and eventually rivers and lakes. The water becomes contaminated and harms soil, plants, and animals.

TURN and TALK Think of ways in which people influence natural systems in your community or region. Do their efforts help the environment or hurt it? Share your thoughts with a partner.

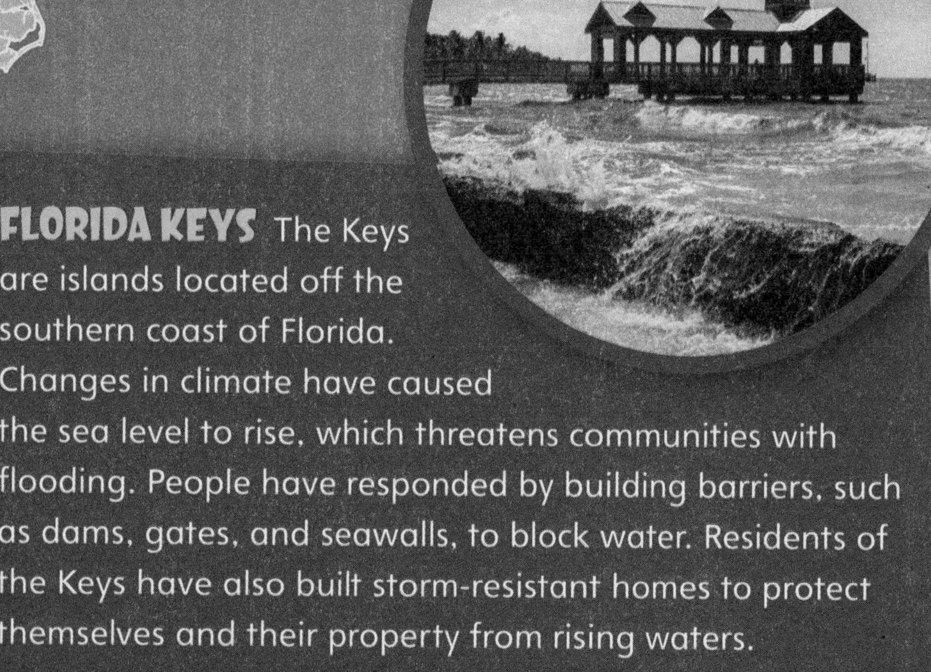

FLORIDA KEYS The Keys are islands located off the southern coast of Florida. Changes in climate have caused the sea level to rise, which threatens communities with flooding. People have responded by building barriers, such as dams, gates, and seawalls, to block water. Residents of the Keys have also built storm-resistant homes to protect themselves and their property from rising waters.

Learning Goal

I can learn more about the theme *Systems* by reading a text that helps me analyze arguments.

Argumentative Text

An **argumentative,** or **persuasive, text** tries to convince a reader to think or act a certain way. Authors use facts either to support an argument or to oppose an argument. Argumentative texts include

- A **claim**, or clear position that the author defends
- **Reasons** that support the claim
- **Facts and details** that support the reasons
- Comments on an opposing claim, or **counterclaim**
- **Appeals** to readers

TURN and TALK How do argumentative texts differ from informational texts? With a partner, compare and contrast characteristics of argumentative texts with those of informational texts. Use the anchor chart to help guide your discussion.

If a text tries to convince you to do or believe in something—it's argumentative!

Be a Fluent Reader Fluent readers read with accuracy, which means they pronounce words properly and do not add, skip, or replace words in text.

When you read text aloud, you may come across unfamiliar words or difficult sentences. To read them accurately

- look for letter sounds and spelling patterns you already know
- apply rules you have learned for letter sounds and pronunciations
- reread the sentence to make sure you did not add, skip, or replace any words

Argumentative Text Anchor Chart

Purpose: To persuade

Introduction

- Claim, or opinion statement

Reasons

- Supporting facts and details

Counterclaim

- Statement of opposing claim

Rebuttal

- Shows weakness of the counterclaim

Conclusion

Arguments appeal to audience's

- Logic
- Emotions, or feelings

Meet the Author

Lee Francis IV is a writer and teacher whose work has appeared in many publications. He leads a company called Native Realities, which creates comics and graphic novels for and about Native Americans and other native groups. He lives in Albuquerque, New Mexico, with his family and dog.

People Should Manage Nature

Preview Vocabulary

As you read *People Should Manage Nature*, pay attention to these domain-specific vocabulary words. Notice how they connect to the author's claim.

geological **habitat**
debris **advocates** **valve**

Read

Before you begin, consider reasons for reading the text to establish your purpose. Use these strategies when you read **argumentative texts.**

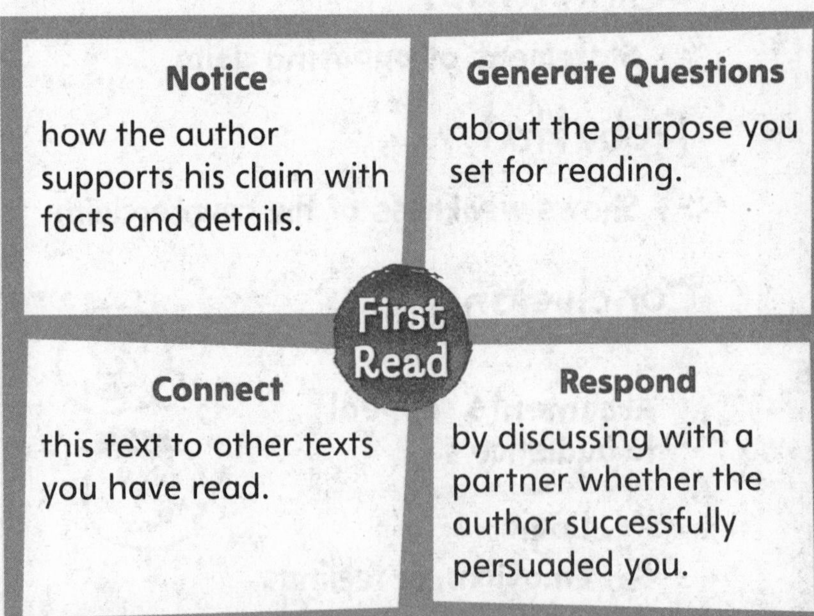

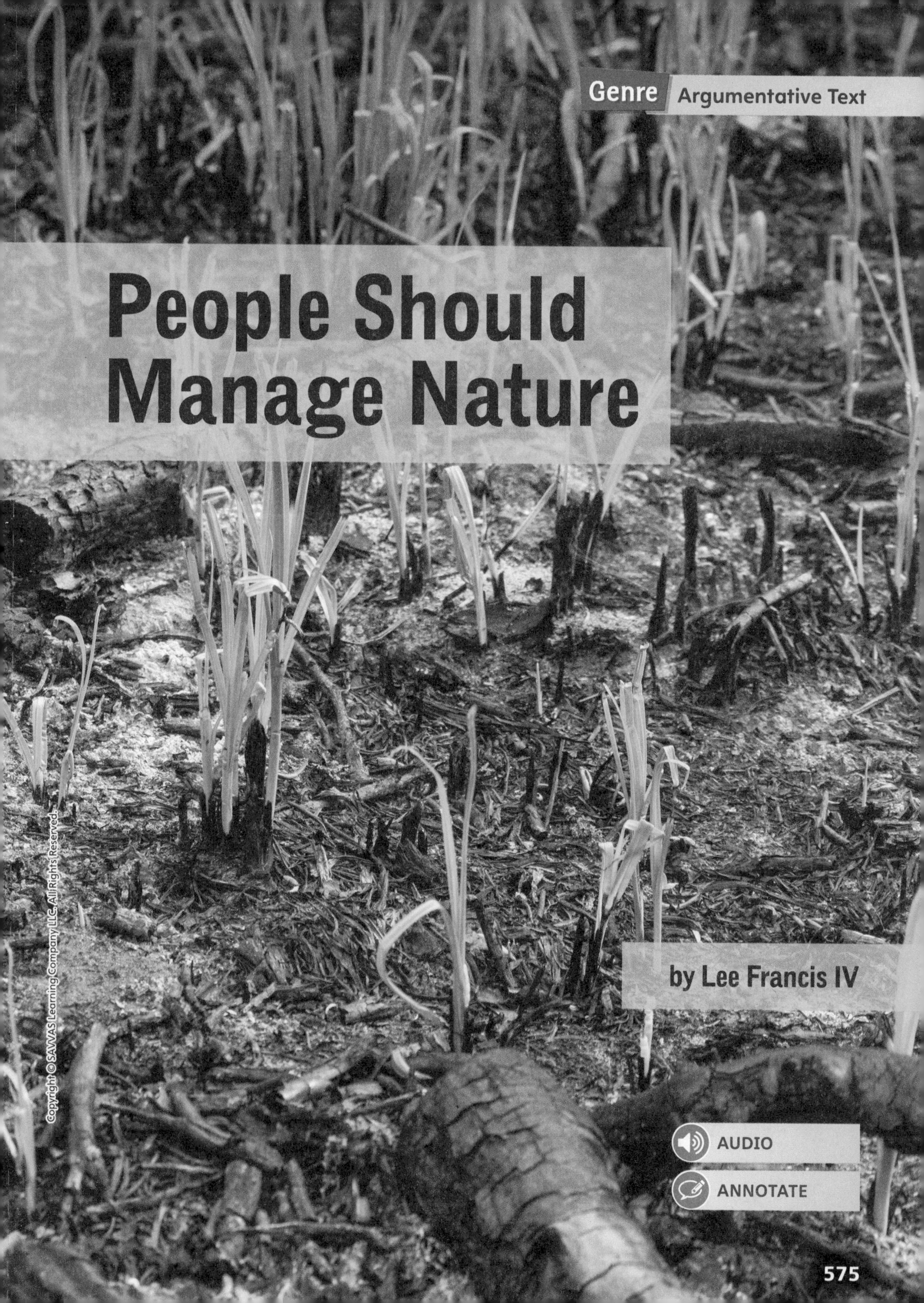

Genre Argumentative Text

People Should Manage Nature

by Lee Francis IV

AUDIO

ANNOTATE

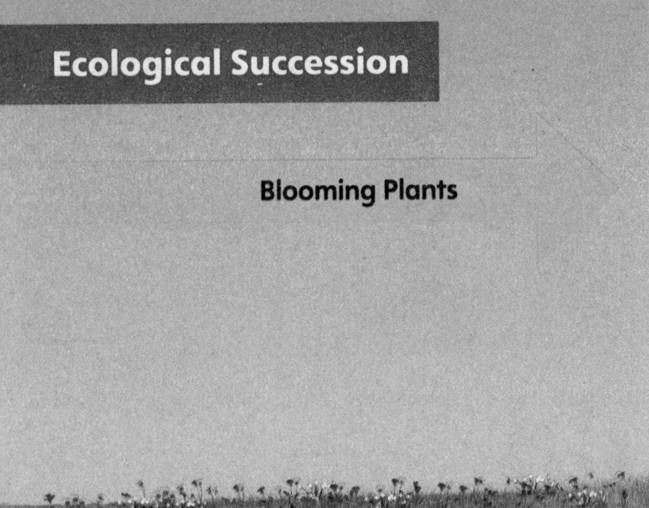

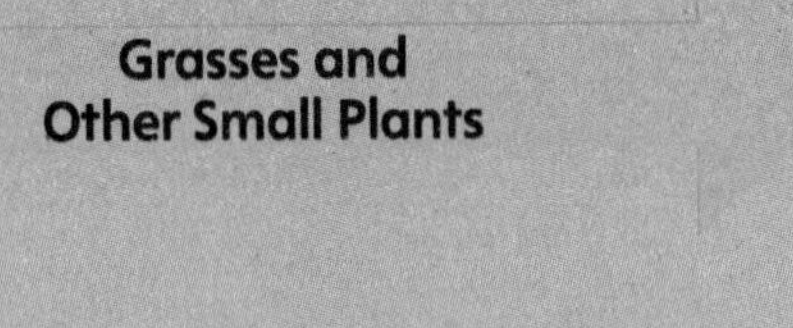

CLOSE READ

Make Connections

Highlight evidence that helps you determine the cause of natural disturbances.

Make a connection about a natural disturbance that you know of or have read about. What caused it?

1 A wildfire burns through an old forest. A flood sweeps across a coastal area. A mudslide buries a wide patch of jungle. When the disaster has passed, the landscape has changed. Many plants and animals are gone. The ones that remain begin to shape their new ecosystem, which includes all the living and nonliving things in the area.

2 A natural disaster is a type of disturbance, or temporary condition that causes major changes in an ecosystem. After a disturbance, plants that remain sprout from seeds or roots in the soil. Other plants move into the area. Over time, shrubs and trees grow, shading out smaller plants. Insects make their homes in decaying plant matter. Small mammals burrow in the ground. Birds return and nestle among the leaves. What once was quite barren becomes rich with life again.

3 Cycles of disturbance and regrowth are common in nature. Many plants and animals have characteristics that help them survive these types of changes. Their populations may suffer losses. But they can eventually bounce back from fire and flood. So when it comes to disturbances, some may argue that we should let nature take its course.

4 However, disturbances can be catastrophic when humans are involved, and humans live in almost all natural areas on Earth. A large natural disaster can kill people and damage property. That is why it is essential that humans practice careful management of nature. Management can reduce human tragedy and still allow diverse ecosystems to thrive.

CLOSE READ

Analyze Argumentative Texts

Underline the author's claim.

Ecological Succession

5 Cycles of disturbance and regrowth are part of ecological succession. That's the natural process of change in an ecosystem over time. In simple terms, this is what happens during ecological succession: blooming plants appear first, followed by grasses and other small plants, then bigger plants, shrubs, and finally trees. Each step allows the next step to happen.

Question for Reflection: What does your local ecosystem look like? In what ways do people control it?

6 Ecological succession happens after a disturbance such as a forest fire. The fire doesn't last long, but it causes significant change. Other natural disturbances include mudslides, floods, droughts, avalanches, and heavy winds or tornadoes. Natural disturbances are the result of environmental elements, weather, and geological processes.

geological relating to the study of Earth's physical properties

CLOSE READ

Analyze Argumentative Texts

Underline details on both pages that introduce an opposing viewpoint, or counterclaim, to the author's claim.

Then underline details that argue against the counterclaim.

habitat a place where a plant or animal normally lives or grows

Fires and Ecological Succession

7 Wildfires offer a good example of how ecological succession works. Wildfires occur in forests, grasslands, shrub lands, and even in wetland areas, such as marshes and swamps. Wildfires frequently break out during the dry season. They are often the result of a lightning strike.

8 Wildfires play a role in many forest ecosystems. Some plants, such as the jack pine tree, need a fire's heat to release their seeds. Fire can also clear away old growth and underbrush, creating a habitat for new plants. This enhances biodiversity, or the variety of plants and animals in a specific area. Long before humans began to settle near or in forest areas, forests developed naturally in response to wildfires.

Fire: People and Nature

9 Today, many people live in or near forests and other areas where wildfires can start. If the fires spread too fast and too far, they can be deadly. In the United States, local, state, federal, and tribal governments have established fire management policies. These policies focus on saving human lives. They also try to balance saving human property with protecting the environment.

10 Fire management has changed over time. Initially, management focused on eliminating all wildfires.

However, this strategy led to many problems. A more successful approach controls wildfires while still allowing some cycles of disturbance and regrowth.

11 In the United States, managing wildfires became a top priority in 1910, following the Big Blowup, one of the largest wildfires in the nation's history. The Big Blowup actually started as a series of smaller fires; officials estimated there were hundreds of them that started in late summer. Months of dry weather were followed by a sudden bout of storms. Lightning, as well as sparks from a train, started numerous fires. Whipped together by hurricane-force winds, the fires burned 3 million acres in Montana, Idaho, and Washington State in two days. The fires killed at least 85 people. Smoke reached all the way to New England, more than 1,900 miles from Montana. Soot reached the country of Greenland, more than 2,700 miles away.

12 The Big Blowup finally ended with the help of 4,000 soldiers-turned-firefighters and a heavy rainfall. Afterward, lawmakers in Montana, Idaho, and Washington, under pressure from the public, began pushing the U.S. Forest Service to adopt a new policy of suppressing, or immediately putting out, any and all forest fires. The policy soon went into effect. Under the new rules, all wildfires were to be put out no later than 10 A.M. the day after they started.

13 Forest Service Chief Henry Grave was in office during and after the Big Blowup. He said that this tough new approach was the best way to protect U.S. forests, the people, and businesses nearby, as well as the nation's economy. (Fighting fires of this size is hugely expensive. In addition, lumber companies wanted to protect timber so they could sell it.)

Make Connections

Highlight reasons that explain why stopping wildfires became a priority in the United States after the Big Blowup.

Do you think wildfire management is helpful or hurtful to our society? Make connections and discuss your answer with a partner.

Question for Reflection:

Have you seen examples of ecological succession in your area? What did you notice?

CLOSE READ

Analyze Argumentative Texts

Underline details that attack the counterclaim that aggressive interventions eliminate fires altogether.

14 The Forest Service received government funding to build new roads into the wilderness so firefighters could quickly reach a blaze. It built lookout towers so workers could see over vast stretches of forest. It hired highly trained fire crews. Later it added smokejumpers, people who jump out of planes to put out fires; bulldozers to drop dirt on fires; and planes to spray flame retardant over forests. Flame retardant helps keep wood and other materials from catching fire. The goal was to use technology and labor to eliminate fire entirely.

15 The policy of complete fire suppression turned out to be a devastating mistake. People failed to understand the essential role that wildfires play in forest ecosystems. Aggressive fire suppression interrupts the cycle of disturbance and regrowth that makes forests thrive. Such forests become more, not less, likely to burn. When forests are so carefully protected, they grow thicker. Trees grow closer together. Dead and fallen trees, no longer cleared by periodic wildfires, litter the forest floor. This debris can easily catch and spread fire. And that can mean less frequent but much larger and more destructive wildfires.

debris the remains of something that has been destroyed

16 That's what happened in 2000. During spring and summer of that year, a long dry spell and a buildup of debris led to massive wildfires. The fires burned more than 6.6 million acres, mainly in western states. That's more than double the average per decade in the United States. Then, in 2006, almost 10 million acres burned across the country.

17 After wildfires, people also cause problems by attempting to "clean" the forest. Workers log and clear trees in burned areas. They sometimes even take trees that are still living. This is known as salvage logging. Advocates say that it will help a burned forest bounce back faster. However, many experts say logging and clearing robs these areas of essential nutrients and resources that will help regrowth. The process not only removes trees but also disturbs organisms in the ground. Heavy equipment compacts the soil. That can lead to erosion and runoff, the draining of water from soil. Erosion and runoff, in turn, can affect nearby water sources. The ashy sediment that the runoff water carries can harm plants and fish in streams, rivers, and lakes. It also harms the animals that eat those plants and fish.

CLOSE READ

Make Connections

Highlight details that tell what happens when people try to "clean" the forest after a fire.

Make a connection to what you know about the world that helps you understand what happens when people mismanage nature.

advocates people who support a cause or policy

Analyze Argumentative Texts

Underline a reason in paragraph 18 that supports the author's main claim. Then underline facts that support the reason.

Question for Reflection:

Have you seen the aftermath of a fire? What did you notice? Can you think of ways humans could help without further disturbing the area?

18 Over the past few decades, the Forest Service has rethought its approach to wildfires. It has taken a hard look at the results of scientific research as well as the clear failure of its no-burn policy. Now the Forest Service uses controlled burns to help maintain forest ecosystems. Controlled burns mimic the natural process of wildfire disturbance. They also reduce the buildup of wood that can cause massive and uncontrollable wildfires. Controlled burns protect people while also promoting ecological renewal. This type of careful management benefits both people and forests.

Barrier Islands and Ecological Succession

19 Barrier islands are long, sandy islands along ocean coastlines. Geological processes built these islands, and ocean waves and winds shape them every day. Steady waves deposit sand to form long beaches. Strong waves during storms sometimes submerge whole islands. Currents erode sand on one end of a barrier island. These currents carry the sand and deposit it on the island's other end. This can cause the whole island to move slowly down the coast. Clearly, disturbance is constant on barrier islands. Because of this, ecosystems remain in the first few stages of succession. Ocean forces often "reset" these ecosystems.

20 Each barrier island ecosystem has distinct features. Beaches on the ocean side remain sandy with no plants. Algae live between particles of sand. The algae provide food for burrowing animals, such as crabs. Winds blow sand toward the middle of a barrier island, forming dunes. Grasses and other low plants take hold on these dunes. Their roots help to stabilize the sand. Salt marshes and mud flats develop on the protected side of a barrier island. Cordgrass grows in these areas. Many fish, sea turtles, and wading birds live within the submerged cordgrass.

21 Tidal activity floods low areas of a barrier island daily. Constant winds blow saltwater onto these islands. These conditions make it hard for shrubs or trees to grow. Larger woody plants only grow on larger islands. Wide dunes on these islands protect the plants. Trees and shrubs on barrier islands are usually evergreen. Their tough leaves provide protection from windy and salty conditions.

22 Small barrier islands have very little fresh water. Plants must get water from rain. Animals either use saltwater or get fresh water from plants. Larger islands have freshwater ponds in areas away from shore. The island of Assateague is a large barrier island along the coasts of Maryland and Virginia. Freshwater ponds on this island support frogs and toads, red fox, deer, and even wild horses. The horses are descendants of domestic horses brought to the island by European colonists.

CLOSE READ

Vocabulary in Context

Context clues are words and phrases that surround an unfamiliar word and help you determine the word's meaning. Look at the word *conditions* in paragraph 21.

Underline context clues to help you determine the meaning of *conditions*.

CLOSE READ

Make Connections

Highlight details that help you make connections to what you have read in other texts about the process of erosion.

23 Storms are particularly damaging to barrier islands. The strong winds of tropical storms blow away sand dunes. Strong waves remove beach sand. Salt marshes and mud flats that were protected by dunes and beach are then vulnerable. Diverse animal populations in these areas may disappear. All ecosystems on a very small barrier island can be damaged by a storm such as a hurricane.

24 Some natural features of a barrier island prevent sand from completely disappearing during a storm. Storm waves move across the whole island in a process called overwash. These waves move sand from the ocean side to the land side. The sand collects on the land side and does not wash away. Scientists have verified that overwash protected sand on Santa Rosa Island in Florida during Hurricane Opal in 1995.

25 Plant life on a barrier island can also prevent the loss of sand. Roots of plants hold sand as waves crash ashore. Roots and leaves shelter dunes from heavy winds. When sand is protected, all barrier island communities can thrive.

CLOSE READ

Barrier Islands: People and Nature

26 Lovely beaches and dunes attract people to barrier islands. They are popular tourist spots, and they support many permanent human communities. Galveston Island in Texas has had people living on it for over 1,300 years. Its current population is over 50,000 people. But barrier island communities face challenges. Natural disruptions from storms can kill people and ruin property. On Galveston Island in 1900, nearly 10,000 people were swept away or killed in a huge storm. This led officials to build a seawall for protection.

27 A seawall is a structure made of concrete or rocks. It is built on the coast to keep communities safe from tides and large waves. A seawall changes the coastline of a barrier island. Instead of sand, waves encounter a hard, unmovable surface. Seawalls and other hard structures can interrupt the flow of sand down the ocean side of a barrier island. This can change ecosystems on that island and on other islands near it.

28 In 1933, engineers built two jetties between Fenwick Island and Assateague Island, off the coast of Maryland. These rocky structures allowed boats to move between the islands. But the north jetty stopped the flow of sand to Assateague Island. The south jetty caused waves to quickly erode the beach on Assateague. The change in the movement of sand actually moved part of the island closer to shore.

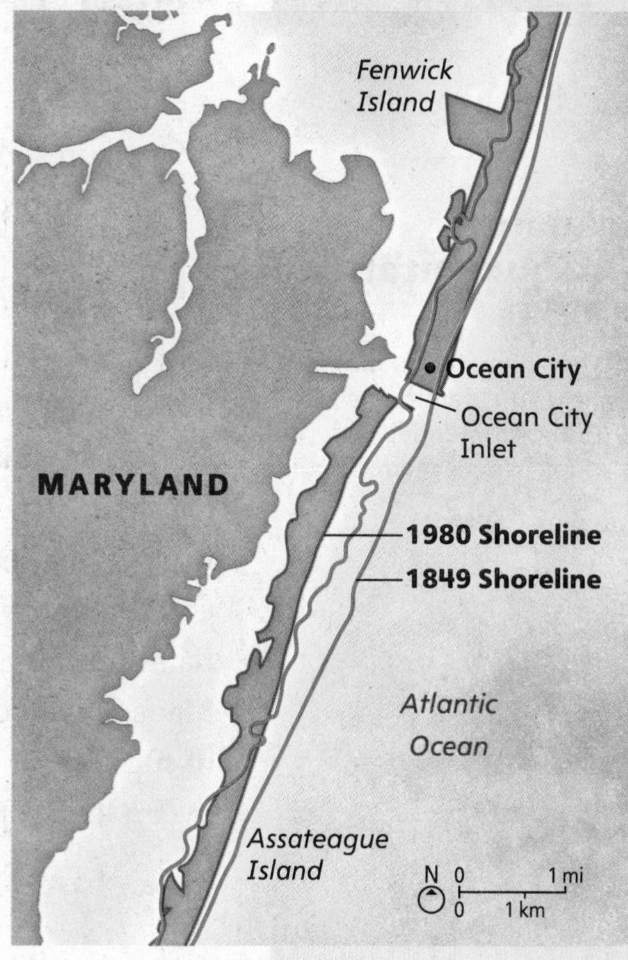

Analyze Argumentative Texts

Underline evidence that supports the idea that people should manage nature to prevent disasters.

CLOSE READ

Analyze Argumentative Texts

Underline details that help you identify the author's intended audience, or readers.

Question for Reflection:
How might people help minimize changes to barrier islands rather than make them worse?

29 Structures like jetties and seawalls improve safety and access for people on barrier islands. And some may argue that this type of management also protects many barrier island ecosystems. Hard structures meant to prevent waves from reaching upland areas also protect dune ecosystems. When dunes are protected, so are mud flats and salt marshes on the land side of the island. Management can actually slow down the rate of cycles of succession. These ecosystems can then remain stable over a longer period of time.

30 Unfortunately, seawalls or jetties can damage the beach ecosystem. Sand can erode more quickly when these hard structures interfere with normal wave movement. So, many communities on barrier islands pay for beach nourishment. Beach nourishment widens a beach by adding sand from other areas. A community interested in beach nourishment generally consults with the U.S. Army Corps of Engineers. The Corps helps the community come up with a good plan. The community then hires skilled contractors to perform the work.

31 During beach nourishment, workers use a floating machine called a dredge to suck up sand from underwater. The workers then steer the dredge toward the center of the beach. They attach a long pipeline to the dredge that stretches to the beach. The end of the pipeline is fitted with a Y-valve, that is then fitted with two more sections of pipeline. This valve allows workers to control the flow of sand to different sections of the beach. As sand is pumped onto the shoreline, bulldozers spread it out.

32 Beach nourishment is expensive. The process of pumping and moving sand is loud and disruptive to beach communities. Having heavy equipment working on a beach interferes with tourism. It is also only a temporary solution to the long-term problem of erosion.

33 However, beach nourishment does restore the important beach ecosystem to a barrier island. This ecosystem prevents waves from damaging roads and homes close to the beach. It expands habitats for barrier island animals. It also enhances recreation and tourism on the island.

CLOSE READ

Analyze Argumentative Texts

Underline a reason that supports the author's main claim. Then underline facts that support that reason.

valve a structure that controls the flow of materials

CLOSE READ

Analyze Argumentative Texts

Underline evidence that supports the author's point on the previous page.

Fluency

Read paragraphs 34–38 aloud with a partner. When you come to a word you do not know, sound out the letters in the word. Use context clues to help you determine the meaning of the word.

34 Restoration of the beach ecosystem has been shown to protect barrier islands from hurricane damage. Officials from the National Oceanic and Atmospheric Administration observed that islands with beach nourishment kept their sandy beaches after hurricanes in 2005 and 2008. Other similar islands experienced heavy erosion. On those islands, beaches and dunes were removed by violent waves and wind. Salt marshes on those islands then became vulnerable to future storms.

35 Restoration of barrier islands in general helps to protect coastal communities from hurricanes. The Barataria Bay island chain off the coast of Louisiana is being restored with funds from the Coastal Wetlands Planning, Protection, and Restoration Act. These islands are a first line of defense when a hurricane hits. They absorb energy from the storm, sparing communities on the mainland.

36 Ecosystems on barrier islands can benefit greatly from human management. After violent natural events, such as hurricanes, human intervention can restore these ecosystems. Barrier island management also helps human communities. It enhances species diversity on the islands and improves safety. In these ways, management is much more beneficial than just letting natural cycles act on barrier islands.

Conclusion

37 Disruptions are common in nature. Some, such as fire and mudslides, are relatively rare. Others, such as wind and waves, are constant in certain ecosystems. Catastrophic disruptions can reset ecosystems to an early stage of succession. These systems were formed to handle these types of disruptions. However, modern human communities were not, and people now live within nearly all ecosystems.

38 To protect lives and property, we must manage nature. If done thoughtfully, management can actually protect and enhance ecosystems. We can slow down cycles of natural disturbance, increasing stable habitats for many plants and animals. We must respect and understand cycles of nature. But with ecological understanding, we can manage nature so that all of life benefits.

Make Connections

Highlight a solution the author provides to the argument about humans managing nature. Connect this solution to solutions in other argumentative texts you have read.

Develop Vocabulary

In an argumentative text, the author tries to convince readers to agree with his or her viewpoint. Authors use precise words to make their claims, reasons, and supporting information clear.

My TURN Find each word in context in *People Should Manage Nature.* Complete the chart to explain how each word relates to the author's argument.

Author's Argument in Context

Word	Author's Argument in Context
geological	Some geological processes cause natural disturbances.
habitat	
debris	
advocates	
valve	

Check for Understanding

My TURN Look back at the text to answer the questions.

1. What makes *People Should Manage Nature* an argumentative text?

2. Analyze the Questions for Reflection that appear throughout the text. What are their purpose and effect?

3. What conclusions can you draw about why people feel the need to manage natural processes and disturbances?

4. Write an argument that disagrees with the author's claim. Support your argument with reasons and evidence.

Analyze Argumentative Texts

An **argumentative** text attempts to persuade readers. The author provides reasons and evidence, including facts and examples, for or against a claim. To analyze an argument, identify the author's claim and intended audience.

1. **My TURN** Go to the Close Read notes in *People Should Manage Nature* and underline the parts that help you identify the claim, supporting reasons and facts, and intended audience.

2. **Text Evidence** Use the parts you underlined to complete the chart.

Claim	
Reason	**Reason**
Facts	**Facts**
Who is the intended audience?	

Make Connections

As you read, make connections to your own experiences, other texts, and what you know about the world or society in general. Ask questions that help you better understand new information in a text.

1. **My TURN** Go to the Close Read notes and highlight evidence that helps you make connections to the text.

2. **Text Evidence** Use your highlighted text to explain the different types of connections you made to *People Should Manage Nature.*

How does the text connect to my life?
Text Evidence
Connection

How does the text connect to other texts I have read?
Text Evidence
Connection

How does the text connect to what I know about the world?
Text Evidence
Connection

Reflect and Share

Talk About It Consider all the texts you have read this week. What natural systems did you learn about? Do you think people should manage these systems? Use these questions to help you prepare an opinion presentation about whether people should try to influence or manage the environment.

Give a Short Presentation Before you begin your presentation, gather information to support your opinion.

- Write a claim, or opinion statement, on a separate piece of paper.
- Choose two or three texts you have read.
- Record direct quotations from the texts that support your opinion statement. Be sure to include the name of the text, the author, and the page number.
- Identify a counterclaim to your opinion, and give text evidence that opposes the counterclaim.

When giving your presentation, speak clearly at a natural rate and volume, making sure to enunciate every word. Make eye contact with your audience.

Weekly Question

How much should people try to influence natural systems?

Academic Vocabulary

Parts of speech are categories of words. Words can be used as more than one part of speech. As a result, words can have multiple meanings.

Learning Goal

I can develop knowledge about language to make connections between reading and writing.

MY TURN For each sentence,

1. **Identify** the academic vocabulary word's part of speech.
2. **Write** your own sentence using the same base word as a different part of speech. Add the part of speech to the chart.

Sentences	Part of Speech
The construction disturbed the peace and quiet of the building's residents.	verb
Mary cycles in her neighborhood every weekend.	
Trisha had a composed and focused look during the test.	

Vowel Changes

Changing the ending of a word can also change its pronunciation. For example, the word *define* is pronounced with a long *i*, but *definition* is pronounced with a short *i*.

Vowels can also change from a long vowel sound to the schwa, or *uh*, sound (*combine* to *combination*) or from a short vowel sound to the schwa sound (*excel* to *excellence*).

My TURN Read each word and add a word part to create a new word. Then identify the vowel sound that changes.

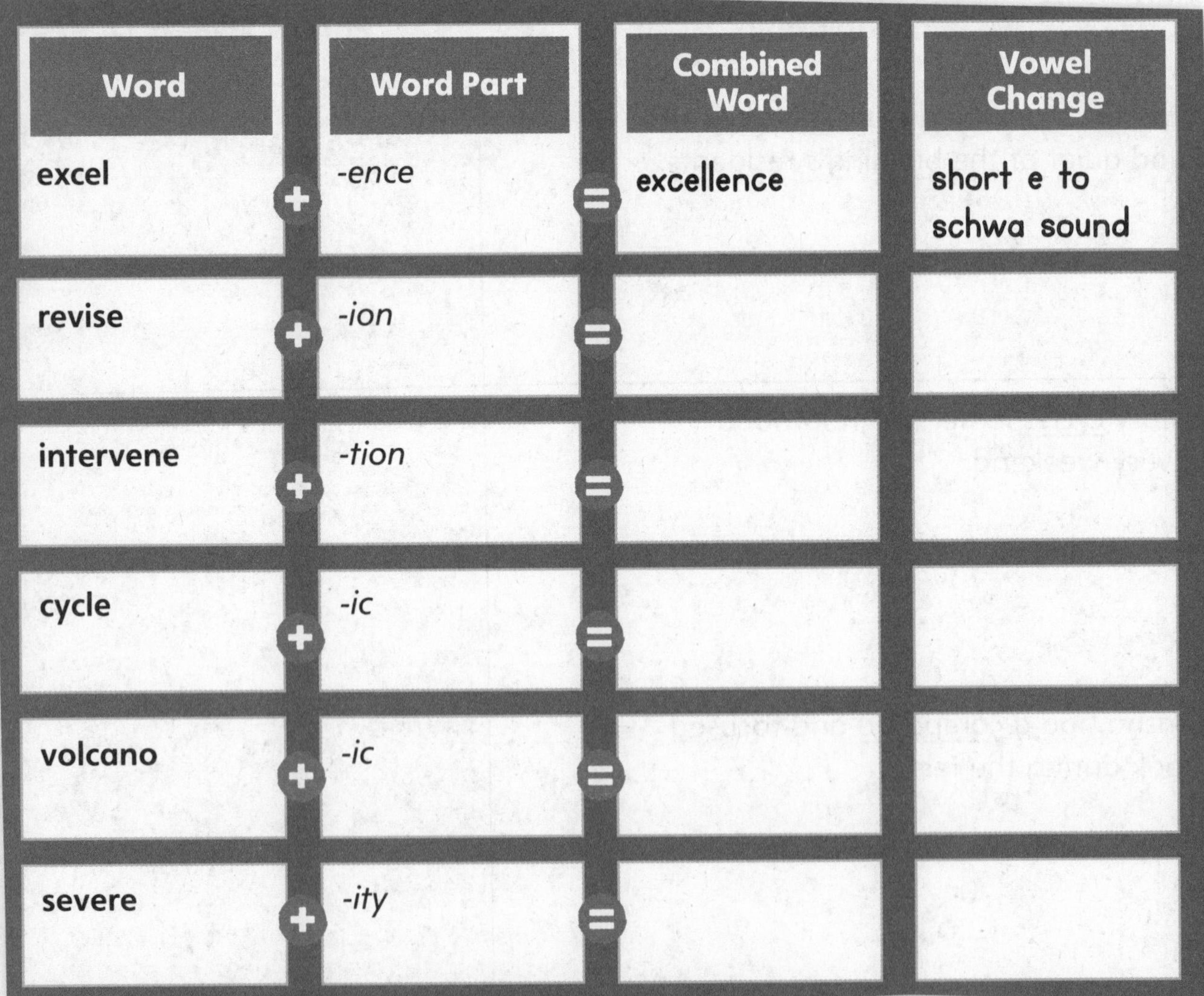

Word		Word Part		Combined Word	Vowel Change
excel	+	*-ence*	=	excellence	short e to schwa sound
revise	+	*-ion*	=		
intervene	+	*-tion*	=		
cycle	+	*-ic*	=		
volcano	+	*-ic*	=		
severe	+	*-ity*	=		

Read Like a Writer

The literary device point of view often determines how authors present information. Some writers use first-person pronouns in argumentative texts to connect with their audience or to reinforce their claims.

Model! Read the text from *People Should Manage Nature*.

> We must respect and understand cycles of nature. But with ecological understanding, we can manage nature so that all of life benefits.

first-person pronouns

1. **Identify** Lee Francis IV uses the first-person pronoun *we* in his conclusion.
2. **Question** Why does the author use this point of view at the end of his argument?
3. **Conclude** He uses first-person point of view so readers feel included in his argument.

Read this sample text.

> If we have patience and trust nature to take care of itself, I believe we will avoid many natural disasters.

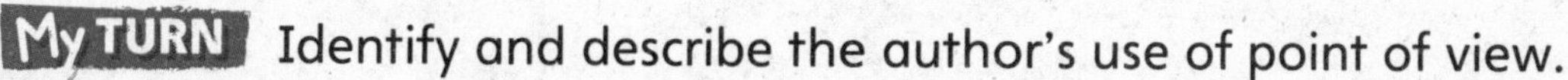

MyTURN Identify and describe the author's use of point of view.

1. **Identify** The author uses ________________________________.
2. **Question** Why does the author use this point of view?
3. **Conclude** The author wants readers ________________________________

____.

Write for a Reader

Some writers use literary devices, such as first-person point of view, to connect with and persuade readers.

My TURN Think about how Lee Francis IV uses first person at the end of *People Should Manage Nature.* Consider how it appeals to your emotions, beliefs, and sense of reason. Now identify how you can use first-person point of view as a tool to persuade your readers.

1. If you were trying to persuade a reader about your opinion on people's management of nature, how would you use first-person point of view?

2. Write an argument about human management of nature using information from the text and some of your own research or background knowledge. Use first-person point of view to connect with readers and emphasize your points.

Spell Words with Vowel Changes

Sometimes adding an ending to a word changes a vowel sound in the word. Vowel changes include long vowel to short vowel, long vowel to schwa sound, and short vowel to schwa sound.

Understanding syllable division patterns can help you spell multisyllabic words. As you spell words, notice where they naturally break into syllables.

My TURN Read the words. Sort and spell each related word pair side by side. Use slashes to divide each word into syllables.

SPELLING WORDS

physical	collide	perspire	deduce
perspiration	cyclic	collision	explanation
deductive	prepare	repeat	sincere
explain	physicality	cycle	preparation
repetition	severe	severity	sincerity

Interjections

Interjections are words that express emotion, or feelings. Interjections are most often used in informal situations. They are rarely used in formal writing.

When an interjection expresses a strong feeling, it is followed by an exclamation mark.

Oh no! I forgot my book report.

Eek! Watch out for snakes!

A strong interjection can also appear after a sentence.

I can't believe you got playoff tickets. **Wow!**

When an interjection does not express a strong feeling, it is followed by a comma.

Great, let's ask the teacher at school tomorrow.

Well, I guess we'll catch the game next week.

MY TURN Edit this draft by inserting the proper punctuation for each interjection.

Hey did you hear about the latest wildfires? Luckily, firefighters put them out before they got too close to our cabin. Whew Ugh the cleanup will be tough and time-consuming. Oops I forgot I'm supposed to pick up bottled water for the volunteers.

Edit for Collective Nouns

Learning Goal

I can use elements of poetry to write a poem.

A **collective noun** names a group of persons or things. A collective noun is singular in form, but it refers to a group or collection. Some common collective nouns include *group*, *collection*, *herd*, *set*, *flock*, and *family*.

Use a **singular verb** and a **singular pronoun** when you use the collective noun to mean the group as a whole.

Sentence	Meaning
The **herd** is exploring its territory.	Every member of the same herd explores the same territory.

Use a **plural verb** and a **plural pronoun** when you use the collective noun to mean each individual in the group.

Sentence	Meaning
The **herd** are exploring their own territories.	Members of the same herd live in different territories, but they are all exploring.

My TURN Write a sentence using the correct form of the verb and pronoun based on the purpose of the collective noun.

1. Purpose: all members of the same **flock**

2. Purpose: individual members of a **family**

My TURN Edit a draft of your poem for subject-verb agreement with collective nouns.

Edit for Irregular Verbs

To form the past tense of a regular verb, add *-ed*. The past participle uses the past tense of the verb plus *has*, *have*, or *had*.

Present Tense Verb	Past Tense Verb	Past Participle
want	wanted	(has, have, had) wanted

An **irregular verb** has a different form for the past and past participle. Irregular verbs are common, but be sure to memorize their spellings.

Present Tense Verb	Past Tense Verb	Past Participle
take	took	(has, have, had) taken
see	saw	(has, have, had) seen
bring	brought	(has, have, had) brought
know	knew	(has, have, had) known

My TURN Edit the paragraph to have the correct form of each irregular verb. Spell each word correctly.

My class take a field trip to the planetarium. We see how stars form. I wish I had knew about this place before, because I would have brung my whole family!

My TURN Edit your writing to have correct forms of irregular verbs.

Publish and Celebrate

When you finish your poem, it is time to share it with the world by publishing it. You can choose to publish by including your poem in a book of poetry, by reading the poem aloud to an audience, or by posting it to a blog or poetry Web site.

My TURN Describe your writing experience. Write legibly in cursive.

My favorite poem was ____
____
____.

I liked using figurative language such as ____________________ because
____
____.

My favorite rhymed lines that I wrote were ____________________________
____
____.

I found it difficult or easy to write a poem because ____________________
____
____.

When I write another poem, I will _____________________________________
____
____.

Prepare for Assessment

My TURN Follow a plan as you prepare to write a poem from a prompt.

1. **Relax.**
   Take a deep breath.

2. **Make sure you understand the prompt.**
   Read the prompt. Underline what kind of writing you will do. Highlight the topic you will be writing about.

   Prompt: Write a poem about the beauty of water during part of the water cycle.

3. **Brainstorm.**
   Brainstorm three ideas based on the topic. Choose your favorite.

4. **Identify precise language.**
   List vivid words about your subject.

5. **Write your draft. Remember to establish a rhythm. Use rhyming words if they accomplish your goals.**
   Use your own paper to write your poem.

6. **Revise and rewrite your poem.**
   Read your poem aloud. Rewrite parts that disrupt your poem's rhythm.

Assessment

MyTURN Before you write a poem for your assessment, rate how well you understand the skills you have learned in this unit. Go back and review any skills you mark "No."

IDEAS AND ORGANIZATION	Yes!	No
I can write a poem.	☐	☐
I can develop rhythm and rhyme in poetry.	☐	☐
I can identify ideas for poems based on meaningful themes.	☐	☐

CRAFT	Yes!	No
I can use figurative language, including personification, simile, and metaphor.	☐	☐
I can use line breaks with punctuation to create rhythm.	☐	☐
I can break thoughts into lines and stanzas.	☐	☐
I can rewrite to select words with appropriate connotations.	☐	☐
I can break the rules of grammar, punctuation, and capitalization to achieve my goals in poetry.	☐	☐

CONVENTIONS	Yes!	No
I can use comparative and superlative adjectives.	☐	☐
I can use italics and underline with titles and for emphasis.	☐	☐
I can use subordinating conjunctions.	☐	☐
I can edit for collective nouns and irregular verbs.	☐	☐

UNIT THEME

Systems

Week 3

"The Dog of Pompeii"

disturb

TURN and TALK

Connect to Theme

In this unit, you learned many new words to talk about Earth's systems. With a partner, review each text and write a sentence about it that best illustrates the academic vocabulary word. Be prepared to tell why you wrote the sentence.

BOOK CLUB

Week 2

from **Earth's Water Cycle**

impact

BOOK CLUB

Week 1

from **Rocks and Fossils**

composed

WEEK 6

Week 4

"Let's Talk Trash" and "It's Time to Get Serious About Reducing Food Waste, Feds Say"

cycle

Week 5

People Should Manage Nature

engineer

BOOK
CLUB

Essential Question

MyTURN

In your notebook, answer the Essential Question: How do elements of systems change?

Project

Weeks 6

Now it is time to apply what you learned about systems in your **WEEK 6 PROJECT: Persuade the Public!**

Persuade the PUBLIC!

Activity

How can you get people to help the environment? A great Public Service Announcement (PSA) could convince them! Write the script for an audio or video PSA that persuades people to improve the environment and describes specific ways they can help. Explain how your advice will create a positive change in one of Earth's systems.

RESEARCH

Research Articles

With your partner, read "Now Hear This!" to generate questions you have about the article. Then work together to make a research plan.

1. Now Hear This!
2. Emergency!
3. Meet FEMA

Generate Questions

COLLABORATE Read "Now Hear This!" Then generate three questions you have about it. Share your questions with the class.

1. ______________________________
2. ______________________________
3. ______________________________

Use Academic Words

COLLABORATE Throughout this unit, you learned words related to the theme, *Systems*. Work with your partner to add more academic vocabulary words to each category. If appropriate, use some of these words as you plan and write your public service announcement.

Academic Vocabulary	Word Forms	Synonyms	Antonyms
disturb	disturbs disturbing disturbance	upset spoil mess up	heal help leave alone
cycle	cycles cycling recycle	series set sequence	individual interruption single
impact	impacts impacted impacting	affect influence sway	ignore overlook disregard
composed	compose composure decompose	built created united	decomposed disconnected taken apart
engineer	engineered engineering reengineer	build design plan	destroy wreck demolish

A Persuasive PSA

People write **argumentative texts** to try to persuade readers to think or do something. Look for these features when you listen to public service announcements

- a claim
- facts that back up the claim
- effective language and media techniques that make the message stick

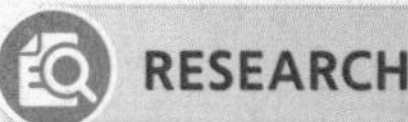

COLLABORATE With your partner, read "Emergency!" Then, answer these questions about the text.

1. What is the writer's claim?

2. What evidence does the writer use to persuade readers?

3. Does the writer provide enough evidence? Why or why not?

Plan Your Research

COLLABORATE Before you research ways to improve the environment, you need to make a research plan. Refer to the chart as you write a claim and plan how you will look for evidence to support it.

Definition	Examples
CLAIM A claim is a statement that tries to persuade a reader to agree with an opinion. An effective claim • defines a writer's goal • is clear and specific • is supported with reasons and evidence One of the examples is an effective claim. The other is not. With your partner, write a claim for your PSA about improving the environment.	• Everybody hates noise! NO • You need to protect your ears by limiting the amount of loud noise you hear. YES! My claim about improving the environment: __________ __________ __________
EVIDENCE Information that supports your claim is evidence. You might include • facts • statistics • quotations • examples	**Fact:** Hearing loss cannot be reversed. **Statistic:** Eighty percent of elementary students use personal music players. **Quote:** Dr. Alana Suarez says, "Ear protection is the key." **Example:** Most music players allow users to set maximum volumes.

List possible sources that could provide supporting evidence for your claim about protecting the environment and Earth's systems.

GREAT GRAPHICS

The information you gather from print and digital sources will help you support the claim you want to prove in your PSA. Sometimes the best way to share information is to create a graph. The type of graph you create will depend on the information you gather. This chart shows three useful types of graphs.

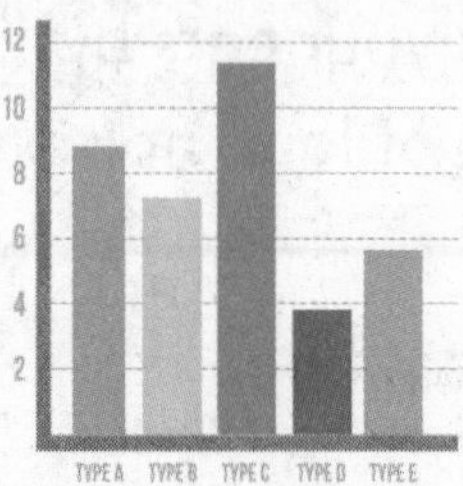

A **bar graph** compares individual pieces of information.

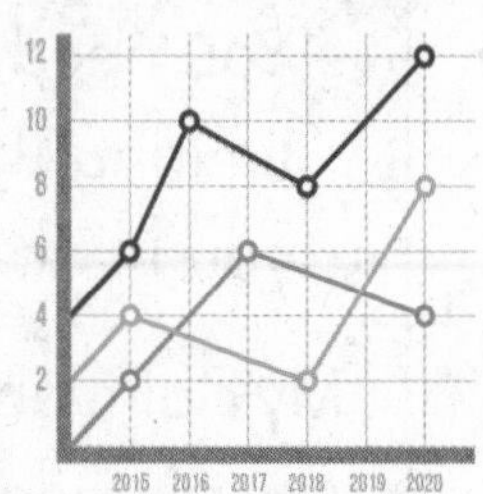

A **line graph** shows the changing relationship between two factors.

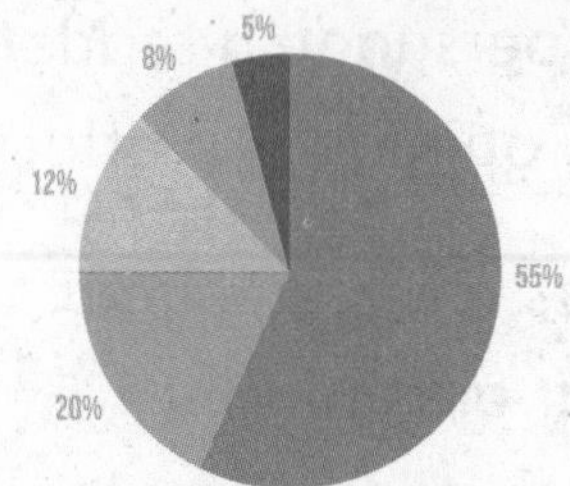

A **circle graph** (also called a **pie chart**) shows percentages, parts of a whole.

EXAMPLE Kevin created this graph to compare different types of noise pollution.

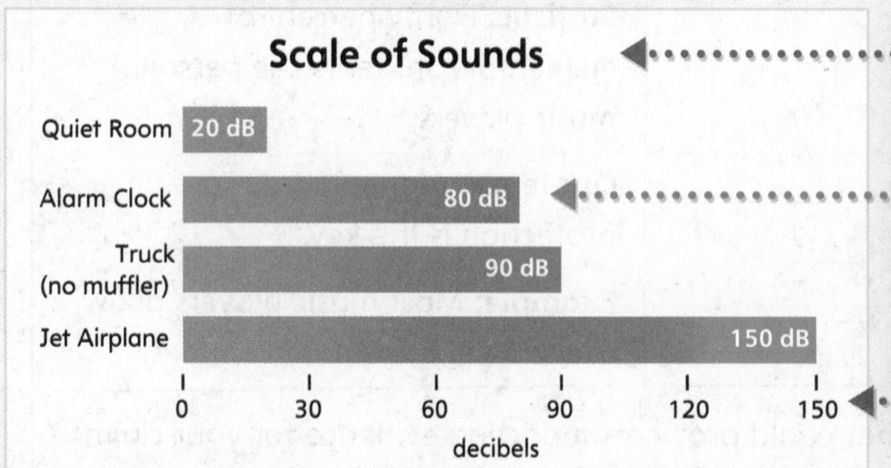

The title tells what the graph is about.

The bars in a bar graph can be vertical or horizontal. Kevin created a horizontal bar graph.

The labels tell you the units of measurement.

COLLABORATE With your partner, think of two graphs you might create to support your claim. Consider the type of information you have and the best way to display it. Take notes in the charts to plan your research.

Graph 1

Type of Graph	
Graph Title	
Possible Sources	
Why is this the best type of graph to show this data?	

Graph 2

Type of Graph	
Graph Title	
Possible Sources	
Why is this the best type of graph to show this data?	

Work together to gather information from the sources you identified. Discuss how you can create graphs to share the data you find.

Send a STRONG MESSAGE

A **public service announcement (PSA)** tries to persuade readers to believe a claim. Most PSAs follow this basic plan.

- The **introduction** presents the claim.
- The **body** of the PSA presents evidence to support the claim.
- The **conclusion** restates the claim and leaves readers with something to think about.

The details in an effective PSA should be facts, statistics, and examples. A video PSA also uses visuals and graphics that support the claim and key ideas.

COLLABORATE Read the Student Model. Work with your partner to recognize the characteristics of public service announcements.

Now You Try It!

Discuss the checklist with your partner. Work together to follow the steps to create a public service announcement.

Make sure your PSA

- ☐ makes a clear, specific claim.
- ☐ presents facts, statistics, quotes, or examples as evidence.
- ☐ follows a logical and persuasive order.
- ☐ includes a strong conclusion that restates your claim.

Student Model

Noise Pollution PSA

Words/Script	Video/Audio
Loud noises can actually hurt your ears forever. Protect your ears by avoiding noise pollution.	*Collage of noisy things, like a jet plane taking off, honking horns, and super loud music*
Sounds are a natural part of Earth's systems.	*Birds tweeting and rain falling on the ground*
Some natural sounds are loud, but they don't last long.	*Thunder in a storm or a dog barking*
We use decibels to measure sounds. An alarm clock ringing is about 80 decibels.	*Bar graph showing different sound levels measured in decibels*
Sounds that last a long time become noise pollution.	*A jackhammer at a construction site*
Dr. Alana Suarez is an expert on kids and hearing. She says, "I see a lot of students who have permanently damaged their hearing by blasting music through headphones."	*Video clip from interview with Dr. Suarez*
Turn down the music to save your ears!	*A student using headphones*

Underline the sentence that states the writer's claim.

Highlight one statistic.

Underline a quotation.

Name Your SOURCES

A **bibliography** is a list of all the sources used when researching a topic. A bibliography helps readers check that facts are reported accurately.

This chart shows the information you should include for different kinds of sources.

Books

- Author. (last name, first name)
- *Title of Book.* (in italics or underlined)
- City, State of publication.
- Publisher, year of publication.

Luyden, Erik. *Noise: The Invisible Menace.* Austin, Texas. Action Press, 2017.

This encyclopedia article did not list an author.

Encyclopedia Articles

- Author. (if available)
- "Title of Article."
- *Title of Book.* (in italics or underlined)
- Date of edition.

"Noise Pollution." *Encyclopedia of the Environment.* 2015.

Look on the home page to find the name of the Web site.

Web Sites

- Author. (if available)
- "Title of Web Page."
- *Name of Web Site.* (in italics or underlined)
- Date of your visit to Web site.
- <URL—Web site address> in brackets

Stone, Kayla. "The Sounds Around You." *Students for Earth.* Oct. 14, 2017. <www.url.here>

RESEARCH

COLLABORATE Read the article "Meet FEMA." Then work with a partner to create a bibliography entry for the article.

COLLABORATE Read this bibliography for a public service announcement. Then answer the questions.

"Measuring Sound." *Encyclopedia of Modern Science*. 2013.

Talpur, Abdul. *Ouch! My Ears! Noise Pollution and What You Can Do About It.* San Diego, California. Zoom Publishing, 2018.

"Wait! I Can't Hear You." *NASA*. September 9, 2016. <https://www.nasa.gov/topics/aeronautics/features/aircraft_noise.internet>

1. What is the most recent source listed in this bibliography?

2. How are the entries in the bibliography organized?

3. Now include two entries for your own bibliography.

Recording TIPS

Your public service announcement will be more effective if you plan your audio or video recording carefully. Your script will help you create a PSA that makes a strong claim and supports it.

These tips can help you create a PSA that meets your goals.

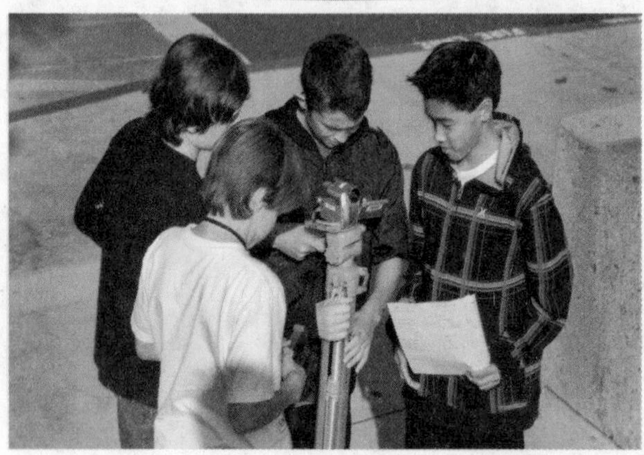

Rehearse First
Practice reading or memorize your text before recording. Speak slowly and clearly.

Include a Variety of Media
Plan to include a variety of slides, videos, graphs, and illustrations.

Change the Camera Distance
Include both close-ups and long shots from a distance to add interest.

Add Titles
Use titles to emphasize important ideas.

Rerecord and Edit
Record multiple takes of your PSA to get the best version. When you edit, choose the takes that are easy to understand.

Use Special Effects Carefully
Too many fancy fades or sound effects can be confusing. Choose just one or two special effects.

COLLABORATE With your partner, discuss how you will record your PSA. Complete the planning chart to guide your decision-making process. For each row, brainstorm and decide on the steps you will take to fill in the plan.

PSA Planning Chart

Ideas to Emphasize	
Variety of Media	
Titles	
Camera Distances	
Special Effects	
Other Notes	

Revise

Revise Claim and Evidence Reread your PSA script with your partner. Have you

- ☐ clearly stated your claim?
- ☐ included strong facts, statistics, quotations, and examples?
- ☐ ended with a strong conclusion?

Strengthen Your Support and Conclusion

The writers of the noise pollution PSA added another statistic to strengthen their message. They also added a conclusion that restates their claim in a memorable way.

We use decibels to measure the volume of sounds. An alarm clock ringing is about 80 decibels. ^ A jet plane taking off is almost twice that loud.

Turn down the music to save your ears! ^ Always pay attention to how loud your environment is. Your ears will be glad you did!

Edit

Conventions Read your PSA script again. Have you used correct conventions?

- ☐ spelling
- ☐ punctuation
- ☐ capitalization of names and places
- ☐ capitalization of titles
- ☐ quotation marks around ideas directly quoted from research
- ☐ a variety of simple and complex sentences

Peer Review

COLLABORATE Exchange public service announcements with another group. Use the chart to review the PSA. Write the claim and then note the key evidence from the text and media. Discuss whether the evidence is strong, and give suggestions for how to improve it.

CLAIM	
EVIDENCE	
SUGGESTIONS	

Time to Celebrate!

COLLABORATE Present your PSA to your class. Whether presenting in person or in a video, remember to make eye contact, enunciate, and speak at a natural rate and volume. Use gestures to make your presentation seem natural. After you present, listen actively to comments and questions from your audience. Was your PSA persuasive? Write some audience reactions here.

Reflect on Your Project

My TURN Think about your PSA. What parts do you think are strongest? Which areas might you improve next time? Write your thoughts here.

Strengths

Areas of Improvement

Reflect on Your Goals

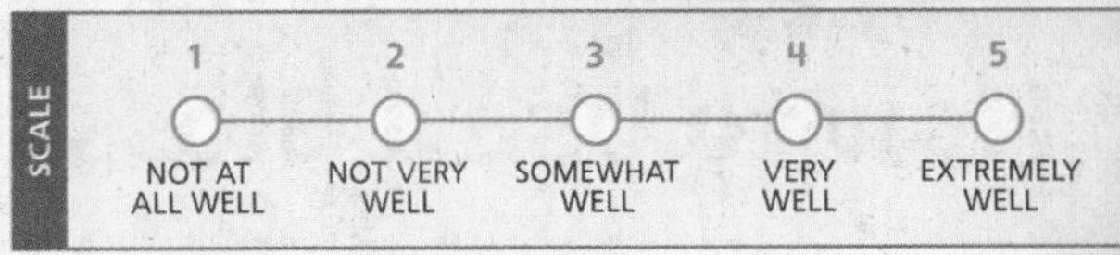

Look back at your unit goals. Use a different color to rate yourself again.

Reflect on Your Reading

Which text from this unit best supports the theme, *Systems*? Why?

Reflect on Your Writing

Review the writing you did in this unit. Which piece of writing expresses your thoughts most clearly? Why?

How to Use a Glossary

This glossary can help you understand the meaning, origin, pronunciation, and syllabication of some of the words in this book. The entries in this glossary are in alphabetical order. The guide words at the top of each page show the first and last words on the page. If you cannot find the a word, check a print or digital dictionary. To use a digital resource, type the word you are looking for in the search box at the top of the page.

The entry word in bold type is divided into syllables.

The pronunciation is in parentheses. It also shows which syllables are stressed.

The part-of-speech label shows the function of an entry word.

a•bun•dant (ə bun′dənt), *ADJ.* existing in large amounts; plentiful. from the Latin word *abundantem*, meaning "overflowing"

The definition shows what the word means.

The word origin tells what language the word came from.

My TURN

Find and write the meaning of the word *tactics*. Say the word aloud.

Write the syllabication of the word.

Write the origin of the word.

How did the origin help you understand the meaning of the word?

TURN and TALK Discuss how you could look up *tactics* in a digital resource.

Aa

ad•vo•cates (ad′və kəts), *N.* people who support a cause or policy. from the Latin word *advocatum*, meaning "summoned"

al•ti•tude (al′tə tüd), *N.* position of height. from the Latin word *altus*, meaning "high"

ap•peal (ə pēl′), *N.* the quality of beauty or interest

Bb

ban•dits (ban′dits), *N.* enemies or outlaws

Cc

coaxed (kōkst), *V.* persuaded someone to do something by words or actions

com•menced (kə mensd′), *V.* began; started

com•mo•tion (kə mō′shən), *N.* a loud noise or activity

com•posed (kəm pōzd′), *V.* formed by putting together

com•post (kom′pōst), *N.* fertilizer made from decayed organic matter. from the Latin word *compositum*, meaning "put together"

Pronunciation Guide

Use the pronunciation guide to help you pronounce the words correctly.

a in *hat*	ō in *open*	sh in *she*
ā in *age*	ȯ in *all*	th in *thin*
â in *care*	ô in *order*	in *then*
ä in *far*	oi in *oil*	zh in *measure*
e in *let*	ou in *out*	ə = a in *about*
ē in *equal*	u in *cup*	ə = e in *taken*
ėr in *term*	u̇ in *put*	ə = i in *pencil*
i in *it*	ü in *rule*	ə = o in *lemon*
ī in *ice*	ch in *child*	ə = u in *circus*
o in *hot*	ng in *long*	

com•rade (kom′rad), *N.* a companion who shares in a person's activities and who is that person's equal

con•den•ses (kən den′səz), *V.* makes or becomes more close; compacts. from the Latin *com-*, meaning "with," and *densus*, meaning "thick"

con•fide (kən fīd′), *V.* trust someone with a secret. from the Latin *com-*, meaning "with," and *fidere*, meaning "to trust"

con•sci•en•tious (kon′shē en′shəs), *ADJ.* diligent; thorough

con•scious (kon′shəs), *ADJ.* aware of an issue or idea. from the Latin *com-*, meaning "with," and *scire*, meaning "to know"

con•tam•i•na•tion (kən tam′ə nā′shən), *N.* the process of infection

con•ven•tion (kən ven′shən), *N.* a formal meeting of a group with particular interests; from the Latin word *conventionem*, meaning "agreement"

crin•kled (kring′kəld), *ADJ.* wrinkled or creased, as a crushed piece of paper. from the Middle English word *crincan*, meaning "to bend"

cus•tom (kus′təm), *N.* an accepted, repeated way of behaving or doing things

cy•cle (sī′kəl), *N.* a sequence of events that occurs regularly. from the Greek word *kyklos*, meaning "circle"

Dd

de•bris (də′brē), *N.* the remains of something that has been destroyed

del•e•gates (del′ə gits), *N.* people appointed to represent others

dem•on•strate (dem′ən strāt), *V.* display something. from the Latin word *demonstratum*, meaning "shown clearly"

dem•on•stra•tors (dem′ən strā′tərz), *N.* people who participate in public protests or marches in support of or against something

de•pos•its (di poz′its), *N.* amounts of something left in one place by a natural process. from the Latin word *depositum*, meaning "put away"

dis•turb (dis tėrb′), *V.* interfere with or interrupt something

Ee

ed•i•ble (ed′ə bəl), *ADJ.* safe to eat. from the Latin word *edere*, meaning "to eat"

em•bod•ies (em bod′ēz), *V.* symbolizes or represents in a clear way

em•pow•er (em pou′ər), *V.* enable or influence

en•com•pass (en kum′pəs), *V.* surround or completely cover

en•dure (en dů́r′), *V.* survive; continue existing. from the Latin *in-*, meaning "in," and *durus*, meaning "hard"

en•gi•neer (en′jə nir′), *N.* a person who plans and builds a machine

en•thu•si•asm (en thü′zē az′əm), *N.* high interest, excitement. from the Greek word *entheos*, meaning "god-possessed"

e•ro•sion (i rō′zhən), *N.* a slow process of being worn away. from the Latin *ex-*, meaning "away," and *rodere*, meaning "to gnaw"

Gg

ge•o•log•i•cal (jē′ə loj′ə kəl), *ADJ.* relating to the study of Earth's physical properties

grace (grās), *N.* ease of movement. from the Latin word *gratia*, meaning "favor"

Hh

hab•i•tat (hab′ə tat), *N.* a place where plants or animals normally live or grow

heed (hēd), *V.* pay attention to; listen to

Ii

im•pact (im′pakt), *N.* a strong effect on something; *V.* to hit with force. from the Latin word *impactum*, meaning "struck against"

in•di•vis•i•ble (in′də viz′ə bəl), *ADJ.* unable to be split into pieces

in•sep•ar•a•ble (in sep′ər ə bəl), *ADJ.* never apart; unable to be split up

i•ron•ic (ī ron′ik), *ADJ.* contrary to expectation

Ll

lim•i•ta•tion (lim′ə tā′shən), *N.* something set within a certain boundary. from the Latin word *limitem*, meaning "boundary"

loam•y (lō′mē), *ADJ.* having a certain mixture of clay, sand, and organic material; having a texture good for growing plants

Mm

man•u•fac•tur•er (man′yə fak′chər ər), *N.* a company that creates items by hand or by machinery. from the Latin words *manu*, meaning "hand," and *facere*, meaning "to make or do"

me•lod•ic (mə lod′ik), *ADJ.* pleasing and harmonious to hear; sweet sounding

min•er•als (min′ər əlz), *N.* solid substances made of one or more simple chemicals

mis•trea•ted (mis trē′ted), *V.* treated in an unkind or cruel way

Nn

no•ble (nō′bəl), *ADJ.* excellent; notable. from the Latin word *nobilis*, meaning "well-known"

Oo

o•blige (ə blīj′), *V.* earn gratitude; do a favor for. from the Latin word *obligare*, meaning "to bind"

Pp

par•ti•cles (pär′tə kəlz), N. very small pieces of matter. from the Latin word *particula*, meaning "small part"

per•se•vere (pėr′sə vir′), V. do something in spite of discouragement

per•spec•tive (pər spek′tiv), N. how someone sees the world. from the Latin word *perspicere*, meaning "look through"

pe•ti•tion (pə tish′ən), N. a formal request signed by many people. from the Latin word *petere*, meaning "to seek"

pon•der (pon′dər), V. think long and carefully. from the Latin word *ponderare*, meaning "to weigh"

prin•ci•ples (prin′sə pəlz), N. general theories or facts. from the Latin word *principium*, meaning "beginning"

pro•vi•sions (prə vizh′ənz), N. materials or supplies. from the Latin word *providere*, meaning "to provide"

Qq

qual•i•fied (kwol′ə fīd), ADJ. has met the necessary requirements to do or be something

quar•ters (kwôr′tərz), N. living space; a place to stay

quell (kwel), V. put an end to something. from the Old English word *cwellan*, meaning "to kill"

Rr

rad•i•cal•ly (rad′ə kə lē), ADJ. in an extreme way

rat•i•fi•ca•tion (rat′ə fə kā′shən), N. a formal act of approval or confirmation. from the Latin words *ratum*, meaning "fixed," and *fecere*, meaning "to make or do"

re•as•sur•ing (rē′ə shůr′ing), ADJ. giving comfort; reminding someone not to worry

re•call (ri kôl′), V. remember

re•lay•ing (ri lā′ing), *v.* passing along

re•sem•bled (ri zem′bəld), *v.* looked like something or someone else

re•sist (ri zist′), *v.* use one's strength of will to defeat or overcome a challenge. from the Latin word *resistere*, meaning "to make a stand"

re•tired (ri tīrd′), *ADJ.* no longer working

re•vived (ri vīvd′), *v.* brought back to consciousness. from the Latin word *revivere*, meaning "to live again"

rev•o•lu•tion•ar•y (rev′ə lü′shə ner′ē), *ADJ.* very different from something that came before

Ss

seg•re•ga•tion (seg′rə gā′shən), *N.* official separation of groups of people based on a characteristic such as race or gender

set•tle•ment (set′l mənt), *N.* a place or region that is settled. from the Old English word *setlan*, meaning "a sitting place"

shat•tered (sha′tərd), *ADJ.* broken into many small pieces; damaged or destroyed. from the Middle English word *schateren*, meaning "scattered"

sol•emn•ly (sol′əm lē), ADV. in a sad and serious way; from the Latin word *sollemnis*, meaning "solemn"

stalk•ing (stôk′ing), *v.* following closely and in a sneaky way

strap•ping (strap′ing), *ADJ.* healthy and strong

sub•stance (sub′stəns), *N.* a physical material. from the Latin word *substantia*, meaning "stand firm"

sup•por•tive (sə pôr′tiv), *ADJ.* encouraging; helpful

sus•pi•cious (sə spish′əs), ADJ. not to be trusted

sym•pa•thize (sim′pə thīz), V. feel or express concern, compassion, and support for someone. from the Greek word *sympatheia*, meaning "feeling together"

Tt

tac•tics (tak′tiks), N. planned actions for a specific purpose. from the Greek word *taktike*, meaning "art of arranging"

ter•rain (te rān′), N. an area of land and its surface features. from the Latin word *terra*, meaning "earth"

tin•gled (ting′gəld), V. felt excitement; felt a prickling sensation

tol•e•rate (tol′ə rāt′), V. allow; accept; put up with. from the Latin word *toleratum*, meaning "tolerated"

trem•bles (trem′bəlz), V. shakes slightly

trick•les (trik′əls), V. flows or falls in drops

Vv

valve (valv), N. a structure that controls the flow of materials

vi•o•la•tions (vī′ə lā′shənz), N. acts that disregard an agreement, law, or rule. from the Latin word *violatum*, meaning "treated with violence"

viv•id (viv′id), ADJ. clear, bright, and lifelike

Ww

wrig•gled (ri′gəld), V. moved by twisting

Text

Candlewick Press
DELIVERING JUSTICE: W.W. LAW AND THE FIGHT FOR CIVIL RIGHTS. Text Copyright © 2005 Jim Haskins. Illustrations Copyright © 2005 Benny Andrews. Reproduced by permission of the publisher, Candlewick Press.

Crabtree Publishing Company
Earth's Water Cycle by Diane Dakers. Used with permission from Crabtree Publishing Company.

Full Circle Literary
Love Amalia by Alma Flor Ada, used with permission from Full Circle Literary.

Lee & Low Books
Artist to Artist from IN DADDY'S ARMS, I AM TALL by Davida Adejouma. Text Copyright ©1997 by Davida Adejouma. Illustrations Copyright © 1997 Javaka Steptoe. Permission arranged with LEE & LOW BOOKS, Inc., New York, NY 10016. All rights not specifically granted herein are reserved.
Spruce and Sepia from TAN TO TAMARIND by Malathi Michelle Iyengar, illustrated by Jamel Akib. Text Copyright ©2009 by Malathi Michelle Iyengar. Illustrations Copyright ©2009 by Jamek Akib. Permission arranged with CHILDREN'S BOOK PRESS, an imprint of LEE & LOW BOOKS, Inc., New York, NY 10016. All rights not specifically granted herein are reserved.

Mitchell Lane Publishers, Inc.
The Bill of Rights by Amie Jane Leavitt. Mitchell Lane Publishers, 2011. Used with permission.

National Public Radio
It's Time To Get Serious About Reducing Food Waste, Feds Say, ©2015 National Public Radio, Inc. NPR audio report originally broadcast on NPR's Morning Edition on September 16, 2015, and is used with the permission of NPR. Any unauthorized duplication is strictly prohibited.

Robinson Literary Works LLC
A Pet for Calvin by Barbara Robinson in Dude: Stories and Stuff for Boys. Used with permission from Robinson Literary Works LLC.

Scholastic, Inc.
From THE WRIGHT 3 by Blue Balliett. Scholastic Inc./ Scholastic Press. Text copyright© 2006 by Elizabeth Balliett Klein, cover Illustration copyright© 2006 by Brett Helquist. Used by permission.
From Elijah of Buxton by Christopher Paul Curtis. Scholastic Inc./Scholastic Press. Text copyright © 2007 by Christopher Paul Curtis, cover Illustration copyright © 2007 by Carlyn Beccia. Used by permission.

Simon & Schuster, Inc.
From Love Amalia by Alma Flor Ada, copyright © 2012 by Alma Flor Ada. Reprinted with the permission of Simon & Schuster, Inc. All Rights Reserved.

Sleeping Bear Press / Cherry Lake Publishing
The Scarlet Stockings Spy by Trinka Hakes Noble used with permission from Sleeping Bear Press.

The Rosen Publishing Group Inc.
Rocks and Fossils by Richard Hantula. Reprinted by permission from Rosen Publishing.

Louis Untermeyer
The Dog of Pompeii by Louis Untermeyer from Best Shorts: Favorite Stories for Sharing, Houghton Mifflin Company 2006. Reprinted by permission from Laurence Untermeyer.

Photographs

Photo locators denoted as follows Top (T), Center (C), Bottom (B), Left (L), Right (R), Background (Bkgd)

10-11 (Bkgd) David Pereiras/Shutterstock.; **11** DrAfter123/DigitalVision Vectors/Getty Images,Denizo71/Shutterstock; **21** LZ Image/ Shutterstock; **52** (TL) Bluehand/Shutterstock, (TR) Adya/Shutterstock, (CR) Xpixel/Shutterstock, (BC) Vangert/Shutterstock; **52** Radionastya/Shutterstock; **53** (TL) Stefan Petru Andronache/Shutterstock, Eric Isselee/Shutterstock, Subbotina Anna/Shutterstock, Smit/Shutterstock, (C) Signature Message/ Shutterstock, (BL) Odua Images/Shutterstock; **56** Used with permission from Marjorie Pinto-Leite.; **86** (TL) Stephen Chung/Shutterstock, (TR) Redpixel. PL/Shutterstock, (T) 501room/Shutterstock, (BR) Imagefactory/Shutterstock, Rtem/Shutterstock; **86** (Bkgd) Skopva/Shutterstock; **87** (T) Patti Jean_Images & Designs by Patti Jean Guerrero/Shutterstock, (CL) Twistah/Shutterstock, (CR) Kmann/Shutterstock; **126** (CR) Grigoryeva Liubov Dmitrievna/Shutterstock, (B) Rawpixel.com/Shutterstock, (Bkgd) Randy R/ Shutterstock; **127** (CL) Wong Yu Liang/Shutterstock, (CR) Monkey Business Images/Shutterstock, (BL) Darren Baker/Shutterstock; **130** Two Poems "Sepia" and "Spruce" Collection TAN TO TAMARIND Poems About the Color Brown. Text Copyright © 2009 by Malathi Michelle Iyengar. Permission Arranged with Lee & Low Books Inc., New York, NY 10016.; **131** DrAfter123/DigitalVision Vectors/Getty Images; **154** (TR) Spatuletail/Shutterstock, (B) View Pictures Ltd/ Alamy Stock Photo, (Bkgd) Jeff G/Alamy Stock Photo; **155** Thomas Barrat/Shutterstock; **158** Photo by Bill Klein.; **190** (Bkgd) Kelly Redinger/Design Pics Inc/ Alamy Stock Photo; 194 NASA; **196** JPL-Caltech/ Institut d'Astrophysique Spatiale/NASA; **198** (Bkgd) Donatas1205/Shutterstock; **200** (C) AP Images, (R) Kuni/AP Images; **203** Maskot/Getty Images; **206** (BL) Meagan Marchant/Shutterstock, (Bkgd) Lightix/ Shutterstock.; **212** Everett Historical/Shutterstock; **213** (B) Library of Congress Prints and Photographs Division Washington [LC-USZ62-7816]; **216** Daniel Harris Photography Detriot.; **246** (T) World History Archive/Alamy Stock Photo, (B) North Wind Picture Archives/Alamy Stock Photo; **247** (T) Victorian Traditions/Shutterstock; **250** Used with permission from Sleeping Bear Press.; **251** Bruce Amos/ Shutterstock; **284** Jim Barber/Shutterstock; **288** Used with permission from Amie Jane Leavitt.; **289** (T) Yulia Glam/Shutterstock, (B) Swim Ink 2, LLC/Corbis/ Getty Images, (Bkgd) S.Dupuis/Library of Congress/ Alamy Stock Photo; **290** (Bkgd) Orini/Shutterstock, Everett Historical/Shutterstock; **292** Artokoloro Quint Lox Limited/Alamy Stock Photo; **293** (CR) World History Archive/Alamy Stock Photo; 295 (CL) CNP Collection/Alamy Stock Photo; **296** (CL) Martha Holmes/The LIFE Picture Collection/Getty Images; **299** Corbis/Corbis Historical/Getty Images; **300** Data from Reporters Without Borders.; **302** (T) Tetra Images/Getty Images; **303** World History Archive/ Alamy Stock Photo; **320** (B) Maurice Savage/Alamy Stock Photo, (Bkgd) LOC Photo/Alamy Stock Photo; **321** (TL) Pictorial Press Ltd/Alamy Stock Photo; **324** Library of Congress Prints and Photographs Division [LC-DIG-ppmsca-48173]; **358** Dan Lewis/Shutterstock; **404** UTBP/Shutterstock; **408** Unguryanu/Shutterstock; **410** Eric Isselee/Shutterstock; **413** (Bkgd) Art Nick/ Shutterstock, Elnur/Shutterstock; **414** Galina Savina/ Shutterstock; **417** Andersen Ross/Blend Images/ Getty Images; **420** (Bkgd) Aleksandra H. Kossowska/ Shutterstock.; **421** Vintagerobot/E+/Getty Images, Robert_s/Shutterstock, Robbreece/RooM the Agency/ Alamy Stock Photo, SergiiKS/Shutterstock; **426** (CR) Ocskay Bence/Shutterstock, (BL) Kavring/Shutterstock, (BC) Tyler Boyes/Shutterstock, (BR) Showcake/ Shutterstock; **426** (Bkgd) Media World Images/Alamy Stock Photo; **431** Vintagerobot/E+/Getty Images; **432** Mike Norton/Shutterstock, (Bkgd) Noppadon Sangpeam/Shutterstock; **433** (TC) Bjoern Wylezich/ Shutterstock, (TR) Siim Sepp/Shutterstock; **434** (TC) Matteo Chinellato/ChinellatoPhoto/Photographer's Choice RF/Getty Images, (TR) Imfoto/Shutterstock, Albert Russ/Shutterstock; **436** Francesco Carucci/ Shutterstock; **437** Russ Bishop/Alamy Stock Photo; **438** (TR) PJ Clark/iStock/Getty Images, (BL) Givaga/ Shutterstock, (BL) Only Fabrizio/Shutterstock, Rob Kemp/Shutterstock; **439** Heather A. Craig/ Shutterstock; **441** Sascha Burkard/Shutterstock; **442** (TL) John Cancalosi/Alamy Stock Photo, (TR) The Natural History Museum/Alamy Stock Photo; **444** (C) Fritz Polking/Corbis Documentary/Getty Image, (CR) Steve Kaufman/Corbis Documentary/Getty Images; **445** Nuttaphong kanchanachaya/123 RF; **446** Maria kraynova/Shutterstock; **447** Isoft/iStock/Getty Images; **449** AA World Travel Library/Alamy Stock Photo; **468** (CR) Naan/Shutterstock, (BL) Azuzl/Shutterstock; **468** (Bkgd) Epic Stock Media/Shutterstock; **469** (BR) Jaros/ Shutterstock; **472** Used with permission from Crabtree Publishing Company.; **473** Robert_s/Shutterstock; **474** NASA; **475** (Bkgd) Volodymyr Goinyk/Shutterstock; **476** (T) Christian Mueller/Shutterstock, (B) Can Balcioglu/123RF; **477** (TR) Vaclav Volrab/Shutterstock, (TC) Chrisdorney/Shutterstock, (C) windu/123RF, (CR) Natalia Lukiyanova/123RF, (B) ivan kmit/123RF; **478** (C) Pzaxe/123RF, (BL) maximkabb/123RF; (BR) Sundraw Photography/Shutterstock; **479** (T) djgis/ Shutterstock; **480** (Bkgd) Ifong/Shutterstock, (C) Tom Biegalski/Shutterstock, (BL) Power and Syred/ Science Source; **481** Ensuper/Shutterstock; **482** (TC) Serg64/Shutterstock, (TC) Iscatel/Shutterstock, (TR) Christophe Testi/Shutterstock, (C) Kirill Smirnov/ Shutterstock, (CR) David P. Lewis/Shutterstock; **482** Ch123/Shutterstock; **483** Vaclav Volrab/ Shutterstock; **484** Dainis Derics/Shutterstock; **485** snapgalleria/Shutterstock; **486** Designua/123RF; **487** Onemu/Shutterstock; **504** (BL) Joe Carini/ Perspectives/Getty Images, (Bkgd) G & M Therin-Weise/Robertharding/Alamy Stock Photo; **505** (BL) Peder Digre/Shutterstock; **508** Used with permission from Laurence Untermeyer.; **542** (Bkgd) Mohamed Abdulraheem/Shutterstock; **547** (Bkgd) Robbreece/ RooM the Agency/Alamy Stock Photo; **548** Happy Stock Photo/Shutterstock; **552** ScottNodine/iStock/ Getty Images; **553** Anna Om/Shutterstock; **570** (TL) Jeffrey B.Banke/Shutterstock, (CR) Photoiva/ Shutterstock, Kovalov Anatolii/Shutterstock; **571** (CR) Fotoluminate LLC/Shutterstock; **575** (Bkgd) SergiiKS/ Shutterstock; **578** (T) Yelantsevv/Shutterstock; **580** (T) Avalon/Photoshot License/Alamy Stock Photo; **583** (T) Hans Blossey/Imagebroker/Alamy Stock Photo; **584** (T) Andrew Holbrooke/Corbis/Getty Images; **586** (T) Charlie Varley/SIPA/Newscom; **587** (CL) Joe Ferrer/Alamy Stock Photo; **589** (T) Andrew Holbrooke/ Corbis/Getty Images; **608** (Bkgd) Sjhuls/123RF; **614** (Bkgd) Ilozavr/Shutterstock; **616** (Bkgd) James Steidl/ Shutterstock; **618** (TL) Marmaduke St. John/Alamy Stock Photo, (BR) Dragon Images/Shutterstock.

Illustrations

16–17 Jeanine Murch; **19, 89, 249, 361, 471** Olga & Aleksey Ivanov; **21–35** Martha Aviles; **55, 157, 215, 429, 573** Ken Bowser; 57–69 Kevin Rechin; 91–109 Juan Manual Moreno; **129, 287, 323, 507, 545** Ilana Exelby; 159–171 Nurit Benchetrit; 200, 585 Karen Minot; **217–229** Ron Mazellan; **246–247** Nate Padavick; **363–385** Peter Hoey; **509–525** John Jovin; **576–77** Peter Bull; **612** Rob Schuster.

NOTES

NOTES

NOTES